The Famous Historie of
Chinon of England

TOGETHER WITH

The Assertion of King Arthure

EARLY ENGLISH TEXT SOCIETY

Original Series, No. 165

1925 (for 1923)

THE
Famous Historie of
Chinon of England, with his
strange aduentures for the loue of Ce-
lestina daughter to *Lewis* King
of *Fraunce.*

With the worthy Atchiuement
of Sir *Lancelot du Lake*, and Sir *Tristram
du Lions* for faire *Laura*, daughter to *Cador Earle of Cornewall*, beeing all
Knights of King Arthurs
round Table.
By Chr. Middleton.

AT LONDON,
Printed by *Iohn Danter*, for *Cuthbert Burbie*, and
are to be sold at his shop by the Royall
Exchange. 1597.

The Famous Historie of Chinon of England

BY

CHRISTOPHER MIDDLETON

TO WHICH IS ADDED

The Assertion of King Arthure

TRANSLATED BY RICHARD ROBINSON FROM LELAND'S

Assertio Inclytissimi Arturii

TOGETHER WITH THE LATIN ORIGINAL

EDITED FROM COPIES IN THE BRITISH MUSEUM
WITH INTRODUCTION, NOTES, AND GLOSSARY

BY

WILLIAM EDWARD MEAD, PH.D.

LONDON:
PUBLISHED FOR THE EARLY ENGLISH TEXT SOCIETY
BY HUMPHREY MILFORD, OXFORD UNIVERSITY PRESS
AMEN HOUSE, E.C.

—

M DCCCC XXV

KRAUS REPRINT
Millwood, N.Y.
1987

OXFORD
UNIVERSITY PRESS

Great Clarendon Street, Oxford OX2 6DP
United Kingdom

Oxford University Press is a department of the University of Oxford.
It furthers the University's objective of excellence in research, scholarship,
and education by publishing worldwide. Oxford is a registered trade mark of
Oxford University Press in the UK and in certain other countries

© The Early English Text Society 1925

The moral rights of the authors have been asserted

Database right Oxford University Press (maker)

First Edition published in 1925

All rights reserved. No part of this publication may be reproduced,
stored in a retrieval system, or transmitted, in any form or by any means,
without the prior permission in writing of Oxford University Press,
or as expressly permitted by law, or under terms agreed with the appropriate
reprographics rights organization. Enquiries concerning reproduction
outside the scope of the above should be sent to the Rights Department,
Oxford University Press, at the address above

You must not circulate this book in any other form
and you must impose this same condition on any acquirer

Published in the United States of America by Oxford University Press
198 Madison Avenue, New York, NY 10016, United States of America

British Library Cataloguing in Publication Data
Data available

Library of Congress Cataloging in Publication Data
Data available

Original Series, 165
ISBN 978-0-85-991903-6

The

Famous Historie of

Chinon of England

PREFACE

THE late Arthurian romance of *Chinon of England*, here reprinted for the first time, from the copy in the British Museum, has there been accessible for a good number of years to students of English romance, but beyond slight incidental mention [1] it has hitherto practically escaped attention. There may, however, still be unsuspected copies in private libraries, like the one that came into the market a year or two ago from the Britwell collection.

Of the author, Christopher Middleton, we have scanty information, but in the *Dictionary of National Biography* he is doubtfully identified 'with the Christopher Middleton of Cheshire who matriculated from Brasenose College, Oxford, 12 Dec. 1580, aged 20'. Of Middleton's literary work apart from *Chinon* there is not much to be said. His first production, printed in 1595, was a translation, with woodcut illustrations, of Everard Digby's *De Arte Natandi*, 1587. His second work was *The Historie of Heaven: containing the Poetical Fictions of all the Starres in the Firmament, gathered from amongst all the Poets and*

---

[1] In the *Dictionary of National Biography*, s.v. *Christopher Middleton*, in A. J. K. Esdaile's *List of English Tales and Romances Printed before 1740. Part I, 1475-1642 ; Part II, 1643-1749*, Bibliographical Society, London, 1912, in F. E. Schelling's *Elizabethan Drama*, 1558-1642, vol. i, &c.

Astronomers, 1596. His third publication was *Chinon of England*, 1597 ; and his fourth, *The Legend of Humphrey, Duke of Glocester*, London, 1600. This rather elaborate work, in 184 six-line stanzas, follows the plan of the poems contributed to the *Mirror for Magistrates*, and is not notably inferior to some of them. It has even been reprinted in the *Harleian Miscellany*.

In the lack of the author's manuscript we have to base our edition of the romance upon the rather slovenly work of the sixteenth-century printer. We do not know, therefore, whether the somewhat numerous instances of carelessness and confusion of various sorts are to be charged to the author, the compositor, or the proof-reader.

In the preparation of the present edition I am indebted to my wife for a careful copy of the entire romance and for assistance in reading the proof, and to the compositors and proof-readers of the Oxford University Press for their vigilance and accuracy. I have also to thank Miss Mabel Day, D.Lit., Assistant Director of the Early English Text Society, not only for reading proof but for attending to various details in connexion with the printing, and, lastly, Sir Israel Gollancz, Director of the Early English Text Society, whose ready co-operation has made possible the publication, not only of the romance of *Chinon of England*, but also of the curiously interesting *Assertio Inclytissimi Arturii* of the antiquary John Leland, and the sixteenth-century translation of the same by Richard Robinson.

Preface

Great care has been taken to ensure an accurate text of the romance, which has been read three times with the original edition in the British Museum. Spelling and capitalization have been carefully reproduced, but in view of the carelessness of the old printers a slight modification of the punctuation has been made in order to bring some light into obscure sentences.

W. E. M.

WESLEYAN UNIVERSITY,
   MIDDLETOWN, CONN., U.S.A.
      September 15, 1924.

ERRATUM

Page lviii, line 8 from bottom *for* Celestina's *read* Cassiopeia's

E.E.T.S.—*Chinon of England.*

CONTENTS

	PAGE
INTRODUCTION	xiii
I. The Vitality of Medievalism	xiii
II. The Survival of Romance	xxi
III. Arthurian Story in the Sixteenth Century	xxv
IV. The Romance of *Chinon*—the original edition	xlvi
V. The Story of *Chinon of England*	xlvii
VI. The Romance of *Chinon* and its Sources	liv
VII. The Supernatural Element	lvi
VIII. Influence of the Classics	lix
IX. Plot and Characters	lx
X. Grammar	lxii
XI. Style	lxiv
XII. Literary Value	lxvii
TEXT OF *Chinon of England*	1
NOTES	69
GLOSSARY	79
INDEX TO TEXT OF *Chinon of England*	81
INDEX TO INTRODUCTION AND NOTES	83

INTRODUCTION

I

THE VITALITY OF MEDIEVALISM

UP to the present time, with some striking exceptions, notably in the field of the drama, comparatively little attention has been given to the medieval survivals in the time of Elizabeth, in so far as they are literary. But investigation discloses what in the aggregate is a large body of material, much of it scattered and hitherto never brought together in orderly fashion, although, beyond question, the literary history of the period cannot be adequately written until account is taken of the lingering medieval survivals.

The average reader assumes, without giving much thought to the matter, that with the invention of printing, the discovery of America, and the Revival of Learning this medieval literature, with some striking exceptions, came to a rather abrupt end. And one must admit that in the course of two or three generations stupendous changes were wrought in the structure of English society, in the forms of worship, in the materials and methods of education, in numberless externals of life, and in the very habits of thought. We not inaptly refer to the period as the age of the Protestant Revolution and, still more expressively, as the Renaissance, the rebirth. And when we fix our attention upon the things that were new we can hardly exaggerate their number or their importance.

But modern science has taught us to doubt the completeness of sudden and cataclysmic changes in society. What seems sudden, as, for example, the French Revolution, has been preparing for generations. What seems to be destroyed and swept away often reappears later in another form. We might, therefore, on general principles raise the question whether we must assume without discussion the utter decay and suppression of medieval habits of thought in the presence of the new tendencies.

As a matter of fact, we find that the Middle Ages died very slowly, for they were in a sense a state of mind, and this state of mind, so difficult to define yet so easy to recognize in its works, persisted long after the flood of newly discovered classic literature had swept over the land and long after the official separation of the English Church from Rome. We must not forget, moreover, that until recently England has been one of the most conservative countries in the world. And four hundred years ago such a country, all unused to radical innovation, would have been quite unlikely to change its habits of thought overnight and to consign to sudden oblivion the favourite tales, the favourite ballads, and the favourite amusements that had long been a part of the national life.

No one can deny that in a thousand ways England had changed in the two centuries between 1375 and 1575. It would indeed be folly to pretend that the general state of society in 1575 closely resembled the state of society in 1475, but that is far from saying that from top to bottom old things had passed away and all things become new.

In endeavouring, however, to present in rough outline some aspects of medieval life and literature still surviving in the period commonly regarded as modern, one becomes painfully aware that the material, though abundant, has not until recently[1] been duly assembled and co-ordinated. Much still remains to be done. In fact, for many years the old, inherited literature was mainly ignored by writers on the history of Elizabethan and Jacobean literature. A well-known sketch of Elizabethan literature proceeds almost as though there had never been a past, and Swinburne's study of Ben Jonson would hardly arouse a suspicion that Jonson was interested in any period, except the classical, outside his own. No reader of a recent interesting account of seventeenth-century English literature would imagine that a great mass of the popular literature in the time of Milton and Bunyan was a modernized survival of medieval romance and poetry.

[1] Two of the most notable works dealing with matters of this kind are *The Cambridge History of English Literature*, edited by A. W. Ward and A. R. Waller, New York and London, 14 vols. (with ample bibliography), 1907 ff.; and the collective work entitled *Shakespeare's England*, Oxford, Clarendon Press, 2 vols., 1916. Important, too, is E. K. Chambers's *The Mediaeval Stage*, Oxford, 2 vols., 1903 and later. Mention should be made also of Courthope's *History of English Poetry*, Berdan's *Early Tudor Poetry*, &c.

Introduction

For this attitude the reason is obvious. The newer literature is of greater interest to the average modern reader, and the historian of literature generally aims to point out what is beginning to dominate the field rather than to follow the sometimes obscure traces of a literature which is vanishing and is at no distant date practically to disappear.

To this vanishing literature we shall come shortly in this brief survey. But meanwhile we shall do well to glance at a few suggestive facts relating to the country as a whole, remembering that the beginning of the reign of Elizabeth was removed from the time of Richard III and from what in one sense we may call the downfall of feudalism by no more than the span of one long life. More than one old man who threw his hat into the air and cheered the Virgin Queen as she passed through the streets of London might have cheered for Warwick the Kingmaker in the fifteenth century and admired the almost royal state in which he lived and feasted. Such an old man would have witnessed the beginnings of printing in England, would have heard the first strange news of the discovery of a new world of untold wealth, might have viewed the lavish splendour of the Field of the Cloth of Gold, might have had a hand in the dismantling of great abbeys like Walsingham or Glastonbury or Fountains, and perhaps seen a few heretics burned alive in the days of Bloody Mary. He would have noted, without doubt, in his later years the great increase in the number of rogues and sturdy beggars owing to the dispossession of small tenant farmers to make way for vast enclosed fields as sheep pastures.

These and multitudes of other facts must not be overlooked when one endeavours to realize conditions in the sixteenth century. But the general aspect of the country must have been much the same as before. The fair large manor-houses of which old Harrison speaks with pride in his survey of England were for the most part yet unbuilt, though there was no lack of great houses and castles, like Warwick and Windsor and Hever and Haddon Hall and Ludlow, and scores of others that had for generations been the boast of the districts in which they were situated. More than one of the monasteries, like Battle Abbey and Welbeck, had fallen into the hands of rich families and been transformed to meet the needs of a luxurious household. But in very large measure the old man could see in travelling from one part of the country to another that the general aspect of the towns and the countryside remained surprisingly unchanged. Despite the barbarity of the Wars of the Roses, these conflicts had caused singularly little destruction of notable buildings, to say nothing of the dwellings of humble folk. Towns and cities were not levelled to the ground in the fashion only too familiar in modern warfare. As a rule, the old city walls still survived, as they do yet in large measure at Chester and York and Oxford and Colchester and Conway, and although a well-directed heavy shot would have caused a serious breach, the old fortifications made a brave show with their towers and their battlements, their drawbridges, and their massive gates studded with iron bolts.

As for the streets, they presented long rows of high-gabled houses of the medieval type, such as we still find here and there in old English towns, in the Shambles at York, in bits of ancient Shrewsbury or Hereford or Canterbury or Tewkesbury. To realize more fully the aspect of an old English town, one must go to the Continent, to Lisieux, to Dinan, to Vitry, to Braunschweig, to Hildesheim, where multitudes of houses and other buildings—allowing for inevitable changes in details—present substantially the appearance that they had in the later Middle Ages. Most notable of all, the beautiful English churches, with their rich glass and their exquisite carvings, were not yet delivered over to the tender mercies of Puritan fanatics, and still exhibited, hardly defaced, the artistic glories that our modern architects strive in vain to equal. The market-places, with their carved butter-crosses, their booths, and their throngs of petty dealers crying their wares, made an impression almost wholly medieval. Even yet, the open markets, as one sees them in various parts of the Continent, seem like a practically unaltered feature of the life of five or six centuries ago.

Before the end of the sixteenth century there were of course many changes in the material aspects of England. Great new houses, on a grander scale than ever before attempted in the island, were built in every part of the country, and English life in general took on a lavishness hitherto confined to a favoured few. Obviously, the wealth of Elizabethan England, drawn from a rapidly increasing commerce and the gold and silver of the New World, had risen to a level hitherto unknown.

As for the people of the Elizabethan time, they were notable for their fondness for brilliant processions, for pageants of every sort, full of glitter and colour, such as had delighted the Middle Ages. Their amusements were in large measure those of generations before—wrestling, cock-throwing, putting the stone, bear baiting, dancing round the maypole, Christmas mumming, and a multitude of other inherited diversions that lasted far into the seventeenth century. That genial scholar, Roger Ascham, the tutor of Queen Elizabeth, published in 1545 a famous treatise on the use of the bow, the primitive weapon which indeed in actual warfare was largely displaced before the end of the century, but which retained great popularity as a healthful means of recreation. Fox-hunting was followed substantially as in the thirteenth and fourteenth centuries. In the Middle Ages hawking had been the favourite sport of the nobility. We even see Earl Harold depicted in the Bayeux tapestry with a hawk on his wrist. Only the wealthiest classes could afford the expense of hawking, but in the sixteenth century and later they still followed it with much of the zest of their ancestors. The tilts and tournaments that had captivated the Middle Ages had indeed largely ceased to be a preparation for serious warfare, but as a diversion they still persisted. The tragic death of Henry II of France in a tilting match in 1559 brought tournaments to an end in that country, but in England they were popular up to the end of the sixteenth century, and under the encouragement of Henry, Prince of Wales, eldest son of James I, they continued for some years in the seventeenth century.

One is tempted to dwell unduly long upon these features of the older life that appeal to the eye, but although there is much more to add we must pass to another type of survivals, those representing the literature. Of these, as already remarked, there is a much larger amount than the popular histories of literature give any reason to suspect.

We may of course admit without hesitation that under the influence of the Renaissance the prevailing note of the literature from 1550 to 1650 is classical,[1] much of it with no trace of medieval influence. Allusions to ancient mythology abound at every turn. In many cases the whole substance of a poem, in so far as lies in the author's power, is classical. But nevertheless, although

[1] The strong French and Italian influence in the same period further strengthened the tendency to imitate classical models.

highly educated writers delighted to spread before the world the fruits of their newly won learning, the themes that had held the attention of the Middle Ages for centuries could not without further ceremony be consigned to oblivion. That dogged conservatism which is ingrained in the English temperament clung to the traditions of the olden time; and while scholars at the universities in their English poems were familiarly addressing Jove and Apollo and Venus, along with the nymphs and satyrs that became indispensable in English poetry for a century and a half; while brilliant wits at court were pointing their sentences with euphuistic phrases —which, by the way, largely drew upon the traditional medieval lore collected in the old bestiaries and lapidaries—humbler folk were reading and telling the old tales of Arthur and Robin Hood and Guy of Warwick and Bevis of Hampton and Merlin the Enchanter.

There is indeed, in the aggregate, a very large body of popular medieval literature, sometimes in the form of ballads, sometimes in the form of verse romances more or less modernized, or of short prose tales, which survived the troubled sixteenth century and still lived in the seventeenth century and beyond it. Much of it has been collected in Percy's *Reliques*, in the publications of the Ballad Society and the Percy Society, in Hazlitt's *Early Popular Poetry*, in Thoms's *Early English Prose Romances*, and so on. But there is still a great mass of scattered material, either in the form of a modernized and abridged prose romance, a short poem, or of a mere allusion that no one has made accessible.

We are liable to under-estimate the amount of this surviving material, since, to a great degree, it lived on in humble surroundings, amid people who had no thought of literary values but only of entertainment.

I cannot undertake here to present in detail—if we are to have due regard for proportion—the evidence for this statement, but I cite a few facts that we should not overlook.

All in all, the most notable contribution of the Elizabethan age to literature is the drama, but practically all of that drama which we now read was produced after 1590. Tentative efforts in the new field were repeatedly made during the first thirty years of Elizabeth's reign. But what on the whole had the popular support during that time was the old inherited miracle and mystery plays, with their

Introduction

conventional scenery and their peculiarly medieval flavour. Probably everybody in England had witnessed one or more of these plays, had shuddered at the slaughter of the Innocents and been thrilled by the reproduction of the scenes of Passion Week. Still more homely and primitive than the mystery plays were the popular Robin Hood plays, introducing the outlaw and Maid Marian, and affording opportunity for pretty rural scenes and ancient rustic sports. These plays became a regular part of the inherited May games.

All these popular representations were rapidly replaced in the closing years of the century by plays of a more artistic and coherent type, with a closely woven plot. The new plays drew their themes from Spain, from France, from Renaissance Italy, from ancient Greece, from ancient Rome. But the Middle Ages were not passed by. To say nothing of Shakespeare's brilliant series of historical plays, all but one of which deal with an age before the discovery of America, a good number of his other plays are a direct outgrowth of medieval legend or tradition. Such is *Cymbeline*, such is *King Lear*, the story of which goes back to Geoffrey of Monmouth in the twelfth century and even earlier; such, in some of their elements, are *Hamlet* and *The Merchant of Venice*. Largely based upon popular fairy tradition transformed by the creative genius of Shakespeare is *A Midsummer Night's Dream*. It would be easy to illustrate at undue length the extent to which the dramatists, either in choice of theme, or in allusion, or in satirical attack, as in *The Knight of the Burning Pestle*, show that the Middle Ages still loom large in their thought.

But we have a number of other important matters to consider; and first the old English ballad. The ballad is a type of literature going back to a far more primitive age than ours. One essential of its popularity is its simplicity and its appeal to natural emotion. We all remember how Bishop Percy in the artificial eighteenth century felt obliged to apologize for the publication of the famous manuscript that bears his name. He had been requested, he says, by many gentlemen 'of learning and character' to undertake the work, and he hoped that their names would 'serve him as an amulet to guard him against every unfavourable censure for having bestowed any attention on a parcel of Old Ballads'.

The manuscript that Percy used had been copied toward the middle of the seventeenth century in a tall ledger-like volume from its 'original of 1420,[1] or earlier'. The manuscript is carelessly written on coarse paper and shows no trace of artistic decoration. It was made, not for show but for use, by some one who cared enough for old ballads to go to the trouble or the expense of bringing together a large number of them in convenient form. But we need not cite the Percy Folio to prove the popularity of ballads in the time of Elizabeth and later. We have only to turn to the specimens quoted in Shakespeare and rival dramatists, to say nothing of other contemporary writers, to see to what an extent the ballad still maintained its popularity. Old favourites like *Chevy Chase* remained to stir Sir Philip Sidney, as he himself said, more than the sound of a trumpet; and the many ballads on Robin Hood long continued to be recited. Constant repetition led to imitation. The ballad form—perhaps the easiest type of verse for the budding poet—encouraged a vast amount of new production, the fruits of which we see in Child's great collection and the bulky volumes of the Ballad Society.

The ballads as a rule tell or imply a story and hence make a natural transition to the romance, whether in prose or verse. In the Middle Ages no popular demand was stronger than that which called for stories. The Church met the demand with a vast number of saints' lives—now buried in the huge folios of the *Acta Sanctorum*, where fact and fiction are impartially blended. Less saintly material found its way into the *fabliaux*, which made up part of the then stock-in-trade of the wandering minstrel or gleeman, who would perform acrobatic feats and sleight-of-hand tricks in the public square, and at the tavern rehearse before hilarious listeners the amorous adventures of ploughmen and cattle herders, of monks and priests and prioresses. As may be imagined, some of these narratives are not excessively delicate, but, on the other hand, they are not seductive. They move in a world so different from ours that we are no more drawn to imitate the actors than we are to imitate the pigs in a sty. The situations are commonly farcical and doubtless brought out the roars of laughter that the narrator aimed to arouse—for the ultimate benefit of his pocket.

In one form or another this kind of entertainment retained its popularity in the time of Elizabeth. Refinement of a sort had become conventional in society, but we need only glance at

[1] A good number of these pieces are obviously much later.

Introduction

a Restoration comedy or at poems written by eminent and doubtless truly religious clergy of the established church to realize that delicacy is a purely relative term. In the seventeenth century women of unimpeachable character exposed their beauty in a fashion that might seem too daring for a cabaret dancer in our time. It is, then, not at all surprising that multitudes of topics commonly ignored in our social gatherings were joyously exploited, and that *risqué* situations in popular tales were relished by women quite as much as by men.

A striking illustration of the frank acceptance of the facts of everyday life is seen in the coarse conduct and speech of even the higher classes of society at weddings, where the universally tolerated freedom of speech was a direct inheritance from earlier generations. Allusions such as commonly appear in the epithalamium, 'sung', as Ben Jonson tells us, 'when the bride was led into her chamber', would now be resented in our lowest circles. Needless to say, the epithalamium is an imitation of classic models, but in its content it follows medieval standards of propriety or what passed for such. We may not be really better than our ancestors, but in speech and conduct we take somewhat less obvious delight in ostentatious nuditarianism.

Even in the seventeenth century a reaction against open impropriety was undoubtedly preparing, and when the Puritans for a few years got the upper hand outward decorum became the rule. But with the Restoration a more than medieval licence swept over the land, and again for a generation men and women of high social standing unblushingly jested on situations such as moved the fourteenth-century Chaucer to repeated apology.

II

THE SURVIVAL OF ROMANCE

WE have already in passing touched upon the fondness of the Middle Ages for stories of all sorts, whether in prose or verse. With the dawn of the sixteenth century the romances that had been the main dependence of the reading—perhaps we ought to say *listening*—public for generations were not at once cast aside. Most of the books printed by Caxton, and a good part of those issued by Wynkyn de Worde, William Copland, and other printers, were books of entertainment, and held their popularity quite as long as modern works of fiction.

We cannot here take up in detail the multitude of popular romances, old and new, that continue the traditions of the Middle Ages. But we must name in passing the famous *Amadis of Gaul*, dating from the middle of the fourteenth century and Englished in 1567,[1] with its successors, *The Exploits of Esplandrian*, son of Amadis, *Lisuarte of Greece*, son of Esplandrian, and so on. Besides these elaborate romances, which were far too bulky and expensive for the ordinary purse, there were many short tales in prose or verse that circulated widely in cheap editions and kept alive in the popular mind some conception, however confused and imperfect, of the heroes of medieval romance. *The Life of Robert the Devil*, with its bad beginning and its edifying close, was known in some form to most readers; and not less famous was the touching old story of *The Knight of Curtesy and the Fair Lady of Faguell*, published by William Copland in 1568. Popular in its turn was the romance relating the adventures of *Helyas, Knight of the Swan*, and telling of the birth of 'Godfrey of Boulyon'. So, too, was the interesting verse romance of *The Squyr of Lowe Degre*, first published by Wynkyn de Worde and later by William Copland and represented by a brief version in the Percy Folio MS.

Some of the earlier sixteenth-century prose romances are written in the plain style that befits a plain man telling a story as he best can. Some of the later romances—such as Lodge's *Rosalynde*, a version of the story told in the *Tale of Gamelyn*, sometimes credited to Chaucer and the main source of Shakespeare's *As You Like It*—are overloaded with ornament and so verbose that the reader is choked in a very sea of words. In the same cloying, gluey style is the tale of *Apollonius of Tyre*, which appears in 1608 as a prose novel under the title *The Painfull Adventures of Pericles Prince of Tyre*. An Anglo-Saxon prose version tells the story in simple and attractive style; and the form in the prose of the *Gesta Romanorum* and in the verse of Gower is interesting and unaffected, but the overwrought and inflated periods of the Elizabethan version put a heavy tax upon a reader's patience.

Much more might be said on the romances of various types, but we must pass in a moment to the Arthurian group. Before doing

[1] Under the title, *The Treasury of Amadis of France*.

Introduction

so, however, we must at least glance at the greatest poetic and romantic achievement of the reign of Elizabeth, Spenser's *Faery Queene*, in some sense itself an Arthurian poem. It is to be feared that this poem is now more admired than read, for most of the great problems that make Spenser's lines throb with intense feeling awaken but slight sympathy in the modern reader, and he cares little about the wiles of Duessa or Archimago, and still less about the Blatant Beast or that portentous dragon which exceeds the measure of all recorded beasts, stretching as he does from one valley over into another. What charms us in Spenser is the endless succession of scenes richly coloured with all the lavishness of the Renaissance and of the Middle Ages. No one has ever more clearly realized the picturesqueness of the great period whose glory was already dimmed and soon to be hardly a memory. In a sense the past age lives again in his verse. And yet the illusion is hardly perfect. The civilization of his time is far more complex in many ways than that of the Middle Ages and more sensitive to new impressions from every side. In a thousand forms the new life pulsates though his entire poem. And although Spenser at times effaces himself in the scenes he portrays, he presently reappears in his own person as the stout Protestant of the sixteenth century.

He essays to write the English of an earlier age, but the more one knows of the English of the Middle Ages the more one realizes that Spenser's English is not the English of Malory or Lydgate or Chaucer or Piers Plowman. Still less is it the English of his own day, but in general it presents no difficulty to one tolerably versed in our older literature, and it is so exquisitely modulated and fitted to the thought that it sets the standard of poetic diction for two centuries.

As for the poem itself, it is of course a succession of episodic romances in verse, somewhat after the fashion of the Arthurian romances that put a knight at the service of a distressed or capricious damsel, to perform at her behest numberless feats that appear impossible. Spenser in a sense systematizes the unorganized types of earlier romance by making a knight represent a particular virtue, such as holiness or temperance or courtesy. Each romance in the series takes its place in an elaborate allegory which the poet manages with remarkable skill. A good part of the machinery of the poem is obviously suggested by well-known medieval material.

Arthurian romance, particularly as represented by Malory's *Morte Darthur*, holds perhaps the foremost place in the poet's thought, though magic elements like those in *Huon of Bordeaux* constantly reappear, and Ariosto and Tasso furnish more than one hint. Almost the entire range of medieval romance comes before our eyes as we read the *Faery Queene*. There is the knight in armour and his richly caparisoned horse; the castle with its towers and gorgeous halls; the combat against false knights; the victory over a monstrous beast. At every turn we meet evidence of complete saturation in the romantic life of the Middle Ages, along with the passionate zeal for religion that marks the crusader, but a religion more pure and undefiled and free from superstition. In reading Spenser we sometimes fail to realize, I think, that the poet in making his knights combat Duessa and Archimago is assailing the very church which is inextricably bound up in the chivalric order. Spenser might perhaps urge that for the church itself he has only affection and reverence, that his sole aim is to cleanse it from corruption. In any case, the more one considers the problem that Spenser had to solve, the more one must admire the skill with which he makes his knights typify the saving grace of his own Protestant religion while at the same time they are in Faery Land in the age of the Catholic crusades.

But there is one striking omission in the *Faery Queene*—monks and monasteries are practically ignored. Now every reader of the romances knows how indispensable a feature of the older life monks and monasteries are; how constantly the knight finds his way to a monastery as he would to a castle, assured that he will there find free-handed hospitality. But in England the monasteries had been put aside as evil things for more than half a century, and a monk was become an accursed creature. Whether Spenser hesitated to bring his spiritual heroes into close relation with monastic establishments—a scruple that apparently caused the dramatists no searching of heart—the fact is that the poet makes practically no use of one of the greatest and most pervasive institutions of the Middle Ages. At most he introduces an occasional hermit—the first one a repulsive hypocrite; the last, a gracious, kindly man, who, in his little house,

'Deckt with greene boughes and flowers gay beseene,'

entertains passing knights 'with entire affection and appearance plaine'. Of the same type is the good old hermit who in his humble abode receives Lancelot and Tristram for the night, just before the great tournament described in *Chinon*.[1]

III

ARTHURIAN STORY IN THE SIXTEENTH CENTURY

WE now turn to a closer examination of the Arthurian literature surviving in the sixteenth century, and we may well begin by noting what place Arthurian tradition holds in the chronicles, and then pass to consider the romances and other pieces that used the same material with greater freedom. For several centuries before Elizabeth came to the throne the legend of Arthur had been dignified by being adopted into ambitious historical works and had won a large place in popular esteem. For the most part the story rested ultimately upon the authority of Nennius and Geoffrey of Monmouth, but many fantastic details had crept in that had no basis in the ancient chronicles or in genuine folk-lore tradition. Yet it is to be noted that with a growing historical and critical sense there was increasing distrust of the magical and supernatural features of the Arthurian story. Such matters were felt to belong to romance rather than to history.

It is needless to repeat here at length what has been admirably presented in a detailed study,[2] but at least an enumeration of the quasi-historical works dealing with Arthur, along with a word or two of comment, is indispensable.

We may well begin with Higden's *Polychronicon*. This is a stupendous work for its time, and it naturally gathers up most of what was to be found about Arthur in Geoffrey's *Historia* and his successors, who need not be exploited here. Fortunately for his fame Higden found a spirited translator in John de Trevisa, whose English version, somewhat revised, was printed by Caxton in 1482, by Wynkyn de Worde in 1495 (?), and by Peter Treveris in 1527.[3]

John Capgrave's (1393–1464) *Nova Legenda Angliae* gives very

---
[1] See Chapter III of the romance.
[2] See R. H. Fletcher, *The Arthurian Material in the Chronicles*, (Harvard) *Studies and Notes in Philology and Literature*, vol. x.
[3] *Dictionary of National Biography*, s. v. *Trevisa*.

scant space to Arthur, in fact, as Fletcher remarks, 'only a single summary sentence', but he briefly recounts later the alleged discovery of the body of the king at Glastonbury. A translation of Capgrave's work in abridged form was brought out in 1516 by Pynson and, unabridged, by Wynkyn de Worde in the same year.[1]

John Hardyng's *Chronicle*, about 1436, draws heavily upon material that goes back to Geoffrey of Monmouth, though the author appears to have used some form of the Arthurian story as found in the *Brut*. To this he added an extended account of the Holy Grail, bringing in also Arthur and the knights of the Round Table.[2] In January, 1543, two editions of Hardyng's *Chronicle* were printed by Richard Grafton,[3] and his narrative, much coloured by the romances, was thus made accessible to the reading public.

More critical than his predecessors is Robert Fabyan, whose *New Chronicles of England and France*,[4] written about eight years after Caxton had printed Malory's *Morte Darthur*, was published in 1516. He rejects as unhistorical the magical elements in Geoffrey's account, and thus adopts the new historical criticism which grew out of the Revival of Learning. But nevertheless he includes the traditional Arthurian story, though taking evident pride in showing that he regards much of it as fabulous.

In general harmony with Fabyan's account of Arthur's exploits is John Rastell's *Pastyme of the People, or the Chronicles of Divers Realms, and most especially of the Realm of England*.[5] But Rastell has no very decided convictions as to the trustworthiness of Arthurian tradition, and he presents the story without vouching for its truth.

The growing tendency to doubt the historicity of Geoffrey's *Historia Regum Britanniae*[6] especially appears in Polydore Vergil's (1470–1555) *Anglicae Historiae Libri XXVI*,[7] which greatly

[1] *Dictionary of National Biography*, s.v. *Capgrave*.

[2] See Fletcher, op. cit., p. 251.

[3] 'Curiously enough, Grafton's editions themselves differ considerably the one from the other', and they were sharply criticized by Stow in 1570. *Dictionary of National Biography*, s. v. *Richard Grafton*.

[4] Ed. Sir Henry Ellis, London, 1811.

[5] London, 1530.

[6] On this matter of the trustworthiness of Geoffrey, see an interesting discussion in Edward Bolton's *Hypercritica* (1618?), sect. v–viii, edited by Spingarn, *Critical Essays of the Seventeenth Century*, i, 85–91.

[7] The first edition appeared at Basel in 1534, folio.

Introduction xxvii

stirred the wrath of conservatives like Stow and Price and Leland. Polydore is entirely in accord with modern scholarship in rejecting the questionable details of the Arthurian story, but in the sixteenth century he had to encounter great opposition.

The most valiant defender of the historical existence of King Arthur against the temperate scepticism of Polydore Vergil is the antiquary John Leland.[1] To defend Geoffrey of Monmouth he wrote a tract entitled *Codrus sive Laus et Defensio Gallofridi Arturii Monumetensis*.[2] But his most ambitious work of the sort is the *Assertio inclytissimi Arturii, regis Britanniae*, 1544. This gathers up every shred of evidence for Arthur's existence that Leland could find, and presents it with a violence that seems to foreshadow the insanity which overtook him in 1547 and ended only with his death in 1552. We may well smile at some of his proofs,[3] but we must not overlook the fact that they doubtless appeared conclusive to the average sixteenth-century reader.

We cannot afford space to present all the late chroniclers who retell the story of Arthur, and it is the less necessary since in general their accounts are substantially the same despite minor variations. But the great production of Raphael Holinshed, *The Chronicles of England, Scotland, and Ireland*,[4] is too important to be omitted. The enormous scale of the work, based upon the ambitious plans of the printer and publisher Reginald Wolfe (d. 1573) made necessary the assistance of various helpers, such as John Hooker, Richard Stanihurst, and, notably, William Harrison, who wrote the famous description of Elizabethan England. Shakespeare's free use of Holinshed is too well known for comment. But of no little interest is the chronicler's version of the Arthurian legends, modified in an unusual way by Scottish traditions.[5] Holinshed hestitates to put implicit faith in Geoffrey, and in general he endeavours to balance his authorities. Space forbids the discussion of details, but the reader will be rewarded who

---

[1] Leyland or Laylande, 1506 (?)-1552.
[2] Published by Thomas Hearne in his *Collectanea*, Oxford, 1715. According to the *Dictionary of National Biography*, it is 'not known to have been printed previously'.
[3] These proofs it is interesting to compare with those offered by Caxton in his famous preface to Malory's *Morte Darthur* in 1485.
[4] London, 1577, 2nd ed., 1587.
[5] See Fletcher's comments, op. cit., pp. 267 ff.

compares Geoffrey's account with Holinshed's. The Elizabethan chronicler is no longer content to follow trustfully the genial historical romancer of the twelfth century and he vigorously slashes the improbable details.

Possibly Holinshed's attitude may have stimulated Richard Robinson in 1582 to put forth his English version of Leland's *Assertio*, which had appeared thirty-eight years before. Robinson's translation was published under the title: *A Learned and True Aſſertion of the original Life, Actes, and death of the moſt Noble, Valiant, and Renoumed Prince Arthure, King of Greate Brittaine.*

In the following year he brought out a very singular little production which affords a striking proof of the vitality in the late sixteenth century of Arthurian tradition in everyday life. The pamphlet, it is hardly more, bears the title: *The Ancient Order, Societie and Vnitie Laudable of Prince Arthur and his knightly Armorie of the Round Table; with a Threefold Aſſertion, frendly in fauour and furtherance of Engliſh Archery at this day. Tranſlated and collected by R. R. Pſal. 133, vers. 1 & vers. 4. London: Imprinted by Iohn Wolfe, dwelling in Diſtaffe Lane, neere the ſigne of the Caſtle, 1583.*

The members of this society had conceived the idea of assuming the names of various knights of Arthur's Round Table. In Robinson's little book, after the dedication, is a brief outline of heraldry followed by a display of escutcheons. The name of an Arthurian knight appears above each escutcheon—fifty-eight in all—and in most cases the initials of a member of the society at the right and the left. Below are two stanzas of four lines each, the first stanza descriptive of the device, the second, complimentary.

The last production of the chronicle class to be noted before the publication of the romance of *Chinon* in 1597 is William Warner's *Albion's England*, the first portion of which, in four books, appeared in 1586. This quasi-historical, quasi-poetical work, though extravagantly lauded by contemporaries, is singularly jejune and almost entirely devoid of romantic detail. To a modern reader it makes no appeal whatever. The author carefully excludes supernatural features from the story of Arthur, and among them the account of the magic boat, so exquisitely described in Layamon and Malory, which conveys Arthur to Avalon.

Michael Drayton's *Polyolbion*, 1613, which with surprising skill

Introduction xxix

narrates the legends associated with various parts of England, briefly touches outstanding features of Arthurian tradition, but it properly lies beyond the range of this brief survey.

With this we conclude our enumeration of works dealing seriously with Arthur as an important historical figure. But before we pass to the actual Arthurian literature surviving or newly produced in the sixteenth century, we may observe that scattered throughout England and Scotland were many localities traditionally associated with Arthur and his knights. Most of these are enumerated in the interesting paper on Arthurian Localities by J. S. Stuart Glennie, prefixed to Part III of the prose romance of *Merlin* printed by the Early English Text Society in 1869. Nothing but an active popular belief, we may safely assume, could have kept alive in the sixteenth century, to say nothing of our own time, all these widely scattered names perpetuating the memory of the great heroes of Arthurian romance. Incidentally, we may here note the well-known round table, eighteen feet in diameter, that still hangs on the wall in Winchester castle, traditionally dating from the time of King Arthur but repainted in the reign of Henry VIII, with alternate red and blue lines radiating from the centre and with the names of Arthur and his knights at the places where each was supposed to have sat.

More interesting from our point of view, however, than the material we have been reviewing is the considerable body of popular Arthurian literature, some of it old and some of it new, that found its way into print in the sixteenth century. The amount of English Arthurian literature in prose or verse unquestionably never equalled the amount in French literature, from which indeed the greater part was translated or adapted. And some of the best of the old verse romances, such as the fourteenth-century alliterative *Morte Arthure*, *Sir Gawain and the Green Knight*, and the exquisite story of Elaine in *Le Morte Arthur*,[1] to say nothing of Layamon's *Brut*, were quite certainly not read in the sixteenth century, though the manuscripts may have been occasionally looked at as interesting curiosities. But in estimating what had really survived we must carefully note the Arthurian romances in prose and verse that had

[1] Preserved in Harleian MS. 2252. No printed edition is known before that of Furnivall in 1864.

the good fortune to be printed. Even here we have difficulty in determining conclusively whether certain pieces were actually printed, as were, for example, the originals of some of the poems preserved in the Percy Folio MS. We can easily see how short pieces printed on one or two unbound sheets might be worn to rags by their very popularity and ultimately disappear, were it not for the happy accident that some one thought to copy them, as did the unknown scribe who brought together the miscellaneous collection in the Percy manuscript. In the process of transmission the language almost inevitably suffered, since obsolete words were ruthlessly dropped and more intelligible though less expressive modern terms substituted.

Turning now to the surviving material in prose and verse, we naturally begin with Sir Thomas Malory's *Morte Darthur*, unquestionably the outstanding masterpiece of Arthurian prose romance and the only one that still remains popular. First printed in folio by Caxton in 1485, it was reprinted by Wynkyn de Worde in 1498, and by his successors in 1529, in 1557, and in 1585, each time in folio; then again in 1585, in quarto. A new edition appeared in 1634, and this supplied the demand of the reading public until 1816, when a new edition was called for.[1] Malory's romance divided the honours with Lord Berners's English version of *Huon of Bordeaux*, the great repository of adventure and fairy lore which, along with Lord Berners's *Arthur*[2] *of Little Britain*, provided some of the material, and in a sense prepared readers, for Spenser's *Faery Queene*.

So great was the fame of Arthur and the popularity of Malory's romance in the second half of the sixteenth century, three generations after the first printing, that that sturdy moralist Roger Ascham feels constrained to break out in a protest so well known that I hesitate to quote it once more, but I hardly venture to omit it. After severely condemning the books and the morals of Italy, he goes on to say:

'In our forefather's tyme, whan Papistrie, as a standyng poole, couered and ouerflowed all England, fewe bookes were read in our

---

[1] I cannot here enumerate the many modern editions, and I note merely Sommer's exact reprint of Caxton's edition, with Introduction and Studies on the sources, vol. i, 1889; ii, 1890; iii, 1891.

[2] Needless to remark, this Arthur has nothing in common with King Arthur besides the name.

Introduction xxxi

tong, sauyng certaine bookes Cheualrie, as they sayd, for pastime and pleasure, which as some say, were made in Monasteries, by idle Monkes, or wanton Chanons: as one for example, *Morte Arthure*: the whole pleasure of which booke standeth in two speciall poyntes, in open mans slaughter, and bold bawdrye: In which booke those be counted the noblest Knightes that do kill most men without any quarrell, and commit fowlest aduoulter[i]es by sutlest shiftes: as Sir *Launcelot* with the wife of king *Arthure* his master: Syr *Tristram* with the wife of king *Marke* his vncle: Syr *Lamerocke* with the wife of king *Lote*, that was his owne aunte. This is good stuffe, for wise men to laugh at, or honest men to take pleasure at. Yet I know, when Gods Bible was banished the Court, and *Morte Arthure* receiued into the Princes chamber. What toyes, the dayly reading of such a booke may worke in the will of a yong ientleman or a yong mayde, that liueth welthily and idelie, wise men can iudge, and honest men do pitie. And yet ten *Morte Arthures* do not the tenth part so much harme, as one of these books, made in Italie and translated in England.'[1]

It is at least possible that the *Morte Darthur* suggested some of the characters that played a part in the festivities at Kenilworth for the entertainment of Queen Elizabeth in 1575, only five years after Ascham's complaint that the book was too much read. In *The Princelye Pleasures at the Courte at Kenelworth ... in the Yeare 1575*[2] we find (pp. 2, 3) verses recited by the 'Ladie of the Lake', who had lived in the Lake 'since the time of great King Arthure's reigne'. On pp. 8-10 we learn that the Lady had been compelled to remain in the Lake by 'Sir Bruse, sauns pittié, in revenge of his cosen Merlyne the Prophet, whom for his inordinate lust she had inclosed in a Rocke'. No such relationship is hinted at in the *Morte Darthur*, and no exploit exactly like this is assigned to Breuse saunce pyte, who is, nevertheless, frequently mentioned. Breuse is credited with several villainous performances in the *Morte Darthur*, such as following a lady to slay her (p. 397, Sommer's reprint) and killing a lady's brother and keeping her at

---

[1] *The Scolemaster* (1570), p. 80, Arber's reprint. Ascham had used some of the same phrases, yet without naming the *Morte Darthur*, in the preface to his *Toxophilus*, 1545, Arber's reprint, p. 19.

[2] London, 1576; reprinted London, 1821. Edited by F. J. Furnivall, with interesting comments, for the Ballad Society, 1871. This latter is the edition here cited.

his own will (p. 407). He may, therefore, have seemed to be a suitable character to be pressed into such service as was desired at the festivities. Literal reproduction of the Arthurian legends was not aimed at, for novelty was the chief feature of the whole entertainment; but the romantic motives and the names were as likely to have been suggested by the *Morte Darthur* as by any Arthurian literature that has come down to us.[1]

In the well-known letter of Robert Laneham describing these festivities appears a remarkable list of the romances in the library of Captain Cox of Coventry, who marched in the procession. Noting only those of immediate interest to us, we find the writer remarking that 'az for King Arthurz book, Huon of Bordeaus, ... Beuys of Hampton ... Sir Tryamoour, Sir Lamwell ... Syr Gawyn ... with many moe then I rehearz héere: I beléeue he haue them all at hiz fingers endz'.[2] To men of this type we doubtless owe the preservation of many of the pieces in the Percy Folio MS. and of the ballads in Child's great collection.

Very different in spirit is the sour-tempered Nashe, who in 1589 bursts out abusively against 'the fantasticall dreames of those exiled Abbie-lubbers, from whose idle pens proceeded those worne out impressions of the feyned no where acts of Arthur of the rounde table, Arthur of litle Brittaine, Sir Tristram, Hewon of Burdeux, the Squire of low degrée, the foure sons of Amon, with infinite others.'[3]

Besides Malory's great romance, which is in a sense a library of Arthurian literature, there is in the aggregate a very considerable body of pieces in prose and verse[4] that claimed the attention of readers in the sixteenth century and to some extent in the seventeenth. To continue with those productions that make Arthur the central figure, we have at least three pieces in verse, preserved in

---

[1] This paragraph is borrowed from the introduction to my *Selections from Malory's Morte Darthur*, pp. xl, xli.

[2] Laneham's Letter was edited by Furnivall for the Ballad Society, 1871, vii, 29, 30.

[3] *Anatomie of Absurditie*, ed. Grosart, i, 14.

[4] As an indication of what has been lost we may note the entry in the Stationers' Registers, 22 July, 1565—22 July, 1566: 'Receved of Richard Jonnes for his lycense for prynting of [a] ballet intituled *a pleasaunte history of an adventurus knyghte of kynges ARTHUR's Couurte*. ... iiij^d'.

the Percy Folio MS., that beyond question are much older than the date of that manuscript (c. 1650) and most likely belong to the sixteenth century, if not earlier. The end of that century is the probable date suggested by Sir Frederick Madden for the ballad of *King Arthur and the King of Cornwall*,[1] a fragment of 301 lines offering singular parallels to the old French romance of *Charlemagne's Journey to Jerusalem and Constantinople*[2] and showing acquaintance, in the incident of the beheading of the King of Cornwall, with material such as we find in *Sir Gawain and the Green Knight*.

Of considerable interest is the picturesque ballad of *The Boy and the Mantle*, with its gleeful exposure of pretended virtue.[3] In variant form, both in this piece and in numerous analogues, the test is made by means of an enchanted horn from which no faithless wife or cuckold husband can drink without spilling. The sources of the story are some three or four centuries earlier than the ballad, of which no early print is known. Nothing in the contents, the form, or the diction points to the seventeenth century as the time when this piece was composed, and the lilt and the tone appear to indicate a date at least as early as the sixteenth century.

As for the very prosaic ballad entitled *King Arthur's Death*,[4] it evidently consists of two pieces loosely joined together, the first running to l. 96, and the second to l. 251. For its material it evidently draws upon the well-known chronicles and the romances, though too vaguely to enable us to identify the sources. There is nothing to show that this too may not be a sixteenth-century production, but little is gained by deciding the matter one way or the other. Malory's prose is infinitely more picturesque than the hobbling lines of this ballad, which proves nothing concerning the actual popularity of Arthur, except perhaps that his fame must have been great to float such verse as this.

In late prose romance the only new production in the Arthurian field after *Chinon of England* is *Tom a Lincolne*, a fantastic per-

[1] *Percy's Folio MS.*, ed. Hales and Furnivall, i, 61 ff.
[2] See Child's *English and Scottish Ballads*, i, 274–83, and also *Englische Studien*, xxxvi (1906), 337.
[3] *Percy's Folio MS.*, ii, 304–11. Cf. *Le Mantel Mautaillié* in Montaiglon et Raynaud, *Recueil Général des Fabliaux*, iii, 1 ff., and Child's comments on No. 29 of the *English and Scottish Ballads*.
[4] *Percy's Folio MS.*, i, 498 ff.

formance in euphuistic style by the well-known Richard Johnson. This 'was entered at Stationers' Hall in 1607,[1] though the seventh edition (1635), which is in the British Museum, is the earliest known to be extant'.[2] Like all of Johnson's romances, it is full of startling adventures which cannot be presented here in detail.

Part I

Tom is the son of King Arthur by an amour with Angelica, the Earl of London's daughter, with whom the king long keeps up relations. Tom is entrusted to a shepherd to be reared, but as he grows older he leaves his sheep, organizes his young companions as a band of outlaws, and assumes the title of the Red Rose Knight. King Arthur begins to hear of Tom's exploits and sends 'three of his approved Knights, namely, Lancelot du Lake, Sir Tristam (*sic*), and Sir Triamore'[3] to induce him to come to court. Here he is royally received and made a knight of the Round Table. Immediately thereupon, commissioned by Arthur, he leads a punitive expedition to Portugal, wins there a great victory, and brings back enormous booty. The English warriors on their return give themselves up to inglorious ease, but Tom a Lincolne begs leave to go abroad for more adventures, and setting out with Lancelot and a hundred knights is driven by a storm to Fairy Land, an island occupied only by women. Needless to say, during their four months on the island both Tom a Lincolne and the hundred knights win the favour of Celia the Fairy Queen and of the ladies of her court, so that there is no longer fear that the island will be depopulated. At length, however, realizing that they cannot remain longer inactive, Tom and his knights take leave of the sorrowing ladies and sail away in search of more adventures.

---

[1] In the romance (Part I, Chapter II) Tom a Lincolne is said to have bestowed the bell known as Great Tom upon the city. Doubtless the hero owes his name to the famous bell, which far antedates the romance and has been twice recast, once in 1611 and again in 1834. See A. F. Kendrick, *The Cathedral Church of Lincoln*, London, 1899, pp. 62-4.

[2] *Dictionary of National Biography*, article *Richard Johnson*. The romance was reprinted by Thoms, *Early Prose Romances*, 3 vols., 1827, 1829. A second edition, revised, not by Thoms, appeared in 1858. In this edition the romance appears in vol. ii, pp. 219-361.

[3] It is to be noted that these same knights appear also in *Chinon*, published at least ten years earlier than *Tom a Lincolne*.

Introduction xxxv

Driven by favourable winds, their ship at last comes to the land of Prester John, who receives them hospitably and inquires much about Arthur's court. Tom a Lincolne loses his heart to the king's fair daughter Anglitora and is delighted to learn that he has only to kill the dragon that guards the golden tree to claim her for his bride. The dragon is thirty feet long, spouts flame, and has three tongues, but in the fight Tom speedily cuts off the monster's three tongues and seven feet of his tail and at last pierces his heart. Flushed with victory, Tom returns bearing on his sword the three tongues and in his hand a branch of the golden tree. He is welcomed with a great feast and then conducted to his lodging by a company of noblemen and other attendants. After their departure appears Anglitora bearing a golden basin of warm perfumed water, washes the dragon's blood from his body, and then spends the night with him as his promised bride. But when Tom sees the king and asks for the hand of his daughter he meets a curt refusal. Anglitora, however, resolves not to give up her lover, and taking her richest jewels she accompanies him early the next morning to his ship, leaving her father disconsolate.

The ship passes the Fairy Island where Queen Celia with her infant son is eagerly awaiting Tom's return, but contrary winds prevent a landing and the hopeless queen throws herself into the sea. Borne by the waves past the English ship, her attire of cloth of gold catches the eye of the Red Rose Knight. He takes her body up into the ship and reads the pitiful letter which is her last message to him. Anglitora also reads the letter and requests that the body be taken to England for burial. This is done. On arrival at Arthur's court the Red Rose Knight and Anglitora are solemnly married and live long and happily in Arthur's court.

Part II

The remainder of the romance may be briefly summarized. When Arthur comes to die he reveals his amour with Angelica. This confession enrages his queen and shames Angelica, who has long been a nun at Lincoln. Tom a Lincolne's wife Anglitora is angered that she has married a bastard and without delay she sets out with her son the Black Knight for the land of Prester John, her father. Tom in his turn also leaves England. Meanwhile Arthur's widowed queen causes Angelica to be put to death and shortly thereafter hangs herself from remorse. Anglitora and her son, attended by a black slave, cross the sea and arrive at a castle, where with indecent haste she becomes the mistress of the castellan and for seven years lives with him. Late in the afternoon of the very day when Anglitora and the Black Knight arrive at the castle the latter sallies forth to hunt. By mischance he loses himself in the thick forest, and though he searches day by day he is unable to find his way back to the castle. In the wood he remains seven years as a wild man.

When Anglitora becomes the mistress of the castellan her blackamoor slave, horrified at her infidelity, determines to seek his former master. By a miraculous chance, not uncommon in Richard Johnson's romances, it happens that, after seven years of fruitless search by the faithful black, the ship upon which Tom a Lincolne has been drifting floats to the very place where the slave is. Conducted by him, the Red Rose Knight Tom, disguised as a palmer, makes his way to the castle, but he is recognized and killed and the slave is fastened in the earth to die. Then appears one day to the Black Knight the ghost of his murdered father calling for vengeance. Without delay the Black Knight sets out for the castle, finds the negro slave half-starved in the earth, and under his guidance penetrates to the chamber where Anglitora and her paramour are sleeping. He kills them both and then raves madly because he has slain his mother. He afterwards kills the Dwarf of the Castle and buries him in the same grave with the negro slave, who dies soon after he is taken out of the earth where he has been fixed. Then the Black Knight digs up the body of his father, buries it with that of his mother in one grave and for three days remains there kneeling and pouring out his laments. While he is sleeping upon the grave the Fairy Knight, son of Queen Celia and Tom a Lincolne, who has also taken to wandering, finds him and awakens him. The two knights soon discover that they are brothers and henceforth they are inseparable. After various adventures they make their way to England, where the king receives them with the greatest honour and holds feasts and jousts for forty days. Then the two knights proceed to Lincoln, where they build a sumptuous minster and a stately tomb in memory of their parents and spend their remaining days in good works.

This romance exhibits many of the familiar traits of Richard

Johnson's productions and, in particular, his fondness for farfetched and impossible adventures with abundant supernatural motives. His wide reading in the field of medieval romance is obvious at every turn, and he makes the most of his knowledge in developing his situations. In no sense is it very original, though it is measurably readable, if one's mood is not too exigent.

If we now turn to the drama, we find that for some reason Arthurian themes made comparatively small appeal to the dramatists of the Elizabethan time, and, although in various plays allusions to Arthurian characters occur,[1] Arthurian plays themselves are singularly few.[2] This is the more remarkable when one considers the dramatic possibilities, for example, of a tragedy on such a theme as the relations between Lancelot and Guinevere.

Of plays based upon the Arthurian tradition the only one actually surviving is Thomas Hughes's tragedy, *The Misfortunes of Arthur*,[3] 1588. This formed part of an ambitious and costly entertainment consisting of allegorical dumb-shows—in which even Francis Bacon had a hand—and complimentary speeches in the fashion of the time, 'presented to her Majestie by the Gentlemen of Grayes-Inne at her Highnesse Court in Greenewich, the twenty-eighth day of Februarie in the thirtieth yeare of her Majesties most happy Raigne'.

Hughes drew mainly upon Geoffrey of Monmouth for his characters,[4] introducing among others Cador, who in our romance

---

[1] Note, for instance, in Shakespeare, *Henry V*, ii, 3, 9, where Dame Quickly says of Falstaff, 'He's in Arthur's bosom, if ever man went to Arthur's bosom'; *Lear*, iii, 2, 95, where the Fool says, 'This prophecy Marlin shall make; for I live before his time'; 2 *Henry IV*, iii, 2, 300, where Shallow says, 'I was then Sir Dagonet in Arthur's show.' This 'show' was mainly an exhibition of archery by men from the city who took the names of Arthurian knights. Cf. p. xxviii.

[2] In Henslowe's Diary, 11, 12 April, and 2 May 1598, a play by Hathway on *The Life and Death of Arthur King of England* is mentioned, but is otherwise not known; and on 29 April, 1597, is noted the name of a play entitled *Uter Pendragon*, the father of Arthur. This also is lost. Not impossibly 'the playe of Valteger', mentioned in Henslowe's Diary 'the 28 of November 1596', may have to do with Vortigern. The play was several times acted, but it has not been preserved. Under date of 13 October, 1599, Henslowe notes the Booke of Trystram de Lyons, which may have been a play.

[3] Edited, with introduction, by H. C. Grumbine, Berlin, 1900.

[4] Although Hughes is the chief author, he appears to have been more or less

is the father of Chinon. But he could hardly escape knowing Malory's *Morte Darthur*, which was famous beyond all other romances in the sixteenth century, and probably to Malory he owed certain details in the forms of proper names, 'the incestuous birth of Mordred, and the slaughter of Arthur and Mordred by each other's hands'.[1] The obvious debt of Hughes to Seneca,[2] the favourite model of the earlier English tragedians, is pointed out in some detail by critics of the play.[1] For modern taste the horrors in this play are somewhat too liberally presented, and probably few but professional students of literature now turn its pages, but simple justice compels us to admit that it has more than one passage of considerable power. When all is said, however, we must agree that the play belongs rather to the closet than to the stage.

Next to Arthur rightly stands Merlin, the enchanter and prophet, who enjoyed great renown throughout the Middle Ages and even long after the reign of Elizabeth. It is to be noted, however, that the English versions of the vast French prose romance of *Merlin* appear to have been little known, if at all, in the sixteenth century [3]; but the fame of the ancient sage and magician was kept alive by popular tradition, by short pieces printed by Wynkyn de Worde and by John Hawkins, all before 1533,[4] by a *Life* written by Simon Forman, the astrologer and quack doctor (1552–1611), and, above all, by the repeated printing of Malory's *Morte Darthur*. Quite possibly to the sixteenth century belongs the prosaic verse romance of *Merline*,[5] 2378 lines. This parallels the fifteenth-century English prose *Merlin* [6] up to the death of Uther Pendragon and presents a somewhat modernized text of the early fifteenth-century manuscript of a verse *Merlin*

aided in the planning and the composition of his play. See Schelling, *Elizabethan Drama*, 1558-1640, i, 265.

[1] Cunliffe, in *Cambridge History of English Literature*, v, 87-9.

[2] *Seneca, His Tenne Tragedies translated into English* appeared in 1581. Translations of single plays were printed earlier.

[3] Such, for example, as the fourteenth-century verse *Merlin* edited by Kölbing, *Altenglische Bibliothek*, iv, 1890; the fifteenth-century prose *Merlin*, E.E.T.S., and Louelich's metrical version of the prose, E.E.T.S.

[4] See my account of the Merlin legend, published by the E.E.T.S. (1899), pp. lxxii ff.

[5] *Percy's Folio MS.*, i, 422-96.

[6] E.E.T.S., p. 57, line 1.

Introduction

preserved in the library of Lincoln's Inn (MS. 150). But no sixteenth-century printed text of this version has come down to us, and if the piece was widely known it left at all events no marked impression.

The chroniclers dealing with Arthur necessarily give more or less space to Merlin, and although their endeavour to narrate sober history leads them to suppress some of the marvels exploited by the romancers, 'it is to be remembered', says Schelling,[1] 'that Grafton, Holinshed, and Stow, sober historians that they were, accepted most of these tales as of equal authenticity with the history of Edward the Black Prince or Henry V himself'.

Edmund Spenser, greatest of the Elizabethan poets, shows in various passages of the *Faery Queene*[2] that he is saturated with the Merlin tradition. And in a famous canto he tells of the wall of brass[3] with which Merlin began to surround the City of Carmarthen just before he was lured to his tomb in the rock by the wiles of the fair temptress. But necessarily the plan of the *Faery Queene* precluded the use of anything beyond an occasional bit of the voluminous Merlin romance.

We must not overlook the fact that Merlin's fame, particularly as a prophet, increased in the seventeenth century and that his name was freely used by almanac makers and exploiters of dubious predictions, but these productions we cannot enumerate here.[4]

One notable work, however, deserves our attention, William Rowley's vigorous and entertaining play, *The Birth of Merlin : Or, The Childe hath found his Father*.[5] By some critics this piece has been dated as early as 1597, but the suggestion made by Daniel, accepted by Fleay and pushed to a conclusion by Howe,[6] that Rowley's *Merlin* owes much to Thomas Middleton's play, *The*

---

[1] *Elizabethan Drama, 1558-1642*, i, 298.
[2] Bk. I, canto 9, st. 4, 5 ; II, canto 8, st. 20 ; III, canto 2, st. 18, 21.
[3] Bk. III, canto 3, st. 6 ff. This is, of course, Spenser's own invention.
[4] See Mead, *Outlines of the Legend of Merlin* (E.E.T.S.), pp. lxxiv ff.
[5] First printed in 1662 as the joint production of William Rowley and William Shakespeare! Edited, K. Warnke and L. Proescholt, *Pseudo-Shakespearian Plays*, 5 vols., Halle, 1883-8 ; also T. E. Jacob, *Old English Dramas*, 1889. It is needless to observe that the association of Shakespeare's name with this piece is nothing but a clever trick of advertising by the first publisher in 1662.
[6] *Modern Philology*, iv, 193-205.

Mayor of Queenborough, makes this date more than doubtful.[1] Fortunately for our purpose, the exact date is not of prime importance. The interesting and suggestive fact is that the tale which was already ancient when Geoffrey of Monmouth took it up should still in the seventeenth century have retained its vitality and served as a nucleus for a dramatic work of much more than ordinary merit.

Sir Lancelot does not belong to the original group of Arthurian characters and finds no place in Nennius or Geoffrey, but he rapidly forges to the front in Arthurian romance until he is second to none. In *Chinon*, although he is not the nominal hero, he is in a sense the dominant character. But in sixteenth- and seventeenth-century English literature in general he suffers great neglect. He holds indeed the foremost place among the knights in the ever popular *Morte Darthur*, but otherwise he almost drops out of sight. In *The Fall of Princes*,[2] a prosaic poem of ninety-six lines that perhaps borrowed the title from Lydgate's *Fall of Princes*, the author asks—

'Where is King Arthur the venturer, with his Knights bold?
or Sir Tristeram, that treasure of curtesye?
or Sir Gawaine the good, with his helmett made of gold?
or Sir Lancelott dulake, a Knight of Chiualrye?'   ll. 73-6;

and although this sort of question was already a well-known formula long before this doggerel was written, we cannot doubt that all the heroes here named were felt to belong to an age far different from the sixteenth century.

The Scottish romance of *Lancelot of the Laik*, dating from the last quarter of the fifteenth century, is 'a translation of a portion of the great French prose romance of "Lancelot du Lac", a portion consisting of from five to seven chapters of the printed versions,

---

[1] Professor C. H. Herford in the *Dictionary of National Biography* states that 'Middleton's connection with the stage cannot be shown before 1599', and it would not be easy to prove that *The Mayor* was Middleton's earliest work. But see Schelling, *Elizabethan Drama, 1558-1642*, i, 296, who accepts 1596 as the date of Middleton's *Mayor of Queenborough*.

[2] *Percy's Folio MS.*, iii, 169-73. Percy infers from the last stanza that 'this song should seem to have been wrote soon after the Death of Henry 8'. Quoted, iii, 168.

Introduction

according to the edition. It is the only version in our language which treats of the first "Lancelot", of which Malory seems to have had no knowledge, he ignores it so completely. The translation deals with the wars between Arthur and Galiot, Lancelot's prowess therein, and his devotion to Guinevere'.[1] But this mediocre Scottish romance was certainly not known to many English readers, if to any, and the modern reader familiar with Malory will wonder why the versifier could imagine that there would be any demand for his own production.

Hardly worth mention is the dull and fragmentary ballad of sixty lines written late in the reign of Elizabeth, possibly by Thomas Deloney, describing Lancelot's fight with Sir Tarquin as narrated by Malory.[2] The ballad appears in the Percy Manuscript.[3] With some variations, Falstaff repeats the first two lines in *2 Henry IV*, ii, 3, and, as the editors of the ballad note,[4] 'it is quoted in Marston's *Malcontent* and Fletcher's *Little French Lawyer*'.

Elsewhere in the Percy Manuscript [5] a *Laudation of Olde Times Paste* assures us that

'no man did greater matters then than Lancelot of Du Lake'.
ll. 3, 4.

But times have changed:

'rich men, alas they know not how
to keepe ne hawke nor hound.
all merriments are quite fforgott,
& bowes are laid aside.'   ll. 55-8.

And here we leave the greatest of the knights of the Round Table, who remains in unmerited obscurity until the coming of Romanticism restores him in part to his wonted pre-eminence.

Gawain fares better than Lancelot. The popularity of the group of romances associated with the name of Gawain, whose early reputation suffers so disastrously in Malory's pages, is attested by the fact that some half-dozen of these romances still survived when the romance of *Chinon* was written, and in them all Gawain is the gracious embodiment of courtesy that we find in *Gawain and the*

---

[1] Margaret M. Gray, Scottish Text Society (1912), p. xiii.
[2] *Morte Darthur*, vi, chs. 2, 7, 8, 9. In Malory, Lancelot's antagonist is Sir Turquyne.
[3] *Percy's Folio MS.*, i, 84.   [4] i, 84-7.   [5] iii, 120-2.

Green Knight. These romances are naturally of varying merit and in some cases show a sad falling off from an earlier version. Strikingly true is this of *The Grene Knight*,[1] which modernizes, abridges, and strangely mutilates the story told in the exquisite old romance. The mysterious glamour of the early fourteenth-century version is dimmed by trivial and prosaic details. So eager is the narrator to tell all he knows that he cannot keep the reader in suspense but, for example, explains at once that the castle at which Gawain arrives in his fateful journey is the home of the Green Knight whom he is seeking. The original version contains 2530 lines: the modernized version has but 516. How late this version is we cannot precisely say. Possibly it may belong to the fifteenth century, but we have it only in the Percy Manuscript. In the old romance the knights of the Round Table wear a green belt in honour of Gawain's exploit (l. 2516 f.). In the Percy version this belt, as the author tells us, explains

> 'why Knights of the bathe weare the lace
> vntill they haue wonen their shoen'.   ll. 503-4.

Undoubtedly the modernizer found himself quite unequal to reproducing in language of his own day the extremely rich and varied phraseology of the old version, and he produced a bald and spiritless abstract, typical of only too much of late medieval romance.

The Turke and Gowin, which belongs to the fifteenth century and reappears in the Percy Manuscript,[2] has come to us in a fragmentary state, though 337 verses have survived. In this romance, which at the beginning reminds us of *Gawain and the Green Knight*, a burly Turk enters Arthur's hall while he is at meat and offers to exchange blows with any one present. As usual, Kay is discourteous while Gawain is gracious and considerate. At length Gawain departs with the Turk and arrives in the Isle of Man, where Gawain performs great feats—apparently underground—in the castle of the King of Man, who maintains a company of giants. The king and a giant even attempt to throw Gawain into a boiling cauldron, but the Turk, who wears a coat that makes him invisible, rescues Gawain and throws the king into the fire and the biggest giant into the cauldron. Then the Turk, with a basin in his hand,

---

[1] *Percy's Folio MS.*, ii, 58-77.   [2] i, 90-102.

Introduction xliii

asks Gawain to cut off his head. When Gawain reluctantly consents, the Turk is transformed into a Christian, and, in due time, at Gawain's request, is crowned King of Man with the consent of Arthur.

Golagrus and Gawain, a romance of 1362 lines in the Scottish dialect of the late fifteenth century, directly or indirectly draws its material from the French *Perceval* and is an interesting example of the group of romances that exalt the courtesy of Gawain in contrast with the crabbed surliness of Kay. Throughout the story Gawain everywhere wins his way by his gracious manner, yet without dimming his glory as a valiant knight. The romance was printed at Edinburgh in 1508.[1] There is nothing to show that the story was known in England, but since it was in print we may well believe that an occasional English reader may at least have turned its pages.[2]

The Marriage of Sir Gawain[3] and the parallel tale, *The Weddynge of Sir Gawen and Dame Ragnell*,[4] treat the same theme as that of Chaucer's *Wife of Bath's Tale*[5] and have affiliations with many other romances. In some form or other this delightful though fragmentary little romance lived through the sixteenth century and thus found its way into the Percy Manuscript.

The Jeaste of Syr Gawayne,[6] a fifteenth-century episodic romance, in part based upon a tale in Gautier de Doulens's continuation of Chrétien's *Perceval*, throws light upon the origin of the hero of the better-known romance of *Libeaus Desconus*, the son of Sir Gawain. The story clearly antedates by several centuries the form in which

---

[1] Reprinted, Edinburgh, 1827, and in *Anglia*, ii, 395 ff.
[2] Another piece may be at least named. *The Avowing of King Arthur, Sir Gawan, Sir Kaye, and Sir Bawdewyn of Bretan*, a poem of 1152 lines, in seventy-two stanzas, dates from the later fourteenth century and is preserved in a fifteenth-century manuscript. Gawain here again is ever courteous and is contrasted with Kay, who is forever boasting. In the sixteenth century this romance apparently slipped out of sight and was forgotten, doubtless because the language was too antique to be easily understood. My only excuse for citing it here is that it affords a good illustration of the way in which a piece of considerable merit might lose popular favour and never regain it.
[3] *Percy's Folio MS.*, i, 105 ff.
[4] Rawlinson MS., ch. 86, Bodleian Library.
[5] For an elaborate study of the theme of this romance and its analogues, see Maynadier, *The Wife of Bath's Tale*, London, 1901.
[6] MS. Douce, Bodleian, 261 (1564).

we have it in the manuscript. By a lucky chance the last leaf of a black-letter edition printed by Thomas Petyt[1] has survived[2] and thus affords conclusive evidence that the romance was known to readers in the second third of the sixteenth century.

The connexion of *Libeaus Desconus*[3] with Arthurian Romance is more or less casual, but clearly the story is more Arthurian than anything else. The hero is the son of Gawain, gotten 'under a forest side', and at the age of fourteen he goes to King Arthur, who, after vainly trying to learn his name, calls him Lybius Disconius (l. 80), knights him, and grants him the first fight that offers. Among the characters are Gawain, Percival, Agravaine, Ewaine, all drawn from Arthurian romance. Arthur himself is mentioned every little while as the recipient of the fruits of the young hero's victories (ll. 745 ff., &c.) Of the six manuscripts of the romance all but the Percy Manuscript belong to the fifteenth century, and the Percy Manuscript version, as Kaluza forcibly argues, is probably a copy of a sixteenth-century edition. He observes[4] that Henry Crosse mentions the 'Libbius' in *Vertues common,wealth, or, The highway to honour* (1600), and Skelton, who died in 1529, does the same in the line,

'And of sir Libius named Disconius'.

The old edition of the romance is lost, but Kaluza goes on to remark that the Percy Folio version of the romance of *Sir Triamore* (who plays his part in the romance of *Chinon*) is, 'except in spelling, a literally accurate copy of Copland's edition', and that a good number of the other romances are obviously copies of old printed editions.

The interesting romance of *Syre Gawene and the Carle of Carelyle*,[5] in 660 lines, recounts Gawain's perilous adventure in the castle of the Carl of Carlisle, who always insists upon instant and implicit obedience and who strikes down Gawain's companions Kay and Bishop Bawdewyn for a slight offence. Gawain's courtesy and scrupulous compliance with the demands of his host win the favour of the savage Carl, who finally conducts Gawain to his wife's bed

---

[1] Petyt's activity extended from 1536 to 1554.
[2] Harleian 5297, art. 32.   [3] *Percy's Folio MS.*, ii, 405-97.
[4] *Libeaus Desconus*, Leipzig, 1890, p. x.
[5] Ed. Madden, Bannatyne Club, 1839.

and bids him kiss her. Gawain obeys and is then taken to the chamber of the Carl's lovely daughter, with whom he passes the night. Next day the three guests, with the Carl's daughter, return to Arthur's court, and Gawain weds her. Arthur makes the Carl a knight of the Round Table and also lord of the region about Carlisle.

This romance undoubtedly embodies material far older than the sixteenth century and has been by Madden derived from the fabliau *Le Chevalier a l'épee*. The English romance here summarized is probably not later than the fifteenth century, but the sixteenth-century ballad,[1] *The Carle off Carlile*, in 500 lines, is doubtless based upon it. An incident not found in the romance but a variant of the beheading motives in *Gawain and the Green Knight* and *The Turke and Gowin* appears at the end of the ballad. When Gawain is about to leave his host he is taken to a room hung about with swords and bidden to strike off the Carl's head. After some hesitation Gawain obeys and to his astonishment sees the Carl, who for forty years has been forty cubits high, now released from his enchantment and restored to the stature of an ordinary man. No one but a knight of the Round Table could work the transformation.

Although, strictly speaking, the story of Tristram and Iseult is for the most part independent of the cycle of Arthur[2] it was in the course of time drawn into the group of Round Table romances, since great heroes like Arthur and Tristram could hardly be supposed to have lived in the same country without occasional association. But for some reason the Tristram story had no great vogue in early English literature, and it is represented only by the thirteenth-century verse romance, and by a large fragment of the prose romance in Malory's *Morte Darthur*, reproducing somewhat more than half of the French original. In the sixteenth century the verse romance had long since been forgotten and nothing remained but the version in Malory, perhaps the least satisfactory portion of the *Morte Darthur*. In view of the toughness of

---

[1] *Percy's Folio MS.*, iii, 272-94.
[2] Some traces of early connexion with Arthurian material appear in the Welsh Triads, in the Mabinogion, and in Englynion. See McNeill's introduction to *Sir Tristrem*, Scottish Text Society, pp. xiv, xv.

popular tradition, it would, however, be surprising if the Tristram story had passed out of memory, since, as Schofield remarks,[1] 'there was no one in the Middle Ages in western Europe who did not know it in some form'; and it appeared in the sixteenth century in various literatures of the Continent—Spain (1528), Italy (1555), Denmark, Germany (Hans Sachs, 1553), again in Italy in 1588, and so on.

Romances based upon the legend of the Holy Grail are not strictly Arthurian, but in course of time they are inevitably drawn into the cycle of the Round Table. Of the English pieces in prose or verse recounting the legend of Joseph of Arimathea—none of them significant as literature—several were printed before 1521. But after that date, except for the version of the Quest of the Grail incorporated in the *Morte Darthur*, the Grail story drops out of sight. The explanation is not far to seek: aggressive protestantism, though it might tolerate a fantastic legend hidden away in a great romance like Malory's, was not likely to welcome, solely for their own sake, religious tales so far removed in spirit from those sanctioned by the Established Church.

With the legend of the Holy Grail we conclude our general survey of Arthurian romance in the sixteenth century and may now turn to the romance of *Chinon of England*.

IV

THE ROMANCE OF CHINON OF ENGLAND, THE ORIGINAL EDITION

In the Stationers' Registers (ed. Arber) is entered under the year 1597 *The History of Chinon of England*, by Christopher Middleton.[2] This was not the first time the name had come before the public, for in Henslowe's Diary is mention of a play called *Chinone of Ingland*, first acted 3rd January, 1595—Henslowe, the manager of the theatre, receiving fifty shillings.[3] According to Henslowe's record there were in all eleven performances, the last on 10th November, 1596. After that date the play disappears, and our

---

[1] *English Literature from the Norman Conquest to Chaucer*, p. 214.
[2] For his other works, see the list in the *Dictionary of National Biography*.
[3] The receipts for the last four performances were respectively 9s., 52s., 17s., 10s.

Introduction

only knowledge of it is derived from Henslowe. Nothing is known of the author. That there is some relation between the play and Middleton's romance is not improbable, but to urge, as does Schelling,[1] that 'no one can question that this was a dramatized version of The Famous History of Chinon of England ... by Chr. Middleton, 1597', is to go beyond the evidence. No edition of the romance is known earlier than the entry in the Stationers' Registers, 1597, and the assumption of an earlier edition is purely gratuitous. That Middleton may have had his romance in manuscript two years before he gave it to the printer is of course possible, and in that case he may have allowed some dramatist to adapt it to the stage, if indeed he did not attempt to do it himself. But beyond such conjectures we cannot go, nor can we venture (on the evidence) to argue that the romance is due to the play. In any case, however, the appearance of the two productions under the same title within the space of two years inevitably suggests various interesting possibilities.

The present edition of the romance, the only one known since 1597, is based upon the copy in the British Museum.[2] This comes from the library of the Earl of Jersey at Osterley Park and has his coat of arms within the front cover, with his name, Victor Albert George Child Villiers. The volume is a small quarto in black-letter, containing forty-seven leaves not numbered, but the order indicated by the signatures at the foot of the pages, D_1, D_2, D_3, &c. The printing is rather carelessly and inartistically done, and in more than one place betrays the lack of a competent typographer, a manuscript corrector, or a trustworthy proof-reader.[3]

V

THE STORY OF *CHINON OF ENGLAND*

Chapter I

IN the time of the famous King Arthur a noble knight named Cador is for his many merits installed in the Earldom of Cornwall. To this knight are born in his advancing years two children, a son

---

[1] *Elizabethan Drama*, i, 202.
[2] Another copy came into the market from the famous Britwell library in 1923 at Sotheby's in London.
[3] See especially pp. 49-63, and 63/34.

and a daughter, both of them endowed with great beauty of body. The daughter, Laura, is as wise as she is beautiful, but her brother, Chinon, is so lacking in ordinary sense that he everywhere passes for a fool, to the great grief of his parents.

Chapter II

The fame of Laura's beauty draws to Earl Cador's court many valiant knights, among whom are two knights of King Arthur's Round Table, Sir Lancelot du Lake and Sir Tristram du Lions, 'two wonders for their worthines'. Amid the throng of admirers Laura is most attracted by Lancelot, and he in turn utterly loses his heart to Laura. With the hope of winning her love he resolves 'to undertake some hardie aduenture', but before he departs he sends her a passionate letter in which he unreservedly offers himself to her. Without waiting to learn her answer he takes formal leave of the court, proclaiming openly why he feels compelled to leave the kingdom. With him, despite the friendly protests of Lancelot, goes also the valiant Sir Tristram.

Chapter III

Crossing the Channel to France the two knights, attended only by two pages, set out on their way. While resting beside a spring they fall in with an aged hermit, who courteously offers them entertainment and tells them that not far away is the court of King Lewis of France, and that the very next day there is to be a contest for three prizes—a rich suit of armour, a gorgeous bed, and, best of all, the king's daughter and heir, the fair Celestina. Next morning the two knights proceed on their way to the court and overtake a knight in golden armour mounted upon a stately black steed. This is the son of the 'Soldan' of Babylon, who has come as a suitor for the hand of Celestina. Another knight, all in black and occupying a sable tent, is Sir Triamore, son of the 'Duke of Brittaine', who has long been the favoured lover of the princess. In the tournament that follows, the Soldan's son carries all before him and then, thinking himself invincible, arrogantly challenges all Christians to meet him in the field. This challenge Sir Lancelot boldly meets and after a terrific combat vanquishes the boaster. Second only to Lancelot in the tournament is Sir Tristram.

Introduction

The great prizes of the tournament are awarded to Lancelot and, of course, among them the fair Celestina. But as Lancelot's heart is fixed upon Laura, he magnanimously bestows Celestina upon her lover, Sir Triamore, reserving the other prizes for his own lady love, and sending them to her by a trusty messenger. Lancelot's exploits lose nothing in the telling and so powerfully impress the young prince Chinon, hitherto indifferent to warlike achievement, that he suddenly begins to lament his wasted youth and persuades his astonished and delighted father to equip him as a knight and send him abroad to win a name for himself.

Meanwhile, preparations are making in France for the marriage of Sir Triamore and Celestina. But Triamore's aged father is eager to witness the wedding, and the king graciously consents to allow the bridal pair to proceed into Brittany for the ceremony, attended by Sir Lancelot, Sir Tristram, and many other knights and ladies.

With a speed possible only in romances the Soldan of Babylon has in the interval learned of the death of his son and landed a strong army which is already encamped around the town where the Duke of Brittany is holding his court. Then, laying an ambuscade four miles outside the city, he awaits the arrival of the bridal party. In the fight that ensues, all except Lancelot, Tristram, and Triamore are slain, and Celestina is carried off as prisoner. Worn out by fighting, the three knights wander many hours in the darkness through the woods until they come upon 'a great worne way', which finally leads them into a dark cave whence issue 'striking cries'. Then out of an adjoining cave suddenly emerges a 'mightie monster' with the face of a woman and the body of a huge serpent, and rolls against the mouth of the cave a great stone, making the knights helpless prisoners.

Chapter IV

While all this is happening Chinon has come to France in search of adventures worthy of a young knight. Ignorant of the country, he rides through deep valleys and dark woods until by chance he arrives before the mouth of the cave where the three knights are imprisoned. Reading the inscription at the entrance he learns that only a 'maiden knight' can release whoever is imprisoned within.

Presently he is confronted by the monster keeper of the cave and almost smothered in the dark smoke issuing from his 'fierie bellie'. In the fierce fight that ensues the brave young Chinon is almost overcome, when suddenly the monster vanishes. Then the great stone rolls away from the mouth of the cave, and the three imprisoned knights come forth. Great is the astonishment of Lancelot and Tristram to recognize in the valiant young man now before them the foolish boy they had left in England. But hardly have they recovered from their astonishment when King Oboram, king of the fairies, appears amid a troop of his attendants and bestows highest praises upon young Chinon, at the same time revealing that the hideous monster was none other than himself. Then he leads the four knights through long underground passages and out into a broad vale, where fastened in a great rock is a costly enchanted sword which is to be his who can pull it out. All try in vain until Chinon easily draws it from the rock. Thereupon the young knight receives rich arms and armour, along with a dwarf as a page, and promises of further help from Oboram.

Chapter V

From his new companions Chinon learns of the capture of Celestina and at once resolves to rescue her. Accordingly, with Triamore in the guise of an enchantress come from far to further the love of the Soldan for Celestina, Chinon and his dwarf go as attendant servants, while Lancelot and Tristram lie in wait for the infidels. Beguiled by the seductive enchantress the Soldan goes at night to an appointed place in the woods accompanied by his chief captains, when Lancelot and the others fall upon their unsuspecting enemies, killing them all but the Soldan, whom they carry away as a prisoner. To the unbounded gratitude of Celestina and Triamore Chinon makes a modest disclaimer and proposes to return to England with Lancelot and Tristram and his prisoner, the Soldan.

Chapter VI

Upon their arrival in England the three are welcomed with joy by all, and particularly by Chinon's aged father. King Arthur himself, to do Chinon honour, summons a solemn meeting of all the nobles

Introduction

and peers of the realm and before the assembly formally dubs Chinon a knight, as he has already proved himself in reality, and appoints him a place at the Round Table.

Chapter VII

After his great exploits Chinon long idles away his time at home, until one day as he lies sleeping on a pleasant bank there suddenly appear two fairies showing him a suit of rich armour and a sword surpassing the one he had pulled out of the rock, and also the vision of a fair maid whose beauty baffles description. This maiden, Cassiopeia, the daughter of Bessarian, chief counsellor of the king of Egypt, has been vainly wooed by a noble named Perosus. Out of revenge he has enlisted the help of an old witch, who has conveyed her through the air far from her home to an unfrequented plain beside the river Nile. Here she sits and sings mournful ditties, when suddenly the wicked witch appears, upbraiding her for her cruelty to Perosus and threatening her with perpetual banishment unless she relents. To pass away the time the maiden keeps sheep, spins their wool, and makes herself homely garments. She sees no hope of escape, though without her knowledge her three brothers, Michander, Terpander, and Theonas are actively seeking her.

Meanwhile, Perosus, not content with the evil he has wrought, falsely accuses Bessarian of treason to the king, and as a proof shows forged letters that the aged man apparently had written to the king's enemies. The king, in a rage, overwhelms Bessarian with reproaches and, without waiting for an explanation, banishes the faithful old man from the kingdom and strips him of his property. Everything appears to favour the success of the plot, but the old witch on looking into her speculative glass discovers that the gods have determined the maiden's release, and hence encloses her 'within the ruine of an olde Rocke hard by the river side'.

Chapter VIII

Having Celestina in safe keeping, the witch now turns Bessarian into the form of a bear and has her attendant spirits hang about his neck a scroll bearing verses promising good fortune to whoever kills him.

While the old man is roaming about, the witch observes in her magic glass the approach of Cassiopeia's three brothers, who by different ways are unawares drawing near to their imprisoned sister. Michander, the eldest, catches sight of her in the midst of the 'cloven rock', and then sees the sides close and hide her from him. To his inquiry what he can do to release her she gives an answer dictated by the witch, directing him to bring from Mt. Taurus in Asia a vial full of virgin's tears that will 'breake the strongest inchaunted bands'. This vial is guarded by a 'sight-killing serpent' and the winning of it will be perilous.

While Michander is on his way, the second brother, Terpander, draws near and, overjoyed to see his lost sister, tries to kiss her hand, when suddenly the rock closes and shuts her from him. With tears she tells him how she has been imprisoned and entreats him to strive to free her. Far away, in the deserts of Arabia, says she, is Arion's harp, 'kept by a man-eating Canniball'. The music of this magic instrument will open the rocks and free her from her prison. Believing this lying tale, dictated, like the first, by the witch, Terpander sets out on his fool's errand.

Last comes the youngest brother, Theonas, and like his brothers sees his imprisoned sister. He in his turn is sent by her on a dangerous errand suggested by the witch. He is to go to a 'perilous island' where, guarded by two harpies, lies on an altar in a temple a golden book containing all known enchantments 'and their severall releases', and with this book he may effect his sister's release.

Chapter IX

After the departure of the three brothers, the fairies bring Chinon to Cassiopeia's prison, and while he wanders along the river he at length hears her singing a mournful ditty as she sits amongst the rocks. At sight of her he breaks out in passionate avowals of love and without hesitation undertakes the task that the maiden, impelled by the witch, imposes upon him.

Chapter X

Meanwhile, the eldest brother, following the directions given him, at length finds in distant Asia the monstrous cockatrice that guards the precious vial of virgin's tears, and, as his bright armour reflects

Introduction

back upon the beast the poisonous rays darting from its eyes, Michander easily gets possession of the treasure. But the so-called tears, warmed by the heat of his hand, soon drive him to frenzy. While Michander is wandering aimlessly, the second brother finds the golden harp, far away in the Arabian deserts, guarded by a monster, part dog and part man. A furious fight ensues, the monster is killed, and the harp carried off. No sooner, however, has Terpander touched the strings than he is struck dumb by the magic sounds.

Last of all comes the third brother, Theonas, to the shores of the perilous island where lies upon the altar of the temple of the enchantress Erganea the golden book of enchantments, kept by two harpies. A short combat puts him in possession of the coveted book, but when he opens it his eyes are blinded by 'a dustie fogge', and he has to grope his way back to the place whence he came.

Chapter XI

While the three brothers are vainly wandering, Chinon by chance meets them one after another and draws upon himself the plague that torments each of them, becoming raging mad, dumb, and blind. Now that Chinon is practically helpless, the witch encloses him, like Cassiopeia, within the cleft of a rock against which she rolls a mighty stone, but fortunately she removes his plagues and restores him again to his wits.

Chapter XII

While Chinon has been wandering in strange lands, his father, the Earl of Cornwall, is plunged in sorrow at the loss of his son, and, unable longer to endure his trouble, one day appeals to King Arthur for aid. The king commands his knights to draw lots for the coveted privilege of joining the searching party. The lot falls to Sir Calor, who, after choosing two companions and taking counsel of Merlin, hastens on his errand. Arriving in the perilous island they soon come upon the giant guarding the cave where Chinon is kept, and after a fierce fight they compel him to free his prisoner, but consent to spare his life in return for his revelation of all that Perosus has plotted.

Chapter XIII

We now return to the brothers of Cassiopeia. When Chinon has relieved them in turn of their troubles and unwittingly drawn the plagues upon himself, the brothers make their several ways back to their sister. One after another they meet their father transformed into a bear, attack the supposed beast and leave him for dead. Meanwhile, there has been fought in Egypt between the king of Egypt and the traitor Perosus a great battle in which the king, aided by Sir Calor's company of Englishmen, puts Perosus to flight. By chance Bessarian, now somewhat recovered, meets Perosus and suddenly seizes upon him, but does him no harm. The conscience-stricken fugitive sees the scroll and with tears falls down before the man-bear, entreating his pardon and promising to lead him to his daughter. By good fortune Chinon, with the English knights, after the battle intercepts the witch as she is fleeing and, on her promise to free her prisoner, spares her life. The witch now transports them to the place where Cassiopeia is imprisoned, frees the maiden and begs forgiveness. This the lady grants; whereupon after the witch has recounted all that Chinon has done for the love of Cassiopeia, the young knight and the maiden pledge themselves to each other. In the midst of the rejoicing appears Perosus leading Bessarian, still in the form of a bear. By the help of the witch he presently resumes his former shape and then returns with the entire company to court. He is then reinstated by the king in his former dignity. Perosus is severely punished, and, as we might expect, Chinon and Cassiopeia are 'matched together in marriage'.

VI

The Romance of *Chinon* and its Sources

A SLIGHT examination of the romance of *Chinon of England* suffices to show that it is mainly a combination of features appearing in earlier romances or suggested by them, and that it is almost wholly a romance of adventures, strange and startling. Moreover, it is in large measure a fairy romance; in some sense, too, an original romance, since the author has tried to put his material together in his own way. Although the sources of much of the romance are obvious enough, in many cases it would

Introduction

be difficult if not impossible to determine which of several possible sources the author actually used. We might not improperly characterize it as a belated Arthurian romance, with an abundant infusion of the sort of matter that appears in *Huon of Bordeaux* [1]— the old French wonder-book translated by Lord Berners and first printed by Wynkyn de Worde—the whole tricked out with an ambitious display of classical learning, or what passed for such.

As is the case in *Huon of Bordeaux*,[2] Arthur is in *Chinon* little more than a lay figure drawn from literary tradition, and his court is the centre about which the chivalric life of his kingdom naturally gathers. Cador of Cornwall, as elsewhere remarked,[3] appears in Geoffrey of Monmouth's *History of the Kings of Britain* and subsequent chronicles and Arthurian romances as one of the great supporters of Arthur, and he is similarly described here.

His son Chinon,[4] the central figure of the story, finds no place in older Arthurian romance, but he has obvious affinity with the hero of the folk-tale of the Great Fool [5] and with many similar heroes of medieval romance. The stories of this type present a young fellow who is of good stock but who, because of his crude early surroundings or his lack of opportunity, appears at the outset as an unsophisticated, awkward, and outwardly unpromising youth. The type varies in detail, but we find it in Peredur of the Welsh *Mabinogion*, in the more familiar Perceval of the romances, in Malory's Gareth,[6] in the Knight La Cote Male Taile,[7] and the hero of *Libeaus Desconus*. With some modifications we may even put into this class such a character as the knight Balin,[8] who alone

---

[1] The first edition of Lord Berner's translation is assigned by Sidney Lee, who edited it for the E.E.T.S. (1882-7), to about 1534; the second edition, now lost, to 1570. The third edition, with somewhat modernized phrasing, was printed in 1601.

[2] See Index of Names in E.E.T.S. edition.

[3] See note to p. 5/1.

[4] Was the name suggested by the famous old castle town on the Vienne?

[5] For *The Lay of the Great Fool*, see Campbell's *Popular Tales of the West Highlands*, iii, 146 ff., and for a summary, Nutt's *Studies on the Legend of the Holy Grail*, pp. 60 ff. Cf. also the stories of Cuchulinn and of Fergus, and of the hero of the romance of *Tyolet*, edited by G. Paris, *Romania*, viii, 40-50. Of course, only the general conception of an unpromising youth who ultimately achieves much links *Chinon* with the *Lay*.

[6] *Morte Darthur*, Book VII. [7] Ibid., Book IX, chs. 1-9.

[8] Ibid., Book II, ch. 2.

among Arthur's knights, although he is shabbily dressed and temporarily under a cloud, can draw the magic sword out of its sheath. Similar instances of the development of notable qualities in some one of unpromising exterior will occur to all readers of old romance.

Among the other personages in *Chinon* Lancelot presents the well-known characteristics of bravery, generosity, and modesty that he displays in Arthurian romance. But Guenevere—the traditional object of his devotion—is not once mentioned in *Chinon*, and Lancelot is presented as madly in love with Laura, daughter of Cador. By a singular and inexplicable slip, however, Sir Calor is introduced as the son of Lancelot and of the fair and chaste Celestina![1] Tristram is, of course, drawn from the Arthurian or the Tristram romances, but we get no hint of his earlier career nor any mention of King Mark or of Iseult. Triamore, in his turn, though doubtless suggested by the well-known romance bearing his name, is put in a new setting.[2] The author seems in general to aim at arousing the reader's interest by presenting well-known characters in novel situations. These three famous knights here serve mainly as a foil to enhance the glory of Chinon. As for Laura, Celestina, and Cassiopeia, they are charming creatures, but their like may be found in any old romance, and we need not seek their prototypes. Nor do the remaining characters offer anything distinctive. Perosus is the well-known traitor type and Bessarian the victim of baseless slander. One of the stock features in many old romances is the false accusation, which, as a rule, is believed as soon as made. The helpless unfortunate is then banished or otherwise punished, and not till long after is the truth made known and the accused vindicated. We cite, as a few examples out of many, King Horn, the slandered empress in *Valentine and Orson*, Constance in the Man of Law's Tale, the legendary Genoveva, and so on. As for the three brothers of Celestina, they have no more individuality than so many automatons.

VII

THE SUPERNATURAL ELEMENT

ONE notable feature of *Chinon*, perhaps even the most characteristic feature, is the lavish use of supernatural agencies—fairies,

[1] See p. lxi.   [2] See note to 16/6.

magic, witchcraft—though there is singularly little of the magic atmosphere. The supernatural had dominated the Middle Ages, and under the intense strain of the Reformation period the old inherited belief in magic and witches and all the powers of darkness was rather intensified than diminished. High and low alike felt that they were encompassed by powers supernal and powers infernal, which either by prayer or by propitiation or by the use of a magic formula might be made to do the bidding of man.

Men of learning and real wisdom, to say nothing of the common folk, believed more or less firmly in the influence of the moon and the stars on the destinies of men, and our old poets abound in allusions to astrology, often too veiled to reach the modern reader. The courses of the planets run parallel with the paths of human life and might point the way to success or failure. No one had explored the mysteries of the skies and of the far away lands across the seas. Who could tell what might be hid there? What fountains of youth, what mountains of gold, what heaps of jewels exceeding the wildest dreams of the Arabian Nights? In such matters exaggeration is easy, but assuredly we may say that in every class of society there was a generally diffused faith in mysterious wonder lands and in medieval superstitions that have long since been relegated to the humblest ranks of our modern communities—in fairies, in witches, in ghosts. Probably Spenser did not seriously believe in the existence of fairies any more than did Shakespeare when he wrote *A Midsummer Night's Dream*,[1] but the Elizabethan age had a profound conviction of the existence of unfathomed marvels and of things never seen on sea or land. Heaven and angels were real and not very far away. And a hot flaming hell, with devils black and horned, was ready to receive the wicked. Alchemy had been scoffed at by Chaucer, but it had survived, just as Christian science and spiritualism and occultism of all sorts have captivated brilliant men and women in our own age of exact scientific research. The learned Dr. Dee, who was on friendly terms with Queen Elizabeth and many of the leading men of England, was a firm believer in alchemy and astrology and augury, and on March 10, 1574-5, he explained the use of his 'famous magic glass ... to her

[1] For an interesting account of the conception of fairies current when *Chinon* was written, see Edwin Greenlaw, *Spenser's Fairy Mythology, Studies in Philology* (University of North Carolina), xv, 105-22.

Majesty's satisfaction'. Very common was the magic use of the Bible and the works of Virgil—perhaps more famous throughout the Middle Ages as an enchanter than as a poet—to forecast future action. It is well known that Charles I, along with the poet Cowley, tried the *sortes Virgilianae* at Carisbrooke Castle in 1648. And John Wesley was frequently guided to a decision by the chance text that his eye rested upon as he opened his Bible.

The sixteenth century was, then, peculiarly favourable to the production of such a romance as *Chinon*, and it is not surprising that we find obvious traces of the influence of *Huon of Bordeaux*. Not only is 'Oboram' a modified form of Oberon, king of the fairies in the old French romance, but there is much reason to think that from the Huon romance came the chief suggestion for the extensive use of fairies and of magic in *Chinon*.[1] There is no certain proof that the author owes anything directly to Spenser, though his example possibly counted for something.

After what has been said above, the supernatural features that appear in *Chinon* call for no detailed discussion. In the realm of the impossible anything may be supposed to happen. One objection, indeed, to introducing magic as an active element in a romance is that everything has to yield to it. The characters can no longer develop under the influence of normal motives, and caprice rules the progress of the story. This is abundantly illustrated throughout the romance, the greater part of which is a succession of marvels. The unexpected constantly happens. Oboram and his magic cave, his attendant fairies, and his swift transformation from loathsome dragon to king of the fairies—all present situations not found in this workaday world. To these we may add the capture of Chinon by the fairies and his passage through the air to Egypt; Celestina's similar journey through the air and her imprisonment amid rocks that open and shut; the various plagues that torment the brothers in performing the tasks imposed upon them by the witch through the mouth of their sister, and the subsequent transfer of these inflictions to Chinon; the transformation of Bessarian into a bear; and, lastly, the release of all the victims from the power of the magic spells.

Moreover, since individual valour is at a disadvantage in con-

[1] Proportionally, if not actually, there is more fairy activity in *Chinon* than in *Huon of Bordeaux*.

Introduction lix

tending with magical power, there is small room in *Chinon* for the interplay of one character upon another. The attention of the reader is forced upon the incidents, which almost necessarily become more and more startling and impossible.

VIII
INFLUENCE OF THE CLASSICS

LASTLY, we may note a feature of *Chinon* which forcibly strikes the modern reader, and that is the varied classical learning lavished upon this short romance. Much of the medieval literature makes free use of classical literature and tradition, but not infrequently the classical elements are strangely transformed in their medieval setting. Witness, for example, the metamorphosis of the myth of Orpheus and Eurydice into the exquisite fairy romance of *Sir Orfeo*. Nothing of the sort appears in *Chinon*. The medieval features still persist, but almost every situation suggests to the author something purely classical by way of illustration. As for the gods, they are the familiar deities of the classical pantheon, and there is no trace of Christianity in the entire romance. Quite likely the author took some pride in his familiarity with ancient literature or at least with some compendium of classic mythology. In any case, he parades his knowledge with the delight of a child showing a new toy. This exploitation of the classics is the peculiar earmark of the great Renaissance. Along with free use of the medieval lapidaries and bestiaries, it is one of the marked features of the euphuistic style; and of euphuism in *Chinon* there is quite enough for modern taste.

Obviously, *Chinon* is mainly addressed, not to the populace, who still delighted in variously modernized and abbreviated versions of the old medieval romances, but to readers who might be assumed to care chiefly for the great writers of antiquity and yet might be enticed into reading a quasi-medieval romance if classical allusions were liberally scattered along the pages. In his procedure the author is merely following a fashion exemplified by Spenser and Chapman and scores of others who found themselves living in an age still partly medieval but were so delighted with the new learning that they could not refrain from dragging it in at every turn.

So numerous are the classical allusions in *Chinon* that we can touch only upon the more notable. A favourite image of Elizabethan poets is that of the horses of the sun, and our author, wishing to indicate the approach of evening pompously refers to 'the fweating Horfes of the weary funne fwiftly defcending from the higheft top of that heauenly hill' (13/3 f.). The armour of the son of the Soldan of Babylon reminds the romancer of the armour of Achilles (15/19), and his heavy lance, of the great shaft that Ajax bore at the siege of Troy (16/35). He is familiar with the 'fweet tuned tongue of heauenlie Tullie' (20/33), and with the story of Aeneas and Dido (20/39, 38/20). Heavy blows in the fight with Oboram make him think of the 'fteele the fmoakie Cyclops forged for the mighty God of wrathfull warr' (28/12). Then he is reminded of the Gorgon's head (29/10); of the sword made by a magician for Julius Caesar (30/21); of the story of Orpheus and Eurydice (35/23); of Alcides and Jason (37/34) and once more of the Greeks before Troy (38/2); of Endymion (40/9); of the furies (41/5); of the dolphins dancing to the music of Arion's harp (41/10); of Medea (41/27); of 'Efopes vngratefull fnake' (44/16); of Diana amidst her undraped nymphs (48/4); of Atlas, the labours of Hercules, and the labyrinth of Theseus (50/4-6); of Arion's harp (50/10); of the harpies (51/8, 58/23); of the wheel of Fortune (52/35); of the golden prize given to the fairest goddess (53/3); of the torments of Sisyphus (53/35); of the giants that piled hill upon hill to build steps up to heaven (54/1); of the poisoned shirt of Hercules (56/9); of 'the throted Dogge whome Thefeus awaked in the Gates of hell' (57/4); again (with much amplitude) of the harp that with its music could move rocks and trees (57/36); of the blinded Oedipus (59/13); of Ajax raging when he failed to get the armour of Achilles; and of Alcides in fury upon the mountain Oeta (60/5).

This rather formidable list is not exhaustive, but it is sufficient to present the striking phenomenon of a writer so full of medieval romance that he is impelled to produce one himself, and so steeped in the Greek and Latin classics that he naturally turns to them for illustrations and comparisons and forces them in superabundance upon his readers.

IX

PLOT AND CHARACTERS

AFTER this rapid survey of the materials of the romance we may well spend a moment in observing how they are put together, and

Introduction

also how the personages of the story are handled. In its construction *Chinon*, like many medieval romances, has no central controlling motive, but is rather a loose-jointed succession of exploits designed to show the pre-eminence of the character who gives his name to the romance.

A glance at our analysis of the story indicates that it is divided into two main parts. The first six chapters take us through Chinon's early youth and his exploits in France. Then the author seems not to know precisely what to do with his hero, and, after allowing him to rest in idleness for some time at home, can think of nothing better than to transport him bodily through the air to the banks of the Nile, there suddenly to fall in love with the imprisoned Cassiopeia, whose face and figure he had already seen in a vision, and to undertake marvellous adventures which lead to her release. The exploits in the East fill the remaining seven chapters and have practically nothing to do with those described in the first part, but the two parts are mechanically brought together under one title. In the first division of the romance, after Chinon has rescued the imprisoned Lancelot, Tristram, and Triamore, he is presented by Oboram with rich arms and armour, but he makes no use of them after his return to England, and he receives from the fairies a new equipment for his exploits in the East. Oboram is not again named. Moreover, Tristram, Triamore, and the Soldan of Babylon disappear from view, and there is only incidental further mention of Lancelot and Celestina. We do not even definitely learn whether the incomparable Laura finally accepts the hand of Lancelot, but possibly the author thought that the two had so fully pledged themselves that further comment was needless.

Although in effect the second half is almost wholly a detached and separate romance, there appears one remarkable and incomprehensible feature which is possibly not due to the author but merely one more instance of the incredible carelessness of the printer[1] or the proof-reader, if such there was. Sir Calor, who has hitherto not been mentioned, is suddenly presented (63/34) as the son of Lancelot and the young and innocent Celestina, though she is devoted to Lancelot's companion in arms Sir Triamore, to whom Lancelot—himself devoted to Laura—has gallantly resigned her.

---

[1] We find startling evidence of the sort of blundering the printer was capable of in the account of the three brothers of Cassiopeia, pp. 49–60.

By no ingenuity can we find a time or place for the alleged origin of Sir Calor, which is morally and chronologically impossible. Celestina had never met Lancelot before he came to France to win by his exploits the favour of Laura; and even if we assume, as we have no right to do, a love affair between Lancelot and Celestina, how can we find room in the story for the eighteen or twenty years required to bring Calor to reasonable maturity? Can we assume that Chinon spent years in idleness after his return from France and before his going to Egypt? And lastly, since Earl Cador is already a tottering old man when his son Chinon is spirited away to Egypt, what must have been his age if we allow time for the birth and education of a knight competent to be the leader of the rescuing expedition which is to restore Chinon to his sorrowing father? Consideration of these facts leaves no other alternative than to assume that Sir Calor is the son of Sir Triamore and Celestina, and even this solution, which removes the moral difficulty, affords no explanation of the chronological puzzle.

X

GRAMMAR

ANY discussion of the style of *Chinon* compels some previous consideration of the grammatical features of the romance. But we can afford little space for details [1] and must present the essentials in compact summary. The modern reader unfamiliar with sixteenth-century English might at first suspect the author to be an illiterate scribbler. But closer study shows that practically every apparent lapse in grammar can be paralleled in the work of the most approved writers of the sixteenth century. Usage in Elizabethan English had not yet been brought to such uniformity as appears in the time of Queen Anne, and considerable differences are found in writings published at about the same time.

On the purely formal side there is little to remark. Inflexional endings, with one remarkable exception, are substantially those of modern English. The *-en* of the infinitive and the plural of verbs, so common in Chaucer, has vanished; *-eth*, the regular ending in the King James's Bible, is not in ordinary use in the third singular indicative present throughout the romance, its place being commonly taken by *-s* or *-es*, though *-eth* occasionally appears.[2]

---

[1] Some items are treated in the notes.
[2] The use of *-(e)s* (third singular indicative) in *Chinon* substantially agrees

Introduction

Nouns are inflected for the most part as in our time, but the possessive of proper nouns is in a few instances indicated by adding *his* after the unchanged noun.¹ The ordinary possessive in -*s* or -*es* is, however, the normal form.² As for *its*, there is no example in the entire romance.

Although on the inflexional side the English of the romance calls for little comment, the syntax is often notably different from that sanctioned by modern usage. This especially appears in the frequent use of a plural subject with a verb apparently singular. As Kellner, however, observes,³ this 'may be simply accounted for by the fact that not only the endings -*es* and -*eth* but also *is* and *was* were used both in the singular and in the plural'.⁴ When compared with the usage of Chaucer and of fourteenth- and fifteenth-century romances in the Southern and Midland dialects, the practice of our author appears at first hardly defensible. But comparison with the usage of his contemporaries shows that he merely does with considerable freedom what others do now and then.⁵

A curious instance of attraction appears in the following: 'fhedding manie fhowers of amber teares, whofe power were able to haue drawne pittie,' &c. 41/3.

We can hardly afford further space for an enumeration of the peculiarities of the accidence of *Chinon*, but we may note one or two illustrations of the use (or misuse) of relative pronouns. Almost any page offers an example. Middle English writers

with the practice of Shakespeare, who uses -(*e*)*s* or -(*e*)*th* 'according to convenience'. Cf. Earle, *Philology of the English Tongue*, p. 66. The most frequent -*th* endings in *Chinon* appear in *hath*, *quoth*, and *doeth*, but we find also *catcheth* 24/21, *fareth*, 37/13, *fpreadeth*, 38/27, *ftandeth*, 49/10, &c. By a singular slip the author, 42/9, presents the following: 'thou . . . that before efteemeft'!

As for participles, we note in *Chinon* the unusual forms *ftinged*, 44/17, *ouercommed*, 56/32, *ftroken* (see Glossary). Cf. forms in the Oxford Dictionary.

¹ Cf. 'Ferdinand his horfe', 17/2, 'Sifiphus hys toyle', 53/35, 'Vlyffes his armour', 60/5.
² See, for example, 18/25, 18/26, 18/31, 18/37, 19/6, 19/24, 19/35, &c.
³ *English Syntax*, p. 48. Cf. also Abbott, *Shakespearian Grammar*, pp. 167, 235 f.
⁴ I have more than a score of examples, such as 'Sailers . . . doth admire', 6/31; 'plannets that guides', 9/38. Cf. also 11/32, 12/35, 16/37, 17/28, 22/18, 28/37, 33/15, 37/21, &c., &c.
⁵ Examination of a few pages of Edmund Spenser's *Present State of Ireland* (Globe edition) yielded four examples. See pp. 615, 622, 626, 641.

frequently omit a relative pronoun where ordinary modern usage retains it. *Chinon* continues the older practice.¹ A good instance of *constructio ad sensum* is the following: 'Thefe wer they of whome we faid afore were by the fubtill fhift of a deceauing Syren cunningly compaffed in that Caue,' 28/39.

In general our author is no model in his use of pronouns of any sort. Note the following: 'her that whofe life', &c. (37/33); 'two or three periured companions who he ... had fuborned' (43/17); 'Shee that by them was thus bound ... haue the Gods ordained', &c. (49/3). A characteristic exhibit of the author's method of using personal pronouns appears in the last paragraph on p. 65.

Throughout the romance the syntax is for the most part left to shift for itself; and in far too many passages words are left loose without grammatical relation with the quasi-sentences in which they are found.²

XI
Style

LEAVING now questions of grammatical form and structure we may venture a few words upon the style of the romance, if we may apply the term style to English such as Middleton writes. One has only to contrast the lightsome grace of Malory, to say nothing of Lord Berners, with the heavy lumbering of Middleton to realize that a great change has come over English prose in the course of a century.

Malory's prose doubtless employs too freely co-ordinate clauses connected by *and, for, then, thus,* and *so*,³ and it is perhaps at times unduly loose and garrulous and needs the variety and compactness that come from occasional suspension and subordination of the members of the sentence. But it is nearly always clear, often exquisitely beautiful, and always free from clumsy involutions and

---

[1] 'Leauing the way fhould lead him backe againe to hys Sifter' (56/12) and often. Browning furnishes many examples.

[2] Note the following, out of many:

The participle *forefeeing* (45/35) has nothing to agree with, and *maide* has no clearly indicated syntax. The main verb is often lacking. Cf. 'who long profeffing', &c. (30/4), 'and then leading', &c. (30/29). In the sentence beginning 'The maide', &c. (45/32) the first twenty words are left without grammatical relation, &c., &c.

[3] Middleton has taken over the old paratactic habit while at the same time imitating the ponderous Latin period.

Introduction

magniloquent verbosity. It shows no trace of the far-fetched euphuistic frippery which, a century later, wraps itself about a thought and smothers its life and movement. Of course, some of the credit for the style of Malory's *Morte Darthur* is due to the nameless charm and finish of his French originals. But so fully does he catch their spirit that the passages which are unquestionably his in matter as well as in form present substantially the same stylistic features as the translated portions of the romance.

Elizabethan euphuism undoubtedly did something to polish English prose style, for normal early Tudor prose, such for example as Latimer's or Tyndale's, tends somewhat unduly to plain, homely, workaday utility and gives too little attention to mere form. Euphuism, in the last third of the century, goes to the other extreme. The form of the sentence is as a rule more important than the content, and the over-ornamented product is essentially artificial and unreal.

To the average modern reader, indeed, nothing is more wearisome than euphuism,[1] with the long-drawn similes,[2] the repetition of a thought in another form,[3] the heaping-up of mere words for the sake of showing off the writer's vocabulary, the forced alliteration,[4] the parade of classical illustrations, and the beasts and birds that haunt the medieval bestiaries.[5] And of euphuism, belated though it is,[6] there is quite enough in *Chinon*.

But euphuism is not the only questionable feature of late sixteenth-century prose. Too many of the later Elizabethan prose writers have no clear conception of the different rhythm pertaining to prose and to poetry and they are continually tempted in their prose to trench upon the domain of the poet. They have, moreover, the vaguest ideas of the form and function of a sentence.

---

[1] It is a surprising fact, showing how dependent old translators were upon their models, that Lord Berners, whose English in *Huon* is so simple, should have introduced to English readers the tortured phrases of the Spanish Guevara, which rapidly became the pest of sixteenth-century English prose.

[2] Cp. in text 9/6 ff., 35/33 ff., 38/27 ff., 43/34-44/28, 58/27 ff., &c.

[3] Cf. in text 35/33, 43/4 ff., 58/27 f., &c.

[4] Incidental alliteration appears at every turn. Some of the more notable instances are found in the following pages: 6/2 ff., 7/33 ff., 11/1-20, 17/7 f., 17/20 ff., 18/2 ff., 20/25 ff., 21, 22/8 ff., 57/37 ff., &c.

[5] See 21/7 f., 38/27 f.

[6] See Earle, *English Prose*, p. 437.

Abundant illustrations may be found in Sidney's *Arcadia* (1590), where exquisite sentences abound beside numberless others that are mere thickets of phrases and clauses hopelessly entangled. Sir Walter Raleigh in his turn pours out his thought in a style that is stately and magnificent but almost unreadable, owing to the inordinate length and complexity of his sentences. With Sidney and Raleigh practically begins the 'flood of ponderous imitations of the Latin period that make much of the prose of the early seventeenth century a terra incognita for modern readers'.

These tendencies and many others are in greater or less degree illustrated in *Chinon*. We may begin with matters purely mechanical. Middleton apparently does not know what a sentence is or should be in form or extent and he constantly tries to crowd too much into it, with little concern for arrangement or length. Many of his attempted sentences are mere aggregations of phrases and clauses with no main verb and no movement. As a rule he advances as if he were wading through glue. His exasperating verbosity as he slowly wallows through phrase after phrase constantly reminds us that he has more words than thoughts. In the length of his sentences he shows no mercy. For example, the romance begins with a quasi-sentence of fifty-nine words—but with no main verb —and this is immediately followed by one of two hundred and six words. The subsequent sentences rarely, if ever, present the brief types constantly found in good modern prose, sentences ranging from ten or fifteen to twenty, thirty, or forty words. They normally run rather into blocks of seventy, ninety, and one hundred and twenty words, and even to shapeless monsters of more than three hundred words.[1] Some of this undue protraction can be in part remedied by a freer use of periods in place of commas, but in general the only cure is a radical recasting of the form. There are too many formal comparisons long drawn out, the diction is painfully prolix and overloaded with epithets,[2] while sometimes it is a mere jingle.[3] There is an excess of participial and relative and parenthetical clauses[4] beginning with *who, when, where,* and in

---

[1] See pp. 8/15 ff., 9/27-10/28, 12/28-14/2, 23/37-24/31, 39/9-40/4, &c.

[2] Cf. pp. 6/11 ff., 13, 14, 23/23 ff., 47/33 ff., &c.

[3] 19/35 (content, confent, intent), 35/36, 37 (meede, deede), 42/15 (maid, difmayed!), 57/32 (confort, comfort).

[4] 11/24 ff., 16/28 ff., 29/26 ff., 54, 58-61, &c.

general an overplus of dependent clauses themselves modified by dependent phrases or clauses, the whole combining to make the sentence limp wearily on until it can go no farther. Illustrations of all these matters meet us at every turn. Dip in at random and we find at once a specimen on page 19/3, no better and no worse than scores of others. To readers of our time wordiness of this sort is little better than mere mouthing. And the worst of it is that the author evidently takes pride in his purple patches, and delights in saying simple things in as complicated and turgid a fashion as possible.

These are regrettable features of Middleton's writing, but we must note that, notwithstanding his usual clumsiness, he is rarely obscure, and he is often content when off his guard to write in a relatively unambitious fashion. At worst he seldom ventures upon the wildly tempestuous rhetorical sea in which the contemporary romancer Richard Johnson habitually disports himself. He does indeed occasionally swell somewhat and soar higher than modern taste approves, but he soon deflates and descends to earth again. Possibly his euphuistic flights were welcomed by Elizabethan readers; to us they appear hopelessly artificial and antiquated.

XII

Literary Value

WE have been compelled to deal somewhat severely with the style of this romance, but we must not allow the unfortunate form to obscure the significance of the romance on other grounds. *Chinon* affords one more proof out of many, too generally overlooked, that the type of literature which had held the foremost place in popular esteem for three or four centuries still made sufficient appeal to induce a writer in the latter days of Elizabeth to bring together famous characters of old romance in new relations. Nothing exactly parallel appears in the course of the entire seventeenth century, though a multitude of medieval romances continued to be reprinted in condensed and variously refashioned forms, and Richard Johnson's *Tom a Lincolne* and the more famous *Seven Champions of Christendom* along with the once widely read romances of Emanuel Ford freely exploited the whole range of old romance for striking situations. *Chinon* never won the popularity attained by Johnson's flowery productions, but at all events it deserves more attention than it has received. The common neglect of the late romances, even by professed students of literature, has gone a little too far. With increasing research it is becoming obvious that the history of English literature in its relations with popular romance is yet to be written; for no adequate account of that literature—to say nothing of the old reading public—is possible that overlooks the fact that the old romances during the seventeenth and eighteenth centuries helped to keep alive the appetite for the marvels of fairyland and the departed glories of chivalry and thus prepared the way for the romantic revival in the eighteenth century.

As an attempt to rival the old romancers in their own field *Chinon* certainly leaves much to be desired, but as an attempt to meet the demand for medieval romance at the end of the sixteenth century by writing an original romance of the old type it is curiously interesting and significant.

THE Famous Historie of

Chinon of England, with his strange aduentures for the loue of *Celestina* daughter to *Lewis* King of *Fraunce*.

With the worthy Atchiuement of Sir *Lancelot du Lake*, and Sir *Tristram du Lions* for faire *Laura*, daughter to *Cador* Earle *of Cornewall*, beeing all Knights *of King* Arthurs round Table.
By Chr. Middleton.

AT LONDON,
Printed by *Iohn Danter*, for *Cuthbert Burbie*, and are to be sold at his shop by the Royall Exchange. 1 5 9 7.

To the right worſhipfull Maſter

Edward Stanley Eſquire.

SIR, were I not more comforted with aſſurance of your Generous diſpoſition, than perſwaded of anie merit on my part, by offering the Patronage of this Hiſtorie to your hands, I ſhould as certainly diſpaire of the acceptaunce, as I am vncertaine whether it bee worthie to bee accepted. From the time of my firſt entraunce in Printing till now, it is the firſt Booke of this kinde I euer had power to dedicate; from my firſt yeres of capacitie to read anie printed thing, my affectionate dutie hath to your W. been dedicated.

Enisham, one of your Lordſhips, was my [A² back] birth-place; and as my Frends there pay dueties for the place they liue in, ſo tender I this here as part of my duteous loue.

The Authour of the Booke hath left it to the wide world without a Patron, perchance eſteeming it vnworthie protection; neyther doo I thinke it in the leaſt part worthie your protection, before whoſe excelent iudgement (ſo daily conuerſant among the moſt iudiciall) it cannot but vaniſh like light ſmoake before a bright flame. All my excuſe is loue, all my requeſt is pardon; which as (I firſt inferd) your noble diſpoſition aſſures mee of. On which foundation building, I ceaſe now to bee more bold.

Your Worſhips, moſt dutifully affectionate:

Iohn Danter.

The famous Hiftory

of Chinon of England, Sonne to Lord *Cador* Earle of *Cornewall*, with his rare atchiuements for faire *Celleſtina*, daughter to *Lewes King of Fraunce.*

In the time of King Arthur the Earl of Cornwall is Cador, already advanced in years and no longer equal to the burdens of his station.

CHAP. I.

How Chinon *the Earle of* Cornewalles *Sonne was borne a foole, and of the excellent ornaments of nature wherewith his faire Siſter* Laura *was beautefied.*

In the beginning of this flouriſhing Kingdome, when *Arthur* then Monarch of this little worlde, with his attendant Knights, whoſe valorous exployts, euery where acted for theyr Countries honour, hath eternized their euerliuing names, euen in the fartheſt coaſts of the barbarous Pagans, where yet in deſpite of conſuming time liues their eternal Trophies as ſpectacles for all poſterities; [B¹ back] In this time liued there in England an auncient Knight, whome this famous king for his many merits and well deſeruing deedes, had inſtalled in the Earledome of *Cornewall*, a dignity as hee thought fitting the deſerts of this famous man, that had ſo often vndergone the furious attempts of the vnciuill Pagans, enemies to God, foes to his countrie, and great hindrances to the then but young plants of ſpringing Chriſtianity, as alſo endeuoring himſelfe euery where to defend the fame of his countrie, then of all other only fame worthy the Honour of his order euery where honored, and the dutie belonging to his Knighthood, which hee alwaies performed, till at the laſt, when the waight of many wearie yeares gan bow his declining bodie downe to the lowly earth, making his oft tried Armour too heauie a burthen for his now war weakned body, his brandiſhing ſword beating down his age fallen armes, and euery supporter of his luſtie limmes beginnes to faile of their former force, he determins to end his life in peace at home, whoſe beginning he had ſpent in warres abroad, incouraging younger men with the ſpectacle of his former valours, couragiouſly themſelues to attempt the like indeuors.

Late in life he is bleſt with two children, a son, Chinon, and a daughter, Laura. The daughter is a pattern of all the virtues and incomparably beautiful.

In which time of his home aboad, the heauens bleſſed him with two goodly Children, a Sonne & a Daughter: but yet as it is the continual courſe of al ruling fortune to mixe with euery good ſome ill, with euerie ſweet a ſowre, & with euery ſunſhine ſhow of promiſing hap, a tempeſtuous ſtorme of ill boading hurt, ſo fared it in the iſſue of this yet vnhappie Prince: for when the ſtealing houres of all ripening time had brought them from their Infant Cradelles to ſome participation of ſencible knowledge, his Daughter, whoſe name was *Laura*, ſo forwardly proſpered in euery Liniament of her beautifull bodie & all eternall quallities of a vertuous minde: [B²] ſo that in ſhort time ſhe became the cenſured ſubiect of all wiſe iudgements, in determination whether nature had better beautefied her bodie, (where indeede ſhee had exceeded her ſelf) or the Gods quallified her mind, wherin they had made her the only ſimilitude of themſelues. No penne that was not buſied in painting her praiſes, though all too little for that purpoſe, and no tongue but was ſtill telling her perfections, though they neuer could attaine them: for too bright was her beautie to be ſhadowed in the couloring cunning of a mortall capacitie, and too high her heauenly minde to be enſtauld with the earthlie weedes of mans baſe wit, that as the toileſome Sailers in the dangerous Seas watching the miſfortunes of a tedious night doth with themſelues mightily admire the gorgeous ſtate of many twinckling ſtars, till when the ſiluer Moone, proudlie riſing from her glorious bed, drawes backe their daſeled eies to behold her more than common countenance: ſo fares it in this age of theirs, where no ſtarre may compare with her ſtate, no face with her faire fortune, nor no grace with the leaſt glimce of her glorie; ſo to leaue to expreſſe that in wordes which could

of Chinon of England 7

not bee comprehended in all wits, neuer did nature before compose of so rude a Chaos so comely a creature: But her Brother, whose name was *Chynon*, outwardly formed in as faire a fashion as might well beseeeme the sonne to such a sire, but in his minde
5 more than a maimed man, wanting that portion of sensible capacity which commonly doth accompany euen the meanest seruillitie: So that by how much his Sister exceeded in extraordinarie wisdome, by so much was hee scanted in ordinarie witte, where in steede of Princely feature was nothing found but
10 foolish behauiour, for high atchiuementes boyish follies: for that which is required in a man, not so much as is commonly found in a childe, vncapable of the rudiments of good [B² back] counsaile, and vnfit to conceiue the commoditie of comelie quallitie: whence as all men with admiration wondred at the one, so none
15 but with commisseration pittied the other, that so well fashioned a body should containe so ill formed a minde; strongly had nature forged hys limbes, which promised his valour, but weakely had the enuious Fates framed his mind, wher was no hope of better. So that heere nature vnnaturally handling so good
20 a subiect had enclosed in the perfecte body of a man little better than the vnperfect soule of a beast, like almost the imitating of an apish artificer, that in faire showes deciphers a formall substance, in curious cunning colours painting a Princely perfection, which satisfies the outward sence as the same, but cannot content the
25 inward conceit, beeing but a bare show: So by euery outward appearance was he iudged well till triall by experience to euery one proued him worse; but how great a corsiue it was to his careful Parents, I leaue it to the*m* to consider whom experience hath taught to conceaue the like inconuenience; great griefe was
30 it to his old father that had beene himselfe full of valour, to see his young sonne, though able, yet vnfit for any such endeuour, which turned his hoped for rest to haplesse ruine, his aged mirth to angrie moane, and what so euer other content, into a contrarie conceit, to see his poore neighbours comfort their seruile liues with
35 the sight of their forward Children, and hee their unfortunate Lord wanting that redresse which those poore creatures in respect of him in such plentifull manner do daylie possesse.

Thus grieuing to remember that which hee cannot forget, and sorrie to haue so discontented an obiect to his aged eies, which

Her brother is well formed and handsome, but he has the mind of a child with the manners of a fool and is a great grief to his father.

8 *The Famous Historie*

he ſtil bewailed, though by no meanes his griefe could be healed, at laſt learnes with patience to beare that which with paines he cannot amend, and [B³] inſtantly ſolicites the great Parlament of heauen, in whoſe diſpoſe reſts the eſtate of all creatures, that in their vnſearchable wiſedome they woulde either open the eyes 5 of his blinded ſoule, forged in the miſtie vale of a cloudy ignorance, or els cut ſhort the vnpleaſant date of his wearie life, and ſo preuent the inſuing ignominie of his future times: where wee muſt now leaue him a while in his follie, till the proceſſe of our Hiſtory bring vs thither againe. 10

CHAP. II.

How two of King Arthurs *Knights ariued in Earle* Cadors *Court, and how* Launcelot du Lake *obtained the loue of faire* Laura.

The fame of Laura's beauty draws to Cador's court a multitude of valiant knights from distant lands, among them two from King Arthur's Round Table, Sir Lancelot and Sir Tristram.

During which time this young Ladie, Daughter to this worthie 15 Earle *Cador*, with the report of her matchles beautie, reſounded in euery eare the welcome ſounde of ſelfe pleaſing loue, and thereby incited many aduenterous Princes and matchles Knightes to forſake their fartheſt Countries with contented trauailes, to confirme with their eyes what had [B³ back] so filled their longing 20 eares, as doth the neuer moouing pole drawe the adamantine touch of euerie ſteely compaſſe ſtill to direct their purpoſe to one point, ſo fared it here, whether declines the glance of al eies, the thoughts of all harts, and the aime of all actions. Amongſt whom arriued two Knightes of the honourable order of King 25 *Arthurs* rounde Table, which was then ſo fullie furniſhed with a peareles troupe of couragious Cauileers, as iuſtly compared with all countries for like company, whoſe names were Sir *Lancelot du-lake*, and Sir *Triſtram du-Lions*, two wonders for their worthines, matchles for their might, and for their curteſie 30 exceeding compare: who amongſt many millions of other braue Gallants there all for one purpoſe aſſembled, proudly oppoſes themſelues againſt all approaching powers both of forraine and homeborne foes that durſt any way ſet themſelues againſt her Soueraignetie, wherein they ſo valiantly behaued themſelues, 35

of Chinon of England 9

especiallie Sir *Lancelot du-lake*, whose vndaunted courage ftroke fuch terror to the hearts of his foes, and won fuch fauour in the fight of his friends, as hee was generallie admired of all, but especiallie of *Laura* whose maiden heart, being nowe touched
5 with the pricke of affection, receaued fo deepe an impreffion as could neuer after be raced forth againe, and l[i]ke [1] as there is no fubftance without his accident, no fire without his fmoake, nor fhadow without his body: fo is there no loue, how clofely foeuer it bee fhadowed, howe cunningly foeuer it bee diffembled, or how
10 farre fo euer remooued, but will by fome meanes manifeft it felfe, which in her proued true; for though her modeft countenance blufhing, afhamed at firft to difcouer the earneft affection of a fo foone conquered louer, labored what in her lay ftill to repres her new mounting thoughts winged with the afpiring defence of
15 a reftles louer: yet like fire the more it is kept [B⁴] downe the fiercer it rifeth, floods the furer they are ftopped the fooner they ouerflow their bankes, and windes the greater that are their oppofitions the more furious are their forces; fo fared it with the laboring heart of this lawles louer, sometimes determining to
20 difclofe with her tongue what lay fo hid in her heart, and then fhe blufhed for fhame: then determined to fmother it in obliuion; and then lookes fhe pale as fainting in difpaire: no minute but there entred into her minde the thought of a thoufand doubtes, no doubt but redoubled her troublefome thoughts, and both
25 more and more doubtes, ftill increafes the vnquenchable fire of her loue-thirfting foule.

In that thinges by howe much they are hard to compaffe, by fo much are more worth being once compaffed, gladly would fhe forget that which moft fhee delighteth to remember, faine
30 would fhee fhunne the fnare that fhee fo willingly runneth into, and defires to winke at that fhee doeth moft defire: On the other fide the worthie Knight difpairing of his good fortune, or els doubting his former force, grew with melancholly demeanor to fpend halfe in difpaire the dayes hee was wont to ouerpaffe in
35 the fulnes of defire, thinking eyther her affections were els where fo throughly fetled as could not be feuered, or his worth merriting demeanor deferued not so much as a fayre afpect from thofe powerfull plannets that guides the diftreffed eftate of his ficklie

Lancelot loses his heart to Laura, and she is not indifferent to him.

But she hardly dares confess the secret to herself, and Lancelot defpairs of winning a prize so incomparable.

[1] Text, *looke*.

foul. L[i]ke [1] as a weary wayfaring man, that tired with the toilfome labor of a tedious trauaile, difpayring with in his time to enioy the end of his iourney, and therefore vseth a fpeedier pace to perfourme his purpofe, fo fares it with the ftill troubled minde of this diftreffed Knight, who determining with himfelfe how he might worke fome meanes that might merrite mercie in the moodie cenfure of that difdainefull Iudge, who as he thought [B⁴ back] with a feuere fentence, would rather pronounce his death than promife his life, determined with himfelfe how he might doe his endeuour to obtain her frendly fauour, which with long confultation hee thus concluded, namely, to vndertake fome hardie aduenture & dedicate his labour to her loue, and fo if peraduenture the happie courfe of all helping heauens did fo profperoufly further his attempts, as that in his wearie plotted way hee might but fortunately finde any worthie worke whofe conqueft might deferue commendations, he fed himfelfe with this hope, that the fetled perfwation of his fure loue confirmed by the dangerous endeuors of his longing life, perfectly prefented to her memorie by the atcheiuements of his worthie victorie, wold fomwhat affwage the fury of her contemptuous conceit, & if not at the firft win her, yet by little & little weare out the blot from her memorie, that detaines his loue from her minde: yet leaft his abrupt departure might be a greater caufe of his difgrace, hee determined before hee went to paint forth that paffion in the vnblufhing lines of an amorous letter, which he could not difclofe with the inforfiue words of a pittie moouing louer, & therefore fequeftring himfelfe from the refort of all company, hee thus in pittiful termes difcouers his pure loue.

But he determines to attempt some 'hardy adventure' to prove his devotion,

[C¹]

and he even addresses a letter to the matchless Laura, avowing his love and pledging himself to prove worthy of her favour.

'Lancelot du-Lake, *to the Soueraigne of his foule, matchles faire* Laura.'

'Laura, *pardon my rude proceeding, in that I fo barely begin with thy naked name, for that thou dimmeft all accents of fayre, and exceedeft all Epethites of wit; the Poets thought Venus fayreft when fhe was naked, for that her beautie, being fufficient of it felfe, fcorned all the artificiall ornaments of rich apparell: And fo of thee, whofe fhaddow fairer than her fubstance, canft not bee fitted*

¹ Text, *Looke.*

of Chinon of England 11

with any ſtile which thou doeſt not farre ſurmount: Looke downe vppon the ſeruile eſtate of a ſubiect ſlaue that, burning in the fierce flame of a neuer dying fire, proſtrates his ſillie ſoule at thy perfections ſhrine, ſo deepely imprinted in his hart, as but the comfort of thy pleaſing ſelfe; no ſalue may eaſe his dying ſmart, [C¹ back] onely thou haſt hurt mee, and ſaue thy ſelfe none can heale mee. Ah, doo not then triumph in my tragedie, becauſe peculiarly from thee proceedes my remedie: nor bee not proude of thine Art, becauſe thus piteouſlie I implore thine aide, but with gentle fauour intertaine what with humble ſubmisſion I intreat, and in requitall of that deede I will impoſe to myſelfe a toile without reſt, a trauell without end, and be a Conquerour without conqueſt, till my ceaſeleſſe paine may deſerue thy pittie, my toileſome trauell procure our truce, and the Trophies of my victorie requite ſome part of thy curteſie: Thus what I doe or what I ſuffer, what I preſently poſſeſſe, or whatſoeuer I ſhall haue, I ſacrifice at thy Altar, as propitiatorie offrings, and with the ſad ſighes of a ſorrowfull hart, cenſe thy ſacred ſhrine, ſtill intreating but this, that thou wouldeſt gently accept theſe rude lines of a rude Louer, and when diſcontented diſtance ſhall diuorce me from thy Angelicall preſence, thou wouldeſt at the leaſt pittie my ſorrow, though thou wilt not ſalue my ſore.

Thine whilſt his owne,

Lancelot du Lake.'

[C²] This Letter he deliuered to a Page attendant vpon him, and whilſt his feruant was gone to conuay it to her, himfelfe went in to take his leaue of the Duke and the reſt of his Noble friends and fellow Knights, where with a tedious diſcourſe he diſcouers the cauſe of his fo ſodaine departure, vowing his deuoted feruice wholly to her honor, for whoſe loue he was now forced to leaue his Country, and feeke ſtraunge Aduentures in forraine Coaſtes, whom they all were forry to forgoe; yet feeing his importance, folemnely commits him and his intended enterpriſes to the good fortune of his ſtill fauourable ſtarres, except Sir *Triſtram du-Lyons* who, for loue of him and honourable care of his folemne order, would needes in defpite of what euer contrarie perſwations, accompany him in his courſe: whom when Sir *Lancelot* had

This letter he sends by a page to Laura and immediately takes leave of Cador to go to France.

with many perfwafiue arguments of forceable friendfhip difwaded from his indeuour, laying open vnto him the great caufe of his dolefull departure, which fo deuoutly hee had vowed to performe, as also what difcontent the abfence of fo many Knights would breed in their King and Captaine *Arthur* of England, whofe 5 royall furnifhed Table had ranfacked the treafurie of the world for to fupply his want: yet all in vaine ftroue his wordes to diffwade the other from his will, for not all the fugered wordes the others oratorie could afford, would anie whit diswade him from his former purpofe: but, in defpite of what euer accident 10 fhould enfue, he would needs accompany him in his iournie, vowing to fuftaine what hardy ftormes of abiect miffortune foeuer fhoulde betide this thrice famous *Lancelot* hys vowed brother, that neuer fhould the burning heate of all fpringing fommer, nor the cruell colde of deade killing winter, weale nor 15 woe, profperous felicitie, [C² back] nor aduerfe extreamitie, funder their foules whilft life did vphold their bodies: Whom when *Lancelot* saw that by no meanes he could difwade, hee gentlie admits his fo long defired company, and with as many thankes accepts it, as the other with millions of offers had 20 vrged it.

His only companion is Sir Tristram, who cannot be perfuaded to allow Lancelot to depart alone.

CHAP. III.

How Lancelot du-Lake, *and* Triftram du-Lions *ariued in the French Kings Court & how* Lancelot du-Lake *ouercame* Roderigo *Duke of Auftria, and wonne the chiefeft prizes in the Turnament, with other thinges that hapned.* 25

The two knights quickly arrive in France and set out on horseback for the court of the French king.

Thus thefe two aduenterers for honor, after they had folemnly tane their leaues, ioyfully fet forwarde on their iournie, & with a profperous winde quickly cuts ouer the calme confenting Seas 30 vnto the bordering rockes that walles their countrie France from the furie of the fometime furging Sea, and after their ariual, being proudly moun-[C³]ted vpon ftately Steedes, ftout of courage, able of limmes, and beauteous in fhow, attended onely with two Pages, who for that purpose they had appointed, takes vppon 35 them the neareft and directeft way that bordered vpon that coaft

of Chinon of England

where they lately landed, & spending the partching heate almost of a whole sommers day wandring through desart woods and manie vnpeopled plaines: till when the sweating Horses of the weary sunne swiftly descending from the highest top of that
5 heauenly hill, whence in his glory hee ouerlookes the mightiest mountaines that the earth affordes, & by their fiery tract summoned the silent night vp to her wearie watch, they began to looke out where they might espy any conuenient place for their purpose, where that night they might repose themselues to
10 rest.

At last after much curious search descending down into the pleasant bottome of a lowlie dale, where by chance ran from forth the bowels of a mighty mountaine a coole fresh spring, whose siluer current shadowed ouer with the heat expelling power
15 of thicke tufted trees refreshes the increase of all adioyning vallies, who weary with wandering, and willing no thing more than such pleasure as there was plentifully promised, they alighted, and rayning all their horses to the big bowes of an aged neighboring Oake, gins with the fresh coole current of that pleasant spring to
20 alay the thirst of their hot stomackes, where they had not long sol[ac]ed¹ themselues in the shade after their great trauaile, but that an auncient Hermite inhabiting the desart roomes of that vnaccquainted corner, walking his accustomed iournie, by chaunce lightes vpon these wearie Knights as they were cooling
25 their weake limmes in the delightsome depth of that pleasant spring, who as ioyfull to see some crea-[C³ back]ture of whome they might be better directed for the furderance of their affaires, as the other was willing to supplie their wants, with that poore prouision that himselfe wanted not, they with curteous salutation
30 entertaine him, and hee curteously regreeting them with the like wishes of good lucke, requires what, whence, and who they were that had so farre wandred from the beaten wayes of those wide Desarts; to whome *Lancelot*, with reuerent regard to his olde age, mildely answers that they were two Knights of the round
35 Table, aduenterers in Armes, that had for the honor of their order, the credit of their countrie, & the loue of their loue worthy Ladyes, vndertaken to trauaile euen as far as sunne and

On their way they descend into a pleasant dale where they meet 'an ancient hermit' who asks them who they are and whence they come.

¹ Text, *solicited*.

14   *The Famous Historie*

feas, the one would giue them light, and the other afford them land.

On learning from Lancelot that they are knights of the Round Table seeking adventures for the honour of their order and the love of their ladies, the hermit tells them that King Lewis of France is not far away and on the morrow is to hold a great tournament, one of the prizes being his daughter Celestina.

'Then,' anfwered the old Hermite, 'are you happely come into thefe Confines: for not far from hence is the great Court of that mighty Monarch *Lewes* of France, that, for the eternall memorie of all fucceeding pofterity, hath for to trie the ftrength, valour, & manhood that all the wide world can afford, appointed three Prifes, the firft a rich Armour curiouflye wrought, and richly bee deckt with precious ftones, whofe worth I cannot in words fufficiently fet forth, with al the habilliaments thereunto belonging; the next a gorgeous Bedde curioufly couered ouer with beaten gold, the fafhion whereof farre exceedeth the worth of the maffie worke, & all the rich adorninges thereunto appertaining; the laft but beft, faire *Celeftina* his daughter and heire, whom I may well call the wonder of our worlde, whofe beautie I will not labour to blafe, leaft fayling in furdering that rare report, I should difcredite my felfe in feeming curioufly to commend that whofe leaft moytie exceeds the higheft reach of any earthly minde: There [C⁴] may you trie the truft you haue in your felues, & cut fhort the proceffe of your long pretended iournie: for that thither will reforte all the flowers of Cheualrie, that now flourifhe ouer the face of the whole world: To morrow begins thefe triumphes, whether in good time you fhall attaine, and for that this day, well nigh done, will not afford you any further trauaile, pleafe it you but to accept the turfie Cabbine of a homely Hermitage, and the fimple fupper of a fillie fequeftered man that, hauing forfaken the vaine delights of his young dayes, hath betaken himfelfe to the melanchollie remembrance of his after life: where to fupplie your want of meate, you fhall haue ftore of welcomes, and when the next morne fhall bring glad tidings of the fwift infuing fun, my felfe will direct you backe thither, from whence you far erred in declining your wearie iournie hither.'

After being hofpitably but plainly entertained in the hermit's cabin the knights start the next morning for the court on a broad highway thronged with travellers.

Thefe two Knights curteoufly accepting the pleafure of this aged Hermite, contented themfelues that night with the vnbolftred bed of a hard hurdle, & when the liuely Larke, a gladfome Harrald to the dawning day, gan with her filuer founding note to difcharge the melanchollie glooming night, hence hafte thefe fame following aduenterers, to practife their

forward indeuours, whom the olde Hermite duelie directes how
they fhould againe get into the great traced way that directlie
would carrie them to the Court and so, with manie praiers for
their good fpeede, committeth them to the charge of him that
5 carieth the care of all creatures: from whence they had not long
trauailed, recounting to themfelues the happie chance of theyr
fpeedie ariuall, but before them ouer an euen leuelled plaine they
might efpie a wide beaten way, beeing full fraught with ftill
approaching trauailers that, like a huge and mightie ftreame
10 fending all [C⁴ back] his force to the fea, turnes all the courfe of
their conueiance to one end, directs their iourney with al fpeed
thither, fuppofing that to be the way that fhould lead them to the
Court, and thofe trauailers wandring thither to be witneffes of the
rare report of thofe deeds of Armes wherof their old Hoast had
15 the other night giuen fuch great commendations: where when
they came, they found it to be euen fo as they before imagined,
and turning themfelues that way whither preffed the ftreame of
the increafing company, At laft they ouertooke a mightie knight
clad in habilliments of gold, such as was the Armour of *Achilles*,
20 mounted on a blacke *Barbarian* Steede, that with his ftately gate
ftoutly contendes to put downe his Mafter in pride, trapped with
the rich pompe of *Perfian* worke, curioufly fet with ftarres like
Diamonds that, playing with the dazeling beames of the golden
Sunne, dimes all the gazing eyes of the greedy beholders: before
25 him rides richly mounted ten Efquiers bearing ten luftie Launces,
and thus martching in as triumphant a ftate as euer did *Caefar*
in the *Romane* ftreets, he comes to the Court, where were readie
prepared all neceffarie circumftances for fuch Knightly feruices:
where before the Court vppon a plaine greene prouided for that
30 purpofe the attendants appointed to bee erected a riche
Pauillion of wealthie wrought Crimfon filke, the ropes of the
fame colour wrought with filuer threds, and what els belonged to
the fupporting thereof was workemanlike wrought of the fame
mettall: there till the time that euery thing was ready for the
35 Tilt he repofes himfelfe, where *Lancelot* longing to know and
proue what was conteined within all this Port boldly gins
inquire of an attendant vpon him what he fhould be, who
anfwered that his Mafter was fonne and heire to the great [D¹]
Soldan of *Babilon*, drawne from his Country with the fame of

At last they overtake 'a mighty knight' in golden armour, mounted on a black steed superbly trapped and acompanied by ten esquires. This is the son and heir of the Soldan of Babylon and a suitor for the hand of Celestina.

faire *Celeſtina*, for whoſe loue hee came thither, to aduenture his life.

<small>Next comes a knight all in black, with a single page, Sir Triamore, son of the 'Duke of Brittaine', already the favoured lover of Celestina.</small>

Shortly after approaches the place another puiſant Knight clad all in blacke, and he, onely attended by a little Page that bore his Lance, erected a ſable Tent, of whom when he required to knowe, it was anſwered that he was called *Triamore*, ſonne to the Duke of *Brittaine*, who for that hee had long affected this beauteous Prince (for whoſe ſake all this was prouided) and ſhee with like affection anſwered his loue, ſeemed diſcontented in himſelfe, that ſhee ſhould bee offered to any but himſelfe.

Next him came many other of whome were too long ſeuerally to dilate. But in the ende when all were ready, & euery thing for theſe ſtately triumphs orderly prouided, the Prizes brought forth, the Iudges ſet, and euery other appurtenance orderly
<small>Among many othercontestants is Ferdinand, heir to the Emperour of Almaine, who soon unhorses a mighty pagan, but is himself overthrown by the Soldan's son.</small>
appointed, the firſt that entred the Liſts was *Ferdinand*, heire to the Emperour of *Almaine*, mounted on a white Courſer, that being artificially arrayed with cunning conceited wings, Peggaſean-like deceaued the earneſt eies of euery beholder, with a ſhowe of fained flight.

Againſt him prepares a Pagan, mightie of body, and cruell of countenance, who furiouſly meeting, like the fatall oppoſition of two Elements, ſhiuers their ſtrong ſtaues, whoſe ſplinters ſpinning in the emptie Aire, with their buzſing ſound, tels the braue encounters of their furious fight from whom they flew, which courſe the Pagan, borne from his Horſe and ſore bruſed with the big bound of his vnweildie body, was conuayed from the place of their Chiualrie, almoſt paſt hope of recouery.

In whoſe reuenge ſtepped forth many mightie [D¹ back] men, hardie and approued Knights, whome this yong Prince with like furie forced to fall with their fellowes : till at laſt like an angry Bore newly rouſed from his drowſie den, buſling vp his big briſſels, as aiming at an act of rigorous reuenge, ſteps foorth the proud Soldans ſonne, and he, pricking his Palfray to the end he might rigoroſly root out the ſpringing hope of this young Prince, clapping as heauie a Launce in his ſtrong reſt as euer *Aiax* fore the walles of *Troy*, ſhiuered for the recouerie of their vnhappie loſſe : euen like the furious ſtroke of two ſtrong ſtreames, that with their tirrible thunder affrights the vnacuſtemed eares of their neare neighbours, meetes in the mideſt of the Liſts the liuely Lordes, where with equall encounters they were both dung downe to the grounde, where *Ferdinand* his horfe, vnhappily falling upon his Mafters leg, fo brufed it as hee was not able againe to recouer his faddle but was conueyed thence: which when the young 5 Soldan perceaued, ftoutlye triumphing in his valiant victory, gins faucely to proclaime a proud challenge againft all Chriftians, for the reuenge of thofe fore punifhed Pagans: which vaine glorious vaunt fo ftirred vp the neuer vanquifhed valour of valiant *Lancelot* as that addreffing him to the fight gins fhew himfelfe at the 10 other ende of the Liftes, as ready to recouer the almoft loft Honor of his Chriftian Countrie, whome fo foone as the Soldan had efpied, fpreading his winges like a greedy Gofhauke houering ouer a fearefull couie of cowardly Fowles, gins addreffe himfelfe to his former demeanor: whome *Lancelot* with fuch courage 15 encountred as, bearing downe both horfe and man to the ground, aftonifhed the vnchriftned flaue with fo fearefull a fall as almoft quite expelled the vitall fpirits from his bigge fwollen breafts: But yet feeling [D²] himfelfe in fo great a daunger of deuouring death, & out of all hope of the pittifull compaffion of his eager 20 enemie, beganne againe to roufe himfelfe, and fpeedily preparing his ftrong fencing furniture, to affay the fortune of a furious fight, cafting ouer his fhoulder a large fheltering fhield and brandifhing in hys hand a keene edged Curtle-axe, gins nowe a foote to affayle him, that before on Horfe backe hee did affault.

25 When *Lancelot* perceaued it, he prouided himfelfe for the like purpofe, and couragioufly encounters this harme hammering Heathen, where betwixt them againe beganne a farre more fiercer fray on foote then was the cruell encounters before with their Horfe, which, continuing very long on both fides confirmed with 30 the fierce falles of their vnwildie weapons, makes at length Sir *Lancelot du-Lakes* armes (weakned with the iffue of much blood, that the Pagan had fpilt with his blowes) almoft to faile of his former forces, which beeing efpied of the Chriftians, and efpecially of the King, who aboue all other, defpifed a Pagan fhould poffeffe 35 fo Princely a Prize as they had there prouided, gins euery where to enquire of that Knight, on whofe ftrength almoft nowe depended their whole eftate, to whom at length word was brought that it was a Knight of King *Arthurs* round Table, whofe name was Sir *Lancelot du-Lake*, to whome all the Confines

The victor now challenges all the Christians and thus draws Lancelot into the lists.

After a hard fight Lancelot slays the pagan prince.

18   *The Famous Historie*

of Chriftendome hardly in Chiualrie afforded a fellow: which ftroke fuch a difmall dumpe into the moodie minde of this difcontented King, to fee the Champion of Chriftendome fo neere vanquifhed, vnder the pittileffe power of a moft hellifh heathen, as almoft driues the bright and Rofiall colour from his afore well 5 coloured Cheekes. [D² back]

Till when this ftill triumphant Knight, fhakeing himfelfe as from a fluggifh flumber, reaches at the Pagan with fuch power as that, at one blow with his well tempered fword, hee quite cuts a funder the ftrong turret that hemmed in his head, & fettling 10 further downe to his harmefull head, batters a funder the filuer wall that fhieldes the principall partes of foul feruing fence : and the reft remayning remnants of that little world, wanting the direction of their greateft guide, altogether faile any further to fence their fainting fellowes from his battring blowes ; which 15 fight bred no fmall content to the almoft fickly foule of the King, who expected nothing leffe then the fo fpeedy death of his fpitefull foe who, beeing by the conquer[or] [1] difarmed of his rich habilliaments, was by the reft of his company quickly conuaied to his curious Tent, and all his attendants fent home with forrow, 20 that whilome flourifhed in fuch hope for felicitie.

Sir Tristram also wins honour in the lists, but no one equals Lancelot.

After this approached many other Knights to trie their fortunes in that fight : from whence Sir *Triftram du-Lions* won the honor of that day, ftill working for greater glorie with more manlike demeanor. Till when the nights blacke fhadow gins fet an end 25 to that dayes bright fhowes ; and fo euery one, expecting the end of their aduentures, thronged to heare the iuft iudgement of that fure cenfuring Senate, forepointed by the King to determine of

Celestina thus becomes the prize of Lancelot.

this doubt, who with one affent after they had highly commended the many valerous deedes of diuers couragious Cauileers, did 30 aboue all wholly attribute the honor of that dayes dutie to Sir *Lancelot du-Lake*, as one that had beft deferued it of them all ; and fo putting him to the King, at whofe hands he was to receaue this renowned reward, he there with no leffe pleafure to heare [D³] the murmering noyfe of the muttering multitude, 35 buzfing the report of his valerous deedes, then with the hope of thofe rich rewardes appointed for the Conquerours meed, receaued

---

[1] Text, *conquered*.

of Chinon of England

at his Kingly hands al thofe robes, of more than eftimable eftate, and whatfoeuer by due was fitting his defert.

Amongft which was that more than faire *Celeftina*, for whom rather than the reft was affembled fuch and fo many mightie men, euen from the furthieft Coafts of al the Efterne Kingdomes to the Wefterne Iles, bound vp in the Oceans bofome: but for that himfelfe had before fetled his feruice to honour that Saint, whofe Idea grauen with the Diamond points of Chriftall caruing eyes in the impregnable table of his fecret [1] heart, whence no furie of newe affaulting force can euer wafh it away, determines in this to winne to himfelfe the report of more worth than by his former acts he had fully atchieued: and therefore with many thankes to his Maieftie, receauing the rewardes of his honour, which nowe lay all in hys power to difpofe, after fome conference fuche as to like affaires are moft fit, calling for Sir *Tryamore*, of whome we before told you that he was fonne & heire to the *Brittaine* Duke, gins thus difcourfe his honorable intent.

'Since', quoth he, 'the vnmerited mercy of euer helping heauen, from the great attemptes of many more mightier than my felfe, hath attributed the honour of this day to the vndeferued dutie of my deed[es] [2]: By the cenfure of which fentence I am to enioy the poffeffion of all this pleafure, whofe efpecial good refts in the glorie of this more than a Goddeffe; yet fince my minde not cappiable of her loues impreffion, becaufe already [3] it retaineth the beautie of another, in fuch fure poffeffion as that no time can trie [4] it, no beu-[D³ back]tie blot it, nor other loue with languifhment lauifh it away, to thee will I giue what I might by right take away, and fo gaine more honour by the voluntary releafe of her loue to thee then I fhould get fame by the forceable detayning of her affections to my felfe. In which I fhall binde thy loue to me as to a friend, her liking as to a fauorer of her fortunes, and further the faire fruite of a yet fcarce blooming bud in the bleffed bofome of anothers beautie'; & fo deliuering her freely ouer to Sir *Triamore* twixt whom there had beene afore fuch fettled likeing of likely loue, to the Kinges great content, the louers full confent, and his owne more furthered intent, he difpofed of the greateft part of his prize: the other feueral

But he resigns her to Sir Triamore, her lover, sending meanwhile his other prizes to England.

---

[1] Text, *fecrert*.   [2] Text, *decdse*.
[3] Text, *alrerady*.   [4] *tire* !

rewardes he determined to fend ouer into *England*, to prefent to
his *Laura*: for whofe conueyance he adreffed a truftie Efquire
of his owne, that from a childe had followed him in all hys
actions of honor : where awhile we muft leaue him to his further
aduentures, and profecute the prefentment of his Prize to his
peareles Parramour, which by his Page was quickly performed:
who flying with the fauorable fortune of well wifhing windes, in
fhorter fpace than commonly acompanieth fuch tired trauellers,
ariued in *England* at the olde Earle *Cadors* Court, where was
then a Royal affembly of Courtlike company: to whom when it
was knowne that there was arriued one ready to tell ftraunge
tydings of the admirable atchiuements of their late fortune finding
friends affembled all to gether to heare thofe welcome wordes
into the Earles great Hall: where both himfelfe, his daughter
and his vnfeemely fonne, as alfo the reft of that Royall refort
orderlie placed with attentiue diligence, quieted themfelues to

The messenger displays the prizes and reports Lancelot's success.

heare expreffed thefe ftraunge exploits: to whofe prefence did
preafe a comely Efquire attended by a [D'] drudging Dwarffe
that was loaded with a rich Armour, who after he had in order
rendred deferuing duty to euery feuerall affemblant, thus
deliuered hys meffage.

'Great Earle to whofe honor wholly fubmites it felfe the whole
worth of his worke, that from the fierce furie of Alians armes
hath brauely born away thefe Princely rewards. Grant pardon
to my rafh refort, and giue licence to my truth telling tonge in
few wordes to difclose the efpecial caufe of my haftie comming':
and then with the honorable accidents of thefe worth worthie wars,
gins he to paint forth the praifes of that famous fight; wherein
from the ftil flowing force of many furious foes, had his matchles
mafter brauely borne away the home brought booties: Which
tale hee fo furnifhed with fitting Epethites and true titles of
aduenterous valour, as neuer fung the fweet tuned tongue of
heauenly *Tullie* in the famous Capitoll of ftill renowmed Roome,
with more applaufiue fpeeches of a truth vrging tale, extolling
the eternized honor of thofe thrice famous aduenterours with
the heauen fcaling ftile of a more than earthly Oration: and
then with the blacke tragicke tunes of ftrange miffortune, fuch
as was the Art framed action of that Thracian Knight, when he
defcribed to doleful *Dido* the true ftory of *Troys* eftate: To

of Chinon of England 21

whose powerfull speech listned the attentiue eare of that pitty Chinon is stirred by Lancelot's valour and gets his father's permission to seek adventures abroad.
mouing Prince of whom we before told, when the happy heauens
disperfing now the sable vale of sad faced follie, that so long in
the darke dungeon of ignominy had lockt vp the happines of his
5 after hopes, being now able in himselfe to see that which before
in another he could not discerne, euen as the Eagle after her age
casts her bill, the Serpent slides off his skin, or the wanton Bucke
his harmles head: [D⁴ back] So he, to the great admiration of
all those worthy witnesses, suddainely starting at the strange tale
10 of this well spoken Page, griuouslie bewailed the lucklesse date
of his forespent dayes that had so sluggishly ouer slipt the young
yeares of his youthfull iollitie in the fabling fancies of childish
follie: wherein hee neyther had discharged the duty of a sonne,
satisfied the honour owing to hys countries seruice, nor won the
15 least part of that worth that by due desert he saw generally attributed to many men of far meaner byrth, & therefore, nowe
turning his former foolish demeanors to more Princely promising
endeuours, he suddainelie sollicited his old sorrow tyred sire, that
hee would thus far further his intent, as to graunt him leaue
20 a while to forsake his natiue soyle, and learne thus to aduenture
for honor in far forraine lands, whose instant intreatie not brook-
ing the deferring of further delay, earnestly vrged his now more
fortunate Father to further so his forward Sonne, as that presently
prouiding all such necessaries as to him was most needefull without
25 any more meanes made for his bootlesse abode, fitly furnished
him in euery point for such a purpose: where euery necessary
being prouided, and himselfe now readie to depart, blessed with
the many praiers of hys ioyfull father to see hys forward sonne
recouered from the helples horror of darke ignorance to the
30 approuing prowesse of Princely pusance, and with the well willing
wishes of all his friendly fauorites, he departs his home to seeke
his so long lost glorie abroad.

  Meane while whilest thus *Lancelot* had sent ouer to hys Meanwhile Sir Triamore, with the consent of Celestina's father, prepares to return home to Brittany with her and his friends Sir Lancelot and Sir Tristram, attended by
Mistris the afore named fauors, speedy preparation was prouided
35 in Fraunce for the solemnezing of this Royall marriage betwixt
Sir *Triamore* and faire *Celestina*: which for that his father then
resi-[E¹]dent vpon his Dukedome was desirous to content his old
conceit with the sight of his sonnes marriage, Syr *Triamore*
earnestly intreated of the King, that he would so farre further his

22 *The Famous Historie*

many knights and ladies.

olde fathers requeſt, as to licence their departure home into *Brittanie*, whereto the old King willingly condiſcended and moſt Royally furniſhed this their ioyfull iourney: whither being attended with ſir *Lancelot du-Lake* and ſir *Triſtram du Lions*, beſides many other aswell valiant Knights as beauty brauing Dames, drawen out from the chiefeſt choice of all that Countrie, merrily ſets forward on their way.

But the Soldan, enraged by the death of his son, hastily gathers an army and lands in Brittany, where he besieges the town of Triamore's father.

In the meane time, the Soldan hearing of the diſgraced death of his ſonne, and certefied by ſome of his eſpials of the pretended purpoſe of theſe Chriſtian Princes were the onely ſharers of that glorie, gins preſently to leuy what forces his Countrie in ſo ſhort a time was able to lend, and imbarking with all ſpeede his Armie, in ſhort time landed all his men vppon the vnhappy Coaſt of *Britanie*, where orderly incamping themſelues about the warlike walls of that ſtrong defended Towne where the Duke with all his attendants kept then a puiſant Court for the welcomming of his ſonne and his beauteous Bride, cutting off all thoſe conueying paſſages that leades any way to their neighbour compaſſing Confines, remoouing all ſemblance of ſuccor from their longing ſight: And being further certefied of the neere approach of that triumphant troope of valiant Victors, that fearing nothing leſſe than ſuch trothleſſe treaſon weares out their iourney with ſuch ioy, as experience in farre meaner mens matters proues paſſing all other pleaſure.

By a sudden and unexpected attack the Soldan slays all of Celestina's guard except Lancelot, Tristram, and Triamore, and takes her prisoner.

Whoſe purpoſe the ſubtle Soldan purpoſing to preuent, in an old ouergrowne wood, ſcituate ſome [E¹ back] foure miles from the Citie, ſlily inſconſes a great Scout both of horſe and foote: who as ſoone as they had encompaſſed this careleſſe company within their ill intending Armes rudely ruſht out vpon them: who for becauſe their comming ſomewhat too ſudden in with the other Knights, could hardly prouide to reſiſt their foreplotted purpoſe, and the numbers ſo far different, as ſcarcely might they affoord one Chriſtian to twenty Pagans, whereby they were forced to a furious fight: In which ſaue onely *Lancelot*, *Triſtram*, and *Triamore* all were ſlaine, and *Celeſtina*, maugre all their force, conueyed away in the fight. Which when they perceaued, like three inraged Lions amidſt the troopes of the Forreſts feareful inhabitants, prayes vppon the curſed carkaſes of theſe vnchriſtened Curres, till when no more fuell was left for their fire, no remainder

of Chinon of England 23

whereon they might worke their further reuenge, nor any other fubiect for their conquering fwords, hope of recouery was paft, becaufe their numbers were too great; the furie of further fight in vaine, becaufe themfelues were too weake; and being defperate almoft, what way to take to find reliefe.

Long time they fpent in difputing what were beft to doo in this extreame danger, themfelues being fore wounded with the many blowes of their ouer numbred foes, their Armour brufed with the oft falling forces of their Foemens fwords, and their weapens almoft all broken in this barbarous battell, incites to their fadde thoughts what fecure meanes they might feeke for their beft fafegard.

Being thus left deftitute welnigh of all defence, they wandred vp and downe the vntrodden wayes of thofe waft woods, one reciting this, another inditing that, and the third mifliking both; till when the [E²] comfortleffe couering of the fad faced night gins hide away the life ioying fight of the lightfome day, when thefe forrowfull fighing foules wandering in the vnpeopled paths of thefe wide woods, fpent all that tedious night in tyred trauels, fometimes ftraying this way, and then ftepping that way againe, till the forrow of their fower chance had almoft quite taken away the ready remembrance of them felues.

At last, as euery forrowe hath an ende, fo had this long night, and the pleafant fpring of the next infuing day gins fomewhat to cheare vp their troubled mindes from the cruell cares of their ouer paffed paines, when determining with themfelues to make fpeedy poft to euery feueral Chriftian Kingdome, and from thence to leuy fuch powers of people as fhould perforce make this heathen Hel-hound again to render vp to their handes this beauty ftaining Bride, whom he had fo cowardly caught away: Till wandring together downe the pleafant fide of a fummer fhowing hill they might efpy beneath in the broade bottome of a difmal dale a great worne way, yet not fuch as accuftomably are the conueyances of peopled beaten pathes, but as it were the fatall footfteps of fome mighty Monfter that with his ill fauored feete had poyfoned the fprouting fpringes of that pleafant Plaine. Which after they had a long time followed, prying euery way what this wonder fhould import, At laft they a farre off might heare the vnaccuftomed cryes (as it fhould feeme) of fome

The three knights plan to rescue her, and proceeding on their way they pass into a difmal dale and at length, following strange cries, they enter a dark den.

tormented foule, that beeing grieuoufly afflicted with fome ftraunge torments made thofe ruthfull moanes to mooue the compaffionate mindes of fome wayfaring wanderer to deliuer her from that great miferie : which they like two loft fellowes in a great growne woode that, with the refounding Ecchoes of theyr [E² back] 5 lowde fcriking cries, brings themfelues after long fearch together againe, who liftning from what likelieft place this fame might growe, at laft vnder the darke fhade of a fheltring Cipreffe that ouerhung the mouth of a craggie Caue (he went out, as it fhould feeme, of the big body of a ruinous Rocke) they might perfectly 10 perceiue the fame to proceede : Whither poafting in all haft, ftriuing who fhould ftand in moft fted for the releafe of this loffe ¹ (as they fuppofed) rudely they together ran downe without regard into this darke Denne, who, as foone as they were in, from out the darke couert of another cabbining Caue ftept foorth 15 a mightie Monfter, framed with the deceitfull face of a faire woman, but the big body of a fubtill Serpent, whofe poyfon fwolne bowelles bearing the breadth of a mighty Tunne was fupported with the ioyntles legs of a Castle carrying Elephant, hands had fhe in forme like a man, but in the fubftance of her frame 20 more than a monfter, a tayle that Serpent like catcheth in the vnprouided trauailers, her backe ftrongly fenced with broad buckling fcales, that proudly oppofes it felfe gainft the tougheft fteele, her force more than could be comprehended within the reach of a reafonable conceit : for fhe (after her Crokadile com- 25 plaints fhe had) drawing the harmeleffe Knight[s] into that fubtill fnare, quickly roules vp againft the mouth of the hole a mightie ftone, which the force of many men could not els remooue, and fo, locking in thefe well meaning men within the compaffe of her loathfome Denne, fhee leaues them to the comfortleffe con- 30 fort of their nowe almost cureleffe cares.

Hereupon a huge monster with the face of a woman and the body and tail of a serpent suddenly appears and rolls a huge stone against the mouth of the cave.

¹ See note.

[E²]
CHAP. IIII.

How Chinon *after his transformation from his foolifhnes betooke himfelfe to feek for forraine aduentures, and after how hee encountred Sir* Lancelot *and Sir* Triftram *in a Forreft, where hapned a ftraunge aduenture, and how* Chinon *pulled a fword from an inchaunted Rocke of ftone.*

By this had *Chinon* croffed the Seas out of his owne countrie, and ariued in *Fraunce* where hee neuer came before, and himfelfe yet ignorant in the courfe of trauaile wandred vp & downe a long time, feeking fome worthy work wheron he might make triall of his ftrength. But for that the defolate Coafts bordering vpon the fea fide afforded no matter for his manly courage, after he had there fpent fome fewe dayes, he takes a new courfe of trauell ouer the vntrodden hilles into the bofome of the next bounding Country.

Which weary way, for that his horfe being young [E³ back.] and not yet vfed to the hard hap of aduentures himfelfe, euen as a childe that, newe fprung from his cradle, can hardly counteruail the worlds weary works, fo fared it with this new Knight, who was greedy of glorie but vnfit to finde it: yet hoping of better hap, drawes out his iourney ouer many high hilles, and then fettles hee downe into the melancholly fhade of deepe darkened valleys, wher before neuer footed any earthly creature, faue foule Serpents, no noyfe but the forrowfull found of the ill boading Owls, no light faue the glimmering of a little beame that fhining through the tranfparant leaues of blacke Cypreffe boughs fhowed him fome comfort amidft this more than the fhadow of death: No meate could hee come by, faue fuch as that vnfruitful earth did afford, nor drinke faue the troubled ftreames of an vnpleafant fpring, that mixed with the vnholfome forts of deade dropping leaues full of the filthy flime of fluggifh Toades, and many fuch vnholfome creatures: his Bedde the ouergrowne moffe vpon the fide of the mountaine; his pillowe the toppe of an vneuen ftone; his couering nothing faue the

Meanwhile, Chinon has arrived in France and wanders in search of adventures.

ouerſhadowing bowes of age trembling trees; his nightly ſleepes often affrighted with the hiſſing of many foule ſnaks, vnacuſtomable antomes to his eares: yet as he that will trauell vpon the ſea muſt addreſſe himſelfe to abide the trouble of euery ſtorme; hee that will enioy the ſweet content of felicitie, muſt needes 5 vndergo all the hard haps of enuious aduerſitie; ſo he that wil in this ſpacious world ſeeke the aduantage of Honour must beare baſe direction of vnſeemely miſſortune.

By chance he wanders toward the vale where the knights are impriſoned,   So this yong Prince after hee had long time wandred thus without the direction of any way, at length eſpies a far off 10 a chalkie path, ſcaling the top of a high hill, whether with much adoe at length he came vnto, [E⁴] and after he had long time climed vpon the ſide of this mount, at length with many wearie ſteps he attains the toppe, from whoſe height hee might againe looke backe at his ouerſpent iourney: following a longe while 15 the broad tract of that beaten way, preſentlie he came to a narrow cut of paſſage out of the ſide of a flintie Rocke, where the high hill ſteepe ore his head troubles the courſe of the winde wandring cloudes, beneath the lowlie bottome of a blacke diſmall Dale, filled with the furious force of aſpyring ſprings that, 20 working from the wombe of the ſea, euen vnto the higheſt toppe of that mightie Promontany, breaks out againe, and with a fierce fall downe into the diſmall Dales makes ſuch a hidious noyſe as when the vnbridled force of the ouerflowing ſea breakes downe the boundes of his neighboring bankes and drownes all the 25 nere placed plaines with his euer-working waters: Yet *Chinon*, ſtill hoping that after ſhowers at length would come a ſunne; after woes, weale; & after theſe hard paſſages, pleaſanter plaines, with as much patience as hee could, ouergoes this griefe he had, and gins at laſt to ſee the farther ſide of his wearie way: 30 from whence looking downe, hee might eſpie a more pleaſant dale; whether deſcending by a downe falling path that went into the bottome of a Hill he gladly at length attained, and there in a more freſher and pleaſanter ſtreame than before of a long time hee had met withall hee ſome what refreſhes him- 35 ſelfe, and beeing content with ſuch fruit as that ſoyle did afforde him, hee goes forwarde on hys iournie, ſtill ſearching for that hee

and before the cave sees the huge stone with   coulde not finde: At laſt he came as hee thought to the mouth of ſome Caue that was fullie filled vp with the ſtronge bulke of

of Chinon of England 27

a mightie bigge ſtone, whoſe hugeneſſe was ſuch as could not be an inscription in verse.
remooued by the might of manie [E⁴ back] men, where, in olde,
almoſt outworne letters, were theſe lines ingrauen.

>   *In priſon here a puiſant wight,*
> 5   *Betraied by cunning craft now lies:*
>   *Whence no man but a maiden Knight*
>   *Can free him from his miſeries,*
>   *Whoſe firſt tried valour muſt aſſay,*
>   *To rid this wretched man away.*

10 Which when he had red and curiouſly conſidered, gins to Presently he is confronted by a monster and has to fight for his life.
reſolue with himſelf to aſſay whether his fortune ſhould bee
ſo good as to performe this ſeruice, where looking round about
for him that did heere in a peremptorie painted challenge keepe
the paſſage of that place, where this Knight whereof mention
15 was there made is by ſubtiltie incloſed, at laſt ſodainelie, but
from whence he ſaw not, there was a huge deformed Monſter,
ſuch as before he ſeldome or neuer had ſeene, whoſe ſhape
neyther imported the proportion of man nor beaſt, but a mixture
of them both; from foorth the furnace of whoſe fierie bellie
20 iſſues, like the aſhes of *Aetna*, many cloudie miſts of darke ſmoke,
that almoſt ſmoothered this famous follower of hardy deedes
before he began the fight; and in this Fogge, armed with the
bulke of a young ſpringing Oake, the fell force of whoſe fall had
beene ſufficient to haue ground him a ſunder, gins vnawares to
25 aſſaile him: which when he perceaued, nimbly leaping backe to
eſchue the heauy ſtroke, prepared in as ſhort ſpace as he could
to prouide himſelfe for this fray, but ere he could be in euery
point armed, gins againe this mon-[F¹]ſter the ſecond time to
aſſault him, which he in the beſt ſort he could deuiſe fought
30 meanes to eſcape, for to vndergoe it he could not: and then,
nimbly conueying himſelfe within the ende of his mighty weapon,
with his well tempered ſworde gins aſſay to worke vppon the
Monſter, but all in vaine, for ſo ſtrongly was it euery where
buckled with inſconfing ſcales, as no more entrance was
35 affoorded for his ſword then if he had ſtroken vppon the hard
face of a flinty Rocke; when the ſubtle ſerpent with a ſodaine
turne gaue the Knight ſuch a heauy blowe with the poyſoned
weight of her ſtrong tayle as perforce beat him downe to the

28   *The Famous Historie*

<small>The fight is long and furious,</small> grounde and almoſt baniſhed the breath from his body: But hee, mindfull of what hee had in hande, to encounter ſo vnnaturall an enemie, long lyes not in that caſe, but nimbly rouſing vp himſelfe againe gins freſhly to aſſaile his enemie: who, ſtill threatning him with the bigg blowes of his vnwieldy weapon, puts him euery way to his ſhift how he might beſt ſhun them.

At laſt ſpying a fit oportunitie, he with his ſword indeuoured to cut aſunder her vnacuſtomed kinde of weapon, which in ſhort time he performed, ſo that now free meanes he had for to aſſay what he could doo vppon her vnwieldy body: But all his labour was loſt, for ſo ſafely was ſhee garded from all entrance, as not the keeneſt ſteele the ſmoakie *Cyclops* forged for the mighty God of wrathfull warre could euer enter into her: when hee, troubled at once with two illes, the furious force of her ſerpentine taile, which now prooues her beſt weapen, and the brimſtone flaming which ſtill iſſued out at the Furnace of her fiery mouth.

At the laſt after much labour, the weary Knight, tyred almoſt with this tedious toyle, gins ſomewhat [F¹ back] to returne backe, to the end he might recouer againe his nie loſt breath; which flight for that the Serpent did not with ſuch eager force purſue, as ſhe was wont to doe in the beginning of their fight, hee made longer ſtay to recouer thereby better ſtrength, & then as two furious fighting Stagges that fetching a farre flight, thereby to encounter with more force, begins againe theſe new olde enuies and with their furious blowes ſo plagued one another, as if the oppoſition of two great Armies had ſent the noyſe <small>but suddenly the monster vanishes, the stone is rolled away, and the three imprisoned knights emerge, released from their dungeon.</small> of their battering Armes from euery reſounding eccho: till at length after the many fierce aſſaults of the furious Knight, hys foyled enemie in a ſudden as ſhe came, vaniſhes away, which he ſuſpecting but to be ſome diueliſh deuiſe, with an intent to ſet vpon him againe at vnawares, gins circumſpectly to prie into euery corner, to the end he might be ſure that no intrapping ambuſhes of her hobgoblin companions might priuily lurk to inſnare his life; when vnwares he perceaued the mighty ſtone ſo meruailouſly laid ouer the Caue of it ſelfe to roule away, and from foorth the hole iſſues out three goodly Knights, two whereof he knew for hys Countrymen and olde acquaintance; but the thirde, which was a ſtranger, he neuer ſaw before; theſe wer

of Chinon of England 29

they of whome we faid afore were by the fubtill fhift of
a deceauing Syren cunningly compaffed in that Caue : where
when Syr *Lancelot du Lake* and hys fellow *Triftram* faw *Chinon*,
that at their departure from *England* they left foolifh in their
5 friendes & his fathers* houfe, miraculoufly tranfformed to
a valiant Knight, and fo luckily there ariued for their reliefe,
no maruaile if with admiration theyr woondering wittes were
drawne into a laborinth of fuch deepe conceites, how this might
come to paffe; that beeing amazed as were thofe ftone turned
10 people, which ga-[F²]zing vppon *Gorgons* heade, coulde hardly
beleeue in their mindes what was fo liuely prefented to their
eyes, till *Chinon* perceiuing their paffion gins thus to waken
them from their drowfie and fluggifhe dreame.

'Fellowes in Armes' (quoth hee) 'the very reporte of whofe *Chinon now*
relates to the
15 valour hath from the heauy weight of obfcure follie rowfed *astonished*
knights the story
my deade drooping thoughtes to the liuely remembrance of *of his transforma-*
tion from a
a higher mounting mind, not happier fhall you be in this your *lumpish dolt*
to a valiant
releafe than I in bringing you reliefe; in that the fucceffion *knight.*
of after growing ages fhall eternize my name for the opening of
20 this worfe than hellifh mouth, and for the vanquifhing of that
more than miraculous Monfter, for that by the one I againe reftored to the world two fuch valiant Knights, and by the other,
rid them of a peftilent plague.

'Stand not in a maze, for I am the man that lately you left in
25 a world of follie, but now, by the power of prouident heauen,
raifed from that deiection.' At laft *Lancelot* (ouercloied with ioy
to fee him thus fortunate, that whilome was fo foolifh) regreetes
his good hap with many ioyfull wordes, fuch as commonlie paffe
betwixt long parted friends at their vnexpected meeting, and then
30 sir *Triftram* likewife falutes hys honorable aduenture, with the
many great thankes and good wifhes of like future good fortune:
then fir *Triamore*, for that he himfelfe altogether vnacquainted
with *Chinon*, although hee had often heard hys friendes, and then
followers in Armes, with mickle griefe to relate the wofull cafe
35 wherein they left fuch a Prince as there they named in *England*:
yet hee begins to enquire of fir *Lancelot* the whole paffed ftorie
of hys friendes eftate, who with ioy repeating, what oft with
forrow hee had seene performed, [F² back] gins certefie him in
euery point according to h[i]s afking, which when fir *Triamore*

vnderſtoode that hee was a Knight of comely carriage and curteous demeanor, he forthwith, with many gentle greetings and more thankes to heauen and him for their happy deliuerie, vowed vnto him all the honor of his actions: Who long profeſſing kindly friendſhippe and duteous indeuor, to deſerue this more then common curteſie, they were preſented with a troope of Fairies, mongſt whome was *Oboram* there King, who eſpecially chooſing *Chinon* from the reſt, began with many wordes of wonder to commend his Cheualry, for that laſt being his firſt Combate he had ſo valiantly behaued himſelf, as had all the chiefe choiſe of powerfull Chriſtendome ſtroue with themſelues to haue exceeded his worth, their Forces all ioyned in one, in reſpect of him, had beene none: And then turning to the reſt of the Knights, tolde them that the Monſter by whoſe deuiſe they were there deceaued was no other than himſelfe, who, for the deſire he had to approue the Proweſſe of this newe come Knight, vndertooke that ſhape, in requitall of which wrong he had prouided a coſtly ſword, which by his Art was faſtned within the cloſe binding body of a ſtrong Rocke, and he of them that ſhould ſtoutly pull it out ſhould for his paines inioy a Iewell of rich price: which ſword was artificially framed for *Iulius Caeſar*, by the cunning craft of a mighty Magitian inhabiting within the deſolate places of thoſe darke vallies, and for that it ſo pleaſed the great Director of all mens dealinges that that worke ſhould come to naught, for that the valiant *Romane* was before the perfection thereof vnluckily ſlaine in the Senate, hee had cloſely referued it to another vſe: But who that ſhould be of al them foure (of which by neceſſity muſt [F³] needs bee one) that as yet was not knowne to himſelfe; and then leading them through the darke ſhades of many light lacking vaultes, ſhewing them the ſeacrets of his cloſe couched Kingdome, bound up within the bowels of the earth: whether when they were a little deſcended they might partly ſee armies of many little Elues come poſting towards him, as ſpeciall attendants on his traine, whoſe buſie fingers woulde gladly haue beene pinching theyr wearie legges, for higher they coulde not reach: but that forbidden by the great charge of their commaunding King, they durſt not aduenture it againe.

Thus after their long walke in thoſe cloſe kept countries, hee brought them at length into a broade vale, in midſt whereof was grauen vp a mighty ragged Rocke, wherein was a faire faſhioned ſword curiouſly contriued of many ſundry mettals, which ſhould ſeeme by ſome or other meanes to haue beene ſtroken thereinto, where this fairie King told them they were all to approue their forces at the pulling of it, and he whoſe lot it ſhould be to win it, for his pains ſhould alwaies were it, whoſe temperature was ſo good as would clearely cut a ſunder what euer ſtone, mettall, or any harder obiect was oppoſed against it; the vertue this, that whoſoeuer wore it ſhoulde neuer be aſſailed by baſe croſbiting of anie ſlie deceitful Inchanter.

And thus with many words extolling the excellencie of the thing, and promiſing good fortune to them whoſoeuer ſhould attaine it, Hee firſt appoints Syr *Lancelot* who, as greedie of this goodly weapon as a hungrie hauke of her pray, ſtoutly ſteps foorth, and laying hold of the ſword with a maine force, offering to vnſheath it, could nothing at all remoue it. The next was ſir *Triſtram*, and he alſo offering to doe his [F³ back] endeuour therein was alſo at the firſt expelled. Next him ſteps *Triamore*, but his force as feeble as the reſt let ſtand ſtill that for which they alſo ſtroue: till *Chinon*, taking ſure hold vpon the hilt, with one hand did more than they were able to effect with all their power: which when he had done, brandiſhing it about hys head, as promiſing therewith to worke ſome extraordinarie wonders, he ſtraight waies by *Oborams* direction was preſented with a rich Armour and all neceſſarie furniture thereunto belonging, borne by two little Elues, which he ſtraight put on, and then girding himſelfe with his new got ſword, makes all poſſib[l]e ſpeede to returne as one longing to approue what thoſe rich habilliments did promiſe: to whome *Oboram* after a long oration of much prefiguring valour and valiant exploytes by him to bee performed, with many offered aſſurances of what readie helpe reſted in his power to performe, 'Whereof', quoth he, 'thou ſhalt ere long ſtand in need,' giues him further, a faire ſhield, compoſed by the cunning of a famous Inchantres, wherein was in rich mettall curiouſlye engrauen a ſtatelye flintie Rocke, ſhiuered in peeces by the power of a naked man, vnder which in letters of gold was in-grauen this poſie, '*Nihil difficile*', & appointing him a Page of his owne bringing vp, a little ill fauored Eluiſh Dwarffe, but

All three try in vain, but Chinon with one hand easily pulls it out, and Oboram at once presents him with rich armour, a shield and an 'Eluish Dwarffe' as a page.

trusty at all assayes, commits him to the keeping of good fauoring fortune, till time and his necessity shall againe bring them together.

[F⁴]

CHAP. V.

How Chinon *and* Triamore *redeemed* Celestina *from the Soldan of* Babilon, *after a most strange maner, with other Noble atchiuementes that they performed in the same exploit.*

<small>Chinon learns of the mishaps of the three knights and plans with Triamore to rescue Celestina.</small>

Thus in a sodaine trance they being back againe conueyed to the place whence he first led them: where they then beginne to acquaint him with all the manner of their triumph in France, the losse of their Lady, the victory of the Pagan, & what els ill hap had betyded them since theyr departure from the King of Frances Court, which tragick tale so whetted the longing lust of this pearelesse Prince, to reuenge the iniuries of those his so happy met mates, as that he straight gins to deuise how hee might best worke some speedy meanes for her deliuerie[1] that nowe was closelie pent vp in delights, farre more worse vnto her than darke Dungeons: [F⁴ back] which with many hammering plots At length hee thus purposed to bring to passe.

'Thou *Triamore*,' quoth hee, 'for that by thy default this Lady so vnluckely lost her libertie, shalt venture with me thus to recouer her, and these my friendes shall in a nother sort employ themselues as I will direct them: then seeing thy yeares are yet young, thy face louely, and euery well fashioned part of thy body fit to further our intent, thou shalt take vpo*n* thee the shape of some inchantres; I & my dwarffe trimmed vp in other apparell will attend vppon thee as dilligent seruants, which thou shalt pretend thou imployest in such secret affaires as none saue such simple slaues will abide to beare: where thou shalt vndertake to procure the likeing of faire *Celestina*, to affect him which for that no welcommer newes can come to his besotted minde than the sound of such seruice, he will easily condiscend to doe any thing that thou shalt direct him to: which beeing done,

---
[1] Text, *deliliuerie.*

of Chinon of England

leaue the reſt to my diſpoſition, and in the meane time theſe my ancient friends ſhall whileſt we worke within attende here without, and the next night when the Queene of ſhades gins in her quiet rule to dimme the glimering ſhow of leſſer lights, in ſome
5 ſecret place that thou (for that the beſt cannot direct vs in this cuntriè) ſhalt appoint to attend our comming; where for the next dayes ariſe we will worke a deede of ſuch worth as ſhall eternize our honour in all ages, and make vnborne Children hereafter to repeat what exceeding valour we, for our Chriſtian Countrie,
10 (ouerloaden with the hatefull burden of barbarous Pagans) performed; and then inſtructing them throughly in euery point of his purpoſe, and carefully prouiding to take away euery obſtacle of aduerſe fuſpition that might any waies be a hindrance to their well intended pur-[G¹]poſe, they meeting all againe on their ſturdie
15 Steedes rides foorth till they came neare to the place whereas the Pagan with all his Armie lay, and there in the ſame place wher by treaſon they were ſurpriſed ſtaies *Lancelot* and *Triſtram* in a thicke Caſtell, couered ouer with thicke leaued hollie, where they might eaſly ſhrowd themſelues from the ſight of all paſſengers:
20 whileſt *Chinon, Triamore,* & hys Dwarffe ſets boldly forward to execute the fore plotted purpoſe; who, comming into the Campe, made it ſtraight knowne to ſome of the Soldans neareſt attendantes what they were, *Triamore* pretending himſelfe to be (as afore we told) an Inchauntrèſſe, that was come from far to
25 further the loue of the great Soldan to faire *Celeſtina*: Which newes, when it was told him, ſounded no leſſe pleaſant in hys eares than *Aue Caeſar* at his Coronation; where charging them ſtraight to be brought to hys preſence, he gins to queſtion with *Triamore* of his ſkill, poſing him in the relation of kings¹
30 paſt as how, when, and where he firſt ſurpriſed that Lady: which *Triamore*, for that himſelfe was an vnfortunate acter in that dolefull Tragedy, could in euery point fitly anſwere him: which the Pagan, ſimply attributing to hys great ſkill, giues thankes to hys gods that in ſo good time had thither
35 directed the ſkilfull Inchantreſſe, by whoſe meanes he hoped not onely to enioy hys new ioyles loue but alſo to performe ſuch prodigious exployts as ſhould redound to the eternal

Triamore takes the diſguiſe of an enchantress come to induce Celestina to love the Soldan.

¹ See note.

dishonour of all Chriftian Countries, and then begins to queftion with him about the recouerie of his loue.

Triamore induces the Soldan to arrange a secret meeting with Celestina in a wood outside the camp.

Triamore, with a fine forged tale, gins tell him that if he would but practife fuch meanes as he fhould appoint, he would fo Inchaunt the louely minde of that fayre Chriftian Princeffe to affect hym as mauger al [G¹ back] the mallice of whatfoeuer oppofing power, fhe fhould forfake father and friends, kinffolks and Countrie, & only bind herfelfe to tarrie with him.

Which foule pleafing found did ring fuch fweete muficke in his rude eares as that he with all fpeede willed her but to determine what was herein to bee done, and he with asmuch expedition would fully effect, if it were to the loffe euen of halfe his Kingdome.

'Then,' quoth *Triamore*, 'this night hath *Cinthia* filled fullie vp her emptie hornes, whofe fauorable afpects will fitly further our purpofe: when therefore the filent night hath fhut the eyes of euery watchfull creature, thou, thy loue, and my felfe muft by fome fuch meanes as thou fhalt beft appoint, be conueyed fecretly from the Campe into the bofome of a neare bordering wood, where wee may clearely fee all the courfe of the ceafles frames of neuer refting heauen: where I with my inuocations and forcefiue Magick fpels will fo Inchaunt the minde of thy beauteous loue as hencefoorth fhee fhall neuer affect any other faue thy felfe;' and then pretending to prepare fuch neceffarie furniture as fhould fit her purpofe, fhe defired that her felfe and her feruants might a while bee remooued into fome fecret place, where they might prouide all thinges fit for their purpofe, and where they might have fome fpeech with the Damfel, which was fpeedily done: for a fecret feruant nerely belong[ing] to the Soldan was appointed to direct them, where by themfelues they had free talk with faire *Celestina*: to whome *Triamore* begins to relate all that had

The disguised Triamore explains the plan to Celestina. The Soldan going to the wood with his chief captains is captured by the three knights and his followers slain. Celestina gives all the credit to Chinon.

hapned them fince their inforcefiue departure, with the happie aduenture of *Chinon* for their deliuerie, and what els had befallen them in that trauel: and then comforts her with the hope of efcape, by theyr thus [G²] plotted purpofe: where long they were repeting their ouerpaffed paines and reioycing in their hoped happines, till time approached of their departure: when the Soldan, not vnmindefull of this matter, fent to the Sorcerer to fee if all thinges were readie for their purpofe: which affirmed that fhee was orderly prouided.

At laſt the lateſt houre is come, when he calling together all the chiefeſt of his Captaines & acquaints them with the caufe, which tended fo much to the furtherance of his defire, & intreating the moſt of them that they would walke with him out into the next adioyning wood to be witneffes of this work: to whom they willingly condefcended, & then, gathering themfelues together, after the watch was fet, they fecretly departed: where the Soldan, ftil thinking on the inioying of his loue, neuer dreampt of any pretended treafon that might thereby infue; but greedily catching like a foolifh fifh at the golden baite, they ftill followe on theyr way till they were come to the place where *Lancelot* and *Triftram* lay hid: where *Chinon* cafting off his diffiguring mafke begins now to fhew himfelfe in his owne likenes, and, with a watch word calling for his fellowes, brauely fets vpon thefe their enemies: where in short time they had fent to hell all the reſt, faue the Soldan himfelfe, and taking him prifoner, carries him away bounde: when *Triamore*, now once againe reuelling in the treafury of his loue, gins with all humble fubmiffion attribute to the honour of *Chinon* all the fore paffed proofe of this their fortunate feruice which they had performed.

But *Celeftina*, that nowe like the *Thracian* Damofell returned with the Lorde of her loue from the difmall Gates of Hell, beginnes with the [G² back] teares of true ioy to proſtrate her felfe at his honorable feete whofe force had againe reftored her from the tedious flauerie of loathfome captiuitie to the pleafant prefence of life feeding libertie, vowing deuoted feruice for this her fecond life: But *Chinon*, difdayning that the foule faced earth fhoulde enioy fo much as a touch of her heauenly hew, with gentle intreatie rayfes her vp, and thus replied to her fuppliant fpeech.

'Fairer', quoth he, 'than is the common compofition of earthly creatures, and therfore of more worth than millions, if I haue ought done in this that hath bred thy content, it is no more than befeemeth the dutie of my degree: Then doe not thus attribute more honor for my meede than is due by deferts to my deed: more is thy fmile towards the reward of a well deferuing worke, than the rich rewards of many millions of an others vowes,

Chinon modeſtly difclaims the honour in a highflown speech and turns her to Triamore, her lover.

more pleafant is the fight of an houres funne, than the fhow of
twenty fhadowed daies: but thy fight exceeding the brighteft
shining funne, that dazels at the mid dayes height the pearcing
beames of euery bright eyes fight, more welcome to vs than
day to the wearie watch, or the repofe of a quiet Inne to a tyred 5
trauailer, graceft our paines with thy prefence. More worth is
his worke that rifles in the rich bowels of the gold growne earth
than hee that drudges in the bottome of a dunghill ditch, and yet
the laft labor is more than the firft: but that the fubiect exceeding in worth excels the reward of his work more than the trauaile 10
graces the thing: but the worth of the fubiect dignifies the defert
of the deede, whereby our credit by thee is maintayned, and not
thy matchles felfe by our might magnified.

'Looke on hym that for thy loue aduentured his life, and the
rewarde of my paynes is this, that they re-[G³]dound to thy 15
pleafure; and for thee *Triamore*, fith now againe thou haft thy
hearts content, remember the eftate of thy old father, as thou
toldeft mee, is compaffed within the circle of yonder befeedged
walles, ftill expecting the fpeedy help of his forward friends:
but yet hath this nights worke fo weakned hys foes as that there 20
is no doubt of further danger.'

<small>All danger now being paft, Chinon proposes returning to England with Lancelot, Triſtram, and the captive Soldan, after conveying Celestina and Triamour 'to their fathers court '.</small>

By this with fuch like chat had they chafed awaie the fable
show of this filent night, and next the funne gins with cheare-
ful countenance to looke vpon the honorable actes of their thrife
prayfe worthy exployts, when by this time they were wandred 25
farre from the place where they firft gaue the onfet to atchiue
this honour: where *Chinon*, calling to him his two countrymen,
giues this carefull charge:

'You two,' quoth he, 'whofe honors accents is euerie where
blazed for your valours, shal henceforth leaue thefe wandring 30
wayes, and returne with me into our Countrie: where I will prefent to my longing Father this Pagan Prince, the firft fruits of
my Mayden manhood, dooing all my humble dutie to hys
Honorable age: but firft in fafety let vs conueye thefe Fayre
friends to their fathers Court and fet them there fafe from further 35
forrow at home that haue fuftained the hard brunt of fell
miffortune abroad, where may as many pleafures attend them
there in peace as honorable accidents happen to me in warres.'

[G3 back]
CHAP. VI.

Of Chinons *returne into England accompanied with Sir* Lancelot *and Sir* Triſtram, *with their moſt honorable entertainment there.*

5   After that hee had thus aduentured for the recouerie of beauteous *Celeſtina* from the handes of the Soldan, that had traiterouſly tane her away from Syr *Triamore,* & ſent them home to her fathers Court to ſolemnize their marriage, *Lancelot, Triſtram* and himſelfe tooke the direct way that led them home into
10 theyr own country, that there they might in quiet tell thoſe thinges with pleaſure amongſt theyr friendes which they had in trouble performed with labour amongſt their foes: In which iournie no occaſion of further let encountered them anie more, but as fareth with ordinary trauailers, they peaceablie paſſe ouer their iournie
15 till they came home into Cornewall to Earle *Cadors* Court, that was not a little glad to ſee the returne of his ſonne, with good hap to anſwere the long expectation of hys faire hope, [G4] he entertaines them with ſuch curteſie, as commonly paſſe betwixt loſt friends at theyr vnacquainted meetings. *The wanderers are received with joy, and even King Arthur summons his court to do honour to Chinon.*
20 *Chinon,* diſcourſing to hys old father the ſtorie of their trauailes, whoſe very wordes breedes new life in the dryed ſinnowes of hys old limmes: as doeth the approaching ſunne cherriſh the decayed winter worne ſtrength of the earths increaſe. *Lancelot,* hee preſents to hys loue the Trophies of his victorie, with many
25 perſwaſions how for her loue hee had aduentured his life in winning thoſe Princely Prizes, the chiefe whereof (whoſe worth exceeded all except herſelfe) he had bounteouſly beſtowed vppon ſir *Triamore*; *Triſtram,* he followes on his friends with the praiſes of them both: firſt, how by their meanes the Lady was
30 atchiued: then, how by *Chinons* deuiſe ſhe was ſecondly attained, with all the whole Hiſtory of their former fortunes: where what ioy was generally receaued, as well of the King himſelfe, whoſe[1] life ſtill laſts in the euerliuing acts of ſucceeding ages, famouſed as much for the renowne of his round table, ˄s *Alcides*

---

[1] Text, *and her, that whoſe,* see note.

38   *The Famous Historie*

for his twelve labors, *Iason* for his iournie to *Calcos*, or the Greekes for theyr triumphes at Troy.

Hee now in the winter of hys waning age, affecting to heare that now of others which before in his youth he had effected the like himfelfe, welcomes home all thefe wearie wanderers, that had beene fo long abroad, writing in the Regifters of other realmes the courage of their own country: as alfo the poore inhabitants of this [h]appy[1] Kingdome, that ioyed to fee their neighboring lands difpoyled of fuch riche rewardes as was brought home by their countrymen. Thus, when euery man had filled his eares with the report, *Arthur*, willing alfo to further the courage of this young Caualeer, fummons a [G⁴ back] folemne meeting of all the Nobles and Peeres of his country to his Court: where when at the time apointed all were gathered together, the King at a Royall banket gins to declare the caufe of this their calling together, that themfelues fhould fee how Princely he had, and would ftill pay the rewards of fuch deferts as by the aduentures of their yong countryman *Chinon* had beene profperoufly performed, and then with Epethites, accents of honour, telling the victorious tale of his fight, as *Aeneas* the Tragicke ftorie of their flight, he concludes hys fpeech with the performance of hys promife, which was the folemne orders he commonly vfed at the inftalment of any of his Knights; and, dubbing him, therewithall appoints him his place at the Table, where a while he remained, as well to comfort the decaying date of his Fathers yeares, whome wreftling age had almoft now layed along in hys graue; and as the Mariegold that neuer fpreadeth her flowers but againft the funne,. So he neuer opened his age dimmed eyes to beholde the chearefull countenance of any creature faue his Son *Chinon*; and like the melancholly Turtle when her mate is from her fight, So fares it with this aged Earle, that neuer fleepes but dreames of hys Sonne, neuer is well waking when he fees him not, & neuer contented with any founds if he heare him not: as alfo the intire affection of hys King and Captaine *Arthur* of England that, inamored with his curtefie, was lo[th][2] to leaue hys company, he was forced a while to refraine his affections, whofe body though[3] it was walled in at home, yet was his minde wandring

Side note: King Arthur dubs Chinon a knight at the banquet and gives him a place at the Round Table, while Earl Cador now adores his valiant son.

[1] Text, *pappy*!   [2] Text, *loft*.   [3] Text, *thought*.

of Chinon of England 39

abroad : which the fates forefeeing, (as do the careful Parents prouide for their forward children) feeke meanes for theyr furtherance in that quallitie whereto they are moft inclined, loath that fo many vertues [H¹] fhould be cooped within the compaffe
5 of a fillie Iland, and not fpread their braunches abroad to the wide world, carefully contriued a meanes to conuaye hym away.

CHAP. VII.

How Chinon was by the Fairies conuaied into Egipt.

Thus hee, fpending the pride of his dayes at home in daliance,
10 letting ruft [e]ate¹ away his well tempered Armour that warres before had fcoured, lying one day vppon a pleafant ouerfpread banke, vnder the couert of a nature framed Canopie, bound together with the bowes of fweet fmelling rofes, vpon whofe pleafant fpraies fate the feuerall forts of muficke making birdes,
15 that with theyr naturall notes calles on inchaunting fleep to poffeffe the quiet organes of his body with all pleafing reft, in the midft of a fweet flumber fuddainely appeares to the view of his drowfie thoughts two airie bodies, fuch creatures as we call Fairies, whome fome [H¹ back] imagine² to be thofe fpirites that
20 fell downe vpon the earth, and fince that time inhabit the feuerall corners thereof, fometimes deluding mens fenfes with the fhowes of that they are not : other, fomtimes fhowing themfelues in the femblances they commonly accuftome to put on, dancing roundelayes ouer the plefaunt meades, fearing the fecrete
25 corners of euerie fhade : in which fort it fhould feeme they found thys Knight, to whom they gan fhewe a rich embrodered armour, curioufly carued and richly fet with all manner of precious ftones, and a faire fword with all the formall furniture thereunto belonging, farre paffing that which before he had pulled out of the
30 Rocke, and therewithall ginnes feed his fancie, that they nourifhed his imagination in the perfecteft ioye of all naturall delight, with the fhow of a faire Virgin, whofe rare countenaunce

While Chinon is leading an easy life, he is one day visited in his sleep by fairies, who show him rich armour and also a fair virgin, daughter of Bessarian, counsellor of the King of Egypt.

---

¹ Text, *cate*.
² The syllable *im-* ends page H¹ back, and is repeated in *imagine*.

promifed more than her outward colour of attire, for that meane were her weeds, fuch as commonly we read of the *Arcadian* Shepheardeffes, whofe perfections haue put to filence fo many pens in labouring to portrait their picture. But her felfe, more than a mortall Maid, looked vppon with the impartial cenfure of 5 a iudging eye, might draw into an endleffe Laborynth the labouring thoughts of an indeuoring wit, ftriuing with it felfe to picture forth her worth. Where awhile we muft leaue him *Endimion*-like fpending his time in this fweete fpeculation, and for a time talke of this rare fight here fhowed hym in his fleep. 10

This fair maid Cassiopeia is vainly loved by Perosus, and he thereupon enlists the services of an old witch who conveys her through the air far away to a lonely plain beside the Nile. Here she sits and sings to the fishes.

This Ladie was daughter to an ancient Lord named *Beffarian*, cheif Counfeller to *Egbatan* then King of *Egypt*, and was there earneftly beloued of a noble Man named *Perofus*, who for that he faw by no way he could compaffe his defire, neither by amorous demeanor of himfelfe, inftance of his frends, nor ear- 15 [H²]neft foliciting deferts of his dumb intermiffiue gifts, could preuaile to drawe towards him the dutye of her loue, he determining by another drift ether to win her to himfelfe or to weare her out of conceit with all other, fecretly gins worke with an old Witch, whofe name was *Eutropa*, who, hyred by him, hammered 20 about to work fome meane how fhe might change the fetled affections of her maidenlyke minde fomewhat to encline themfelues to his intent: which when by no meanes fhe could bring about, fhe ftraight works a way to remoue her quite from all companie, to liue on the vnpeopled Plaines among brute beafts; 25 and to that ende aiming her actions, by meanes of an ayrie Spirit attendant vppon her, fuddenly conueyed her from the Courtly prefence farre off to an vnfrequented Plaine, fcituate by the Riuer *Nylus*, where fhee perceiuing her felfe difplaced, but feeing no reafon of her remooue, ftraitwaies begins to confider 30 with her felfe what luckles occafion might thus croffe her in her hopefull courfe, and when after long fearch in the felfe knowen records of her inward confcience, fhee could finde no readie reafon, how her offences fhould anie wayes haue procured fo great a punifhment as this vnnaturall diuorfe, not onely from the 35 comfort of her kindred but all other frends, hauing with all humble dutie alwaies honored her fuperiors & wyth carefull curtefie intreated her inferiors; beeing euer held as the myrour of good demeanor. And thus finding her felfe as cleare from

of Chinon of England 41

those vengeaunce-meriting sinnes that drawes downe the heauie
wrath of all-iudging Gods so sharply with such seuere plagues to
punish the offences of men, shedding manie showers of amber
teares, whose power were able to haue drawne pittie from the
5 steely hearts of hell-holden furies, fits her downe by the side of
that siluer streame [H²back] that with his seauen heads still sends
fresh supplie to the all eating sea, and tuning her voice to the
bubling musick of his gliding course, & to the flocking sortes of
sundry fishes, that like the dancing Dolphins at the sweete sound
10 of *Arions* Harpe gather themselues together,

She singes this Dittie.

Ye free borne people from th' inthralling bands,
That we poore soules perforce are subiect to:
You glide with pleasure ore these golden sands,
15 *And feeles no hope of weale nor hap of woe.*
Time, fortune, foes, nor any other power,
Changes, casts downe, or turnes your sweet to sower:
But we whome nature wrought vnto the best,
Triumphant time still tosses vp and downe:
20 *And they whome former fortune whilome blest,*
Cruell missfortune with a suddaine frowne:
Casts from a throane where sur'st we seeme to dwell,
To worser woes than death, dispaire, or hell.

Thus whilest with this song shee sought to please her sorrow, The witch upbraids her for
25 sodainely this wicked woman (by whose meanes shee was brought rejecting the love of Perosus
thether) carried through the emptie aire in fierie flaming care, and tells her she must remain in
such as was that secret searching *Medea*, amidst the sable shadow exile till she relents.
of the silent night, ouerroad so many tops of hilles to finde those
hearbes that in the age worne limmes of a bloodles man cals
30 backe fresh spring to keep againe his residence in that body: who,
presenting her selfe vnto her in the accustomed shape at other
times shee vsually shewed her selfe, begins at her first entrance [H³]
to disclose vnto her the manner of translation from her father
and friends vnto these peopleles plaines, confessing her selfe both
35 to be Author and actor of this diuellish deuise: ' where,' quoth
she, ' for the coy countenances that so oft thou haste repayed to
the pitty moouing perswations of him that, for thy loue well nie

loft, weares out in woe the dayes, and watches with tirrible torments the night, that in euerie fentence he fpeakes fo oft cites thee by thy proper name and himfelfe, with bare conceit that hee hath thee whom by confent he rightly fhould haue had, pines awaie, poore foule, in the phificke fits of a paffionate louer. In whofe reuenge', quoth fhee, 'I haue here feated thee by thy felfe, far from the refort of men, where defolation fhall here teach thee to tell thy felfe that thou art now worfe than wilde beasts, that before efteemeft of thy felfe better than faire framed men: where,' quoth fhe, 'till thou canft call backe thy proude prefuming thought to pitty his cafe that for thee fpends his life in fuch care, here fhalt thou haue thy abode, and be as far from any confolation of others as thou art from comforting of him;' and fo fodainely leauing her againe to her felfe fhe departed.

To pass away the time, Cassiopeia keeps sheep and makes clothing with their wool. Meanwhile, her father Bessarian sends his three sons in search of their sister, and Perosus tells the king that Bessarian is plotting treason.

At which abrupt Oration the maid feemed at the firft difmayed: yet at length comfortes fomewhat more her conceit, in that fhe knew the meanes of her remoue; and fo at last, after fhee had long remained there in that people wanting world, to efchue the occafion of harme and the effect of idlenes fhee betooke her felfe to carefull keeping of fome fimple natured fheepe, where of that place was ftored, of whofe wooll fhe now begins to fpinne her felfe fome homely atire, that was wont to be robed in the richeft aray that nature and Arte could afford; and in the meane time (the weary workes preuenting all occafions of further [H³ back] misfortune that might els in the continuance of time haue croffed theyr intent) workes meanes to difcredit her wofull Father, who now deftitute of all his children,—his daughter, the hope of comfort to hys declining age, and hauing three goodly fonnes, whome nature had euery way furnifhed with gifts fitting their degrees, whofe names were *Michander*, *Terpander* and *Theonas*: all these had hee employed in the queft of their fifter, when as his foes, taking the aduantage of their time, *Perofus*, that was alfo a Counceller, gins fecretlie to informe the King of certaine treafons pretended to his life and land by *Beſſarian*, father to thys new fhepheardeffe, of whome before wee tolde you: to the end that hauing vnfurnifhed him of the Kinges fauour, himfelfe might the eafier effect what occafion foeuer fhould be offered, and the poore father left deftitute of all meanes to further his fonnes affaires: which the king at the firft

of Chinon of England   43

was loth to beleeue, both for that he had had fo long tryall of
the faithfull feruice old *Beſſarian* had alwaies performed, as alfo
that hee fuppofed that fuch fubtiltie could not harbour in a filuer
coloured head: 'for that', quoth he, 'Serpents alwaies lurke in
5 young greene tufftes & not in winter wythered graffe, age
abolifhes deceits as it abandons vaine delights, & as the bodie
waxes weake, by fo much more doth the minde waxe ftrong,
as being nowe freed from all the intifing affections in hys age,
whereunto the vaine pleafures of this wicked world did ftill intife
10 him to in his youth': whereunto the other, ready to replie with The credulous
frefhe inforfiue argument, fhewes ftraight to the King the inter- charge, substan-
miffiue letters that fo long had paffed too and fro betwixt forged letters
Beſſarian and many of his Maiefties enemies for the effecting of testimony, and
their treafons, to which he had fo cunningly [H⁴] counterfetted braids the inno-
15 the oldmans hand as if himfelfe had fubftancially fet it downe; cent old man.
and the better to proue euery feuerall circumftance of this his
furmifed tale, hee prefently produces two or three periured companions, who for that purpofe hee had fubborned: whofe fub-
ftantiall tale tooke fuch effect and fo farre incenfed the King, that
20 in all hafte fending for the old guiltleffe foule, who was fo farre from
pretending this ill that, notwithftanding all the croffe occafions
that fo vnluckely had hapned vnto him, he fpends all his time
intending ftill naught but hys Soueraignes good: where when
hee came, the King, breaking foorth into impatience, beginnes
25 with traiterous names to vpbraid him, who, God knowes, was fo
farre from inuenting it that he ftudied nothing more than the
preuenting it: and then vnripping vnto him the forged treafon,
fhewing him the counterfet letters figned by his own hand, the
feuerall circumftances prooued by fuch fufficient witneffes as there
30 pretended themfelues to be, impatient of excufe, and therefore
vtterly denying to heare his further anfwere, ftill vrged by the
enuious inuented perfwafions of his fubtill enemie, gins thus to
bewray his hatred.

'Experience', quoth he, 'hath taught us, and the dayly proofe
35 of ftill prefent time offers occafions to our eies of new examples,
how in brute beafts the countinance of long time groundes perfect loue, as the filly dogge that, brought vp at hys Mafters
trencher, in his kinde remembers his curtefie and, whiles nature
lends him libertie of life, indeuors himfelfe ftill in all duty to

requite it; and fhall then man, their reafonable ruler, be worfe
than thefe reafonles thinges, by him fo ruled? herbs, trees, and
other vegitable creatures increafing from the earth, to them that
with care manure their roots & prune their branches, render
fruit for a reward, [H⁴ back] the beaftes they in their fu[n]drie [1] 5
kindes requites their owners coft, as one with his fkinne, another
with hys fleece; one with his huffe, and another with hys horne;
one with hys labour, and another with hys loue; and fhall not
then he whome God hath made as Mafter of all thefe creatures
exceede them in his reafonable raign, that fubiect themfelues 10
reafonles to be ruled? Since firft I came to fway the heauie
Scepter of this great Kingdome and tooke into my hands the
tuition of fo many people as inhabite thefe fpacious plaines of
wide weft *Egipt*, [I] haue nourifhed thee euen in my bofome:
neareft haue I kept thee to my felfe, becaufe I would draw thy 15
affection from all other, & hafte thou now with *Efopes* vngratefull
fnake, ftinged him in the breaft, that fo carefully fought to preferue
thee in his bofome.

Continuing his abuse, the king banishes Bessarian.

' Can it be that vnder the reuerend fhow of fuch honourable
age fhould reft the vndeferued thoughtes of vnreuerent reuenging 20
rage? Is there founde foule droffe in faire gold, bad fhowes on
good fubftances, & can there be fuch hatred in fure hearts?
I, I, I fee the fayreft fommer fhine hath his fodaine fhower, the
beft bloffome is oft times fooneft blafted, & the trueft friend
prooues oft the moft trecherous foe: But as no man commends 25
the funnie morning, nor the fhowrie night, the fruftrate hope of
his fruite, for the bad blafted bud: fo let euery man efpecially
condemne the foules fecret friend when he turns to a fore ferch-
ing foe: which *fimile* I to thy felfe muft now applie, that vnder
the faire fhow of friendfhip haft fecretly gone about to ouerturne 30
my eftate & bring this welgouerned common weale to a ruinous
decayed wracke; which fault is fo apparant, both by thine owne
hand fufficiently fet foorth, as alfo confirmed by the Teftament
of others, as that my pacience, fcarce contein-[I¹]ing it felfe within
the boundes of euill behauiour, cannot abide to heare any excufe, 35
and therefore will I againft thee pronounce this heauie doome
for thy ill deferuing deedes; the punifhment of death were

[1] Text, *suudrie*.

of Chinon of England   45

a pleasure to thee, so that so I should ease thee of a great deale
of sorrow; if thou shouldest still continue in thy best state thou
wert likely to sustaine, and therefore from henceforth like
a cursed creature shalt thou wander in the world and eate the
bitter bread of banishment in a forraine soyle, that whilome
liuedst so sweetly in thine owne naturall seat, and so foreuer
I banish thee from the compasse of this Kingdome, to burie thy
siluer haires in sorrow, that haddest such hope to harbour them in
their graue with ioy.'

At which wordes the olde man not able to speake for the abundance of teares that stopped vp the way of his wordes, was forced to leaue him without further replie and, hopeles of any helpe, patiently to departe. By this time had the King (more to punish his suppofed amis,) seazed vpon all his goods, to the ende he might leaue him no succour to saue himself abroad: which when he saw, sorrowfully sighing to himselfe, desperately departes away without any further following the King for the repeale of this his punishment, and straight way betakes himselfe to hys trauaile : which when *Perosus* perceaued how they now had brought euery thing euen to the bent of their own bow, gins glorie to themselues in their likely prosperitie, purchased by the hard hap of an others aduersitie : but on a sodaine *Eutropa*, the Witch by whose counsell all this trecherie was contriued, looking further into the matter what was likelie to follow, by these meanes perceaued in the speculatiue glasse, how that the rightful reuenging gods had by many means determined her releafe : as first by *Chinon*, whom for [I¹ back] that purpose they had brought out of England : then by her brethren, who had vndertaken to search all the world for their sister, and lastly by her father, whose giltles banishment could not long be concealed, & the*n*, beeing called home to hys former place, would seeke such meanes for her recouerie as their power coulde hardly preuent ; and therefore to escape these insuing illes [s]he thus determined to deale. The maide who though she was from thence far remote, and in a place whether lay no ordenarie passage yet, foreseeing how at length that all would hit vpon that way inclofes by her wicked workes this faire Damsell within the ruine of an olde Rocke hard by the riuer side, vpon whose bankes before shee made her abode: where accompanied with shadowes of naturall creatures hauing

Unable to speak for grief, the old man departs.

The witch, meanwhile, perceives in her magic glass that Cassiopeia will be released and hence encloses her 'within the ruine of an olde Rocke hard by the riuer side'.

faire womanly faces like her felfe, that feemed to outward fence of the far beholders to make her merrie with melodious muficke, but to her felfe fhe found it far contrarie, proouing nothing els but a harfh difcord of mifliking founds; which outward femblance was for this purpofe by them prouided that it might fomewhat 5 fatiffie any idle beholder, to fee that her prifon was rather a pleafure than anye fuch paine as fhould mooue the mindes of men to venture any thing for her releafe; where, poore foule, fhee now coopt vp in a Cage that before tooke her pleafure vpon thofe fpacious plaines, like to the beguiled bird that, vnwares 10 falling into the Fowlers gin, is nowe caged vp in a little compaffe, that whilome was wont to play vpon the broad branches of euery fpringing Plant.

CHAP. VIII.

Bessarian is transformed by the witch into the form of a bear, with a scroll about his neck promising good fortune to whoever kills him.

How Beffarian *her father was by the Witch turned into the likenes of a Beare, and how* 15 *hee met with his fonnes in that fhape.*

Thus hauing determined of her, they ftraight waies begin to ftriue with themfelues how they might deuife fome drift to remooue the feare that they had of her Fathers rifing againe to his former ftate, which by the meanes of *Eutropa* the Witch they thus 20 contriued.

Shee, calling to counfaile her attendant fpirits, by whofe meanes fhee brought to paffe all this matter, gins giue them feuerally in charge to vfe their Artes in plaging of this poore man, which they fhould fo furely effect as no hope fhould be left 25 of any more comfort to come vnto him: where beating together their hell bred braines, they thus concluded with themfelues, that they would chaunge hym from the fhape of a man into the big body of an vgly Beare, [I² back], and fo let him die a beaft that was borne a man; and further yet to aggreuate hys woes, 30 which might notwithftanding this enuie haue an end, they intended in his difguife to haften on hys death, leaft by fome croffing occafions, as oftentimes are ufually feene vnexpectedly fall out for the releafe of Magicke bandes, which they thus determined when they had wrought their willes in his tranfformation, 35

of Chinon of England 47

about his necke they hang a fcroule, wherein were written two
verfes which were thefe:

> *He whofe good hap fhall kill this beare,*
> *That man fhall haue his hearts defire.*

5 Thinking by this meanes the better to drawe on euery mans
might to the effecting of their former plotted purpofe, for that
all men by a naturall inftinct ar greedie to get any hope of pur-
fuing their purpofes, though oft times they doe it with the danger
of theyr liues: where the oldman turned after this manner *The old man*
10 wanders through the woods, clogged with the burden of felfe *suffers great misery in his*
feeling forrow, and in difpayre of reliefe fettles himfelfe to that *wandering. Meanwhile*
thraldome without hope of releafe. Many were the miferies in *Cassiopeia's three brothers*
this fhape hee fuftained, as the many hungry dayes that in fpite *are seeking her, and the eldest*
of himfelfe he was forced to fpend for that his ftomacke was not *at length spies her 'in the*
15 vfed to feede vpon fuch filthie carion as thofe beafts accuftomably *midst of a clouen Rocke'; but*
deuoure; the raw reftleffe nights without couert hee muft now *suddenly the rock closes and*
continue; the want of his friends, and feare of hys foes, with *shuts her from his sight.*
a countleffe company of more griefes than the capacitie of man
can conceaue was conteyned in him, being then as a beaft,
20 fauing that ftill he retayned the vfe of his reafonable foule,
which they by no meanes could make to mifcarie.

In the meane time the Witch, now in the [I³] midft of her bufines,
feeing in her fpeculatiue Glaffe (wherein fhe vfually faw what
accident foeuer was likely to happen) the approach of her
25 Brethren, who (by tracing vp and downe in the World) were
fome of them come neere (at vnwares) to the place where fhe
was, poafted her felfe with all fpeed, the better to profper
her purpofe, and with violence inforces a fpirit (one of her owne
Attendants) to vfe the organes of her bodie to an ende which her-
30 felfe had deuifed; that was to fend fundrie wayes her Brethren,
who were like feuerally to come thether where now their Sifter
did foiourne.

And by that time this Hag had brought this purpofe to paffe,
Michander her eldeft Brother (that now almoft wearied with
35 walking vp and downe among the high, defolate Hills) had
framed his iourney towards that Riuer the which with his
fwelling waters moyftens once euerie yere those pleasant
Egyptian Plaines, to refrefh his tyred limmes in the coole

The Famous Historie

ſtreames of that pleaſant Current, bathing his ſweet bodie in thoſe refreſhing Springs; ſuddenly in the midſt of a clouen Rocke he eſpies ſitting a companie of faire Creatures, whereof one (exceeding all, lyke the Huntreſſe amidſt the naked troupes of her attendant Nimphs) hee quickly ſtartes vp and hies to the place where he ſuppoſed they ſhould bee: to which as hee came nearer, hee might perceaue the middlemoſt Ladie, that ſo farre exceeded the reſt, to be *Caſsiopeia* his Siſter, for whom he had made ſuch ſearch; when in an extaſie of ioye, ſtanding ſtill as not able at the firſt to vtter the ſudden mirth of his minde, the enuious Stone cloſes his ſides and ſhuts them al from his

He hears her call him by name and learns her plight. The witch then moves her to send him to the Taurus mountains for a vial full of virgin's tears that have power ' to breake the strongest inchaunted Bands'.

ſight. At which ſudden accident, his ſenſes, as farre caſt downe as before they mounted themſelues with the hope of recouering his Siſter, gins with himſelf [I^s back] deuiſe what this matter might meane, till from the Rocke hee heard one pitifully call him by hys owne name; which at length he perceiued to be the voice of his Siſter whom before he had ſeene: and anſwering againe to her ſudden call, ginnes demaund by what meanes he might come vnto her. To whom ſtraight ſhe anſweres, that there was no paſſage to that place; for that, by the wicked worke of an enuious Inchantreſſe, ſhe was there ſo ſurely incloſed, as neither force of man, edge of weapon, violence of fire, nor any other earthly meanes whatſoeuer the World could affoord was able to auaile, except himſelfe would aduenture one thing for her deliuerance. And then ſhee coniures him by the dutie he ought to his Father, the loue to her his Siſter, and the care of preſeruing their Kindred, that he ſhould vndertake this Aduenture: which he with more earneſt deſire offers to doo than ſhe could with her former reaſons perſwade hym too, deſiring her to tell him his taſke, that he might ſlip no time, but in al haſt hye him to the performance of this thing, which was like ſo highly to pleaſure the*m* both, her with comfort, and him with content. To whom ſhe thus begins to vnfold her intent.

'Under' (quoth ſhe) 'that topleſſe Hill which we call by the name of *Taurus*, that with his length gyrdells in the wyde Continent of flowring *Aſia*, vnder the roote of an euerlaſting Lilly, ſtands there a Uiall full of Uirgins teares, that encou*n*tred with the like croſſe as I am now (poore Soule) in, and before her releaſe dyed there for ſorrow; to whoſe eternall memorie, againſt

of Chinon of England 49

the infectiue rage of this ouer ruling power, the Fates haue there
referued that powerfull Potion, whofe Uertue is to breake the
ftrongest inchaunted Bands; and fo Shee that by them was thus
bound while fhee liued haue the Gods ordained as an In-[1⁴]
ftrument to vnbinde them now fhe is dead. But the still
working wits of thefe wicked wretches, hatching nothing but
harme, intending nothing but what is ill, and perfourming
nothing but that which tends to our plague, haue, to preuent
that which is thus prouided, ftrongly garded the ground where
thys Uyall standeth, with the power of a fight-killing Serpent,
fuch as we call a Cockatrice, against whom no power is able to
preuaile.'

At which words [Mich]ander,[1] breaking her from hir furder dif- *The deluded youth at once goes in search of the magic vial.*
courfe, ginnes to perfwade his fifter a little with patience, and ere
long hee doubted not by hys meanes to work her libertie. And *Then comes the second brother, who, directed by his sister (controlled by the witch) goes to Arabia to get Orion's harp, the music of which, he is told, will effect her release.*
thus like the greedie Grey-hound that fuddenly fets out to follow the
swift footed Hare, flies he to attaine his purpofe, beleeuing as his
forrowfull Sifter did, that there had been that vertue in the water,
but it was onely the deceipt of her deadly Enemie, that determined to make away all her Bretheren, whofe indeuours were
elfe likely to worke her releafe: and therefore (as before wee
faid) inforced her tung to tattle that which her minde did not
meane, whereby fhee might bee theyr deaths in feeking to doo
her good.

Not long after [Mich]ander [2] had thus betaken himfelfe to his
iournie, with hope that her releafe from that place fhould repay
the defertes of his paines, comes to her the fecond brother,
whofe name was [Terp]ander,[3] and hee as the firft, ioyfull to fee
the ende of hys iournie, which was the fight of hys fifter, begins
after the manner of newe met friendes to refalute her, and as he
offered to haue kiffed her hand for ioy of his good happe,
fodainely the Rocke fhutting her from him deuorces a funder
both their defires; to refalute whofe proffered kindneffe, fhe,
fpeaking from her prifon, telles him with teares the manner of
her [1⁴ back] inclofure, intreating him by all the true loue that
nature workes in the mindes of men that he would vndertake
fome meanes for her freedome; which he readier to offer than

---

[1] Text, *Terpander*.   [2] Text, *Terpander*.
[3] Text, *Micander*.

E

shee willing to inioyne, calls to hys solemne vow all the Gods of Heauen and Guiders of Earth, that were it a greater toyle than to number the sands of the Shore, the droppes in the Sea, or the starres in the Skie, more heauie than the burden of *Atlas*, more toylsome than the Labours of *Hercules*, or more tedious than the Laborynth of *Theseus*, hee would with ease vndergoe it, with courage performe it, and with pleasure proceed in it: and therefore hastened her forward (poore Soule) to pronounce hys harme.

She gins tell him that ' in the Deserts of *Arabia* rests [*A*]*rions*[1] Harpe, brought thether by the meanes of an Inchauntresse, to releafe from the thraldome of such subiection as now I am in, a valorous Knight, whom another Magitian had there imprisoned: and sayling by some crosse occasion to persourme the purpose whereunto it was brought, there still remaines, but kept by a man-eating *Canniball*, hauing neither the forme of a man, nor the fashion of a beast, but compound of them both. Him' (quoth shee) 'if thou canst ouercome, and bring backe that well tuned Instrument, at whose stroakes the dauncing Dolphin delighted beares on his backe wofull [*A*]*rion*[2] from the furie of the fierce swelling seas, when by the Pirates he was cast among the waues; The sound whereof wilbe sufficient to vndoo the doores of this diuelish deuice: for which deed thou shalt be blessed, and I borrowed from this punishing prison'. Which said, the forward young Man, loath to loose time by standing on reply, gets speedily from the place and hies him to his labour.

Lastly comes the youngest brother, who in his turn is sent to get from a temple in a perilous island a golden book full of enchantments.

[K¹] After whose departure, by chance (as did both the first) comes *Theonas*, the yongest and last of these brethren, who, at a sudden seeing his Sister there inclosed in the Rocke, gins as did the other to resalute her with such louing looks as accustomabl[y][3] passe betwixt longing frends at their first meeting; wher, after manie words on both sides, *Theonas*, wondring why shee should sit so still in her seate and not offer the like curtesie he intended to her, gins to draw neerer the place where shee was when, on a sudden, the Rock (closing together) denies his nearer approach: at which, shee sorry within and he as sad without, gins both of them distil as manie amber teares from their christal eies as might haue dissolued againe the

[1] Text, *Orions*.   [2] Text, *Orion*.   [3] Text, *accustomable*.

craggie cliffes of thofe pittiles Rockes. At length fhee (as afore
to the other two) gins tell him the manner of her life, and
intreates his aid for her releafe, telling him of a perilous Iland
that was fometime kept by a skilfull woman named the wife
Erganea, where on an Altar in a Temple (there built vnto
her name) lies a golden Booke, 'in which (quoth fhe) is contained
all the Enchauntments that Arte can affoord, and their feuerall
releafes again, kept by two Harpies (fuch were thofe monftrous
birds with whom *Alcides* fought, and for his conflict with them
was fo great, it was accounted as one of the xii. Labours
hee atchieued): thence if thou canft but fetch it away, it wil be
the only meane to worke my releafe, and end thy long defires
and tedious labour'.

Wheretoo the yong man attentiuely harkening, as one that longed to eternife his name to fucceeding pofterities for the perfourmance of fome fuch famous Worke, makes fmall delay to profecute this bufines, with comfortable promifes of fairer dayes, cheering and comforting her minde, leaues her to the mercy of [K¹ back] her Foe, till his happie returne make her more fortunate. *He hastens away, deceived like his brothers.*

Thefe feuerall Aduentures by her impofed on her Bretheren, had this Witch before prouided, only for a meane to deftroy all them that fhould in this labour indeuour themfelues, and perforce made her tongue the vnwilling Inftrument to incite them to this ill: who otherwife intended their indeuours onely for her good.

CHAP. IX.

How Chinon *came to the Rocke where the Ladie was inchaunted, and what happened thereof.*

And now comes Chinon, brought by the fairies for the rescue of Cassiopeia. After wandering beside the river he hears her singing a mournful ditty.

In this time the Fayries (by whofe meanes *Chinon* was conueighed out of *England*) had brought hym to the place where in the Vifion whileft he lay afleep vnder the Arbour in *England* they fhewed him the faire Shepheardeffe, and had taken their leaue, telling him how (by his meanes) that Ladie (now in Captiuitie) was to be releafed, but how manie dangers hee muft firft paffe through, left him there to folow his farder fortune, with great promiſes that after labour he ſhould finde reſt, after [K²] ſtormes calmes, and after frowning aduerſitie ſmyling proſperitie: and ſo on a ſudden vaniſhed away. When he (ſeeking vp and downe for her, whome by no meanes he could find) wondring how ſo rare beutie could be bred in ſuch a homely ſoyle, whereas 5 the Earth was vnfruitfull for want of tillage, the Trees vnorderly bearing frute for lacke of pruning, and the ſeuerall Beaſts diſagreeing in their owne kindes for want of ordering; plainly the true definition of ſolitarie deſolation that, oft abounding in all things, is cauſe of decay to euerie thing. At laſt, as hee 10 wandered along the Riuer, he heard excellent muſique, and a more excellent voyce tune forth this Ditie:

> *How ſweete a thing is this Content*
> *To which poore countrie Swaines are born?*
> *Theſe falls of Fortune they preuent,* 15
> *And other hard miſhaps doo ſcorne.*
>
> *Oh how thrice bleſſed had I beene,*
> *If (but obſcurde in countrie weedes)*
> *Thoſe mightie men I nere had ſeene,*
> *Whoſe loathed loue my ſorrow breedes?* 20
>
> *But ſuch is the vnconſtant ſtate*
> *Of this ſtill-changing Worlds delight,*
> *Making the meane a Princes mate,*
> *Croſsing high hopes with low deſpight.*
>
> *Which makes my Soule (in ſad deſpaire)* 25
> *Die here ten thouſand times a day,*
> *Woond vp within a world of care,*
> *Whence nought can it releaſe away.*

Following the sound he at length finds her sitting amid the rocks and in rapture addresses her. But the wily witch controls her tongue as she replies.

[K² back] When hee, following the ſound of the voyce, at length found her where ſhe was ſitting in the hollow ſide of 30 a Rocke, hemmed round about with a ſhow of ſuch creatures as her ſelfe, to whom *Chinon* ginnes thus to bewray himſelfe.

'Ah thou more than thy ſelfe, in that thou retaineſt too heauenly a forme for anie earthly frame, How impartiall are the Fates that turnes the neuer ſtanding Wheele of Fortune, to grace 35 with ſo continuall a Sunne this Soyle, and lowre with obſcure showres on other places. Goddesse of these Plaines, that giuest more grace to these fields than did the Goddesses to the place where they pleaded for the golden Prize, Hadst thou liued in those dayes when young *Apollo* loued, then hadst thou been the Paramour of Learnings Prince, and guided his will that now gouernes the World. For thy sake am I transported from the furthest place of the wide western World into these cynged Plaines of euer ouer dried *Egypt*. For thee will I follow the aduentures of Armes, so that when for thy sake I haue fought the World, and with my sword engraued (in neuer changing characters) thy God like name in the farthest corners of all-breeding Earth, where no consuming fire, cutting sword, nor eating eternitie shall euer weare awaye thy memorie, so that for my labour thou wilt reward me with thy loue.'

When with exceeding passion he had deliuered these speeches, with more than common admiration he paused, like one that were suddenly amazed wyth the showe of some vnacquainted sight, stood a long while as in a traunce: when as the wylie Witch, perceiuing this new come Companion likely to marre what shee and false *Perosus* (by their practises) had been so long a making, beginnes to take once more [K³] the charge of her tongue, and thus boldly begins to tie him to his taske.

'Faire Knight', quoth shee, 'whose willing minde to doo me seruice wins more reward than I am able any wife to bestow, If I were what now I am not, then would I doe what now I doe not, with fauour requite thy forward fortunes; but thus it is': and then she begins in a long Historie to relate her frowning fortunes. First drawne from the Court, then perforced long time by her selfe to dwell solitarily vpon that vnpeopled soyle, and lastly, when shee began to comfort her selfe, with that country content, then solitarily to shut her vp in that place, where was no passage fo[r]¹ any people to come to her, and she depriued of all power to come out to them; & then telling how there rested no hope of redresse, if that for her sake some mighty man would not vndertake a trebble taske, worse than tormented *Sisiphus* hys toyle.

Which words wrought such a desire in the minde of this forward Knight, as vowing to performe more mightie deedes

Cassiopela relates her sad story and begs his assistance, which he is more than ready to give. But the old witch prepares to thwart him.

¹ r partly erased.

than thofe deedes of the olde Giantes that heaping hill vpon hil affayd the height of heauen, he inftantly begins to intreat that in this her charge fhe would admit of him as her Champion.

At which wordes the Hag, that all this while had hid her fubftance in an inuifible fhade, gins vrge her to impofe vpon him all thofe plagues fhe had appointed the other three and, when hyr perfwafiue Oration was fcarce done, hys eager minde, that alreadie was working for fo faire a rewarde, like the towring hawke, that fwiftly takes the aduantage of the fearefull foule, fares hee, that proud to himfelfe fo faire a Saint fhould fo foone accept of his feruice, and imploy him in fo ferious a peece of feruice as was the remedy of her releafe, flies with al fpeed to effect hys purpofe; [K³ back] and fhee, poore foule, hoping well that one of her workmen would at laft returne againe with the reward of their worke, with comfort contents her felfe to abide the end: where wee muft a while leaue her (very melancholily meditating with her felfe, howe fhee might beft fpende her time in that wicked Prifon, thinking euery houre to bee a whole yeare, and euery yeare a thoufand, till fhee had heard againe fome newes of her fearching feruants, that had fpred them felues all abroad in the wide world, to feeke her fome meanes for to mittigate her miferie and reftore her to her former freedome againe) and nowe a while follow our feuerall Aduenturers for her aide, that by this time had trauailed far from the place where they firft tooke in hand this iournie.

[K⁴]

CHAP. X.

How thefe brethren came to the feuerall pla-
ces appointed by the fifter, and of their ad-
uenture there.

The eldest brother after long search finds the magic vial guarded by a monster cock with the tail of a crocodile and fiery eyes that dart poison.

[Mich]ander,[1] the eldeft brother, who firft vndertooke this charge, iournying through the fpacious plains of *Afia*, hopeleffe to finde: for that beeing long fince hee came to the fide of the mountaine where hee was promifed to finde this viall of teares, and had almoft fought euerie feuerall corner of the fame, and yet could

[1] Text, *Terpander*.

of Chinon of England 55

finde no likelyhood of any fuch matter: Notwithftanding, loath to leaue vnfought any place where fhewed any appearance of fuch a matter, At laft he faw a farre off the rifing as it were of an Alablafter Rocke that halfe ouerfhadowed a hole, artificially cut
5 into the fide of the hill: whether, hying him apace to fee what thereby might be meant, came at laft to the place, and there at the firft, feeing nothing that might any waies auaile him, was about to depart againe, till hearing fomewhat hafting [K⁴ back] it felf foorth of the hole, he ftood ftil to fee what it might bee; at
10 laft appeares vnto him the forepart as it were of an ouergrowne Cocke, but farre greater than any of that kinde, that with his fierie eyes poyfons euery obiect he fees; againft whofe force [Mich]ander¹ had prouidently prouided a bright Armour of fteele, which couered euery feuerall part of him, on whome when he
15 looked, the reflexe of hys fight, fending back againe the dart of poyfon to himfelfe that hee threw out at another, powerfully poyfoned himfelfe. The hinder part of this beaft was framed after the manner of a Cocodriles tayle, fuch as are commonly refident about the bankes of *Nilus* in Egipt, that with the force
20 thereof had beene able to haue brufed the beft prooued Armour: with which, when by the retorquation of hys ouer fight he had loft the vfe of his eyes, hee luftily laid about, till fuch time as the vpper part of hys bodie, forceably fwelling with the inwarde working poyfon, made him fo vnwildie that now, vnable to weald
25 his body any more, was forced to fall downe, and with the power of the poyfon fhortly after died: which when [Mich]ander² perceaued that his foe was fo foone foiled, taking it to be the place of which his fifter had foretold, by reafon that in her difcourfe fhe difcribed vnto him fuch a like keeper of that precious water as
30 was this fame that there kild with his owne weapon lay dead before him, gins diligently to fearch vp and downe for the thing it felfe, which at laft on the other fide of the rocke he perceaued: where vnder a faire Lillies roote ftoode the treafure for which he had fpent fo much paines: which when he faw, hartely thanking
35 thofe helping heauens that had fo mightely, not only preferued him from the force of hys foe, but alfo helped him to the inheritance of that hee fo much defired, goes boldy forward to the place where hee [L¹] faw this Lillie fpring, & taking away

Fortunately the youth's bright armour reflects the poisoned glances of the beast's eyes back upon its own body and presently ends its life.

The youth now eagerly seizes the coveted vial which, warmed by the heat of his hand, soon poisons his whole body and drives him to frenzy.

¹ Text, *Terpander*.   ² Text, *Terpander*.

the viall which he, poore foule, tooke to be no other than the teares of a virgin, that by fuch kind of meanes as his fifter had difcribed vnto him was placed there, and about to returne with ioyfull newes of his fifters deliuerance, hee had not gone farre from the place where firft hee founde it ere the Viall, beginning to warme with the heat of his hand, fodainely, by vertue of the venomous water therein inclofed, infufed fuch a contagious heate into euery feuerall vaine and finnow of his body as that wherewith the poyfoned fhirt was that inraged madding *Hercules*: So this poore man, that for his good meaning was thus recompenfed with ill meafure, inraged with the extreame paine of his inuenomed limmes, gins fall into a frantike humor, leauing the way fhould lead him backe againe to hys Sifter, and, furioufly, without regard of himfelfe, gins reuenge hys iniurie vpon fenfles and brutifh beaftes, that had now loft all the power of a man.

This was the end the forceres had intended fhuld betide to him, that in hope to fetch his fifters blis fhuld there finde his owne bane and by fome meanes or other kill himfelfe, or els, vnable fo with reafon to rule himfelfe, fhould fall into the daunger of fome wilde beaft who, without pittying his cafe, might caft hym away: where we muft leaue him in his lunacie and come to the fecond brother, who by this time was attained to the appointed place, fcituate in the bofome of the *Arabian* deferts: where vpon a Cypreffe branch he might a far off difcerne the golden inftrument on whofe trembling ftringes the beauteous beames of the funne delights to dally. There vnderneath this difmall fhade, for that now the funne at the Zenith of this Sphere dartes downe his perpendicular beames with fuch force vpon the face of the earth as [L¹ back] makes euery creature feeke to fhelter himfelfe in the coole fhades: for which caufe this monfter was then crept vnder the Cipreffe fhadowes and ouercommed with the heate of the aire was then falne a fleepe: to whom when [*Terp*]ander[1] came neere, diligently vewing each feuerall part of his deformed body, for that the Inftrument hung high vpon the tree, and without ftyrring this ftubborne beaft could no waies be come by, prepares himfelfe after the beft manner hee could to Combat with this Curre and, when he had buckled on his Armour, made readie his

[1] Text, *Micander*.

weapon and was now encouraged to encounter with hys enemie, gins with fome fuch noyfe as then hee made to roufe hym from hys reft.

When as the Canniball, like the throted Dogge whome *Thefeus* awaked in the Gates of hell, fends out fuch a hideous crie as affrighted the neighboring Birdes and Beaftes that inhabite that part of the world with his terrible founde and, fhaking of himfelfe, gins fhew in his vpper parts the perfect forme of a Dogge with long eares; which long dangling eares, that exceeded the fubftance of the greateft fpaniels, hung well nie downe to his middle. From the middle downeward he had the fhape of a man, big boned as are thefe wilde people that, liuing lawleffe in fuch vnruled places, feeding themfelues after their fafhion vpon the fat of the earth, out growes the common fort of well guided people; and taking vp from the earth a great Iron club, fuch as was in his iudgement too big to be fwayed by a man, without any warning gins fall to his weapon: where betwixt them two was begun a dangerous fight & long time continued with vncertaine hope of fucces, till [Terp]ander[1], nimbly efchueing the weight of his weapons fall, gins get within his reach, & fo carues his fkinne and [L²] bones with his well tempered fword which for that purpofe he had only prouided, that in fhort time hee made him with the great iffue of blood that fell from hys wounds fo weake as he was not able any more to beare the waight of his blowes but was forced to fall vnder his foe: which when [Terp]ander[1] perceaued he ftraight waies difmembers him of all his limmes and leaues nothing behinde for his helpe but the naked bulke of his body; and then, reaching downe from the tree that fatall inftrument (which the Witch to another end than hee aimed at had prepared) gins turne back his courfe, and with that Confort, hie him home to comfort his fifter. *Seizing now the magic harp, the victor touches the strings, but is at once struck dumb.*

As thus hee was trauailing to his long wifhed for place of ariuall, fodainely hee determined with him felfe to trie what was the harmonie of that famous inftrument, that with his found coulde call the cenfeleffe trees from their rootes, remooue the craggie Rockes from their Cliffes, mitigate the reuenging

[1] Text, *Micander*.

wrath of brutiſh deuouring beaſts, compoſe concord betwixt the Lambe and the Lyon, the Hound and the Hare, the Fawcon and the ſillie foule: whoſe ſtrings he had no sooner touched, but determining with himſelfe to ſing ſome delightſome Ditty to the ſweete tenth of theſe ſiluer ſounding ſtringes, for ioy hee had compaſſed his deſire. The powers of his tongue denying any more to execute their office, hee was ſodainely ſtroken dumb, which was the plague this witch had pretended ſhould light on him by the Magicke made ſound of this Inſtrument, which was nothing els but an illuſion, as were all the reſt, to draw theſe brethren into danger; where we wil leaue him, making what ſhift his dumb demeanes affordes him to trauell homeward, and come now at laſt to the third brother, *Theonas*, that by the fauorable hope [L² back] of winde and weather was nowe ariued vppon the perillous Iland: where, comming into the Temple of *Erganea*, the wife Inchauntreſſe, that was richly adorned with all peculiar thinges therevnto belonging. At the vpper end thereof vppon an Altar of clear Chriſtal that was couered with a curious cloth of gold, ouer whome was hung the perfect picture of an ancient woman, which woman was the forenamed *Erganea*, there twixt two golden Candleſtickes that were filled with two continuall burning Tapers cenſing the Temple with ſweet fauours, lyes a golden book which was kept by two harpies, monſterous byrdes, halfe Women, and halfe Serpents, that with their winges ſo beats the young aduenturer as hee was ſcarce able to abide theyr force.

But as hee that looking ſtill vpon the goles is better incouraged to goe forward, hee that ſees the harbour takes greater paines to get home, hee that is neare an end of his labour thinkes all the paines but little hee hath to ſpend: So fares it with *Theonas*, that looking vpon the end whereto hee had endeuored himſelfe, thinkes the paines but a pleaſure hee indured, & in ſhort time ſo behaued himſelfe as that he had ouerthrowne one of hys enemies, and then, like the Hart, that by caſting his horne renues his ſtrength, the Eagle by looſing his bill ſtrengthens his flight, ſo he at the ſight of hys fall begins to fight a freſh, and in ſhort time had the like ſucces of the one as before he had found in the other: ſo that nowe there was no partition betwixt him and his pray, but that he might take away the booke, to which when

Lastly comes the youngest brother, Theonas, and upon the perilous island finds the temple where upon the altar lies the enchanted golden book, guarded by two harpies.

Eagerly opening the book the youth releases

of Chinon of England 59

hee came, opening it that hee might bee an eye witnes what was *a 'dustie fogge' that fills his* there included, in ſteed of thoſe powerfull ſpels that there he *eyes as with* ſhuld haue read, from out the cloſure thereof came ſuch a duſtie *'pitchie smoake' and blinds them.* fogge as filling his eies with a [L³] blacke myſt like vnto pitchie
5 ſmoake he was ſuddenly ſtroken blind, and there left to grope his way back, that came thether with the perfect vſe of his eyes. This Booke (as were both the reſt) was nothing els but a deceipt of the Inchauntereſſe to draw thether one of thoſe Brethren, where (in ſtead of releeuing their Siſter) they might
10 inthrall themſelues. Thus poore *Theonas* (euen in the prime of his Spring) hauing loſt the vſe of this light, (which is the eſpeciall comfort of mans life) wanders vp and down like old forſaken *Oedipus* in his exilde life: where we muſt a while leaue him in this pitteous caſe with hys Bretheren.

CHAP. XI.

15   *How* Chinon *met with theſe Bretheren ſeue-
       rally one after another, and what became
       thereof.*

By this time was *Chinon* come to the place where we firſt left *Chinon now by* [*Mich*]ander¹ mad after hee had taken vp the Violl of Water: *chance meets the first brother,*
20 who ſeeing him fare ſo with himſelfe, rending vp trees by the *crazed by the* rootes, tearing vp mightie ſtones from theyr places where *magic vial of water, and after* they ſtood and tumbling them downe from the [L³ back] tops of *being attacked by the madman* high hills into the bottomes of deepe vallyes, who (notwithſtanding *throws him down and takes* his misfortune) kept ſtill the Viall about him vntouched; to *away the vial.*
25 whom *Chinon* came, wondering to ſee what man ſhould walke that waye, [and] begins to queſtion with him about the manner of his comming thether. To whom the mad man far vnlike him-ſelfe (for that before he was courteous, but now contrarie to his kinde hee had changed his countenance to hair-braind crueltie
30 and in ſtead of courteous behauiour anſweres him in rayling opprobrious tearmes) at² the length begins with force to aſſaile him as an enemie; which *Chinon* perceiuing, cloſing with the mad man as hee came to incounter with him forceablie, caſts him downe, & taking from him the Viall of water, which all

---

¹ Text, *Therſander*.   ² *and* needlessly inserted before *at*.

this while hee had kept clofely in his handes, beginnes to looke what it fhould be the poore foule had in fuch requeft, when fuddenly, by the like mifchance that the other was changed, himfelfe was with Lunacie prefently poffeffed: and raging like *Aiax* after his foyle for *Vlyffes* hys armour, or mightie *Alcides* when on the Mountaine *Oeta* he built the Altare whereon himfelfe was facrificed, tearing his clothes from his backe, the hayres from his head, and launcing with deepe wounds the limmes of his bodie, releafes [*Mich*]ander[1] from the plague wherwith he was poffeffed, and brings it vppon himfelfe. Which the other perceiuing how hee was deliuered from that daunger, pittied the wofull eftate of this worthie Man, but helpe him hee could not, for that fuch was his inuincible ftrength, now by the force of his furie much more augmented, which force neither man nor beaft, ftocke nor ftone, nor any other creature whatfoeuer was able to ftand in hys hand; fo that in fhort time, what with his vnorderly tracing through vnfrequented paffages to finde fu-[L[4]]ell for his fire, and his fwift paces that ftil ouer-went the other wearie, wearie man, who had tyred himfelf before in his furie, *Chinon* was quite gone out of his fight: whom wee muft now leaue after the recouerye of his wits, trauelling home againe into hys owne Countrey, to feeke out fome other meanes for the releafe of his Sifter, and follow *Chinon*, who raging and rauing like an angrie Lion at laft ouer-takes [*Terp*]ander,[2] who (poore man) as quiet for the forrow he had loft the vfe of his tongue as the other vnruly in his rage, feeing him a farre off, ftaid ftill to expect the euent of his fudden [a]pproach[3]; when the madde man, comming to him, gins with vnfeemly behauior to abufe the other poore diftreffed Soule, and wyth force pulling from him the Inftrument which he was loth to loofe, though by it he had incurred fuch a difplefure, yet at laft *Chinon* (farre ftronger than the other) perforce pulls it away and, affaying with his fingers to ftrike the ftrings, was at the firft found thereof ftroken dumbe, whereof as foone as *Chinon* was poffeffed [*Terp*]ander[4] was ftraight waye releafed. Which infirmitie when *Chinon* perceaued in himfelfe, redoubling the rigour of his handes for the vfe hee had loft of his tongue, gins furioufly to fall vpon [*Terp*]ander[4] and

---

[1] Text, *Tirpander*.
[2] Text, *Micander*.
[3] Text, *epproach*.
[4] Text, *Michander*.

of Chinon of England　　　61

beate him for being the Authour of his ill: which the other perceiuing, farre vnable to fuftaine the ftrength of his ftroake, makes meanes to efcape his hands, which by his fwift flight hee foone attayned. So in fhort time ridding of himfelfe enough 5 from the feare of this foe, hee for his owne fafetie takes home the neereft waye hee could finde into hys owne Countrey.

In the meanetime *Chynon* wandring wyldly thus about the World all careleffe where hee went, becaufe how foeuer hee turned euerie where [L⁴ back] lay his way, at laft comes downe 10 vnto the Sea fide, where by chaunce he findes a Boate readie furnifhed with all prouifion neceffarie for the Sea; who (after the manner of fuch madde men) leaping thereintoo (though ignorant what to do or careles whither to go, more than to fatiffie his mad humor) launched from fhore, and making fhift to fet up his faile, 15 was quickly conueyed farre from the fight of anie Land into the midft of the merciles feas, fayling too and fro manie dayes not fearing to be drownd, becaufe he perceiued nothing: nor expecting anie place whether to goe, for that he fcarce knew where he was, either at fea or on fhore. But at the laft (flying 20 with his Barke before the Winde) he was fuddenly driuen on fhore vpon an Iland, where (leaping a land) he betooke himfelfe to trauaile vp into the countrie to fee what people it did affoord: where he had not long trauelled, but a farre off vpon the fide of a Hil he efpied one fadly fitting by himfelfe, 25 towards whom he made what haft he poffibly could.

Now both mad and dumb Chinon wanders to the seaside, and leaping into a boat drifts wherever it carries him. Driven at last to an island he goes ashore and there meets Theonas, the youngest brother. Him he deprives of his magic book and of his blindness, and thus draws the third plague upon himfelf, while Theonas goes in search of his sister and brothers.

This was the yongeft Brother of thofe three, that before we told ye of was ftroken blind by looking into the inchanted Booke; to whom when he came, fuddenly fnatching the Booke out his hande (after hys fond furious fafhion) opens the clafpes to fee 30 what was therein contained, when fuddenly iffued out fuch another fogge as that wherewith *Theonas* was ftriken blinde, and in like manner bedazels his eyes: when prefently *Theonas* was againe reftored vnto his fight, and wondring to fee there fo goodly a man poffeffed with fo manie plagues at once, ginnes 35 then with himfelfe confider how it fhould come to paffe: who, for that himfelfe was vnacquainted with what had happened to his other Bretheren, could geffe at none but that which lately he was punifhed wythall [M¹] himfelfe: one, for that the reafonleffe Man (for all thefe troubles wherewith hee was tormented) could not (by his meanes) be brought within the compaſſe of quiet behauiour, thought it beſt to prouide ſome meanes for his owne eſcape, and leaue hym there to the mercie of GOD, that would not be ruled by the meanes of a man; ſo he betooke himſelfe to his Iourney, where we muſt alſo leaue him (ridde by thys meanes of a miſchiefe) retourning to ſeeke hys Bretheren, and take ſome other order for their inchanted Siſter.

The witch is disturbed that the three brothers are reſtored to health, but rejoices that all the plagues have fallen upon Chinon, whom she fears moſt. She therefore shuts him up in a rocky priſon, but restores his wits. Meanwhile, Earl Cador, grieving over the loss of his son, induces King Arthur to send a party in search of Chinon.

The Inchauntreſſe now (that all this while ſawe the iſſue of this matter), greeuing that her cunning ſhould be ſo croſſed and yet ioying that all theſe puniſhments were light vppon his head whom ſhe before feared more than all the reſt, ſet all her wits aworke, to deuiſe a meanes how ſhee might (now hauing him at ſuch a vantage) make him ſure for euer eſcaping out of her hands againe; foreſeeing that by his meanes all this ſcattered Kindred were likely to be reſtored againe to their former eſtate. And therefore (by her power) incloſes him within the clift of a Rocke, againſt which ſhe rouled vp a mightie ſtone ſuch as the force of manie ordinarie men was not able to remooue: and ſo, leaſt by any meanes he might be recouered out of this inchaunted Caſtle, ſhee places as Porter before the doore thereof a mightie Gyant, twice as great and grim as the ordinarie kynde of ſuch ouer-growen Creatures vſe to bee. Where, when hee was incloſed (ſuppoſing him now ſafe enough from anie reſort that ſhould bring him releefe) ſhe was content all his plagues ſhould ceaſe, and hee (the more to aggreuate his griefe) be reſtored againe to his wits; which was effected as ſpeedily as deter-[M¹ back]mined.

No ſooner was he cloſely ſhut vp into that vncomfortable Cabin, but all his Inſtruments (by whoſe meanes he came by thoſe croſſes) as his Water, his Harpe, and his Booke vaniſhed away, and he himſelfe reſtored (as I before ſaid) againe to the ſame eſtate of ſenſe as he was before, his libertie onely excepted: where we muſt now awhile leaue him in his melancholy Cell, and retourne againe into *England*, to ſee the ſorrow of olde *Cador* Duke of *Cornwall*, for the ſudden departure (without taking leaue) of *Chinon* his Sonne.

of Chinon of England 63

CHAP. XII.

How Arthur *of* England *fent three of his Knights to fearch for* Chinon, & *how they found him.*

Cador Earle of *Cornwal*, whilſt that theſe things were thus by
5 this diueliſh Inchauntreſſe effecting, ſtil ſpent his yeares in ſorrow for the ſudden loſſe of his Sonne, and at laſt (wearied with too much grief) he intended to make ſome friendly meanes to the King, for to haue his royall fauour [M²] and helpe for his recouerie. Therefore on this determining, he repaired one day
10 to the Court, and there finding the King and all his Knights, as carefull for his croſſe misfortune as himſelfe, gins in very humble manner (yet with honourable regard) thus to intreate his Maieſtie:

'Moſt royall Souereigne (for whom from my firſt able yeares
15 my ſeruice hath been imployed) vouchſafe me in my decayed yeares this Kingly comfort: Send foorth (I beſeech you) ſome of his worthie fellow Knights to ſeeke *Chinon* my Sonne; who, albeit he hath yet deſerued little either of your Grace or of them, yet his forward endeuour hath alway ſhowne he would much
20 more ere this haue merited, had not enuious fortune croſt him in this ſort.'

To whom the King and all his Nobles preſent did moſt willingly condiſcend. Then, calling together al the Knightly companie of his Round Table, declared to them Duke *Cadors*
25 requeſt and his owne readineſſe to haue it vndertaken: who all were not onely [ready] to goe in Queſt of *Chinon*, but each man manifeſted his more than common earneſtnes by taking offence if anie one were named beſide himſelfe. To ende this controuerſie, the King thus prouided, that euerie man ſhould drawe
30 his Lot, and on whom ſoeuer it fell that Knight ſhould foorthwith chuſe hym two Fellowes from the reſt of the Companie, and ſo they three ſhuld take vpon them this deſired trauaile. The Lots accordingly were made, and euerie one of the Knights drew, and the Lot fell upon Sir *Calor*, who was Sonne vnto Sir [*Triamore*]¹
35 and the beauteous *Celeſtina*, Daughter to the King of *France*,

A company chosen by lot and headed by Sir Calor goes on the expedition, taking counsel from Merlin before departing.

¹ Text, *Lancelot du Lake.*

whofe Parents *Chinon* before valiantly refcued, beeing betraid and taken in the hands of the trecherous Souldan.

[M² back] But before their departure, it was thought conuenient (for the better furtherance of their Iourney) to take fome counfell of *Merlin*, who then liued accounted as a Prophet in 5 *England*, and (by his fkill) could tell of fecrete things forepaft, and hidden myfteries to come.

Merlin, beeing fent for by the Kings commandement, came to the Court, and fhewes them in a fpeculatiue Glaffe the manner of his departure out of *England*, the manie troubles hee had 10 endured in hys Iourney, and now at laft opens at large the whole manner of that great miferie whereuntoo he is now brought by the meanes of that fubtill Inchauntreffe: telling them further that, except they made verie exceeding great fpeed for to procure his releafe, hee was likely to dye there for want of releefe, being 15 there detained from all neceffaries fit to fuftaine a man, or at leaft hauing of thofe neceffaries a verie fhort pittance allowed him.

Following Merlin's directions they at length arrive before the cave where Chinon is held as prisoner. Sir Calor then overcomes the fierce guardian and releases Chinon. The giant keeper thereupon exposes all the plotting of Perosus; and the knights lay their plans to defeat him.

Merlin, haftening them forward on their iourney, promifed all the cunning he could affoord for their fpeedie conueyance, which 20 he effectually perfourmed, fo that in fhort time they were arriued in this perillous Iland : where, after long fearch for the place wherein *Merlin* did promife they fhould finde their friend, at laft they might efpie this monftrous man, iaylour to that vnfortunate Knight, ftretching himfelfe at the mouth of the Caue 25 wherein *Chinon* was kept. To him they made all poffible fpeede; and firft of all Syr *Calor*, addreffing himfelfe to fight, gins, before hee offered violence, with curteous greetings to falute hym gently, demaunding what he was that liued fo defolately in that vnfrequented Iland. To whom the detefted and currifh 30 Carle made this vnmannerly aunfwere:

[M³] 'I am,' quoth hee, 'as thou feeft, one within whofe clawes thou and the reft of thy fawcie companions haue compaffed yourfelues : if therefore you will fubmit your felues to my mercy, then will I thus difpofe of you heere within a hollow Caue 35 hewne out of this craggie Rock, wherein lyes inclofed a knight fuch a one as you are, who for the like offence that you now haue offered, is condemned to the eternall flauerie of perpetuall imprifonment ; within fhall you fpend your hatefull liues, and when

for hunger you are welnie ſtarued, fall freſhly then to eate one anothers fleſh: but if you ſtubbornely ſtand out againſt mee, thus will I diſpoyle you in renting your curſed limmes peece meale a ſunder, or els faſtning you ſeuerall to the big bulks of
5 ſome of theſe trees; where when the imperiall puniſhment of haſtning hunger ſhall ſeaze vpon your ſelues, you ſhall there be inforced to eate your owne fleſh, that might here haue fed vpon another;' to whom Syr *Calor* thus anſwered:
'Foule vglie fiend, wee come not to kneele to thee, but to
10 force thy ſubiection to vs, and for the releaſe of a Chriſtian Knight that thou keepeſt Captiue within thy power.'
At which wordes the Giant, ſeeing them addreſſe themſelues to fight, preſently beſtirs himſelfe, and taking an Iron mace (which to that ende the Witch had prouided) lets driue at
15 Sir *Calor* with all the might he could, from which he nimbly leaping away eſchued the force of the fall, when as the other knights comming in to reſcue ſir *Calor*, before the Giant could againe get vp his weapon from the grounde, they had ſo mangled hys limmes, as he was now far vnable to fight, but
20 falling proſtrate downe before them, humblie intreats for his life: which they were willing to graunt, as not ſeeking the loſſe of him but [M³ back] the life of their friend: to whome the Giant gins relate all the manner of the impriſonment of *Chinon*, and at the laſt opens the doore of the Caue and calles him out to his
25 friends, who, reſaluting one another with ſuch friendly greetings as are vſuall at ſuch aduenturos accidents, take their iournie from thence vp into the Countrie, and for that the Giant had tolde them in hys former diſcou[r]ſe of the manner of *Chinons* impriſonment, how that *Peroſus*, for whoſe loue all this had come
30 about, had in Egipt taken Armes againſt the King, for that his treaſon beeing diſcouered he intended to recal old *Beſſarian* from his baniſhment, and that his power ſo daylie increaſed as that it was now far greater than the Kings, they intended to ſhape their iournie thetherwards and help the king in his warres
35 againſt this traiterous rebbell: where wee muſt let them goe forward a while in their iourny, and returne againe to our three aduenturers for their fiſters libertie.

CHAP. XIII.

How Beſſarians *ſonnes met with their Father in the ſhape of a Beare.*

[Mᶜ]

Meanwhile, Beſſarian's ſons, now fully reſtored to health and strength, are on their separate ways home. By chance, one after the other they meet and attack the man-bear, their father, who narrowly escapes with his life. On the mountains Beſſarian meets Peroſus—juſt put to flight by the English knights—and seizes him.

After that theſe three yong men were againe reſtored to their former eſtate, [*Mich*]*ander*[1], the firſt of them trauailing homewards to ſeeke againe his ſiſter, meetes by the way his tranſformed Father, who, not a little glad to ſee his ſonne, though the other, taking him for no leſſe than he ſeemed, made ſome haſt to fly from him, till looking backe and perceauing the ſcroule about his necke, for the regaining of his harts deſire ſtrikes his poore father with ſuch a blow as, breaking his ſword vpon the ſcalpe of his head, he was forced to flie for want of weapons, fearing leaſt the Beare ſhould haue fallen freſhly vppon him beeing tyred, when, as God knowes, the fillie man, aſtoniſhed with the ſtroke, was rather afraid of an vnnaturall deaths wound by his ſonne then willing to proſecute any reuenge for the ſame.

Not long after [*Mich*]*ander*[1] had thus hurt his Father, comes that way the ſecond brother, who in like caſe, meeting with the Beare and hoping by his death to obtaine his deſire, gins with a Boreſpeare hee had in his hand eagerly to aſſayle him, in ſo much that in [Mᶜ back] ſhort time hee had grieuouſly wounded hym, but the head of his weapon by chance breaking off, hee was forced to flie as did his brother: to be ſhort, the Witch that intended by the meanes of ſome of theſe ſonnes to make away their father, after that the firſt two had fayled, brought thether the third, who, eager to accompliſh his deſire, promiſed by the ſcroule that hung about hys fathers necke, begins a freſh fight, & ſo wounded his fillie ſire, as that for want of blood which hys weapon had lauiſhly lanched out, hee was forced to fall downe, whome *Theonas* ſuppoſing to be dead, left there to follow his deſire.

In the meane time, whileſt theſe thinges were thus in dooing, had there beene fought a great battaile in Egipt, betwixt *Egbaton* their king and *Peroſus*, the traitour of whome before we told you:

---

[1] Text, *Terpander*.

of Chinon of England 67

where by the meanes of the Englifhmen the King ouercame, and *Perosus* was put to flight: who, for his fauegard forfaking hys Countrie, betooke himfelfe to the Mountaines: where, after hee had long traueiled, hee by chance met with *Beffarian* tranfformed, as afore wee haue told you, who hauing fomewhat recouered himfelfe after the wounds of his fonnes, fearing leaft his foe fhould at his fight flie away, layes fodaine holde vpon him.

At which *Perofus*, beeing afraid feeing himfelfe affailed, gins make all the meanes hee could for hys efcape: but the other, loath to requite him euill for hys ill dealing, in fteede of fuch rauinous behauiour as com[m]only [1] is found in fuch like beafts, gently fawnes vpon him, fhewing himfelfe rather willing to helpe him than readie to hurt him.

When *Perofus*, calling to mind hys former offence in the bewitching of the old man, and feeing by the writing about his necke that this was he whome hee [N[1]] had fo cruelly croft, falles downe before him & with fubmiffiue teares intreats his pardon: to whome the Beare, though vnable to fpeake yet with dumbe demeans fhewing the effect of his minde, anfwers in dum tokens what he could not tel in plaufible words: to whom *Perofus* there promifed that, would hee but follow him, hee would foorthwith conduct hym to the place where hys daughter was imprifoned, & where he hoped alfo to meet with her by whofe meanes all this was brought to paffe.

In the meane time, *Chinon* and his fellow knights, following their foes from the fight, by chaunce intercepted *Eutropa* the Witch as fhee was flying awaie, whome prefently they intending to kill, & fhee knowing very well their crueltie, fell downe before them, humbly afking pardon for her life, and in requitall thereof fhee would reftore to liberty her for whofe fake *Chinon* had fuffered all this extreamity, than which *Chinon* defiring nothing more graunts her requefts, whom fhee prefently tranfportes to the place where *Caffiopea* lay imprifoned: where when they came, they found her three brethren dilating vnto her theyr feuerall ill luckes; whome as foone as they came the Witch releafed from the bondage of the Rocke and falling downe on her knees afkes hartie pardon for her amis, to whome the Lady, glad of her releafe, ftraight forgiues that offence; and then *Eutropa* telling

In a fright Perosus recognizes in the bear the man he has so cruelly wronged, and with tears begs forgiveness. Bessarian answers in dumb tokens, and Perosus conducts him to his daughter. Chinon and his knights intercept the Witch but spare her life on her promise to restore Cassiopeia. This she does, and also extols the merits of Chinon. Perosus is punished. Bessarian is restored to his former shape and his honours; and Cassiopeia and Chinon are united in marriage.

[1] Text, *comnonly*.

F 2

her the great perrill *Chinon* had ouerpaffed for her loue, fhee with all curtefie falles downe at hys feete, fubmitting her felfe for requitall thereof to be difpofed at hys pleafure, whom he taking vp from the ground, offer[s][1] himfelfe like wife to her.

In the meane time, whileft thefe folkes were thus reioycing, comes in *Perofus* leading of the tranfformed olde man, and humbly there afking pardon of [N¹ back] them all for his offence, telling them the manner how he had found the old man, who was by the meanes of the Witch prefently reftored to his former fhape; and then returning all backe to the Court to certifie the King of their feueral affaires. *Beffarian* was then againe reftored to his dignity & *Perofus* fauerely punifhed for hys offence, & *Chinon* and *Cassiopia*, by the confent of their frends and mutuall loue of themfelues, were matched together in marriage.

FINIS

[1] Text, *offering*.

NOTES

1/1. Title-page. The elaborate title is singularly misleading: 'The Famous Hiftorie of Chinon of England, with his ftrange aduentures for the loue of Celeftina, daughter to Lewis, King of Fraunce.' This seems plainly to indicate that Celestina is the object of Chinon's devotion, whereas in fact she is reserved for Triamore. On the other hand, Cassiopeia, who awakens the passionate love of Chinon, is not mentioned before the beginning of the second half of the romance.

3. *Enifham*. Eynsham, about midway between Oxford and Witney.

3. *Iohn Danter*. According to Arber's edition of the *Stationers' Registers*, v, 230, Danter printed and published in London from 1591 to 1597. His widow published in 1599 and 1600. He had a house in Hosier Lane, near Holborn Conduit.

For a brief sketch of Danter see *A Dictionary of Printers and Booksellers*, London Bibliographical Society, 1910, pp. 83, 84. According to this account, all his work 'was very badly printed'; and of this assertion our romance affords striking proof. Phoebe Sheavyn's *Literary Profession in the Elizabethan Age* (pp. 68 ff.) remarks that for the lower forms of literature he was the printer most popular. 'He was evidently rather poor and struggling, glad to print for the stationers and glad to get hold of popular things, cheap to buy and produce, and regularly saleable.'

In the *Stationers' Registers*, ed. Arber, v, 187, we are informed that 'he was suppressed as a Master Printer 10 April 1597 . . . and was dead before 6 Oct. 1600.' His reputation for honourable dealing left much to be desired.

For the seizure of his press, see *Stationers' Registers*, i, 580, and for other references, see v, 183.

5/1. *Cador, Earle of Cornewall*, appears in Geoffrey of Monmouth's *Historia Regum Britanniae*, ix, 1, 5, 15, as a duke and a valiant leader against the Saxons. He naturally figures also in Wace's metrical version of Geoffrey's *Historia* and in Layamon's adaptation of Wace's *Brut*, but with the title of earl, as in our romance. Cador is furthermore mentioned three times in the vulgate prose *Merlin* (E.E.T.S., pp. 640, 655, 656), as one of Arthur's barons 'bolde and hardy', and active in the great campaign against the Romans, but there is no hint that he is or is to be Earl of Cornwall. He appears also in Malory's *Morte Darthur*, bk. v, chs. 2, 3, 6, 7, 8, as 'Syre Cador of Cornewaile'. In bk. xxi, ch. 13, his son Constantine is made king of England after Arthur. In our romance the author carelessly designates Cador as earl or duke, with no attempt at consistency. See Index of Names.

For a discussion of Cador in the Chronicles, see Fletcher, *Arthurian Material in the Chronicles*, Index; *Harvard Studies and Notes*, vol. x.

6/32. *miſfortunes*. The text reads *miſfortunes*, but the original form was discovered after the pages were made up.

8/8. *inſuing*. The earliest example of this word (under the form *ensuing*) in the Oxford Dictionary is assigned to the year 1604.

8/29. *Triſtram du-Lions*. Here we have Lions for Liones(ae). Cf. Malory's *Morte Darthur*, ix, ch. 10, 'Sir Tristram de Liones that was in Brittany'. Modern scholars are unable to determine the situation of Lyonesse.

8/31. *many millions of other braue Gallants*. If we may trust our author, we must assume that more millions were to be found at Arthur's court than in all England at the time of the Domesday survey! For another instance of the author's generous use of millions, see 12/20.

9/6. *no ſubſtance without his accident*. See Locke's comment on substance and accident in *An Essay Concerning Human Understanding*, Bk. II, ch. 13, sects. 19, 20.

For some account of the gradual substitution of *its* for *his* after A. D. 1600 see Trench, *English Past and Present* (ed. Mayhew), pp. 148-52.

9/37. *a fayre aſpect from thoſe powerfull plannets that guides the diſtreſſed eſtate of his ſicklie ſoul*. Astrology, we need hardly remark, was seriously studied as a science throughout the sixteenth and seventeenth centuries, but it lost nearly all credit after Swift's famous satire on Partridge the astrologer in the *Prediction for the Year 1708*.

11/25. *went in to take his leaue*. Lancelot's sudden departure to 'ſeeke ſtraunge aduentures in foraine coaſtes' without waiting to find what the answer is to be to his avowal of love is thoroughly typical of the ways of suitors in medieval romance.

11/29. *forced to leaue his Country*. To the modern reader the obligation is not obvious.

12/7. *for to ſupply*. Cf. *for to trie*, 14/6, *for to assay*, 28/9. This use of *for to*, now obsolete or vulgar, dates back as early as the twelfth century, but it was going out of fashion at the end of the sixteenth. Cf. Oxford Dict., s.v. *for*, A 11; Abbott, *Shakespearian Gram.*, sect. 152; Kellner, *Hist. Outlines of Engl. Syntax*, sect. 295.

12/13. *Lancelot his vowed brother*. That is, his sworn brother in arms. For perhaps the most striking medieval example of this type of relationship, see the romance of *Amis and Amiloun*, ed. Kölbing, Heilbronn, 1884; cf. also *Sir Eger and Sir Grine* in the *Percy Folio MS.*, ed. Hales and Furnivall, i, 354-400, especially after l. 46.

12/18. *ſaw ... admits*. The mixture of present and past tenses in the same sentence, so characteristic of the style of *Chinon*, is of course merely a continuation of a common feature of M.E. writing.

Cf. 'had ... tane ... and cuts', 12/29; 'rides foorth till they came', 33/15; 'rayſes her up and thus replied', 35/31, &c.

12/29. *tane*. Cf. 37/7. For the disappearance of the *k*, see Wright, *English Dialect Grammar*, p. 248.

16/6. *Triamore, ſonne to the Duke of Brittaine*. This is a decidedly new origin for Triamore. In the romance of *Sir Triamour* he is the son of Ardus, king of Aragon. For a convenient analysis of the romance see Wells, *Manual of the Writings in Middle English*, 1050-1400, p. 121; and in greater detail, Ellis, *Early English Metrical Romances* (Bohn), pp. 491-505.

Notes

In the romance of *Sir Launfal* Triamour is the name of

> 'The kinges daughter of Oliroun
> . . . .
> Her father was king of Faerie . . .,
> A man of mickle might'.

For a text of the verse romance of *Sir Triamore*, see Hales and Furnivall, *Percy Folio MS.*, i, 78-135.

16/8. Prince = princess. For similar use of *prince* as applied to a female sovereign, see Oxford Dictionary.

17/28. *then.* Here as in Shakespeare and other Elizabethan writers *then* and *than* are freely interchanged. See Abbott, *Shakespearian Grammar* (Index), and the glossary to *Chinon*.

18/30. *cauileers.* This word is cited in the Oxford Dictionary under the year 1470 in the form *caualers*, and under 1598 in Barrett's glossary of terms of war as Italian, *cauaglere* (for English *knight*); but the passage in our text appears to present one of the earliest instances of its use in *connected* composition in the sense of knight.

19/27. *to thee will I giue*, &c. Lancelot's generosity in surrendering his prize to Triamore may be compared with his similar generosity in giving up to Sir Tristram the prize he has won in a tournament, as recounted in Malory's *Morte Darthur* (ed. Sommer), pp. 394-411.

20/20. *affemblant.* The Oxford Dictionary defines this word as 'semblance, appearance, show'; but here it seems to mean each individual in the assembly.

22/10. *Princes were.* The text here seems to be improved by supplying *who* before *were*.

22/13. *in fhort time landed all his men.* We are not told how short the time was, but in view of the fact that the messenger to the Soldan had to traverse the entire length of the Mediterranean, to say nothing of the time required for equipping and transporting the army, we see that we have a situation possible only in romance.

24/9. *he went out. He* seems loosely to indicate the wailing sound coming out of the den, though the author refers to 'cryes', 'moanes', and 'ecchoes'.

24/13. *loffe.* This word must be wrong, and there is a temptation to read *lasse*; but *lass*, though already used for some two hundred years before *Chinon*, appears to belong to poetry while prose employs *damsel*. Some word has probably dropped out, and *loffe* should perhaps be *loft*. In any case the sense appears to be—'the release of this lost (or tormented) soul', cp. l, 1.

24/16. *a mightie Monfter, framed with the deceitfull face of a faire woman, but the big body of a fubtill Serpent.* The belief was widely prevalent in the Middle Ages that the serpent which tempted Eve had the face of a woman; and Raphael follows the tradition in his famous picture of the Temptation in the Garden. Incidentally, we may note that in ancient times 'paintings and bronze and silver statues of the new god Glycon, in the form of a snake with human face, exhibited by Alexander of Abonuteichos to his faithful followers, were to be procured in Paphlagonia and the neighbouring districts.' Alexander was exposed by Lucian. See Friedländer, *Roman Life and Manners* (Tr. by Freese and Magnus), ii, 299.

In *Libeaus Desconus*, ll. 2094 ff. (ed. Kaluza), where Libeaus has entered the enchanted palace and there won a victory, a serpent with the face of a woman encircles him and kisses him, thereupon turning into a lovely maiden. Cf. also Ariosto, *Orlando Furioso*, canto xxxiv, 79.

24/19. *Caſtie carrying Elephant.* The tower or castle borne upon the back of an elephant is referred to in romances and other works from 1380 till the appearance of our romance in 1597. Note the four examples under *Castle* in the Oxford Dictionary, antedating the publication of *Chinon*.

It is needless to call attention to the famous London public house, the 'Elephant and Castle', which belongs to a period far later than our romance.

24/30. *conſort.* This reading, in the sense of 'company', is probably right. The same play on words occurs in 57/32.

25/6. *Chinon*, text, *Chiuon.*

26/3. *vnacuſtomable antomes.* Is *antomes* here used loosely and inaccurately for *anthems* in the sense of music or sounds? The spelling *antems* is found in the sixteenth century. See Oxford Dictionary, s.v. *anthem.*

26/22. *Promontany* = promontory. This word, not elsewhere found, and not noticed in the Oxford Dictionary, is quite possibly nothing more than the blunder of a hurried printer who might easily mistake in a badly written MS. an *o* for an *a* and an *r* for an *n*.

27/6. *no man but a maiden Knight Can free him*, i.e. no one but a knight newly made, one without experience. Cf. 'my Mayden manhood', 36/33, and see Oxford Dictionary, s.v. *maiden*, ii, 5, d.

28/5. *his vnwieldy weapon.* The author is inconsistent in the gender he gives the monster. In the next sentence the beast is a female!

28/14. *when hee. Hee* is left dangling with no verb, but the sense is clear enough.

29/28. *wordes, ſuch as commonly paſſe*, &c. A favourite expression of our author. Cf. 37/18, 50/31, 65/25.

30/7. *Oboram there King.* As already observed in the introduction, the author of *Chinon* evidently drew largely upon the romance of *Huon of Burdeux*, in which Oberon, king of the fairies, plays a leading part. In this romance (ed. E.E.T.S.), pp. 380 ff., we find a possible source of the adventure of Chinon in Oboram's domain. After many exploits Huon sails to the Castle of Adamant, high upon a rock. At the entrance a gate bears an inscription announcing that the castle can be entered only by the worthiest of all knights (p. 380) and that he must fight the great serpent which guards the place. Huon fights, as Chinon does, and finds that his weapon makes no impression (p. 382, cf. *Chinon*, 27/36 f.). 'And the serpent, when he felte hymselfe stryken cast his tayle abought Huon by such fors that Huon ouerthrew to yᵉ erthe.' Chinon gets a blow from the serpent he is fighting with (27/38) 'as perforce beat him downe to the grounde and almoſt baniſhed the breath from his body.' Further details vary, but of course Huon, like Chinon, wins the fight.

Oberon appears also in an important role in *A Midsummer Night's Dream*, assigned by Sir Sidney Lee to 1595, two years before *Chinon* was printed. Spenser introduces Oberon *F. Q.* II, canto 1, st. 6, and along with him Sir Huon. In II, 10, st. 75, he uses Oberon's name to designate the not altogether fairy-like Henry VIII. Ben Jonson's masque, *Oberon, the Fairy Prince*, belongs to the year 1610. See also Sidney Lee's Introduction to *Huon of Burdeux* (E.E.T.S.), pp. l, li, for the place of Oberon in Elizabethan literature.

For an interesting discussion of Oberon (Auberon), with valuable bibliographical notes, see Lucy A. Paton's *Fairy Mythology of Arthurian Romance*, pp. 124-35.

30/18 ff. *fword.* The incident of the sword pulled out of the rock was most likely suggested by the exploit of Arthur in Malory's *Morte Darthur*, Book I, ch. 3; and Malory's account is obviously based upon the vulgate *Merlin* (E.E.T.S.), pp. 98-107, which gives a more picturesque story than Malory's. For numerous other parallels, see note in my edition of Malory, pp. 248, 249 (Athenaeum Press Series).

Compare also the futile attempts of the knights of the Round Table, all except Balen, to pull out of its sheath a sword brought by a damsel sent by 'the grete lady Lylle of Avelyon.' Malory, *Morte Darthur*, Bk. II, ch. 1, 2. For a list of marvellous swords, see Lucy A. Paton's *Fairy Mythology*, p. 199, note.

30/21. *which fword was artificially framed for Iulius Caesar.* The dragging in of the name of Julius Caesar is not wholly due to Middleton's invention. In the romance of *Huon of Burdeux* (E.E.T.S.), p. 72, Caesar is named as the father of Oberon, and hence we can account for the sword in the possession of the Oboram of our romance.

For other legendary tradition concerning Caesar's sword, see Geoffrey of Monmouth's *Historia*, Bk. IV, ch. 4, 5.

30/25. *the valiant Romane was ... flaine in the Senate.* So too in *Huon of Burdeux* (E.E.T.S.), p. 412, we read, 'Tydynges came to the knowlege of kynge Oberon that his father, Iulius Cesar, was slayne and murderyd within the senat of Rome.'

31/25. *rich Armour.* The sword and armour that Chinon receives from Oboram may be compared with the gifts conferred upon Huon of Bordeaux by Oberon—a magic cup and horn, and a suit of armour. See romance of *Huon of Burdeux* (E.E.T.S.), pp. 76-8, 169.

31/39. *Dwarffe.* From the most ancient times, when one of the kings of Egypt gives minute directions for the safe keeping of a dwarf who is to be brought down the Nile to be one of his favourites, and even long after the date popularly accepted as marking the close of the Middle Ages, dwarfs were a common feature of a court, and they not unnaturally often appear in medieval romances. As a rule their temper is none of the best, and they often make up for their diminutive size by their insolence. Cf. e. g. Chrêtien de Troyes, *Erec*, ll. 140 ff.; the *Mabinogion* story of *Geraint*, based on *Erec*, &c. See also Schultz, *Das Höfische Leben zur Zeit der Minnesinger*, vol. i, Index; Paul, *Grundriss der Germanischen Philologie*, Index, &c. Visitors to the Prado Gallery in Madrid will recall Velasquez's famous painting of the dwarfs of the Spanish court.

32/9. *fodaine trance.* The author's favourite device for transporting his characters from place to place is to take them through the air. Cf. 41/26, 51/31, 67/32. For this he doubtless drew upon his classical knowledge.

32/18. *farre more worfe.* For numerous examples of old double comparatives, see Abbott, *Shakespearian Grammar*, p. 22, and Kellner, *Historical Outlines of English Syntax*, pp. 159, 160.

32/24. *a nother.* For examples of *nother,* with *n* transferred from the article *an,* see Oxford Dictionary, s. v.

33/23. *Triamore pretending himfelfe to be . . . an Inchauntreffe.* In dealing with pagans, Christian knights in the romances commonly lie freely. Note also the pious conversation between Lancelot and Guinevere when they are caught together, Malory's *Morte Darthur,* Bk. xx, ch. 3, and his subsequent talk with King Arthur, ch. 14. In most medieval romances morality is quite divorced from religion.

33/29. *pofing him in the relation of kings paft.* May we assume *kings* to be a misprint for *things*?

35/23. *the Thracian Damofell,* i. e. Eurydice.

36/16. *for thee.* This is the reading of the text, but the first *e* is dotted and looks like an *i.*

37/8. *her father's Court.* But the plan was to marry her at *his* (Triamore's) father's court. See 21/35 ff. and 36/35.

37/19. *vnacquainted.* An obsolete meaning (cited in the Oxford Dictionary) is *unusual, strange.* Here the meaning appears to be *unexpected.*

37/23. *Lancelot, hee prefents to hys loue the Trophies of his victorie.* But these trophies, we are told (p. 20), he had already sent by a messenger!

37/31. The exact meaning of the lines following *where what* is not clear, and the passage is certainly corrupt. But the sense appears to be that the joy felt by the company in general was shared by King Arthur himself, whose life still lasts, &c.

If line 33 is taken to refer to Celestina, it yields no very intelligible meaning.

38/1. *Calcos.* A blunder for Colchis, the scene of Jason's famous exploit in winning the Golden Fleece.

39/9. *fpending the pride of his dayes at home in daliance.* This sort of easy life the Middle Ages judged very harshly. See Chrétien de Troyes, *Erec,* and the corresponding tale in the *Mabinogion* of *Geraint the son of Erbin.* For comment on *verligen,* see Schultz, *Das Höfische Leben,* ii, 1 and Förster's edition of the *Erec* of Chrêtien de Troyes (*Rom. Bibl.* xiii), pp. xvii, xviii.

39/24. *fearing the fecrete corners.* Miss Day, Assistant Director of the E.E.T.S., suggests that the reference is to the marking out of fairy-rings, made by *searing* the grass. This may be correct, but fairies are commonly supposed to have made the rings by dancing in a circle, and there is no evidence that fairies' feet are hot enough to sear anything. Possibly we should read *fearing.*

39/32. *fhow of a faire Virgin.* This well-worn motive, which in medieval romances often set hearts in a flutter, calls forth Chaucer's good-natured satire. His Sir Thopas sees an elf queen in a dream and then rides madly off in search of her. In the *Mabinogion* the emperor Maxen Wledig dreams of a maiden of marvellous beauty and after long journeying finally discovers and wins her. Cf. also Dunlop's *History of Fiction* (ed. Ellis), i, 260.

Kittredge, *Gawain and the Green Knight,* p. 136, notes as ' one of the most familiar of all Arthurian *donnés*—the lady who loves Gawain without having seen him. . . . I might have said one of the best known in all literature. " C'est là un trait que se rencontre dans nombre de fictions romanesques depuis a plus haute antiquité."'

40/11. *Beffarian.* It is at least possible that this uncommon name may have been suggested by the name of the famous Johannes Bessarion (*b.* 1395?

Notes 75

d. 1472), titular patriarch of Constantinople, who had a great reputation as a philologist and philosopher.

40/21. *change the fetled affections.* The help of a witch or a sorceress to gain the affections was often invoked in ancient and medieval times. A famous instance in medieval literature is *Dame Sirith.* For an easily accessible text, see Cook's *Literary Middle English Reader,* pp. 141–58, or MacKnight's *Middle English Humorous Tales in Verse,* pp. 1–24.

41/4. *teares, whofe power were able.* A typical case of the author's syntax.

41/6. *that filuer ftreame.* If the romancer had ever seen the Nile he would perhaps have written *muddy* !

41/6. *feauen heads.* 'In ancient times the Delta was watered by seven branches; now there are but two, the other ancient branches being canals not always navigable.' *Encyclopaedia Britannica,* 9th ed., s. v. *Egypt.*

41/10. *Arions Harpe.* See note to 50/10.

41/28. *ouerroad.* A relative pronoun referring to Medea is obviously required to complete the sense.

42/4. *confent* in original text.

42/5. *poore foule.* For other instances of this expression in *Chinon,* see 41/13, 46/8, 48/38, 50/8, 54/13, 56/1, 60/2, 60/24.

42/26. *workes meanes.* The passage is needlessly obscure, but it becomes reasonably clear if we supply ' the witch Eutropa' as the missing subject of *workes.*

44/14. *weft*—west, or waste, desert. In this passage either meaning yields in effect substantially the same sense, for all west Egypt is waste, and people cannot to any great extent inhabit ' these spacious plaines '.

44/20. *vndeferued.* We may perhaps assume in the king's mind the meaning—' thoughts that I have not deserved '.

44/23. *I, I, I fee.* Doubtless the first two *I*'s are exclamatory, the modern *ay.*

44/35. *evill.* Misprint for *ciuill.*

45/25. *fpeculatiue glaffe.* Cf. 47/23, 64/9. The crystal globe, used for discovering secret or future things, was extremely common in the sixteenth and seventeenth centuries. The famous Dr. Dee, in the time of Queen Elizabeth, used it very extensively. See the sketch of his life in the *Dictionary of National Biography.*

45/36. *inclofes . . . within the ruine of an olde Rocke.* Bespelled princesses are a commonplace of romances and fairy tales. See e. g. Kittredge's discussion in *Gawain and the Green Knight,* pp. 115 ff., 237–56; Schofield, *Libeaus Desconus* (Harvard), *Studies and Notes,* iv, 47 ff. ; Nutt, *Studies on the Legend of the Holy Grail,* p. 195.

46/29. *an vgly Beare.* Bessarian's transformation into the shape of a bear recalls Vergil's account of the magic of Circe at the beginning of Book VII of the *Aeneid.* With this may be compared the story in the *Odyssey,* v, 146, of the transformation by Circe of the companions of Odysseus into swine. The classical student need not be reminded of the manifold shape shiftings in *The Golden Ass* of Apuleius.

In view of the obvious acquaintance of Middleton with the romance of *Huon of Burdeux* it is perhaps not without significance that on p. 111 (ed. of E.E.T.S.) Oberon changes Malabron into the shape of a bear which afterwards carries Huon on his back up the Nile, and that in the same romance, p. 592, a monk tells Huon that certain other monks whom he has seen have been changed by divine displeasure into the likeness of bears, were-wolves, &c.

Worth noting, too, is the fact that in George Peele's farce, *The Old Wives' Tale*, printed in 1595, two years before *Chinon*, appears Erestus as a tottering old man at a cross, where he tells the two brothers who are seeking their sister that the sorcerer Sacropant,

> 'Did seek the means to rid me of my life.
> But worse than this, he with his 'chanting spells
> Did turn me straight into an ugly bear,' &c.
>   Peele's Works, ed. Dyce, p. 447.

Similar marvels are common in folk-tales and in primitive belief. See e. g. Grimm's *Hausmärchen*. For numerous details on transformations of all sorts, see A. Nutt, *The Voyage of Bran*, vol. ii (Grimm Library); Maynadier, *The Wife of Bath's Tale*, London, 1901; Kittredge, *Gawain and the Green Knight*, Cambridge (Mass.), 1916, and *Arthur and Gorlagon* (Harvard) *Studies and Notes*, viii, 170–1; and, particularly, Leubuscher, *Über die Werwölfe und Tierverwandlungen im Mittelalter*, Berlin, 1850; Lucy A. Paton's *Studies in the Fairy Mythology of Arthurian Romance* (1903), pp. 23, 24, 100, 101, 192.

48/4. *the Huntreſſe*, i. e. Diana.

48/11. *the enuious Stone cloſes his ſides.* The conception of rocks that open and shut may have been suggested to the author by the classic myth of the Symplegades, which appears in the legend of the Argonauts. The Symplegades were two cliffs or rocky islets at the entrance to the Black Sea from the Bosphorus, that continually smote each other and crushed all that came between them.

For further discussion and references, see A. C. L. Brown, *Iwain*, in (Harvard) *Studies and Notes*, viii, 81 ff., and, in particular, Lowrie, *Journal of American Folk-Lore*, xxi, 106 ff.

48/35. *Taurus, that ... gyrdells in the wyde Continent of flowring Aſia.* Her geography is somewhat vague. The Taurus mountains are only on the south side of Asia *Minor*.

49/3. *Shee* is, of course, the object of *ordained*, but grammatical correctness is not a matter of special concern to our author.

49/11. *Cockatrice.* 'A fabulous serpent whose breath and look were said to be fatal'.

49/31. *offered to haue kiſſed her hand for ioy.* His *sister's hand*, after his long and agonizing search!

50/10. *Arion's Harpe.* Cf. 41/10. The tale of Arion riding upon the back of a dolphin is taken from the well-known story of Arion told by Herodotus, i, 24, and repeated by Aulus Gellius, xvi, 19, by Hyginus, *Fab.* 194, &c. The 'pirates' who in *Chinon* cast him into the sea were really the sailors on the ship conveying him home to Corinth.

54/1. *the olde Giantes ... heaping hill vpon hil*, i. e. the Titans, who attempted to scale heaven by piling Ossa upon Pelion.

55/21. *retorquation.* Not cited in the Oxford Dictionary, though *retorqued*, *ppl. adj.*, 'twisted or turned back', is found.

55/21. *ouer ſight.* These two words are doubtless to be taken as one, in the sense of *ſight* or *glance*.

56/5. *Viall, beginning to warme.* The story of this magic vial is possibly suggested by the myth of the poisoned shirt of Hercules, which, as we see, 56/9, the author has in mind.

56/12. *leauing the way ſhould lead him.* For the common omission of relative pronouns in Elizabethan English, see Abbott, *Shakespearian Grammar*, sect. 244.

56/15. *that had now loſt,* &c. Obviously, *that* refers to *himſelfe*, i.e. Michander.

57/4. *Canniball.* On this word, see an article by Trumbull in *Notes and Queries*, ser. v, iv. 171.

57/9. *forme of a Dogge.* The dog-man was possibly suggested by the dog-headed Anubis of the Egyptians or more probably by the Cynocephalus, mentioned by Pliny, which may be the well-known baboon.

58/5. *the ſweete tenth of theſe ſiluer ſounding ſtrings.* The tenth is 'the interval between any tone and the tone represented on the tenth degree of the staff above it'.

58/14. *hope,* for *helpe?*

58/15. *where, comming.* The construction is badly broken, but it is made intelligible enough by suppressing the comma and changing *comming* to *he came*.

58/19. *ouer whome.* The antecedent of *whome* is clearly *Altar* or *cloth oſ gold*. Cf. *Dogge whome,* 57/4. For other instances of *who* or *whom* personifying irrational antecedents, see Abbott, *Shakespearian Grammar*, pp. 179–81, and Morris, *English Accidence*, Index.

60/16. *in hys hand,* i.e. if his hand seized them.

61/5. *takes home the neereſt waye,* i.e. takes the nearest way home.

61/10. *findes a Boate.* May we suppose that this story of the boat that receives the mad Chinon is a reminiscence drawn from Malory's *Morte Darthur*, Book xvii, ch. 13, of the wandering ship in which Lancelot is carried, or is it suggested by the vessel in which Huon of Bordeaux is transported with incredible swiftness through the sea? Cf. *Huon of Burdeux* (E.E.T.S.), pp. 439 ff.? It is, however, needless to remark that the rudderless boat is a commonplace of medieval and, particularly, of Celtic romance. See my note in Selections from Malory's *Morte Darthur*, p. 259; A. C. L. Brown, *Ivain* (Harvard) *Studies and Notes*, viii, p. 96, note, and Lucy A. Paton, *Studies in the Fairy Mythology of Arthurian Romance* (*Radcliffe College Monographs*, xiii), p. 16.

61/26. *we told ye of.* For the use of *ye* both as nominative and as accusative in Elizabethan English, see Abbott, *Shakespearian Grammar*, sect. 236.

62/17. *clift of a Rocke, againſt which ſhe rouled vp a mightie ſtone.* Cf. Oboram's cave (24/27), where the monster—Oboram in disguise—'quickly roules vp againſt the mouth of the hole a mightie ſtone'.

63/4. *were thus ... effecting.* Note this interesting form of the passive, still in use but gradually disappearing.

63/34. *Sir Calor ... Sonne vnto Sir Lancelot du Lake and the beauteous Celeſtina.* For a discussion of this absurdity, see Introduction, sect. vii.

64/1. *whoſe Parents Chinon ... reſcued.* We may, perhaps, safely assume (cf. 22/2 ff.) that Celestina's parents accompany her on the way to the castle of Sir Triamore's father, where she is to be married. But in the attack on the company by the Soldan's men we are told (22/34 f.) that 'fave onely *Lancelot, Triſtram,* and *Triamore* all were flaine', and Celestina conveyed away. No mention is made of her parents. In Chapter V we learn how Chinon and Triamore rescue Celestina from the Soldan, but here too there is no mention of her parents.

64/5. *Merlin.* The great prophet and enchanter is a mighty supporter of King Arthur and has marvellous powers which are exploited in the romance of *Merlin,* published by the E.E.T.S., but in that romance there is no mention of the 'speculative glasse'. See note to 45/25.

For an outline history of the Merlin legend in English and other literatures, see my account in the introduction to the E.E.T.S. edition, London, 1899.

65/13. *an Iron mace.* The usual weapon of giants, who, as a rule, are a very stupid lot. Commonly, the giant strikes out fiercely with the mace, which sticks in the ground, and before he can recover it his diminutive but more nimble foe has overcome him.

68/4. *offering himſelfe.* *Offering* for *offers.*

GLOSSARY

a, *prep.*, on, *leaping a land*, 61/21. Cf. *ashore, afoot,* &c.
aboad, *sb.*, abode, 6/11.
abode, *sb.*, stay, 21/25.
accuftomably, *adv.*, customarily, usually, 23/33, 50/31.
amis, *sb.*, error, fault, 45/14, 67/37.
antomes, *sb.*, see note to 26/3.
approve, *vb.*, test, try, prove, 31/5.
arife, *sb.*, rising, 33/7.
artificially, *adv.*, artistically, skilfully, 30/21.
affemblant, *sb.*, 20/20. See note.

banket, *sb.*, banquet, feast, 38/15.
bewray, *vb.*, make known, 52/32.
bootleffe, *adj.*, unprofitable, 21/25.

care, *sb.*, car, 41/26.
careful, *adj.*, anxious, troubled, 7/28.
cenfe, *vb.*, burn incense before, to perfume, 11/18, 58/22.
chiualrie, *sb.*, feats of arms, 16/27.
cocodrile, *sb.*, crocodile, 55/18.
comfortable, *adj.*, comforting, 51/17.
conceit, *sb.*, thought, conception, fancy, favorable opinion, 21/38, 24/25, 29/8, 40/19, 42/3.
conceited, *adj.*, ingeniously devised, 16/17.
confort, *sb.*, accompaniment, company, 57/32.
corfiue, *sb.*, corrosive, i.e. annoyance, grief, 7/27.
couloring, *adj.*, embellishing, 6/29.
countinance, *sb.*, (improperly) for *continuance*, 43/36. See Oxford Dictionary, s. v. *countenance*, III, † 11.
crofbiting, *sb.*, deception, cheating, 31/10.
croffe, *adj.*, perverse, contrarious, 63/11.
croft, *pp.*, opposed, thwarted, 67/16.
curtle-axe, *sb.*, a short broad cutting sword, a cutlass, 17/23.
cynged, *pp.*, singed, scorched, 53/7.

daunger, *sb.*, power to harm, 56/19.
declining, *vbl. sb.*, turning, diverting, directing, 14/33.
demeanes, *sb.*, behaviour, demeanour, 58/12, 67/19.
defart, *adj.*, desert, 13/22.
dimes, *vb.*, dims, dazzles, 15/24.
difpofe, *sb.*, disposal, 8/4.
drift, *sb.*, scheme, plot, device, 46/18.
dumpe, *sb.*, dejection, depression, 18/2.
dung, *pp.* (of *ding*), struck, beaten down, 17/1.

eies, *sb.*, eyes, 6/35.
enftauled, *pp.*, invested with, 6/30.
epethites, *sb.*, phrases, expressions, 20/31, 38/19.
efchue, *vb.*, avoid, escape, 27/26, 65/16.
efpials, *sb.*, spies, 22/9.
efterne, *adj.*, eastern, 19/5.

farder, *adj.*, farther, 51/36.
fond, *adj.*, foolish, 61/29.
forceflue, *adj.*, powerful, 34/22.
foyle, *sb.*, defeat, 60/5.
fraught, *pple. adj.*, filled, 15/8.
furdering, *vbl. sb.*, furthering, 14/17.

gin, *sb.*, snare, 46/11.
gins, *vb.*, begins, 27/10, 28/19, and often.
goles, *sb.*, goals, 58/27.
gofhauke, *sb.*, a large short-winged hawk, 17/12.

hap, *sb.*, chance, fortune, prosperity, 6/15.
harrald, *sb.*, herald, 14/37.
huffe, *sb.*, hoof, 44/7.

inforflue, *adj.*, compulsive, convincing, 34/33, 43/11.
infconfing, *adj.*, protecting, covering, 27/34.

80 *Famous Historie of Chinon of England*

inftantly, *adv.*, earnestly, 8/3.
infuing, *adj.*, following, coming next, 8/8, 23/24.
intermiffiue, *adj.*, coming at intervals, 40/16, 43/11.

kinde, *sb.*, nature, 59/29.

leaft, *conj.*, lest, 10/22.
let, *sb.*, obstacle, hindrance, 37/13.
luftie, *adj.*, strong, massive, 15/25.

mauger, *prep.*, in spite of, 34/6.
meanes, *sb.*, intercession, 63/7.
mifliking, *adj.*, unpleasant, unharmonious, 46/4.
moytie, *sb.*, part, 14/18.

ought, *vb. pret.*, owed, 48/26.
oueroloied, *pp.*, surfeited, satiated, 29/26.
ouerfpent, *pp.*, finished, brought to an end, 26/15.
ouer-went, *vb. pt.*, outstripped, 60/18.

paffengers, *sb.*, passers by, 33/19.
perforced, *pp.*, compelled, 53/28.
phificke, *adj.*, natural, 42/5.
port, *sb.*, state, retinue, magnificence, 15/36.
portrait, *vb.*, portray, 40/4.
pofe, *vb.*, question, 33/29.
pofie, *sb.*, motto, 31/38.
preafe, *vb.*, press, 20/18.
pretended, *pp.*, intended, 14/21, 22/10, 35/11, 42/34, 43/21, 58/8.
promontany, *sb.*, promontory, 26/22. See note.
puifant, *adj.*, puissant, mighty, 22/16.
pufance, *sb.*, puissance, power, 21/30.

raced, *pp.*, erased, 9/6. See Oxford Dict., s.v. *race*, v.³
refraine, *vb.*, to put a restraint or check upon, 38/36.
regreete, *vb.*, to resalute, 29/27.
remove, *sb.*, removal, 42/17.

renting, *vbl. sb.*, rending, tearing, 65/3.
refort, *sb.*, coming, visit, 20/25. 62/24
retorquation, *sb.*, twisting or turning back, 55/21.
rigour, *sb.*, violence, 60/36.
rosiall, *adj.*, rosy, 18/5.

foituate, *adj.*, situated, 22/26.
fcriking, *adj.*, shrieking, 24/6.
fillie, *adj.*, innocent, simple, mere, humble, 14/27, 39/5, 43,'37, 58/3, 66/13, 28.
fodaine, *sb.*, sudden, 45/22.
fower, *adj.*, sour, 23/21.
ftroken, *pp.* (of *strike*), struck, 27/35, 31/4, 59/5, 60/33, 61/27, also striken, 61/31.

tane, *pp.*, taken, 12/29, 37/7.
temperature, *sb.*, temper, 31/7.
teftament, *sb.*, testimony, oath, 44/33.
then, *conj.*, than, 17/28, 18/36, 27/35, 66/15. But also than, 19/4, 66/7. See note to 17/28.
thether, *adv.*, thither, 47/31, 50/11, 59/8, 66/26.
throughly, *adv.*, thoroughly, 33/11.
tuition, *sb.*, care, keeping, governance, 44/13.
turtle, *sb.*, the turtle dove, 38/30.

vnacquainted, *adj.*, unfamiliar, 18/23. 37/19
vndeferued, *adj.*, unworthy, 44/20. See note.
vnwildie, *adj.*, unwieldy, 55/24.
vale, *sb.*, veil, 21/3.

were, *vb.*, wear, 31/7.
weft, *adj.*, west or waste. See note to 44/14.
whether, *adv.*, whither, 8/23, 26/11, 30/32, 45/35, 55/5, 61/18. But 27/11 requires the modern sense of whether, and 61/13 has the modern form *whither*.
woond, *part. adj.*, wound up, enveloped, encompassed, 52/27.

INDEX TO TEXT

Achilles, armour of, 15/19.
Aeneas, 20/38, 38/20.
Aetna, 27/20.
Ajax, 16/35, 60/5.
Alcides. *See* Hercules.
Arabia, deserts of, 50/10, 56/23.
Arion's harp, 41/10, 50/10 ff.
Arthur, King, 5/6, 8/25, 17/38, 38/11 ff., 68/1 ff.
Atlas, burden of, 50/4.

Babylon, Soldan of, 22/8 ff., 32/5 f., 33/22—35/18, 36/32, 37/7; his son, 15/18, 18/21.
Bessarian, counsellor to the King of Egypt, 40/11, 43/2 ff., 46/14 ff., 66/1 f., 67/4 ff.
Brittany, Duke of, 16/7, 19/16, 21/36, 22/16.

Cador, Earl of Cornwall, 5/1 ff., 8/12 ff., 20/9, 37/15, 38/3 ff., 62/35, 63/4 ff.
Caesar, Julius, 15/26, 30/21.
Calcos (Colchis), 38/1.
Calor, Sir, 63/34 ff.
Cassiopeia, daughter of Bessarian, 39/32—42/27, 45/37 f., 48/8—59/9, 67/33, 68/13.
Cave of Oboram, 24/9 f., 26/39, 28/36 f., 30/30 f.
Celestina, daughter of Lewis, King of France, 14/15, 16/1, 19/3 ff., 21/36, 22/35, 32/4 f., 33/25 ff., 34/32, 35/23, 37/6, 63/35.
Chinon of England, son of Cador, Earl of Cornwall, 6/12, 7/3 ff., 21/2 f., 25/1 ff., 26/26 ff., 29/3—39/7, 46/27, 51/27—54/13, 59/15 —65/28, 67/25—68/16.
Cockatrice, 49/11, 55/11.

Dido, 20/39.

Egbaton, King of Egypt, 40/11, 42/34—45/17, 66/33.

Egypt, 39/8—40/12, 44/14, 53/8, 66/33.
Enisham, 8.
Erganea, 51/5, 58/16.
Esop, 44/16.
Eutropa, the witch, 40/20—42/14, 45/22—51/22, 53/19—54/4, 58/8, 62/8, 63/5—65/14, 67/26—68/9.

Fairies, 30/7 ff., 39/7 f., 51/30.
Ferdinand, 'heire to the Emperour of Almaine', 16/15, 17/2.

Gorgon, 29/10.

Harpies, 51/8, 58/24.
Hercules, 37/34 (Alcides), 51/9 (Alcides), 56/9, 60/5 (Alcides).
Hermit, 13/22 ff.

Jason, 38/1.

Lancelot du Lake, 8/29—13/33, 15/35, 17/8—22/34, 25/4, 29/3 ff., 31/14, 33/17, 35/14, 37/2 f., 63 note.
Laura, daughter of Earl Cador, sister to Chinon, 6/19 ff., 9/4—11/21, 20/2, 21/34.
Letter, Lancelot's, to Laura, 10/31 ff.
Lewis, King of France and father of Celestina, 14/5 f., 17/34, 18/33, 19/35, 21/39, 22/2.

Medea, 41/27.
Merlin, 64/5 ff.
Michander, brother of Cassiopeia, 42/30, 47/34 — 49/25, 54/29 — 56/15, 59/19, 60/9, 66 f.

Nile, river, 40/29, 47/36, 55/19.

Oboram, king of the fairies, 24/16, 27/16—31/30.
Oedipus, 59/13.
Oeta, 60/6.

Perosus, 40/13 f., 42/33 ff., 45/19, 53/20, 66/34—68/12.

Roderigo, Duke of Austria, 12/24.
Rome, 20/33.
Round Table, King Arthur's, 8/26, 17/38, 38/24, 63/24.

Sisyphus, 53/35.
Stanley, Edward, 3.
Sword, fastened in rock, 30/18; attempts to pull it out, 31/16 f.

Taurus, 48/35.
Terpander, brother of Cassiopeia, 42/30, 49/28 f., 56/22—58/11, 60/24—61/4, 66/18.
Theonas, brother of Cassiopeia, 42/31, 50/28, 58/13—59/14, 61/26 f., 66/26 f.
Theseus, 50/6, 57/5.
Tournament to win Celestina, 14/6, 16/15 ff.
Triamore, Sir, son of the Duke of Brittany and lover of Celestina, 16/6, 19/15 ff., 21/36—22/35, 29/32 f., 31/19, 32/4—37/28, 63/34.
Tristram du Lions, Sir, 8/29, 11/33, 12/22 ff., 18/23, 22/4 f., 25/4, 29/3 f., 31/18, 33/17, 35/14, 37/2 f.
Troy, 16/36, 20/39, 38/2.
Tullie, 20/33.

Ulysses, 60/5.

INDEX TO INTRODUCTION AND NOTES

Amadis of Gaul, xxii.
antomes, 72.
Apollonius of Tyre, in Anglo-Saxon, *in the Gesta Romanorum*, in Gower, xxii.
Arions Harpe, 76.
Arthurian story in the sixteenth century, xxv–xlvi.
Arthurian themes in drama, xxxvii.
Arthurian tradition in the Chronicles, xxv–xxix.
Arthur of Little Britain, xxx, xxxii.
Arthur's 'Round Table', at Winchester castle, xxix.
Ascham, Roger, his treatise on the bow, xvii; his censure of Malory's *Morte Darthur*, xxx f.
affemblant, 71.
Astrology, 70.

Babylon, the Soldan of, lxi.
Balin, Malory's, a type of Chinon, lv.
Berners, Lord, his version of *Huon of Bordeaux*, xxx, lv; his *Arthur of Little Britain*, xxx, xxxii; his style, lxiv.
Bespelled princesses, 75.
Bessarian, lvi, 74.
Boy and the Mantle, ballad of the, xxxiii.
Brothers, sworn, 70.

Cador, Earl, xxxvii, lv, lvi, lxii, 69.
Caefar, Iulius, 73; slain in the Senate, *ibid.*
Calor, Sir, lxi f.
Canniball, 77.
Capgrave, John, *Chronicle*, xxv.
Cassiopeia, lvi, lxi.
Caftle carrying Elephant, 72.
cauileers, 71.
Caxton, William, xxi, xxv, xxvi, xxx.
Celestina, lvi, lviii, lxii.
Chapman, the classics in, lix.

Charlemagne's Journey to Jerusalem and Constantinople, romance of, xxxiii.
Charles I and the *sortes Virgilianae*, lviii.
Chaucer, his *Man of Law's Tale*, lvi; his attitude toward Alchemy, lvii; his language, xxiii, lxii.
Chinon of England, romance of, xxviii, xxxiii; original edition of, xlvi f.; analysis of, xlvii–liv; sources of, liv–lvi; supernatural elements in, lvi–lix; influence of the classics on, lix f.; plot and characters in, lx–lxii; grammatical features, lxii–lxiv; style of, lxiv–lxvii.
Comparatives, double, 73.
Copland, William, xxi, xxii.

Danter, John, 69.
Dee, Dr., attitude toward alchemy and astrology, lvii.
Deloney, Thomas, ballad on Lancelot, xli.
de Worde, Wynkyn, xxi, xxii, xxv, xxx, xxxviii, lv.
Dog-man, 77.
Drayton, Michael, his *Polyolbion*, xxviii f.
Dwarffe, 73.

Elizabethan age, medieval character of, xv f.; amusements in, xvii; the classics in, xvii f.; popular literature in, xviii f.; the drama in, xviii f.; ballads in, xix f.; stories in, xx; coarseness of, xxi.
Esplandrian, The Exploits of, xxii.
Euphuism in Elizabethan age, lxv; in *Chinon of England*, lxv.
Eynsham, 69.

Fabyan, Robert, *New Chronicles of England and France*, xxvi.

84   *Chinon of England*

Fairies in the sixteenth century, and in *Chinon of England*, lvi ff.
Fletcher, *Little French Lawyer*, xli.
Ford, Emanuel, romances of, lxvii.
Forman, Simon, *Life of Merlin*, xxxviii.
for to fupply, 70.

Gamelyn, The Tale of, xxii.
Gareth, Malory's, a type of Chinon, lv.
Gawain and the Green Knight, Sir, xxix, xxxii, xxxiii, xli f., xlv.
Gawain, popularity of romances relating to, xli ff.; *The Grene Knight*, xlii; *The Turke and Gowin*, xlii; *Golagrus and Gawain*, xliii; *The Marriage of Sir Gawain*, xliii; *The Jeaste of Syr Gawayne*, xliii; *Syre Gawene and the Carle of Carelyle*, xliv f.
Geoffrey of Monmouth, xix, xxv; doubts concerning historicity of his *Historia Regum Britanniae*, xxvi, xxvii; defence of by Leland, xxvii; use of by Thomas Hughes, xxxvii; in *Chinon*.
Glennie, J. S. Stuart, his account of Arthurian localities, xxix.
Grafton, Richard, printer, xxvi.
Great Fool, folk tale of the, relation to *Chinon of England*, lv.
Grene Knight, The, xlii.

Hardyng, John, *Chronicle*, xxvi.
Harrison, William, his description of Elizabethan England, xxvii.
Hawkins, John, xxxviii.
Helyas, Knight of the Swan, xxii.
Higden's *Polychronicon*, xxv.
Holinshed, Raphael, *Chronicles*, xxvii f.
Holy Grail, xlvi.
Hughes, Thomas, his *Misfortunes of Arthur*, xxxvii; his use of the *Morte Darthur* and of Seneca, xxxviii.
Huon of Bordeaux, Romance of, influence upon the *Faery Queene*, xxiv; popularity in sixteenth century, xxx, xxxii; relation of *Chinon* to, lv, lviii.

infuing, 70.

Jeaste of Sir Gawayne, The, xliii.
Johnson, Richard, xxxiv, xxxvi, lxvii.

Kenilworth, festivities at, in 1575, xxxi.
King Arthur and the King of Cornwall, ballad of, xxxiii.
King Arthur's Death, ballad of, xxxiii.
Knight of Curtesy and the Fair Lady of Faguell, The, xxii.

La Cote Male Taile, lv.
Lancelot, Sir, relatively unrepresented in late Arthurian romance, xl; romance of *Lancelot of the Laik*, xl f.; Deloney's ballad on, xli; a leading character in *Chinon of England*, lvi, lxi f.
Latimer's style, lxv.
Laura, daughter of Cador, lvi, lxi f.
Layamon's *Brut*, xxix.
Leland, John, his defence of Geoffrey of Monmouth, xxvii; his *Assertio Inclytissimi Arturii*, xxvii.
Le Morte Arthur (15th century), xxix.
Libeaus Desconus, xliii, xliv, lv.
Lisuarte of Greece, xxii.
Lodge's *Rosalynde*, xxii.
Loving an unseen maiden, 74.
Lying in romances, 74.
Lydgate's *Fall of Princes*, xl.

Mabinogion, lv.
Mace, 78.
Madden, Sir Frederick, xxxiii, xlv.
Maiden Knight, 72.
Malory's *Morte Darthur*, xxvi, xxx ff., xxxviii, xli, xlv, xlvi, lv; the style of, lxiv f.
Marriage of Sir Gawain, The, xliii.
Marston's *Malcontent*, xli.
Medieval literature, character of surviving popular, xviii ff.; miracle and mystery plays, xviii f.; ballads, xix f.; medieval survivals in the time of Elizabeth, xiii ff.; modern neglect of, xiv; material survivals, xv f.
Merlin, romance of, xxix, 78.
Merlin, romances dealing with, xxxviii f.; in the *Faery Queene*, xxxix; popularity in seventeenth century, *ibid.*; William Rowley's play, *The Birth of Merlin, ibid.*
Middleton, Christopher, Preface, xlvi f.; his style, lxiv–lxvii.
Middleton, Thomas, his play, *The Mayor of Queensborough*, xl.

Index to Introduction and Notes 85

Midsummer Night's Dream, A, lvii.
Misfortunes of Arthur, The, Thomas Hughes's tragedy, xxxvii.
Morte Arthure, The alliterative (14th century), xxix.

Nashe, criticism of romances, xxxii.
Nennius, xxv.
Nile, seven branches of, 75.

Oboram, king of the fairies, lviii. lxi, 72.

Painfull Adventures of Pericles, Prince of Tyre, The, xxii.
Perceval, xliii, lv.
Percy, Bishop, xix f.
Percy Folio MS., xix f., xxii, xxxii, xxxiii, xli, xlii, xliv.
Perosus, lvi.
Polydore Vergil, Anglicae Historiae, Libri XXVI, xxvi.
Prince = princess, 71.
Promontany, 72.

Raleigh, Sir Walter, style of, lxvi.
Rastell, John, Pastyme of the People, xxvi.
Relative pronouns, omission of, 77.
Renaissance, the, xiii; literature, xvii f.; the classics in, lix.
retorquation, 76.
Robert the Devil, Life of, xxii.
Robinson, Richard, his translation of Leland's Assertio, and his account of The Ancient Order, Societie and Vnitie Laudable of Prince Arthur, xxviii.
Rocks that open and shut, 76.
Romances, popularity of, in Middle Ages, xx f.; survival of, in sixteenth and seventeenth centuries, xxi ff.
Rowley, William, his play, The Birth of Merlin, xxxix.
Rudderless boats, 77.

Serpent with woman's face, 71.
Seven Champions of Christendom, The, lxvii.

Shakespeare, xix, xxii.
Sidney's Arcadia, style of, lxvi.
ſpeculatiue glaſſe, 75.
Spenser's, Edmund, Faery Queene, Arthurian tradition in, xxiii f.; other medieval elements, xxiv; monks and monasteries in, xxiv; debt to Huon of Bordeaux, xxx; Merlin in, xxxix; fairies in, lvii; the classics in, lix.
Squyr of Lowe Degre, The, xxii.
Stationers' Registers, xlvi f., 69.
Sword pulled out of rock, 73.
Syr Orfeo, lix.

tane, 70.
Tenses, mixture of, 70.
Tenth (in music), 77.
then = than, 71.
Tom a Lincolne, romance of, xxxiii-xxxvii (analysis), lxvii.
Trance, 73.
Transformations into animals, 75.
Treveris, Peter, xxv.
Trevisa, John de, xxv.
Triamore, Sir, romance of, xliv; character in Chinon of England, lvi, lxi f.; note on, 70.
Tristram, Sir, xxxii, xlv f., lvi, lxi, 70.
Turke and Gowin, The, xlii.
Tyndale's style, lxv.

Unwarlike knights, 74.

Valentine and Orson, lvi.
Vergil, magic use of, lviii.
Vial, magic, 77.

Warner, William, his Albion's England, xxviii.
Weddynge of Sir Gawen and Dame Ragnell, The, xliii.
Wesley, John, his use of biblical texts selected by chance, lviii.
Witch's aid in love, 75.
Wolfe, John, printer, xxviii.
Wolfe, Reginald, printer, xxvii.
Worde, de, see de Worde.

Ye as nominative and accusative, 77.

Robinson's

Assertion of King Arthure

with the Latin Original of Leland

PREFACE

IN reprinting the work of Leland and of his translator Robinson I have endeavoured to reproduce the spelling, capitalization, and punctuation of the original printed copies. Both Leland and Robinson were familiar with the typographical conventions of their time and may safely be permitted to reappear in their old-fashioned garb, if not in facsimile.[1] The old punctuation is not uniformly consistent, according to modern notions, but the variations are relatively unimportant. In many passages the punctuation is surprisingly modern and practically in accord with present-day usage. In Middleton's *Chinon*, on the other hand, the original punctuation contributes materially to the confusion caused by the abnormally long sentences.

It was my original intention to annotate Robinson's translation throughout, and thus at the same time to annotate Leland's *Assertio*; but on further consideration I decided that since the chief reason for reprinting Leland's little treatise and the English translation was to give some notion of the attitude of educated men in the sixteenth century toward the question of Arthurian origins, elaborate annotation would hardly warrant the trouble, to say nothing of the expense of printing.

For the transcription of the text of Leland I am indebted to a professional copyist, and for that of Robinson's version,

---

[1] Leland's *Assertio* is excellently printed in clear roman type. Robinson's translation is in large measure in black-letter interspersed with passages in roman and in italics. The variety of type used in the reprint may perhaps give some idea of the typographical variations of the original.

in large measure to my wife. Miss Mabel Day, D.Lit., Assistant Director and Secretary of the Early English Text Society, has attended to various details relating to the printing, and has assisted in reading the proof with the originals in the British Museum; and although proof-reading is rarely infallible, I trust that the present reprints adequately represent the texts on which they are based.

In conclusion, I wish to offer my sincere thanks to Sir Israel Gollancz, Honorary Director of the Early English Text Society, without whose co-operation this work would not have been possible.

W. E. M.

WESLEYAN UNIVERSITY,
    MIDDLETOWN, CONN., U.S.A.
    September 15, 1924.

CONTENTS

	PAGE
INTRODUCTION	vii
RICHARD ROBINSON'S *Assertion of King Arthure* . .	1
The Epistle	3
Table of Names of Authors	11
Certain memorable Notes inserted since the Translation	12
Names of Kings and Knights	14
Robinson's Text	17
JOHN LELAND'S *Assertio Inclytissimi Arturii* . . .	91
NOTES TO RICHARD ROBINSON'S *Assertion of King Arthure*	153
GLOSSARY TO THE *Assertion*	154
INDEX TO ROBINSON'S *Assertion of King Arthure* AND TO LELAND'S *Assertio Inclytissimi Arturii* . . .	155

INTRODUCTION

JOHN LELAND's argument for the historical existence of King Arthur, the *Assertio Inclytissimi Arturij Regis Britanniæ*, published in 1544, and the translation of the same by Richard Robinson, published in 1582, may most conveniently be considered together. The reprint of the *Assertio* is based upon a copy in the British Museum,[1] and that of Robinson's translation of the *Assertio* upon a copy also found in the British Museum.[2] 'All of Leland's works', remarks the *Dictionary of National Biography*, ' are now very rare.' The library of Harvard University has a copy of Leland's *Assertio* and of Robinson's translation, but such a possession is a marked exception. For all practical purposes both the *Assertio* and Robinson's English version have been inaccessible to most scholars for generations. In view of the decay of classical studies it is possible that Robinson's quaint translation may prove not merely curious but useful to modern readers who desire to know in some detail the popular opinion in the sixteenth century concerning King Arthur.

The essential facts in the lives of Leland (1506?-1552) and of Robinson (*fl.* 1576-1601) are presented in the *Dictionary of National Biography* and, except in barest outline, need not be repeated here.[3] Leland was educated at St. Paul's School, and received his B.A. at Christ's College, Cambridge, in 1522, when only sixteen years of age. He later pursued his studies at All Souls College, Oxford, and at the University of Paris, returning to his native land with a mastery of Latin and Greek and a competent

---

[1] The British Museum has four copies of the *Assertio*, including one on vellum—all dated 1544.
[2] The Museum has two copies of Robinson's translation, published in 1582.
[3] The antiquary Edward Burton brought out in 1896 *The Life of John Leland*, with a biography of his works. See also the *Cambridge History of English Literature*, iii. 374 ff.

acquaintance with French, Spanish, and Italian. In 1533 he was appointed King's antiquary and was busily occupied from about 1534 to 1543 in an antiquarian tour about England, during which he gave particular attention to the monastic libraries. Out of the wreckage caused by the dissolution of the ancient monasteries he was able to rescue some valuable manuscripts, but, to his great distress, a vast number were lost or wantonly destroyed. Shortly after his long peregrination, which took him into every corner of England, he published his *Assertio Inclytissimi Arturij* in his thirty-eighth year. But the overstraining of his powers at length broke down his reason, and in his forty-sixth year he died, after having been long insane.

Leland was the first notable antiquarian in England, and as such deserves all honour.[1] Doubtless as a scholar of recognized rank he hesitated to make any serious contribution to scholarship or literature by using the vernacular, and he followed the example of Erasmus and Sir Thomas More by publishing in Latin all the works that he brought out in his lifetime, with the single exception of his account of his search for antiquities, which appeared in a quaint English dress. Leland wrote Latin with the ready fluency of a scholar trained in the traditions of the Renaissance and naturally employed it in the *Assertio*, though the nature of his topic compelled him to adopt many terms unknown to classical literature. Notwithstanding his learning he lacked the special equipment and the keen critical sense that are required in dealing with the thorny question of Arthurian origins; and his disquisition upon Arthur is more notable for heat than light.

His wrath had been stirred by the scepticism of Polydore Vergil, his contemporary rival trained in the schools of Italy, who approached the history of England with a critical temper and raised doubts as to the trustworthiness of many features of Arthurian tradition, particularly as presented by Geoffrey of Monmouth. Leland came to the defence of Geoffrey in his *Codrus sive Laus et Defensio*

---

[1] But we must not overlook the impression that Leland makes upon some scholars in our time: 'The truth is, Leland was a superstition. He received the inordinate praise which is easily given to those of whom it is said that they might achieve wonders if they would. The weight of his learning which he carried was thought to be so great that he could not disburden it in books', &c. Charles Whibley, in *Cambridge History of English Literature*, iii. 374.

Gallofridi Monumetensis contra Polydorum Vergilium.[1] The investigation on which this piece was based served in part as a preliminary study for Leland's *Assertio Inclytissimi Arturij*, which bristles with far-fetched authorities. Despite the parade of learning in the *Assertio*, the modern student, although he may on other grounds believe in the reality of Arthur's historical existence, will doubtless not take too seriously the 'proofs' there presented, many of which are only a proof of the author's inability to weigh evidence. In our day the interest both of Leland and of his translator Robinson lies in the fact that they doubtless represent the attitude of average sixteenth-century English readers towards Arthurian legend. When perusing Arthurian romances they perhaps flattered themselves that they were in a sense reading history. This attitude was not universal, but in a relatively uncritical age like the sixteenth century it must have been far more prevalent than would now be possible.

As for Leland, there can be no doubt of his intense conviction. He is in no sense a cool, dispassionate judge, but a heated advocate, and he eagerly seizes upon any supposed fact that can be pressed into support of his thesis. Writers of more critical judgement than himself he treats with scant courtesy, if indeed he does not regard them as intentionally dishonest. His greatest antipathy he reserves for William of Newbury or Gulielmus Parvus, as he calls him, and for Polydore Vergil, both of whom, by the way, are highly esteemed by modern historical students. A good instance of his own critical method appears in his amusing scruples regarding the bones of the 'Giant' as being those of Gawain,[2] though he is ready to take 'the auctoritie of forraine and of our owne writers that such did inhabit Albion'. With this we may compare his reasoning about Arthur's seal (pp. 39–44). He finds (49/15 ff.) that Mordred's death in battle was a just reward of his treachery. What lesson Arthur's death in the same battle suggests he does not tell us. He rises to his highest rhetorical levels in describing the battle on the Kentish coast when Arthur returns from France (p. 45), and, singularly enough, he is able to present the *ipsissima verba* of Arthur's address to his soldiers (pp. 45, 46). For some reason, he imagines that

---

[1] Published, apparently for the first time, by Thomas Hearne in vol. v of his *Collectanea*, 5 vols., Oxford, 1715.

[2] pp. 29, 30 of Robinson's English version.

Arthur addressed Gawain thus: 'You the moſt praiſe worthy garland of warlike proweſſe', &c. (p. 46/15 ff.). Leland is indeed so carried away by his enthusiasm that his demonstration of Arthur's existence contains wellnigh as much romance as sober history.

From Leland we now turn to his translator Richard Robinson. The list of titles of the works produced by Robinson shows that the greater portion consists of translations and the remainder of compilations.[1] He is far less known than Leland, and rightly so.[2] He is in no proper sense an original writer or even a scholar when compared with Leland, though in the fashion of his time he is an inveterate pedant, as sufficiently appears in the Dedicatory Epistle prefixed to his version of Leland's *Assertio*. This Epistle, with its exuberant and irrelevant piety (pp. 3-6), and its ridiculous babble about the bow, which he connects with the Bow of Promise set in the clouds after the Deluge, affords an excellent index of Robinson's mind—religious, fanciful, and incapable of coherent, logical thinking, to say nothing of historical research.[3] He is obviously trying to win the favour and support of the Worshipful Society of Archers to whom he dedicates his translation of the *Assertio*. Upon their patronage and that of other men of wealth depends his very existence. He is a typical example of the honest, industrious hack writer of moderate skill, compelled to work like a slave for the income of a beggar.[4]

In translating Leland's *Assertio* he endeavours to present the substance of the original, but his version, like most Elizabethan translations,[5] is obviously not meant to be a word for word equiva-

---

[1] See the sketch of Robinson in the *Dictionary of National Biography*.

[2] Another Richard Robinson (*fl.* 1574) was a minor poet, the details of whose life are obscure. Sir Egerton Brydges confounded the poet with the compiler in his sketch of Leland and of Robinson. Cf. *The British Bibliographer*, i. 109-35.

[3] His most interesting addition to Leland—derived from his learned friend Master Steven Batman—is that Arthur is descended from Joseph of Arimathea! See pp. 12, 13.

[4] 'Richard Robinson, who produced many indifferent versions of dull Latin works for various publishers, appears to have received no money payments at all. The proceeds of a certain number of copies to be disposed of by himself to friends and patrons—eked out, if luck willed, by a dedication fee—formed his only remuneration.' Phoebe Sheavyn, *The Literary Profession in the Elizabethan Age*, p. 101.

[5] Cf. *Cambridge History of English Literature*, iv. 3.

Introduction

lent for the Latin but a readable paraphrase. As a rule he appears to be unable even to transcribe correctly the Latin verse that he borrows from Leland, though possibly he flattered himself that his variations were improvements upon the originals.

Precisely what led Robinson to translate the *Assertio* we do not know,[1] but we may plausibly assume that the existence of the Society of Prince Arthur, to which he dedicates his work, was a sufficient incentive. This was a company of gentlemen who practised archery as a diversion and presumably were interested in a demonstration of the historical existence of the hero who gave his name to their order.

In the following year, 1583, doubtless encouraged by the reception accorded to his translation of the *Assertio*, he brought out a small pamphlet entitled *The Auncient Order, Societie, and Unitie of Prince Arthure*. This little book is in the main a treatise on archery, translated from the French.[2] After the dedication is a brief outline of heraldry followed by a display of escutcheons, fifty-eight in all. The name of an Arthurian knight appears above each escutcheon, and in most cases, not in all, initials, presumably of members of the Society—'E. P.', 'T. C.', 'I. P.', &c.—are placed at the right and left of the escutcheons. Below the several escutcheons are arranged pairs of stanzas of four lines each, the first stanza descriptive of the device, the second complimentary.

Following the escutcheons appears *A Breefe Repetition of the Table Rounde*, in two pages, indicating the character of the original Round Table and the duties pertaining to it.

Then comes an account of the development of archery from the earliest times, in the form of three Assertions. 'The First Assertion and is Sacred Hiftoricall' is an abstract in lame verse (nine pages) of Jewish history from Adam to Christ, with particular reference to archery.

'The Second Assertion and ys Prophane Hyftoricall' is mainly

---

[1] We may note that Robinson had already translated in 1577, five years before his translation of the *Assertio*, *A Record of Ancyent Historyes entituled in Latin Gesta Romanorum, Translated, Perused, Corrected, and Bettered*. This work is doubtfully credited to John Leland. It ran through six editions, the latest appearing in 1601.

[2] On page A⁴ back we find: 'Thus much concerning knowledge of Armes blazoned: Wherof (the French Author vncertaine by name) on this maner introduceth', &c.

an epitome (seven pages and a half) of Greek mythology, with mention of famous ancient archers, Apollo, Paris, Hercules, and princes such as Commodus, Domitian, Cyrus.

'The Third Assertion, Englyſhe Hyſtoricall' (nearly ten pages) presents a summary of English history with especial reference to the part archery has played.

Obviously, in work like this there is small opportunity for originality, and there is no great striving for literary effect. To us the chief interest of Robinson's version of the *Assertion* of Arthur and his account of a society imitating in his own time the traditional Round Table of King Arthur is that they enable us in some degree to measure the popularity of Arthurian tradition in the sixteenth century.

Incidentally, we may add that the existence of such a company of gentleman archers in the last quarter of the sixteenth century is also a striking proof of the vitality of the tradition of the prowess of English bowmen on the field of battle; a tradition that kept alive even in Charles II's time a 'fraternity of bowmen, flourishing and rejoicing in the patronage of a queen'.[1]

After this brief survey of Robinson's career we need spend little time upon his style, for nothing that he wrote is in any proper sense a contribution to literature. But in simple justice to him we must admit that he had learned to write reasonably clear and intelligible prose.[2] His sentences are not notably graceful, but they are not unduly long and they are far less involved than the unwieldy periods that continually recur in the work of Sir Philip Sidney or of Sir Walter Raleigh. But we must note that his prose is better when restrained by the comparative sobriety of the Latin he is translating than it is when he essays such an untrammelled flight as appears in his Dedicatory Epistle. Fully to realize the possibilities of his style, however, one must read some of his verse. Rhythm and melody count for nothing. His sole aim appears to be to crowd a certain number of syllables into a line, and if the

---

[1] *Bishop Percy's Folio MS.*, ed. Hales and Furnivall, i. 9.

[2] Like his contemporaries he is fond of alliteration. Note this sentence from his Dedicatory Epistle: 'Chuſing a cheefe & moſt perſpicuouſe, a valiant and most victoriouſe, a couragiouſe and most conquerouſe, a religiouſe and moſt redoubted Royall ſoueraigne King Henry the eight, as ſole ſupreme Patron and protector thereof againſt the cankered curriſh kinde of caueling carpers.' 7/30 ff.

Introduction

metre breaks in the process, so much the worse for the metre. To read his verse aloud gives about as much pleasure as chewing sand. But the reader may judge for himself and test the specimens found on pp. 10, 19, 30, 35, 51, 58, 81–2. His grammar presents the usual characteristics of late Elizabethan prose and calls for no special treatment. He is fond of the awkward genitive forms, such as 'Cerdicius his comming', 24/5; 'Mordred Arthure his nephewe', 25, marginal note, &c.[1] But he also uses freely the ordinary modern possessive form. Perhaps the most interesting grammatical usage found in Robinson's version is the employment of uninflected *it* as a genitive, which appears also in Shakespeare's *King John*, II. i:

'Go to it grandame, child.
Give grandame kingdom and it grandame will
Give it a plum, a cherry, and a fig.'

Robinson's example is: 'Of it owne accorde it beares both Grapes & Corne', 55/25.

---

[1] Cf. the side-notes on p. 46, &c., &c.

Insignia Illustrium Patronorum, huius opusculi selectorum.

D. ARTVRVS BARO Gray, de VVilton.

D. HENRICVS SIDNEY, Illustrissimi Ordinis Garterij Miles, vnus Consiliariorum D. Reg. & in Principatu Walliæ Præsid.

Magister Thomas Smith D. Reginæ Custumarius Principalis, in Portu London.

Eccles. 10. cap. Gloria Diuitum, Honoratorum, & Pauperum, est Timor Dei.

A
Learned and True Affertion of

the original, Life, Actes, and death of
the moft Noble, Valiant, and Renoumed Prince
Arthure, King of great *Brittaine.*

Who fucceeding his father *Vther Pendragon,* and right
nobly gouerning this Land fixe and twentie yeares,
then dyed of a mortall wounde receyued in battell,
together with victory ouer his enemies. As
appeareth Cap. 9. And was buried at
*Glaftenbury. Cap.*12.An.543.

Collected and written of late yeares in lattin, by the
learned Englifh Antiquarie of worthy memory
Iohn Leyland.

Newly tranflated into Englifh by *Richard Robinfon*
Citizen of London. *Anno Domini.*
1 5 8 2.

VBIQVE   FLORESCIT.

LONDON
Imprinted by Iohn Wolfe, **Dwelling in**
Diftaffe Lane, ouer againft the **Signe**
of the Caftell. 1 5 8 2.

H

Infignia Illuftrium Patronorum, huius
opufculi felectorum.

D. ARTVRVS BARO
Gray, de VVilton

D. HENRICVS SIDNEY, Illuftrifsimi Ordinis Garterij Miles, vnus Confiliario-
rum D. Reg. & in Principa-
tu Walliæ Præfid.

[*Gray coat of arms*]   [*Sidney coat of arms*]

AT VINCIT PAVPERIEM VIRTVS   QVO FATA VOCANT

Magifter Thomas Smith *D. Reginæ
Cuftumarius Principalis, in
Portu London.*

[*Smith coat of arms*]

FAMA FIDES OCCVLVS

Ecclef. 10.cap. *Gloria Diuitum, Honoratorum, & Pauperum, eft
Timor Dei.*

[For the coats of arms, see collotype facsimile facing the title-page.]

To the Right Honorable Lord ARTHVRE
GRAY, Baron of Wilton, Lord Deputie
& Liefetenant Generall for the Queenes
Maieſtie in Ireland:

To the Right Honorable Sir H ENRY SIDNEY, Knight
*of the Honorable Order of the Garter, & Preſident for
her Maieſtie in the Marches of Wales:*

To the Right worſhipfull M. THOMAS SMITH, *Eſquire, &*
Chiefe Cuſtomer for her Maieſtie in the Porte of London : & to the Worſhipfull Societie of Archers, in London yearely celebrating the renoumed memorie of the Magnificent Prince ARTHVRE & his
Knightly Order of the Round Table:

Grace, mercy, & Peace in the Lord Euerlaſtinge.

HAVING in mindefull memorie (*Right Honourable, and
Worſhippful*) that mercifull couenaunt of peace, by our
omnipotent Creator towardes all fleſh thus manifeſted (*I do ſet* Gen. 9.
my Raine Bowe in the cloudes, & it ſhall be as a to*ke*n betwene me
5 & the earth*) promiſing hereby neuer to deſtroy the ſame any
more by waters: how much ought ma*n*kind ſpecially, enioying
by this peaceable pact, from Heaue*n*, Earth, & the Sea, aboundance of benefittes ; feare God in his holines, loue one an other in
righteouſneſſe, and vſe theſe benefittes with thankfulneſſe to the
10 aduauncement of his glory. For this Bowe, this Rainebowe
I ſay of his couenant, and pledge of his peace, left vnto vs fro*m*
the deluge (as *Ariſtotle* affirmeth) *Naturally appeareth by* Ariſt. meteor
reflection or giuing backe of the light of the Sunne, from a cloude lib*er* 3. Cap. 1.
oppoſite, or againſt the ſame. So our heaue*n*ly God, the Father Trac. 2.
15 of light, and giuer of grace, departeth with the light of his manifolde mercies vnto mankinde, from the oppoſite cloude of his

4   THE EPISTLE

displeasure. Againe, this Bowe of his co- [A² back] uenant
and pledge of his peace, (as it is saide by *Albertus*) *To be
so much lesse in appearance, as by how much the Sunne is higher
in the Heauens, and contrarie wise so much greater, as the Sunne
is lower to the earth*: So much lesse be the mercies of God 5
minded of man, as his mightie power appeareth out of our sight,
and againe so much greater seeme his mercies vnto vs, as his
mightie power is nere vs in sight. Thirdly according to
Aristotle, this Rainebow of his couenant & pledge of his peace,
As it appeareth in the Spring time, in Sommer, in Autume & 10
in Winter, euening & morning, but specially in Autumne: So is
the performance of his mercifull couenant, and peaceable pacte
at all times apparant, but specially in *Autumne*, that is when
mankinde laboureth most to leaue sinne, and bring-forth fruites
of good life as I saide, fearing God in his holinesse, louing one 15
an other in righteousnesse, and vsing his benefittes with thank-
fulnesse. Thus and to this end graunting his couenant, our
omnipotent Creator and gratiouse God ordayning Man ruler
ouer his Creatures in earth, yet vnder his protection in heauen,
hath not onely bounde vnto him all humaine societie, but hath 20
also substituted euen his liuetenauntes godly rulers ouer the same
to the foresaide effect for the aduauncement of his glory, confirming the same couenant with the aucthoritie of his holie worde
2. Reg. 7. on this manner. *I will ordaine a place for my people of Israell. I.
And I will plant him, and I will dwell with him. II. And he* 25
*shall be no more troubled. III. And the children of iniquitie
shall not vexe or afflict him any more. IIII.* By his word here
he promised that which by his deede he performed to our forefathers, Adam in Paradise, *Gen.* 1. Noah and his children,
Gen. 9. Abraham & his seede, *Gen.* 12. But louing his elect, 30
and hating their enemies, he performed his promise vnto Iacob
in his prouidence, and vnto Laban in his iudgments, *Gen.* 30.
So did he in like manner vnto Ioseph, and his vnnaturall
brethren, *Gen.* 37. Yea in his prouidence laying his right hand
vpon Ephraim, and in his iudgement his left hand vpon 35
Manasses, *Gen.* 48. Whereby as he prospered and [A³] pro-
tected his holy ones in peace and warres against their enemies,
we reade also in the deuine histories from time to time how and
by what ordenarie meanes of power, force, and defence, he

reached vnto his feeble flocke his mightie arme to the difcomforture of the enemie & vtter fubuertion both of their power & pollicie, according to his promifes aforefaide. Heere then memorable and praifeworthie is the prouidence of this moft mightie *God*, who promifing helpe vnto the Iewes againft the Gentiles, vfed no kinde of fpeach fo much as this, *That he would* Deut. 32. *bend his Bow and dye his fhaftes in bloud.* As who fay, God will make the Iewes fhoote ftrong fhootes to ouerthrow their enemies : or at the leaft, that fhooting is a wonderful mightie thing, whereunto the high power of God is likened. This bow a weapon of defence, the Raine Boe a token of truce : This Bow in peace a pleafure, the Raine Bowe a figne of ferenitie : this Bow in warres a paine to the enemie, the Raine Bow at al times and to all people *Gods toaken betwene him and the earth.* The one an inftr[u]ment of mercy, the other of deftruction : the godly haue both as their comfort and fauegarde by Gods protection, the vngodly either wanting the one or hauing both, haue them to their confufion and fubuertion by his reiection. As we reade of King Saul, that he was flaine of the Philiftians being Reg. 31. mightie bow men : and with him alfo his Sonne Ionathas who as the fcripture faith neuer fhot fhaft in vaine. And that the kingdome of Ifraell after Sauls death came vnto King Dauid : who after he was King, decreed by the firft ftatute which he enacted, *That all the children of Ifraell fhould learne to fhoote* 2. Reg. 1. *in the bowe*, according to a law made many a day before *vt patet in libro iuftorum*, a booke not now in vfe to be founde. In his booke of Pfalmes as hee faide *He was at peace with them that hated peace.* So named hee the bow and arrowes in diuers manners & meaninges, as in his Pfal. 7. verf. 13. & 14. Pfal. 11. verf. 2. Pfal. 18. verf. 13. Pfal. 21. verf. 12. Pfal. 45. verf. 6. Pfal. 49. verf. 9. 64. verf. 3. & 4. 76. verf. 3. 91. verf. 5. 127. verf. 4. & 5. [A³ back] Finally in his 147. Pfal. verf. 6. Praying to God for deliuerance from his enemies and for their deftruction. *He faith, fhoot thine arrowes and confume them :* So yet that *He neither trufted in bowe nor fworde, but in the power of God.* Hee affirmeth it Pfalme 44. verf. 6. And to conclude that he had rather liue in a godly peace then to warre againft the wicked, he faith in the 119 Pfal. verf. 15. *As at a marke he will ayme to walke in the wayes of the Lord.* Of this

6 THE EPISTLE

minde was not King Iofias, who though leading a godly life at home in Iuda, yet going vniuftly to fight againft Nichao King of Egipt, was rather friendly dehorted by him from his purpofe then otherwife, faying : *Leaue off to worke agaynft the Lord which is with mee leaft he do flay thee, which admonition Iofias not regard- ing as fpoken from God, tafted in deed of Gods iuft iudgment : for being fhot thorow with arrowes he was wou*nded *to the death incontinently*. I could at large here call to minde the commendation of this peaceable practife of fhooting which once I as a rawe fcholler reade ouer in *Toxophilus,* and at times by tasked leffons interpreted in latine here and there; but for breuitie, I refer your honours, and worfhipes vnto the Hiftories there, of the Ethiopian king, and Cambyfes king of Perfia. Of Sefoftris and his archers. Of the Meffagetanes which neuer went without their bowe and quiuer neyther in peace nor in warres. Of Policrates and his one thowfand archers. Of the Scithians (whofe whole fubftance and riches of a man being a yoake of Oxen and a plow, a Nagge and his dogge, his bowe and his quiuer) were inuincible againft *D*arius and other Monarckes. To be fhort, the Grecians, Perfians, Athenians, and the Romanes, whofe fhooting in peace and warres was worthie of praife and fame. Neyther here ought I nor will I omit with filence the deferued fame of our Anceftors in fauouringe this exercife in this our little England long agone liuing and of latter time, though breefly, referring your honours & worfhippes vnto the hiftories at large, as of Brute and his Troianes the firft Brittaines, before and after the ariuall of Iulius Caefar, Claudius, & Vefpafian Emperoures [A⁴] and they Romanes: after them the Saxons vntill the time of Vortiger, the vfurping murtherer, who (Gods prouidence fo working for them, and his iudgement vpon him) by the two Brethern and valiant Brittaines Aurelius firnamed Ambrofe, & Vther Pendragon, being burned in his Caftell in Wales, was occafion of the Brittaines more happier eftate afterwardes. But here yet by the way (*Right honourable and worfhipfull*) as I applaude in this their well doing, fo it had beene a thing of Brittaine moft worthelie to be wifhed, for that Prince himfelfe leffe opprobrius, of all me*n* more praife worthie, and moft pretioufe in the fight of God : if the ferpent Tyrus had wanted here his vennime vncurable, though his

4 Reg. 23.

5

10

15

20

25

30

35

DEDICATORIE 7

fleſh proued medicinable againſt all other poyſons (as ſaith Cardanus in his booke of Comfort.) I meane if Vther Pendragon had wanted that ſerpentine poyſon of adulterie, Nigromancie & murther (things odible to God and good men:) when that moſt in-
5 comperable King Arthure of great Brittaine for his princely proweſſe, valiant vertues, and triumphant victories yet prooued more Royally renoumed throughoute all the worlde in his time and to his poſteritie. The Hebr[e]wes with greate and not vndeſerued titles extolled their Iudas Maccabeus. Homer the glory of
10 all Greeke Poets left Hector and Achilles moſt commendable vnto the worlde. Neyther by leſſe diligence did the Grecians adorne with praiſe Alexander the moſt mightie conquerour. And the Romanes aduanced the noble actes of their Cæſar to the Skyes not enough. The Burgonians profoundly praiſed Godfrey of
15 Bulloyn (for his noble valiancy) as the ſcourge of the Sarazens in his dayes. And as euery one of thoſe are commended with due deſert: ſo in like manner there were neuer Brittaines wanting of excellent learning and exquiſite knowledge to leaue with carefull diligence and credible commendation, the progenie, life,
20 proweſſe proſperitie, and triumphant victories of our ſaid auncient Arthure worthely publiſhed vnto the worlde. And as Alexander [Mag-[1]] [A⁴ back] would haue none to purtract him but Apelles, nor any but Lyſippus to engraue him in braſſe, nor any but Pyrgotiles to worke him in pretiouſe ſtone: So
25 where in not three, but many Artizans as learned Gildas, William of Malmsbury, Nennius, Diuionenſes, Graius, Ioſephus, Geoffrey of Munmuth, Silueſter Giraldus, &c. performed their worthie workmanſhippes in our Arthure Maur (to vſe the Brittaine phraſe:) euen one Engliſh Leyland for his learned laboure
30 laudable, hath perfectly poliſhed him in all poyntes. Chuſing a cheefe & moſt perſpicuouſe, a valiant & moſt victoriouſe, a couragiouſe and moſt conqueroufe, a religiouſe and moſt redoubted Royall ſoueraigne King Henry the eight, as ſole ſupreme Patron and protector thereof againſt the cankered
35 curriſh kinde of caueling carpers. By cauſe his elder brother being named Arthure, he him ſelfe a moſt chriſtian King for all heroicall vertues commendable, the rather ſeemed to fauour

---

[1] Printed as the catchword, but not repeated on A⁴ back to begin the new page.

8   THE EPISTLE

and further the aduancement of the fame of his moſt renoumed aunceſtor this fame our ancient Arthure and the knightly traine of his rounde table. Hereupon by patent of his princely prerogatiue ordayned, graunted, and confirmed hee vnto this honorable Citie of London, free election of a Chieftaine and of 5 Citizens repreſenting the memory of that magnificent King Arthure, and the Knightes of the fame order, which ſhould for the mayntenance of ſhooting onely, meete together once a yeare, with folemne and friendly celebration therof. So much in his noble minde preuayled all prouident care of 10 princely proweſſe, valiancie, cheualrie, and actiuitie, that he not onely herein imitated the examplers of godly K. Dauid for his Iſraelites as before, and of that noble Emperour Leo in ouerthrowing idolatrie, and exalting archerie maugre the mallice of that Romane Antichriſt, and all his members: but alſo 15 inuincibly maintayned the praiſeworthie practize of this ſhooting in peace & wars by the examples of his princly progenitors. As after the [B] conqueſt, of K. Henry II. alias Beauclerck ſo ſirnamed, the firſt furtherer of K. Arthures benificencie, valiant Edward ſirnamed long & firſt vizitor of the faide Kinges tombe, 20 valiant and victorius Edward III. & *IIII*. bountious and liberall Richard *II*. good and gratiouſe Henry the V. wiſe, politique, iuſt, temperate, and graue King Henry the *VII*. his father. Neither hath this ceaſed in the branch, that flouriſhed in the bole : but by the milde, religiouſe, and gratiouſe King Edwarde 25 the *VI*. and now laſt of all by the Phenix of feminine ſex, our moſt redoubted Heſter and gratiouſe foueraigne Ladie Queene Elizabeth laudably laſteth in force and effect: whoſe highneſſe ſo many yeares humbling, not exalting her ſelfe the more by reaſon of her power, wholy fetteth her ſubiectes in 30 peace, preferring the fame. Now therefore (*Right honourable and worſhipfull*) as duetie bindeth euery degree to further the welfare of this bleſſed peace, and the profit of this excellent practiſe: proceede I humbly befeech you with noble Nehemias and thoſe godly fuperuiſors with dutifull diligence, with the one hand 35 holding your boes, and with the other hand as good laborers for your Prince & publique wealth, to beare the burdens of your vocation, towards the buylding of this earthly Ieruſalem, euen from the morning ſpring till the Starres come forth. Con-

2 Reg. 1.
Anno 730.

Heſt. Cap. 13.

2 Eſd. 4.

DEDICATORIE 9

tinually I fay accuftome your felues to feeke this peace of the
gofpell and to enfue the fame, ryde on I fay with renoume vpon
that *White Horfe whofe fitter hauing a boe and a croune giuen him* Reuel. 6.
hath promiffe from the mightie power of God, that he fhall go
5 *forth conquering and fhall ouercome.* That Chrift our King
of the vniuerfall Church with his croune and fepter, and with the
fhaftes of his mouth or worde and gofpell of peace may pearce
throughout the worlde to the aduancement of his glory which
fhal fit on the raineboe in his maieftie to iudge all Nations, (as
10 the feare of his holyneffe, mutuall loue in righteoufneffe, and
thankfulneffe for his benefites may moue all men) I haue
trauieled in the tranflation of this booke out of Latin into
Englifh, with all humble & [B back] true harted reuerence,
befeeching God to affift you right honourable Lord *D*eputie with
15 his omnipotent power, that as an inuincible Iofua you may continually *bring in the people to the due knowledge of God, and* Deut. 31.
obedience of our Prince: & as a notable Nehemias in true feare
of God without feare of foe buylde vp this earthly Ierufalem to
the perfection of that perpetuall peace, promifed in the heauenly
20 Ierufalem. Finally that you right honourable Lord Prefident,
and you right worfhipfull Mafter Thomas Smith with your
worfhipfull affociates, *Dayly praying for the peace of this* Pfal. 121.
Ierusalem, as the amitie thereof is fweete by the vnitie of your
mindes : So that, *Hoc fit longiffime vt periucundum fic cohabitare* Pfal. 132.
25 *fratres in vnum,* I according to my humble duty hartely do pray
vnto God, crauing pardon of your honours and worfhippes
generally for this my bold dedication. And befeeching you fauour-
ably to accept the fame in furderance of my poore ftudy of
dutifull well wifhing towardes my Prince & countrie : I humbly
30 and hartely befeech the eternall & omnipotent God to multiply
his manifolde mercies vpon your honours & worfhips, that being
all of one dutifull minde in God towardes the maieftie of our
moft facred foueraigne lady (vnder her long liuing in peaceable
profperitie) we may after this life attaine vnto that peaceable and
35 perpetuall kingdome of Heauen to raigne as coheires with
Chrift our Lord in the glory of his Father.   AMEN.

Your Honourable Lordfhips, and worthie Worfhips
moft humble and faithfull poore Orator
RICHARD ROBINSON,
Citizen of London.

I. L. *Ad Candidos Lectores.*

Delituit certé multis Arturius *annis,*
 Vera Brittannorum, Gloria, Lumen, Honos:
Diſpulit obſcuras alacer Lelandius *vmbras,*
 Sydereum mundo reſtituitque iubar. 5
Plaudite Lectores ſtudioſa caterua diſerti,
 Preſtitit officium candidus ille ſuum:
Hinc procul at fugiant Codrino felle tumentes,
 Ne proprio crepitent ilia rupta malo.

I. L. To the Syncere Readers. 10

Many yeeres ſurely *Arthure* hidden lay,
 Of Brittons, the Glory, Light & Honor true:
Cheerely hath *Leyland* driuen darke ſhadowes away,
 And yeelds the world bright ſhining *Sun* to view.
Of Learned Readers, reioyce yee ſtudious Crew, 15
 He ſincere did his Duetie bounden fulfill:
Farre hence flee thoſe their ſpyte which ſpew,
 Leaſt their Inteſtines burſt with their owne ill.

[B² back]
The Table of the names of thofe *Authors*, whofe teftimonies this prefent *Booke vfeth.*

Foraine writers.

5 Lucanus. ⎫
  Iuuenall. ⎬ Poets.
  Martiall. ⎭
  Cornelius Tacitus.
  Paulus Diaconus. ⎫
10 Claudius Gallus. ⎪
   Iohannes Anneuillanus. ⎪ Hifto-
   Valerius. ⎬ rio-
   Boccace. ⎪ gra-
   Diuionenfis. ⎪ phers
15 Ponticus Virunnius. ⎭

Brittaine writers.
Theliefinus.
20 Ambrofius Maridunenfis.
Merlinus Caledonius.
Melchinus.
Patricius Gleffoburgenfis.
Gildas Bannochorenfis.
25 Anonymus.
Nennius.
Samuell.
Beda Girouicanus.

Brittaine writers.
Afferius Meneuenfis.
Gulielmus Meildunenfis.
Galfridus Monemuthenfis.
Aluredus Fibroleganus.
Henricus Venantodunenfis.
Iofephus Ifcanus.
Siluefter Giraldus.
Matheus Parifius.
Iohannes Chyfiftoriographus.
Gulielmus Paruus.
Iohannes Fiberius.
Thomas Vicanus.
Ranulphus Higedenus.
Mattheus Florilegus.
Iohannes Burgenfis.
Thomas Melorius.
Scalechronica.
Chronica Durenfia.
Chronica Gleffoburgenfia.
Chronica Perforana.

2. Cor. 13.
Nihil contra veritatem agere poffumus, fed pro Veritate.

Prou. 12. *Labium Veritatis firmum in perpetuum.*
30 *Prou.* 21. *Teftis autem mendax peribit.*
Efdra 3. 9. *Super omnia autem vincit Veritas.*

[B³] *Certaine memorable Notes inserted into this Assertion since the Translation thereof. By Ric. Ro.*

AS *Pliny* faith, *Ingenui pudoris eft fateri per quos profeceris:* So I muft freely confeffe the friendly helps of thofe which profited me in this purpofe.

Firft by conference with Mafter *Steuen Batman*, a learned Preacher and friendlie fauourer of vertue and learning, (touching the praife worthie progenie of this *K. Arthure*) he gaue me this affured knowledge on this manner taken out of his Auncient records written at *Aualonia*.

Verfes found in certaine Cronicles, wherein were difcourfes had of *Aruiragus* king of *Brittaine* 45. yeeres after the natiuite of *Chrifte*.

> *Twelue men in number entered the Vale of Aualon :*
> *Iofeph of Aramathia was the chiefeft flowre of them.*
> *Iofeph the fonne of Iofeph, his father dia attend,*
> *With other tenne : and Glafton did poffeffe.*

There alfo, this writing did witneffe, that *K. Arthure* of greate *Brittaine* defcended of the ftocke of yᵉ faide *Iofeph* viz. *Helarius* the Nephewe of *Iofeph* begate *Iofue*, *Iofue* begate *Aminadab*, *Aminadab* begate *Caftellors*, *Caftellors* begate *Manaell*, *Manaell* begate *Lambord* and *Vrlard*, and *Lambord* begatte a fonne that begate *Igerna* of which woman, king *Vther Pendragon* begate the noble and renoumed *King Arthure*. Whereby it plainely appeareth, that *K. Arthure* defcended of the ftocke of *Iofeph*.

Againe, like wife of the fame kindred (whereof *K. Arthure* came) proceeded thefe auncient *Brittaines* alfo.

Peter the Cofen of *Iofeph* of *Aramathia*, king of *Arcadia*, begate E*rlan*, *Erlan* begate *Melianus*, *Melianus* begate *Arguthe*, *Arguthe* begate *Edor*, *Edor* begate *Lotho* which maried to wife fifter of *K. Arthure*, of whom *Lotho* begate 4 fonnes, to wit,

Walwanus Agranaius, *Guerelies*, and *Garelies:* all which were noble men of authoritie in Brittaine where they dwelt.

[B³ back] Moreouer he fhewed me out of his auncient records the interchaunges of king *Arthures* armes which hee gaue in three chiefs, from the firft to the third: viz.

His firft armes he bare in a fhield *Gules*, (red) three *Serpentes*, *Or*. gold.

His fecond hee bare in a fhield *Vert*, (greene) a plaine *Croſſ- argent*: in chiefe the figure of the *Virgin Marie* with *Chrifte* in her armes.

His third and laft in a fhield *Azure*, (blew) three c[r]ownes, *Or*, (gold.)

But after knowledge of thefe feuerall armes, I had intelligence of a certaine French booke, wherein he is reported to [h]aue giuen in a fhielde *Azure* (blew) 13. Crownes, *Or*. gold.

This booke beeing in an Englifh mans handes, I was not fo defirous to fee it, but he as willingly fhewed it & lent it me. There was in it portracted both the feuerall names, fhieldes, and feuerall armes in colours alfo depainted of all *K. Arthures* knights and vnder euery one the commendation due vnto him by his cheualrie. Which becaufe the engrauing of their armes was very chargeable, & the circumftance of matter more then I could in fo fhorte time publifh in the Englifh tongue: I was enforced to content me with this briefe collection concerning *K. Arthure*, and with the names of 16. kinges, one Duke, and 149. knightes, fo many as were therein printed. viz.

Of King Arthure himfelfe it faith
Directly vnder his fhield thus.

King Arthure did beare in his fhield *Azure* (blew) 13. Crownes of golde. He was a greate conquerour, and of noble and valiant proweffe, hee inftituted the order of the rounde Table in the kingdome of greate *Brittaine*: Unto the which he appointed all his chofen knightes at Whitfontide yeerely to come, and holde their Homage of him by the fame order.

[B⁴] Now followeth the names of thofe knightes

And firſt how many kinges.

Kinges.

1 Le Roy Meliadus.
2 Le Roy Ban de Benock.
3 Le Roy Boort de Gauues.
4 Le Roy Karados.
5 Le Roy Lac.
6 Le Roy de Clares.
7 Le Roy Vrien.
8 Le Roy Lottho de Orchany.
9 Le Roy Ryon.
10 Le Roy Pelinor.
11 Le Roy Baudemagus de Gorre.
12 Le Roy Pharamondo.
13 Le Roy Galganoys de Norgalles.
14 Le Roy Aguifant d'Efcoffe.
15 Le Roy Malaquin d'outre les marches de Gallounne.
16 Le Roy Claudas.

I

1 Le Duke de Clarence.

Knightes.

1 Meffier Lancelot du Lac.
2 Boort de ga[nn]es.
3 Gawain d'Orchany.
4 Meffier Triftran de Lyonnoys.
5 Lyonet de Ga[nn]es.
6 Helias le Blanc.
7 Hector des Mares.
8 Bliomberis de Gauues.
9 Gaherriet.
10 Keux le Senefchall.
11 Meffier Yuaine.
12 Bruor le Noir.
13 Baudoyer le Coneftable.
14 Agruall de Galles.
15 Segurades.
16 Patris le Hardy.
17 Efclabor le Meffoniez.
18 Saphar le méfcognieu.
19 Sagremor le defree.
20 Gyron le Curtoys.
21 Seguram le Brun.
22 Galehault le Blanc.
23 Le Morholt de Ireland.
24 Danayn le Roux.
25 Amilan de Seffougné.

26 Brallain.
27 Brallain que lon difoit le Cheualier a[ux] d[eu]x efpees.
28 Gallehaulte.
29 Lamorat de Lyfthenoys.
30 Brunor de Ga[nn]es.
31 Le bon Cheualier de Norgalles.
32 Henry de Ryuell.
33 Meffier Gullat.
34 Gueherres.
35 Aggrauaine le Orguilleux.
36 Mordrec de Orchany.
37 Gyrfflet.
38 Dodynel le Sauaige.
39 Yuain le Auoutre.
40 Ozement Coeurhardy.
41 Gualegantine le Galloys.
42 Gaherriet de Lemball.
43 Mador de la porte.
44 Bamers le forcene.
45 Dynadam de Eftrangor.
46 Herret le filz de lac.
47 Artus le petit.
48 Cinglant Rochmont.
49 Artus lesbloy.
50 Guallogrenant de Windezores.
51 Kandelis.
52 Merangis des portz.
52 Gauuaine le franc.
53 Gnades le fort.
54 Pharas le Noir.
55 Pharas le Roux.
56 Iambegues le Garruloys.
57 Taulas de la mountaine.
58 Abandam le fortune.
59 Damatha de folime*n*t.
60 Amand le bel Ioufteur.
61 Ganefmor le Noir.
62 Arphin le Dire.
63 Arconftant le adures.
64 Le Beau courant.
65 Le laid hardy.
66 Andelis le Roux ferré.
67 Bruyant des Ifles.
68 Ozenall de Effrangeé.
69 Le Cheualier de Efther.
70 Le Varlet de Gluyn.
71 Heroys le ioyeux.
72 Fergus du blanc lieu.

15

73 Lot le Coureur.
74 Meliadus del Efpinoy.
75 Meliadus a[u] noir [œ]il.
76 Ayglius des vaux.
77 Iamburg du Chaftell.
78 Meffire Clamorat.
79 Surados des fept fontanes.
80 Le Varlet au Circle.
81 Kaedins de Lonizein.
82 Lucane le Boutellier.
83 Brumer de la fountaine.
84 Lenfant du pleffies.
85 Perfides legent.
86 Sibilias aux dures mai[n]s.
87 Sinados le Efile.
88 Arphazat le groz cœur
89 Le blonde Amoreux.
90 Argahac le Beau.
91 Normaine le Pelerin.
92 Harmaine le felon.
93 Tofcane le Romane.
94 Landone le Leger.
95 Le fort troue.
96 Le Noir Perdu.
97 Le fortune de lifle.
98 Le fee des Dames.
99 Le Forefter de De*n*newich.
100 Le Chaffeur de o[u]tres les marches.
101 Ieyr & Landoys de Rufe.
102 Geoffroy le Lancoys.
103 Randowin le perfien.
104 Froyadus le Gay.
105 Rouffelin de la autre mo*n*de.
106 Gurrant le Roche dure.
107 Arm. on. ouuerd ferpent.
108 Ferrand du tertre.
109 Thor le filz de Arez.
110 lupin des croix.
111 Ydeux le fort Tyrant.
112 Bolinian du Boys.

113 Le bon Cheualier fa*n*s paour.
114 Brouadas le Efpaignoll.
115 Brechus fans Pitye.
116 Malignain.
117 Le Cheualeur de Scallot.

[B⁴ back]

118 Melias de l'Efpine.
119 Agrœr le fel Patrides au Circle d'Or.
120 Mandius le noir.
121 Perceuall de Gallis.
122 Aeuxdeftraux.
123 Lamant du Boys.
124 Melianderis de Sanfen.
125 Mandrin le Sage.
126 Kalahart le petite.
127 Sadoc de Vencon.
128 Perandon le pauure.
129 Verrant de la Roche.
130 Le Brun fans ioy.
131 Bufterin le grand.
132 Le Cheualier des fept voyes.
133 Gryngaloys le fort.
134 Malaquin le Galoys.
135 Agricole Beau grand.
136 Gualiandres du Tettre.
137 Margondes le Rongo.
138 Kacerdius de la Vallee.
139 Nabon le fel.
140 Talamor le Voland.
141 Alibel de Logres.
142 Dalides de la Ryuier.
143 Arain du pine*n*.
144 Arganor le riche.
145 Melias le Beau Cheualier.
146 Meliadus le Blanc.
147 Malaquin le gros.
148 Meffier Palamides.
149 Alexander le Orphelin.

{ Summa totalis 166 Knightes. } whereof { Kinges 16. Duke 1. Knightes 149.¹ }

Kinges

3. Text, *Gauues.*

Knightes

2. Text, *gauues*, 5, 30, Gauues.
27. Text, *an duex.*

75. Text, *an noir œil.*
81. *Lonizein* for *Lonizern*?
86. Text, *maius.*
100. Text, *ontres.*
136. Text, *du Tettre* for *du Tertre*?

¹ A miscount for 150.

Befides notice of thefe I vfed in my tranflation
from time to time, the helpe (of Mafter *Iohn Stow*, &
*Maeſtr Cambde*n diligent fearchers in antiquities)
for the interpretation of thofe hard brittifh and
Welch Townes or names of places, which neither
Mafter Leyland the Collector of this Affertion had
expounded perfectlie, neither I my [felfe¹ the
tranflator could otherwife of my
felfe haue perfourmed. For the
which I am to gratifie them
as the others alfo before
recyted.

¹ Text, *felfe*.

The Aſſertion of K. Arthure.

EVident it is, by the ſpeciall agreement of Greeke and Latine writers, that *Hercules* was borne of *Alcmena*, by the adultery of *Iupiter*. But by what manner of perſon, or how mightie in times paſt hee was, I ſuppoſe is euen of the meanely learned better knowne, then that at this preſent needeth any further Inſinuation. And very many others there were borne in adultery, (as by the Auncient Hiſtory largely appeareth) whoſe proweſſe at home, and in warres, notably excelled. Amongeſt whome also our *Arthure*, the chiefeſt ornament of *Brittayne*, and the onely myracle of his time, floriſhed famouſly. May I therefore bee ſo bolde by good leaue of *Gulielmus Paruus*, yea and ſo of his most mightie ſucceſſour in place, *Polidorus*, euen with condigne praiſes to commend my countryman *Arthure*: and with the ſame dilligence to leane vnto the Brittiſh hiſtory interpreted by *Geoffrey* of *Munmouth* a man not altogether vnlearned, (what ſoeuer otherwiſe perſons ignorant of antiquitie, which thinke themſelues to haue knowledge, ſhall say) as vnto a firme defence, rather then vnto the fond fables or baſe ſtuffe of forraine writers. Truly, in fables which haue crept into the hiſtory of *Arthure*, I doe not more delite, then *Polidorus*, the Judge. But to bee afraide of any man by reaſon of his greate age, or eloquence, or authoritie, finally as like a fooliſh forſaker of the truth, I ſhoulde ſo leaue her partes vndefended: that certainely will I neuer doe: An other way, do equity, honeſty, the rule of fame, and heerehence a iuſt loue to my country, yea truth it ſelfe (then which one thing, nothing more deare I loue) fully moue me: But yet neither thinke I to wage battaile with yᵉ Learned: In meane time, yet by good reaſon it ſhall be free for me, to make moſt famous the ſtate of my countrie, and ſpecially the partes of truth, euen with ſinguler

[margin: William Paruus & Polidorus Virgilius, two aduerſaries of K. Arthures fame.]

[margin: The Authors good purpoſe in this worke.]

dilligence, expedyte induſtry, cheerefull labour, prompt counſell, quicke iudgment, yea, and finally by all meanes. Therefore, truſting in the good will, humanitie, and courteous fauour of the honeſt readers, I will now attempt ſomewhat more, circumſpectly to finde out *Prince Arthures* Originall, euen from the very egge.

  Eſt locus Abrini ſinuoſo littore ponti,
   Rupe fitus media, refluus quem circuit æſtus,
  Fulminat hic laté, turrito vertice Caſtrum,
   Nomine Tindagium, veteres dixere Corini.

A place there is ith' winding ſhoare of th' Abryne Sea by name,
 Scituate in middeſt of a rocke, wheare ebbing tyde the ſame,
Enuironeth. A Caſtle here with towery top ſhines bright,
 (By auncient Corniſh men ſo called) which Tintagill tho hight.

  A Conſtant fame is there giuen out by the voyce of manie, and alſo confirmed with the wrytinges of Learned men, that *Gorloys* the Gouernour of *Cornewale* had heere his habytation for him, and his. He had to wife *Igerna*, a woman no doubt of moſt louely Feature, but of an Improbate or vitious Chaſtitie. Hether ſomewhat oftener for recreation of his minde, repayred *Vther*, kinge of the *Brittaines*, and ſurnamed *Pendragon*: So called for his Serpentine or ſubtile wiſedome, (as I ſuppoſe) whoſe friendlie wellwiller *Gorloys* alſo was.

  Architrenius in his fifth booke (if I count aright) writes theſe verſes.

  Hoc trifido mundum, Corinei poſtera ſole,
   Irradiat Pubes, quartiqu*e* puerpera Phœbi,
  Pullulat *Arturum,* facie dum falſo adulter
   Tintagoll irrumpit, nec amoris *Pendragon* æſtum,
  Vincit, & omnificas *Merlini* conſulit artes.
  Mentiturqu*e* Ducis habitus & Rege latenti,
  Induit abſentis preſenti *Gorloys* ora.

The after coming youth, lightens the world of Coriney
 With his three clouen ſonne ; & ſhe that brought forth at that day

<small>Vther Pendragon king Art. father.</small>

K. Arthure

The fourth Phoebus, broght forth Arthur, *whilst the adulterer he*
[2] *Euen* Tintagol *so false of face brake in most wickedly.*
Neither Pendragon *vanquished the flaming fire of Loue,*
But Merlins *artes so manifold by counsel seekes to proue:*
5 *And counterfeites the Dukes attyre (as while the King did glose*
Thus) He put on the present face of absent Duke Gorlois.

CUstome, acquaintance, and companying together doe sette loue one fire. And becaufe as a certaine Poet fayth (Lis est *Twixt Comelinesse and Chastitie, greate Debate there seemes to bee.*) Lust gotte the mastery ouer *Igernaes* Chastitie: Wherevppon also afterwardes *Arthure* was begotten of her, together with a beautifull virgin, named *Anna.* It must not heere be omitted whereof *Hector Boetius* makes relation: namelie that *Vther* at length slue 15 *Gorloys*, as hee was fighting in the behalfe of *Nothaleos* Gouernour, agaynst the *Saxonnes*, and forsaken of him, that euen the rather hee might more freely obtayne his will of *Igerna*. But the name of *Arthures* is knowne to bee noble with the Romaynes, yea and also familyer amongest them: that from hence *Iuuenall* 20 the *Poet* in his third *Satyre* writeth these.

_{Ouid Epist. 9.}

_{Vther Pendragon begat Arthur of Igerna the wife of Gorloys, Gouernour of Cornwale, and also a Virgin named Anna.}

Cedamus Patria, Viuant *Arthurius* istic, & *Catulus*.

*Fr*om *our Countrie depart let vs: There* Arthure *liue &* Catulus.

Samuell the Brittish writer describeth the starre *Arcturus* 25 so called *Per Cappa ad vrsam*, alluding, that hee taketh his name or signification thereof from the Greeke Originall. But here it ought not to redounde vnto *Arthures* preiudice or reproch, that the father being an adulterer did leaue after him a sonne borne to valiant courage, prosperitie, & triumphant victories: 30 seeing he was not in fault, that he the lesse proceeded from lawfull matrimony, seeing that he afterwardes proued both a valiant and honest person.

_{Originall of Arth. name.}

Nam genus & Proauos, & quæ non fecimus ipsi,
Vix ea nostra puto.

_{Ouid 13. lib. Metam.Fab. 1.}

*For kindred & forefathers, eke which we
Have not begun, I scarce thinke ours to be.*

<small>Iohn Stowe.

Then an ancient Cittie, which was neere faint Albones, the foundations where of are yet apparant.</small>

How greatly alfo the childe profpered in vertue, it then appeared, what time his father (who had florifhed in ftrength, Counfell and Iudgemente alfo not without Glorie) de-[2 back] parted out of this life at *Verolamium*, having ordayned beefore, the dignitie Royall vnto his bafe gotten fonne, becaufe he had none borne in lawfull matrimony.

Chap. ii.

K. Arthures Coronation.

<small>Iohn Stow.
What time Arthur was crowned.
A. D. [5]16.
Graius a writer his testimony.
Iohn Stow.</small>

The hiftory of *Brittaine* affirmeth that *Arthure* began his Raigne ouer the Iflandes of this kingdome in the xv. yeare of his age, and was crowned of *Dubritius* Bifhop of the City of *Caerlegion* vpon *Vfke* in *Wales*. Iohannes ye writer of the golden hiftory feemeth to accounte vpon xviii. yeeres when *Arthure* afcended vp to the Roayll feate. *Scalæcronica*, of which booke (as I am moued by coniecture) one *Gray*, was Author, doe say, that *Arthure* receaued the dignitie of his crowne at *Venta* alias *Caerguent* now called *Winchefter*. The two rulers of the *Pictes* and *Scots* viz. *Lotho*, vnto whome *Anne* the fifter of *Aurelius Ambrofius*, king of *Brittaines* was maried, and *Conranus*, vnto whome *Ada* the fifter of *Anne* was efpoufed, began to enuy at the fame fo ioyfull profperitie of *Arthure*: for <small>Two Rulers of the Pictes afpire vnto Arthures kingdome.</small> both of them, but efpecially *Lotho* afpyred vnto the Dominion of *Brittaine*. Heereuppon followed afterwardes, that hee ioyning vnto him *Ofca*, otherwise *Occa*, a moft filthye person, made warre againft *Arthure*. At length the matter came to hande ftroakes, and the *Pict* beeing ouercome, had the worfe fucceffe, partly by the helpe or furtherance of the most inuincible *Hoel*, who plaied the Captaines parte there.

<small>Battle and victory ouer Arthur his enemies by</small> The little booke of the Empyre of the *Brittaynes* and *English* men vpon the *Scottes* their friendly wellwillers, affirmeth this victory to bee obtayned at *Yorke* by the saide *Hoel*. And that

K. Arthure

(the *Scotles* beeing vanquiſhed) *Arthure* left the auncyent Dominions (by petitions beeing ſo moued) vnder the rule of his friende *Auguſellus*, whom hee made *Gouernour* ouer them. Neither did better fortune happen vnto the *Saxonnes*: when as
5 *Colgrino* the Duke was ſlaine, and *Baldricus* with *Childricke* fledde away. After victorie enſewed Concord. *Lotho* [3] yeelded him ſelfe vnto the *Brittaynes*, *Mordred* and *Galloambieuinus* the Sonnes of *Lothon* by *Anne*, beſought *Arthure* of favour & pardon by wonderfull meanes, and at length were made friendes.
10 In the meane ſeaſon had *Arthure* married *Guenhera* daughter vnto *Cadorus* the Duke of Cornwale, a woman of rare beawtie. Afterwards also he ſubdued vnto him the *Saxones* with moſt bloudy battels.

margin: Hoel his friend.

margin: Arthure married Guenhera the daughter of Cadorus Duke of Cornwaile.

Chap. iii.

The XII. Battelles fought by *Arthure*.

15 *Nennius* the *Brittaine* a writer of good and auncient credit, amongſt many others maketh moſt lightſome mention of his battels: whoſe wordes although by the negligence of Printers and iniurie of time, they be ſomewhat diſplaced, yet notwith-
20 ſtandinge becauſe they make much for our preſent matter, and bring with them a certaine reuerent antiquitie, I will here ſet them downe, and in their order. *Arthure* fought in deed againſt thoſe *Saxones*, with the gouernours of the *Britaines*, but he himſelfe was generall. The firſt battell was at the entraunce of the ﬂoude called *Gleyn, alias Gledy*. The ſecond, third, fourth,
25 and fift, was vpon an other ﬂoud called *Dugles*, which is in the Countrie of *Lynieux*. The ſixt was vpon the ﬂoud which is called *Baſſas*. The ſeauenth was in the wood *Caledon*, that is, *Catcoit Celidon*. The eight in the Caſtle of *Gwynyon*. The nynth was fought in the Cittie of *Caerlegion* vpon *Vske*. The
30 tenth on the Sea ſhore, which is called *Traitheurith*, otherwiſe *Rhydrwyd*. The eleauenth in the hill Which is called *Agned Cathregonion*. The twelfth in the mount *Badonis*, wherein many were ſlaine by one aſſault of *Arthure*. Thus farre wit- neſſeth *Nennius*.

margin: 1, 2, 3, 4, 5, 6, 7, 8, 9, Iohn Stow 10, 11, 12. Some iudge this to be Bathe.

35 *Iohannes* the wryter of the golden hiſſtorie ratifyeth the ſelfe

margin: Iohn the writer of the

The Assertion of

[margin: golden hiftory.] fame truth touching the twelue battels fought againft thofe Saxones.

Aluredus Fibroleganus, the hiftoreographer alfo declareth the like.

[margin: Henry of Huntington.] And fo thefe are the wordes of *Henry* firnamed of *Hun-* [3 back]*tington* in the fecond booke of his hiftory. *Arthure* the warrier, in thofe dayes the Captaine generall of foldiours, and of the rulers in *Brittaine*, fought moft valiantly againft the *[margin: King Arthure Xij times General, and Xij times Conquerour.]* Saxons. Twelue times was he generall of the battell, and twelue times got he the victory. And there alfo. But the battels and places wherein they were fought a certaine hiftoriographer declareth.

Henry of *Huntington* feemeth here to haue hitte vpon the breefe hiftory of *Nennius*, the name of whofe exemplar (as it feemeth) was not fet downe. Herehence came that filence. Neyther was that booke common in mens handes at that time, and in this our age is furely moft rare: onely three exemplars *[margin: Iohn Rhefus a louer of Antiquitie.]* do I remember that I haue feene, *Iohn Rhefus* a louer of Antiquitie, & the fame a diligent fetter forth thereof, hath a little booke entituled *Gilde*, which booke (fo farre as I gather by his fpeach) had not to Authour *Gildas*, but *Nennius*.

[margin: Iohn Stow.] The *Elenchus* or Regiftred Table of the librarie at Batle Abbey, accounteth the hiftorie of *Gildas* among there treafures, I haue diligently enquyred for the booke: but as yet haue I not found it. The Reporte is, that the exemplar was tranflated or carried to *Brecknocke* there to be kept.

Now muft we report the Battels.

[margin: Iohn Stow.] The writer of the life of the reuerent *Dubritius*, Archebifhop of the Cittie *Caerlegion* vpon *Vsk*, not vnelegantly, doth com- *[margin: What time Arthure fucceeded Vther his Father.]* memorate fuch like matters. When at length *Aurelius* the King was made away by poyfon, (and that *Vther*, his brother ruled a few yeares) *Arthure* his Sonne by the helpe of *Dubritius* fucceded in gouernement, who with bold courage fet vpon the *[margin: Arthure could not cleane roote all the Saxones out of Brittaine.]* *Saxones* in many battels, and yet could he not vtterly roote them out of his Kingdome. For the *Saxones* had fubdued vnto them felues the whole compaffe of the Ifland which ftretcheth from the water of *Humber* vnto the Sea *Catteneffinum* or *Scottifh* Sea. For that caufe the Peares of the Realme being called

K. Arthure 23

together, he determined by their counfell what he might beft do, againft the [4] irruption of the Pagane *Saxones*. At length by common counfell he fendeth into *Armorica*, (that is to say, the leffer *Brittaine*,) vnto King *Hoel* his Ambaffadors, which aduer- 5 tifed him at full, touching the calamitie of the *Brittaines*, who comming with fiftene thoufand of armed men into *Brittaine* was honorably entertayned of *Arthure*, and *D. Dubritius*: going vnto the Cittie of *Lincolne* befeeged of the *Saxones*, hauing fought ye battell, there were fix thoufand of *Saxones* which 10 eyther being drowned or wounded with weapons, dyed. But the others flying away vnto the wood of *Caledon*, being befseged by the *Brittaines*, were conftrayned to yeeld themfelues: and pledges being taken for tribute yearely to be paied, he gaue them leaue with their fhippes onely to returne into their Countrie. 15 Afterwardes within a fhort time the *Saxones* were afhamed of the league made: and hauing recouered their ftrength, they made their league as voyde, and befeeged the Cittie *Badon* rounde aboute, which now is called *Bathe*: this when *Arthure* hearde of, hauinge gathered his hoafte together, and beholding the 20 Tentes of his enemies, he fpake thus vnto them.

Becaufe the moft vngodly *Saxones*, difdaine to keepe promife with me, I keeping faith with my God, will endeuoure to be aduenged of them for the bloud and flaughter of my Citizens: Let vs therefore manfully fet vpon thofe Traytours whom by 25 the Mediation of Chrift out of all doubt we fhall ouercome with a wifhed triumphe. And hee rufhing vpon the ranckes of the *Saxones*, beinge helped by the prayers of *Dubritius* in ouer- throwing many thoufandes, obtayned the victorie: and the few which fled this garboyle, he caufed them to yeelde to his mercy.

30 *Boccace* in his booke of Lakes and Marifhes, thus wryteth. *Murais* that Lake fo called famous is, by the victory of *Arthure*, King of *Brittaine*: for men fay that the *Scottes*, *Pictes* and *Irifhmen* being by him befeeged, were compelled to yeelde themfelues there. The fame Authour in his viii. booke of 35 *Famoufe Perfonages* maketh a notable mention of *Arthure* being moued with a certaine [4 back] Godly zeale, to the end he would not with vnthankfull filence ouerpaffe, fo mighty a perfonage, and fo worthie a man. Neyther here are thofe thinges which appeare in the Cronicles of a certaine writer

[Side notes: Hoel King of Brittaine aides him with a powe[r] of 15000 men. Lincolne befeeged by the Saxones. Their flaughter and f[l]ight. Bath befeeged by the Saxons. K. Arthure feekes to be aduenged of the Saxones. His wordes. His victorie ouer them. Boccace mentioneth of Arthure. M. Camden.]

24   *The Affertion of*

<small>Cerdicius the Saxon helde warre with Arthure.</small> of *Digion* differing from our purpofe. *Cerdicius* hauing more often conflict with *Arthure*, if he were one moneth vanquifhed, he more fharply affaulted in another moneth. At length
<small>Arth. friendly to his foo.</small> *Arthure*, with irkfome toyle fo being awearied, after the xii yeare of *Cerdicius* his comming (by fealtie to him fworne) gaue him the Country *Auonia* Southwarde and *Somaria* : which part *Cerdicius* called *Weft faxony*.

<small>William of Malmfbury.</small> *Gulielmus a Medulphi curia* both a gallant writer, and alfo a learned, and which thing firft in his hiftory (he as moft faithfull) in his firft booke of the Kinges of *Britaine* mencioneth,
<small>Arthure fore diftreffed had it not bene for Ambrose a Romaine.</small> bringeth in by the way thefe teftimonies, of *Arthure*. And now truly had it come to an euill paffe with the *Brittaines* (as he vnderftoode) had not *Ambrofe* onely of the *Romans* bene left aliue, (who after *Vortigerus*, was *Monarke or King*), with the furpaffing exployt of warlike *Arthure*, repreffed the outragioufe barbarouse enemies¹ of the Kingdome.

<small>Gildas.</small> Moreouer hetherunto feeme thefe things to pertaine, which in the fragmentes of *Gildas* the *Brittaine* are reade after this manner. The *Brittaines* like conquerours take courage to them, prouocating their enemies to fight, vnto whom by the Lordes good pleafure the victorie fell euen to their defire. From that time, otherwhiles the Citizens, otherwhiles the enemies got the vpper hand, that in this people it might be approued, how the Lord after his accuftomed manner, dealt with this prefent *Ifraell*, and whether he loued the fame, yea, or no, euen vnto the yeare of the feege of the mount *Badon*, and laftly almoft of the petty fpoylers there, in no litle hurlyburly, whereas euen I my felfe was borne. Thefe faith *Gildas*. Behold the flaunderer is now prefent, and as one cruell of eye fight, requireth a reafon of
<small>Aduerfaries quarrel againft Arthure.</small> me, why *Gildas* remembreth not *Arthure*, if he were then liuing. To thefe I anfwere, that I will hereafter fpeake of *Gildas*. In meane time the aduerfarie calleth to minde, that *Gildas* when the [5] battaile was fought at *Bathe*, was but an Infant : By reafon whereof euen his Actes done or not done of him, fomewhat flenderly are vnderftood by the aduerfarie.

<small>William of Malmesburie a friendly writer.</small> *Gulielmus a Medulphi Curia*, a little before, beareth fo honourable a teftimonie of *Arthure*, that fmally it fhall differ, whether, if

---

¹ Text, *enemines*.

K. Arthure 25

not fuperiour, yet as equall hee reputed him with *Ambrofe*. But *Nennius* an Authour of no bad credite, so much perfourmed in fauour of *Aurelius Ambrofius* as *Gildas* in the fauour of Arthure : Uiz. that leauing out the name of the one, hee might attribute vprightly by iuſt caufe vnto the other all honour, concerning the battle fought at *Bathe*. But neither doe thefe alone performe this : There are a number of good authours, which confirme the felfe fame matter with a certaine iuſt Authority. Except in meane time, he be fo vniuſt a Iudge, that he allowe of nothing, bee it neuer fo credible, which fmelleth not of *Tullie* or *Liuy*, when he him felfe in meane time fmelleth I know not what of *Æmilius* : Which thing fhall not difpleafe me, when I fhall vnderſtand, that hee franckely confeffeth this matter. In the meane while I wil recyte the teſtimony of that *Iohn* which concerning *Arthure* write the golden hiſtorie. This yeere beeing the tenth of *Cerdicius*, king of the Weſt *Saxones*, did arife *Arthure* among yᵉ *Brittaines*, a moſt valiant warrier.

Nennius in fauour of another.

Chap. iiii.

K. Arthures expedition towardes the French.

The fixte booke of the *Hiſtory of Brittaine* fpeaketh copiouſly touching things done by *Arthure* in *Fraunce* : vnto which countrie he went not, before hee had forefeene (as it feemed then in deede) with aduifed counfell, the immunitie or difburdenance of *Brittaines* troubles. He had to Nephewe one *Mordred* by name, fonne of *Lotho*, king of the *Pictes* & of *Anna* fiſter of *Aurelius Ambrofius* king of *Brittaine*. Unto this man, becaufe hee was moſt neareſt in bloodde, and familiar in acquaintance, did hee committe all his kingdome, together with *Guenhera* his moſt louing wife. For *Mordred*, in refpect of forti-[5 back]tude or magnanimitie, was moſt commendable, and befides this for his quicke and prompt witte, in accomplifhing his affayres : which vertues, had hee not obfcured with most ardent luſt of ruling, and offence of adultery, (but in meane time at firſt kept clofe for feare) hee had in deede beene worthie to haue beene accompted amongſt the moſt famous perfonages. Nowe had *Arthure* entered into

Mordred Arthure his Nephewe, put in great truſt.

His vertues mixt with vices.

Fraunce, and the Gouernors being fubdued, hee had left a notable teftimony of his proweffe there. Behold, now commeth a fauage Tyraunt, cruell and fierce, who had rauifhed *Helen* the neece of *Hoel* of *Armorica*, or the leffe *Brittaine* (ftolen away and brought out of *Brittaine*) at the coafte of *Fraunce*, and where vpon fhe died. *Arthure* could not take well this fo heynous a reproach done vnto *Helen*, and ftraight way gotte the Tyraunte by the throate, that hee vtterly deftroyed this greate and horrible Monfter. And not longe after did *Hoel* caufe to bee erected a facred Tombe for *Helen* in the Iflande where fhe died, and a name fitly giuen vnto the place where *Helens* Tombe was made, which ferueth euen till this daye. The Cronicles of the writer of *Digion* in *Burgonie*, doe with greate commendation extolle *Arthure* warring in *Fraunce*, by thefe like wordes.

Arthure for nine yeeres fpace, fubdued *Fraunce* vnto him, hauing betaken his kingdome and *Queene* vnto *Mordred* his Nephew. But he defiring ambitioufly to raigne (yet fearing only *Cerdicius*) gaue him, to the end hee fhould fauour his doinges, feauen other prouinces. viz. *Sudo Saxony* or Southfex, *Sudorheiam* or Southery, *Berrochiam* or *Barckefhyre* : *Vilugiam* or *Wiltfhier* : *Duriam* or *Dorcetfhier* : *Deuoniam* or *Deuonfhier* : and *Corineam Cornwale*. And *Cerdicius* confenting vnto thefe (fending for y*e* englifhme*n*) reftored his prouinces, and was crowned after the manner of the countrie at *Wintchefter*. But *Mordred* was crowned ouer the *Brittaines* at *London*. And fo *Cerdicius*, whe*n* he had raigned three yeeres, died, while *Arthure* yet remayned amongeft the *French* : vnto whome *Kinrichus* fucceeded. In the Seauenth yeere of whofe Raigne *Ar*-[6]*thure*, returned into Englande. Thus farre out of the *Cronicles*. Thefe which I haue nowe recited, haue not onely their antiquitie, but alfo credite, and with a certaine circumftance are confonant to the Hiftory.

And that I may fomwhat more friendly fpeake in fauour of *A*[*r*]*thures* Tryumphes ouer the French, there are (befides thefe) many thinges, which I with a certaine zeale doe omitte altogether. But yet, that muft I as it were touch by paffing ouer the reft : viz. that it is manifeft by the infcription of *Arthures* greate Seale (concerning which wee will in place conuenient fpeake circumfpectly) that he was made famous by the firname of a French man. And neither was this donne without manyfeſt occaſion, at any time. For, as touching the Antiquytie and euen moſt ſure knowledge of the Seale, ſo euidently, I doubt not, but that I may aſſuredly beleeue (ſo their appears vpright Iudges heerein, and which are ſkilfull in auncient monumentes) that I ſhall proue by notable reaſons, the ſame was proper, peculier and naturall, and proceeding from the workemaſter. But these thinges more rightly appeare in there place. I will at this inſtant onely heereto adioyne one *Valerius*, which remembreth vs of thirtie kingdomes vanquiſhed by *Arthure*. For in thoſe dayes a greate company of Gouernoures helde vnder their Iureſdictio*n* the Iſlands together with *Fraunce* and *Germany*.

Valerius reporting that K. Arthure vanquiſhed 30. kingdomes.

Chap. v.

K. Arthures Familier Cheualyers, or knightes.

SOme man woulde peraduenture here looke for, that I ſhoulde alſo with a mightie praiſe blaze on the victoryes of *Arthure*, touching which the hiſtorie of *Brittaine* reporteth. Hiſtoriographers doe contend in this behalfe, and the controuerſie, as yet reſteth vnder the Iudge. But I will declare nothing raſhly: For ſo much as it appeareth most euidently, that both obſcure and abſurde reportes haue crept into the hiſtorie of *Arthure*: which thing is [6 back] of the curious ſorte eaſily found faulte with. But this in deede is not a cauſe ſufficient iuſt, why any man ſhould neglect, abiect, or deface the Hiſtorie otherwiſe of it ſelfe, lightſome and true. Howe much better is it (caſting awaye trifles, cutting off olde wiues tales, and ſuperfluous fables, in deede of ſtately porte in outwarde ſhew, but nothing auayleable vnto credite, beeing taken away) to reade, ſcanne vpon, and preſerue in memorie thoſe thinges which are confonant by Authorytie. For, that which nowe a long time is embraced of Learned men with greate conſent: ought not in what ſoeuer moment of time barcking againſt it, together with faith or credite thereof, to be quite taken away.

Otherwiſe the Hiſtory had not hetherto remained in ſo greate reputation. Therefore, becauſe it is a worke of greater importaunce, than wee preſentlie are in hande with, exquiſitely, curiously and perfectlie to difplaye all the deedes of *Arthure*:

K. Arthures knights of his round Table.
Hoel the firft knight.

let vs for this feafon omitte the *Romaines*, and let vs aduance with penne his famylier friendes. *Hoelus* Gouernour of *Armorica*, or the leffe *Brittaine* in this famous Company of Nobles, by a certaine righte of his, requyreth the next place from the firft: 5 Concerning whofe comming into *Brittaine*, and warlike proweffe, we haue formerly written in the chapter of the warres accomplifhed by *Arthure*.

Gallouinus the fecond knight.

Hetherunto enfewe *Mordred* and *Gallouinus*, Brethren Germaynes vnto *Arthure* by bloodde and familiarity alyed. Of 10 which two, this firft at length, like a periured perfon and the fame a Reuoulter neuer enough difcommendable (that I fpeake nothing of the crime of his adultery) was flayne in battle. One *Hector Abrinus* beeing thereof fcarce a true witneffe, and as I gather with iudgement, more rightly firnamed *Alaunicus*. But 15 the fecond, being alwaies a man conftant, performed moft faithfull diligence both in all forraine warres, and alfo fpecially in that conflict at *Dorcefter*, aboute the returne of *Arthure* out of *Fraunce* into *Brittaine*, who was chiefe next vnto him againft Mordred. *Melchinus* the Brittifh Poet [7] blaifeth the fame of 20

Two writers aduancing the fame of Gallouinus.

Gallouinus. The fame doth *Iohannes Anneuillanus* in his booke intituled *Architrenio* a worke not vnelegant, namely by thefe verfes.

  Et Walganus ego qui nil reminifcor auara
  Illoculaffe manu: non hæc mea fulgurat auro,   25
  Sed gladio dextra: recipit, quo fpargat, & enfes;
  Non loculos ftringit, nec opes: in carcere miles
  Degener & cupide, tumulato rufticus ære,
  Et me bella vocant Et tua forfitan vrget
      Solicitudo: vale.   30

And Walgan I with couetous hand nought distribute which haue
This my right hand fhines not with gold but with the fword
 fo braue
It takes that it may diftribute, euen fwordes not bagges it bendes,
Nor wealth, though I a Knight diftreft, yet not vntrue to friendes, 35
Ne yet in countrie liued I like a couetoufe mucke fcrape:
But now the warres away call me vnto my wonted ftate,
 And thine affaires alfo,
 Perhappes vrge the thereto: *Farewell.*

K. Arthure 29

ALfo that Hiftory of *Arthure*, in deede *Fabulus* (which commonly is carried about written in the mother tongue) affirmeth that *Gallouinus* was buried in a certaine Chappell at *Dorcefter*. In which poynt what manner booke foeuer it be, it 5 miffeth not the marke altogether, as the booke entituled *Scalæ-cronicon* makes manifeft relation: and yᵉ inhabitantes of yᵉ Caftle do now repute his bones almoft Gyantlike in ftead of a miracle. And that long fince in the time of *Lucius Magnus* there was a Chappell founded in the Caftle of *Dorcefter* and 10 dedicated vnto our Lord and Sauiour Chrift: what time *Fugatius* and *Damianus Brittaines* preached the Gofpell as by the *Annales* or yearly recordes of the fame Cittie (bearing a reuere*n*t figure & refemblance of Antiquitie) it doth plainely appeare. That it may be moft acceptable, and befides that moft true which I haue 15 aboue inferred, touching both the death and buriall of *Galouinus*: it fhall not through me ftand, that the iudgement of *William de Medulphi Curia* as touching the death and buriall of this *Gallouinus* (by reafon of his fortitude neuer [7 back] enough commended) fhould eyther weare out of memory or vtterly perifh. 20 Wherefore I efteeme it worthie the labour here to fette downe his wordes out of the third booke of the *Kinges* of *England* that herehence the difcreete Reader might euen fully try as it were at a tutchftone the fincere brightneffe of true gold, from that which is counterfeite.

25 Then in the Prouince of *Wales* which is called *Roffia* was founde the Sepulchre or Tombe of *Gallouinus* or *Walwine*, which was the Nephewe not degenerate of *Arthure*, by his fifter. He gouerned (in the Coaft of *Brittaine* which to this day is called *Waluuthia*) as a Knight moft famous in proweffe: but being (of 30 his brother, and the Nephew to *Hengiftus* concerning whom I haue fpoken in the firft booke) driuen out of his Kingdome, did firft to their great detriment recompe*n*ce his banifhment, iuftly pertaking praife with his Unckle, for that he put off or auoyded the downefall from his Country then ruinoufe. But 35 *Arthures* Tombe was at no time feene, wherevpon Antiquitie of foolifh dreames and fables, did vainely furmife that he would yet come againe. But the burying place of the other (as before I set down in the time of *William* the first *King* of *England*) was found fourteene foote long vpon the Sea coaft, where (as

Gallouinus buried at Dorcefter.

His bones Giantlike. Accordinge to the record of Glaftenbury the names are Fagauus and Diruuianus. This Lucius being created the firft Chriftan King in England liued about the yere after Chrift 182. William of Malmesbury his iudgment of Gallouinus.

His wordes of reporte.

The Assertion of

The manner of Galouinu. his death, after the reporte of W. Malmsb.
William of Malmsbury.

some men affirme) he was wounded of his enemies and cast out of shipwrake: certaine persones haue saide, hee was slaine by the Citizens at publique banquet. So saith the Authour *Gulielmus Meildunensis*, as concerning *Gallouinus*. But I (if it might bee lawfull for me as a puny) would make tryall of my strength with these weapons, against this authour *Meildunensis* so olde and most beaten Souldier, to bestow & beare of the blowes. *viz.* It is not like to be true, that men of Gyantlike height (as I gather by ye graue 14. foote long) were then liuing in the dayes of *Gallouinus*. Wherefore vndoubtedly in mine opinion it is more credible that it was the graue of some *Gyant* inhabitinge the countrie. For that first such did inhabit *Albion*, it appeareth both by auctoritie of forraine and of our owne writers. The one of which two his credit I folowing, namely *Iosephus* of *Deuonshire* a Brittish *Poet*, most absolutly elegante by all [8] meanes, (hauing taken out of his *Antiocheides* a work immortall, these few verses) I will vse them as testimony for breuitie sake.

Iohn Leylands opinion to the contrarie.

His proofe out of a brittish Poet named Iosephus.

His Brutus auito
Sanguine Troianus, Latijs egressus ab oris
Post varios casus confedit finibus, orbem   20
Fatalem nactus, debellatorque Gigantum,
Et terræ Victor nomen dedit.

A Troian Brute by auncient bloude, ariued from Romaine roade
After sundry hazardes, and, here in these coastes aboade
And hauing got his dest[i]ned land, subdued the Gyants fell   25
As Conquerour he left his fame vpon the earth to dwell.

Architrenius in his fixt booke of *Gyantes* inhabiting *Albion* recyteth thefe.

Hos auidum belli *Corinei* robor auerno
Præcipites misit: cubitis ter quatuor altum.   30
Gogmagog Herculea suspendit in aere lucta,
Antheumque suum scopulo, detrusit in æquor.

These Corineus his puysant strength (of eager moode to fight)
To hell sent headlong: Gogmagog of twelue cubites height,

*By him (like Hercules wrafling) into the aire was throwne
His Antheus eke and from the rocke in feaes was caft
adowne.*

NEyther am I ignorant that in times paft there was on ye fea
fhoare a Caftle called *Galouine*, touching which the Authour
Meildunenfis as aboue hath written: whofe footefteppes are as
yet apparant. But that was not the habitation of the Gyant, as
neyther perhappes of that *Galouine* of *Arthures*, but of fome
latter vycegerent bearing the fame name. But y^t which he
mentioneth of *Arthures* Tombe at that time, is moft true. No
one man more curioufly fearched forth, at any time all the
treafures of the library at *Glaftenbury*. This onely was here
wanting in him towardes knowledge, that he dying about the
firft yeare of the Raigne of *Henry* y^e *fecond King of England*,
knew nothing of *Arthurs* tombe. For fo much as ye fame
tombe was found afterwards in ye beginning of ye raigne
of *K. Richard coeur de lyon*. But I returne with[1] *William*
Meildunenfis into favour, [8 back] out of the which as yet I haue
not openly fallen: By whome a man as in his age moft learned
in all kind of Good letters, and of finguler wit, diligence and
care in fearching forth Antiquitie, I confeffe and in deede that
franckly muft affirme my felfe to haue beene oftentimes helped
in the knowledge of Antiquitie. Undoubtedly it is a poynte of
honeftie to acknowledge by whom a man profiteth. It liketh me
well, here, vnto the conclufion to adde the notation which
I myfelfe gather of the name of *Gallouinus* out of the *Brittifh*
language. *Walle* fignifieth ftraungers or walfh, *Guin, Album*, or
white. Like as if a man by this phrafe would defcribe a comely,
elegant and beawtifull perfonag: except a man more rightly
thinke that he tooke his originall from the *Saxonifh* rude language, as *Walwine* fignifieth *Gallus Amicus, Leoffwyn Charus
Amicus,* and *Aldwyne Vetus Amicus*.

Now approcheth *Augufellus*,[2] of whom we haue aboue
fpoken a fewe wordes. Who was in fo feruent fauour with
Arthure, that hee was deferuingly made a beneficiall Gouernour
ouer the *Scottes*. This man rendered like for like.

William of Malmsbury a moft curious and painful fearcher of Antiquitie.

William of Malmsbury.

The interpretation of Gallouinus his name.

Augufellus the third knight.

---

[1] Text, w^e (apparently), but evidently meant for w^t = *with*.
[2] See note.

32   The Aſſertion of

Iohn Stow. An auncient Cittie in Kent nere Sandwich the ruins of it yet remaine.

The Proweſſe and valiant aduenture of him, one Graius a writer witneſſeth.

Being ſent for amongſt many other *Princes* to the end he might performe him ſelfe a companion with *Arthure* in his expedition towardes *Fraunce*, ſo farre refuſed hee not his enioyned charge, that with greate example of valiancie there manifeſted, and retorning home on the Coaſt of Richborow with much more proweſſe, (*Mordred* beinge ouercome in ciuil wars and there put to flight) he falling amongſt the Hoaſtes with bloud & lyfe endaungered, valiantly behaued himſelfe: as ye Authour of thoſe bookes *Schalechronica* (one *Grayius* as I ſuppoſe) is none euil witneſſe at al thereof. And becauſe touching the chuſing out, or election of thoſe Princes (vnto *Arthure* being obedient) we haue formerly made promiſe: it auaileth here to ſignifie that there were many & notable elections, not ſpoken of by him.

Iohn Stowe.

But that was moſt notable of all, which appeared in *Iſca* or *Exceter* otherwiſe in the Cittie of *Caerlegion*, or *Cheſter* vpon Vske. What time it was proclamed vnto wars againſt y^e *French*. But what haue the *Muſes* to do with *Mars*? vndoubtedly [9] either little or nothing. And yet if there were a iuſt familiaritie betweene them, they ſhoulde rather wiſh well vnto *Mars*, that for his ſake they might deſeruingly giue *Arthure* greate thankes, who either reſtored or inſtituted a Learned Quier of Eccleſiaſticall perſons in the ſaide cittie of *Caerlegion*: if *Geoffrey* of *Munmouth*, *Iohn Burgenſis*, and *Roſſus Verouicenſis* declare the trueth. This in meane time appeareth plaine by the hiſtorie of *Anonimus* the writer, that *Amphibalus*, Iulius, & Aarona martyres did worſhip *Chriſt*, and alſo had learning in eſtimation in the ſaide cittie of *Caerlegion* or *Cheſter* vpon *Vske*. From whome agayne credible it is that others receiued the ſame letters from hand to hande. There is alſo (if we may beleeue credible reporte) in the treaſuries at Cambridge at this daye, a Table of the priuiledge by *Arthure* ſometime confirmed to the furderance of ſtudents. But as yet haue I not ſearched out the credite of this deede.

Wryters. Geoffrey of Munmouth. Iohn of Borow. Roſſus of Warwicke. Anonimus a writer.

Iderus the 4. knight, neare of blood vnto Arthure.

Iderus ſometime a ſpeciall fauourer of *K. Arthures* court comes nowe to the number of thoſe *Cheualyers*. This man beeing neare alyed in blood vnto *Arthure*, performed many valyant examples of proweſſe, and continually did cleaue to his *Princes* ſide. And at length, by what hap I knowe not, (hee dying,) left a ſpeciall wellwiſhing vnto *Arthure*: who alſo care-

K. Arthure 33

fully accomplifhed his funerall at *Aualonia*. I haue reade at *Glaftenburie* a little booke of the antiquitie thereof, gathered very dilligently by a certaine Moncke of that place : In which booke he declareth many thinges of *Arthures* good will to-
5 wardes this man departed : and of yᵉ liberalitie or beneficiall goodneffe (for yᵉ fame his cofens fake) beftowed vpon religious perfons there inhabiting. Of late there did hang a Table at a pillor within yᵉ Church of Glaftenburie, which accounted *Iderus* amongft the Benefactors and reftorers of the Church at
10 *Glaftenburie*. *Lancelot* a man moft famous requireth place euen amongft yᵉ moft excellent *Cheualyers* to be giuen him. Unto which defire I eafilie graunt as one readie to fpeake this in his commendation : that hee was a certaine vpright and faithfull friende of *Arthures*. His valiancy appeared largely at yᵉ battle
15 which [9 back] was fought betweene *Mordred* the traytor and *Arthure*. He liued in deede after the battle, & as I reade once or twice, conueyed vnto *Guenhera* (mourning at *Arthures* death) the bodie from *Amberfburie* vnto *Glaftenburie*. But *Gyraldus* feemeth fincerely to attribute his buriall in one place or other
20 at *Glaftenbury*, as in his *Speculo Ecclefiaftico* : & in his worke *De Inftitutione Principis*, appeareth. Although it rather feemeth to me in mine opinion yᵗ he tooke his firfte tombe at *Amberfburie*. *Carodocus* a name of noble proweffe martiall, followed *Arthure* in his expedition towardes *Fraunce*. And returning
25 homewarde was flaine, as it feemeth on the coaft of *Richborowe*, in the ciuill battle. The Cronicles of the porte of *Dorcefter*, a worke fauoring of antiquitie makes mention of *Caradocus*. The inhabitants of the Caftle there euen at this day after a forte renewe the memorie of *Caradocus*, affirming
30 that they haue in their Cuftodie I knowe not what Lyneamentes of his. And not fo contented, they fette foorth *Arthures* Courte, and *Guenheras* lodging. Nowe ruffleth in the number and traine of *Arthures* noble warriors. But I, (fo yᵗ it be done without offence to them, becaufe I haue onely taken vpon me to
35 name the moft excellenteft of them and to praife them) haue purpofed to ouerpaffe the refidue, yet otherwife praife worthie, and laft of all to adioyne that *Cadorus* of *Cornewale*. Hee was of the moft noble progeny of the kinges of *Brittaine*, and gouerned the people in the Mountayny foyles of *Cornewale*.

His beneficency towardes the Church at Glaftenbury.

Lancelot the fifth knight.

A faithfull friend and aduenger of iniury done by Mordred vnto Arthure.

Syluefter Giraldus his teftimonie of his buriall at Glaftenburie.

Carodocus yᵉ fixte knight Whofe fame the Cronicles of Dorcefter extoll.

Cadorus the 7. knight, of the moft noble pro-

K

genie of the kinges of England.
A ſtoute defender & preferrer of his princes dignitie.
Conſtantine his ſonne ſucceeded Arth.
Gildas his teſtimony of Conſtantine a degenerate child a murtherer of Innocentes.

Undoubtedly he was a ſtoute defender of his princes dignitie and had perpetuall familiaritie with the *Brittaines*. At length when hee dyed, hee left after him a ſunne named *Conſtantine*: (who after the Death of *Arthure*) was made Ruler ouer *Brittaine.* Hee, (to the ende they following their fathers example in times paſte ſhoulde not aſpyre vnto the kingedome) cauſed the ſonnes and Supporters of *Mordred* the traytor and Nephewes of *Gallouinus* to be ſlaine with the ſworde. But either this fact or the like doth *Gildas* the *Brittaine* ſhewe in theſe wordes. Of which ſo wicked a miſchiefe, *Conſtantine* the Tyrants vncleane whelpe of *Damonia* [10] was not ignorant, who this yeere after yᵉ horrible oth made, from which he againe ſwarued (that he would not worke any iniuries vnto the Citizens, ſwearing firſt by God, then by the mother of Chriſt, and therwith taking all the companies of holy ones to witneſſe) did notwithſtanding by blooddie ſword and ſpeare ruſh into the tender breſts of two mothers and cruelly perced the bowelles or intrayles of two princelie youthes, vnder yᵉ ſame religious *Amphibalus* & of ſo many ouerſeers euen ſtanding at yᵉ very Alter, whoſe armes (being without armour which no one man at yᵉ time more valiantlier vſed then they) hee cruelly cut off euen ſtanding at the Alter, and with his Speare violently toare them in peeces. But they ſhall crie for reuenge vnto God, before the high throne of his Maieſtie in the day of iudgement and at the Gates of thy city (Oh Chriſt) ſhall they hange vp their reuerend banners of pacience and of faith. Hetherto haue wee ſpoken of his Knightes or Cheualyers.

Chap. vj.

K. Arthures Rounde Table.

NOwe is there very conuenient place to bringe in amongeſt other thinges, a fewe, but choſen, excellent, finally magnificent teſtimonies of *Arthures* round table and of his good cheare. Unto theſe had not all noble men acceſſe: But onelie they, viz

   Lucida quos ardens euexit ad æthera Virtus,
   Virtus ſola virens nullis moritura diebus.

K. Arthure

Whom Vertue cleere aduanced to the skies,
Euen Vertue alone which florishing neuer dies.

THis stately sturre (as they say) he somewhat more often solemnized. But specially in the cittie of *Caerlegion*, or *Chester* vpon *Vske* which place he notably esteemed of. The same did he at *Venta Simenorum* alias *Winchester*, & at *Camalet* in Somersetshire. The Common vnlearned sorte of writers supposeth, that *Venta* to bee called by another name, that is to saye, *Camelet*. But I passe not vpon the iudgement of the common sorte. The publike [10 back] reporte of them which dwelt at the lowermost parte of the hill *Cancaletum*, or an olde forte, is, that *Murotrigum* or the Towne now called *Somerton*, spreadeth, aduanceth, and solemnely settes foorth the fame of *Arthure* sometime inhabiting the Castle. Which Castle of olde time was both most statelie and also most strongly buylded, and in a most high or loftie prospect. Good Lorde, what and howe many most deepe Ditches are there heere? How many vallyes are there heere out of the earth delued? Againe what daungerous steepenesse? And to end in fewe wordes, truly me seemeth it is a mirackle, both in Arte and nature.

Iohn Stow. Vsuall places where K. Arth. kept his rounde talbe.

On this side Somerton neare vnto Glastenbury is the village Sutton & Camelet an old forte. K. Arthure inhabited a castle at Somerton.

> At seges est vbi *Troia* fuit stabulantur in vrbe,
> Et fossis pecudes altis, valloque tumenti
> *Taxus*, & astutae posuere Cubilia vulpes.

But corne there is where Troy *did stand, & cattle there abound,*
Stalled in towne with ditches deepe, in trench mounting from ground,
There Yew trees grow, & subtile Foxes made their cabbins round.

ANd in deede this is the interchaunge of humane affayres. Heerehence had *Ilcester* that auncient Towne this calamitie. Heereupon doth the customary traffique there beholde the cleere welspring with heauie eyes, and weepe their fill. There the inhabitants plow the ground, and euery yeere finde by seeking for them, Golden, Siluer, and Brasen peeces of money, expressing the images not very liuely of the *Romanes*. Wherof euen I my selfe haue had a few giuen mee of those inhabitants.

The Assertion of

Frauncis Lord Hastings Earle of *Huntington* an excellent ornament of those noble youthes about the King of England, & somtimes my benefactor in good learning, as heire of y^e *Piperells, Bottrells*, & of the *Hungerfordes*, hath in his possession the ruined old cotages of *Camelet*, together with ye large grounds adiacent. *Iohannes Anneuillanus* ye writer in his *Architrenio* extolleth *Arthures* rounde table for ye excellency therof. The same doth *Volateranus* in his thirde booke of *Geography*, in these wordes. *He also being plentiful at home, vsed amongest his nobles a rounde table that there should be no contention, through ambition for seates.* At *Venta Symeno* alias *Winchester* in ye castle most famously [11] knowne, standeth fixed ye table at the walle side of ye kinges Hal, which (for ye maiesty of *Arthure*) they cal ye round table. And wherefore? Becaufe neyther the memorie nor felowship of the round Trowpe of Knightes as yet falles out of Noble mens mindes, in the latter age of the world. *King Edward* firnamed the longe, as fame telleth, made much of that rounde order of Knightes. To those vses was the round table instituted and framed, (if it be worthie of credit) and that it was with three feete made of perfect gold. There bee which write that one Mortimar by name, spent and consumed away those treasures. That thing yet by the way is most certaine out of the historie of *Thomas Vicanius*, that *Roger Mortimer* helde a very great feast or banquette at *Kenelworth*, whether as he of noble minde sent for most excellentest Cheualiers, or Knightes, as it had beene vnto *Arthures* round table of Knightes: Hereupon were very many tokens of knightly prowesse set foorth in deede: which the diligent posteritie shal with great desire reade expressed in wrytinges. But now so long a while, from this Cheualrie of *Arthure* and his trayne, I passe ouer to his godly disposition.

Marginalia:
- Iohannes Anneuillanus, a writer, extolleth K. Arth. round table.
- K. Arthures round table where it standeth.
- K. Edward the first made much of that round order of Knightes in his time.
- Roger Mortimer, solemnished the same order at Kenelworth.

Cap. vii.

King Arthures Godly Difpofition.

WIth how greate and how fincere deuotion hee was enclyned towards the Chriftian Common wealth, it appeareth plainly by the authoritie of auncient writers. He vfed the familiaritie of *Dubritius* Bifhoppe of the Cittie of *Caerlegion* or *Chefter* vpon *Vfke*, a man both of finguler learning and alfo of continencie in life: fo farre forth that he throwly felt as victor in the battel at *Bathe*, his prayers auaylable. Furthermore *Dauid Meneuenfis* a man no doubt of exquifite holyneffe, as then felt both the fauour and liberallitie of *Arthure*: fo farre forth that the people *Meneuenfes*, report the Bifhoppes fea to haue bene by them receyued as by *Arthures* meanes tranflated from the Cittie of *Caerlegion* or *Chefter* vpon *Vske* vnto them. *Iltutus* a man of incomperable lyfe being companion of thefe two [11 back] hearing that of finguler magnificence of his, & zeale towardes God, was bolde (as the fetter forth of his life writeth) not onely face to face to goe fee *Arthure*, but alfo to falute him and haue communication with him. Through which (in deede boldneffe) much leffe offended he the *Prince* feeing that he both gaue him very greate thankes and alfo an honeft rewarde. *Arthure* (if auncient writers and conftant fame do reporte the truth) had depainted in his Martiall target, the fimilitude of the virgin *Mary*: which target he vfed in many battels, and fpecially in that battell at *Bathe*. In fuch tryfling matters I do not much force to write. But by the way, that is not a thing vnworthie to be heard of the godly, which *Samuel* the writer of Brittaine, and *Difciple of Elbodus* the Bifhoppe, (who flourifhed about nyne hundreth yeares agoe) thus maketh mention of, concerning *Arthures* expedition or rather peregrenation. *Arthure* went vnto *Ierufalem* when as he tooke with him the figne of the Croffe of wood in memory of his Sauiour, whereof the fragmentes are at this day referued in *Wedale* a towne of *Lodoneia*, fix miles from *Mailros*. Finally he exceedingly efteemed of thofe Church men at *Glaftenbury*, as partly I haue aboue faide in *Idero*, and as I will here more largely fhewe. *Siluefter Gyraldus* in his booke *De Inftitutione*

[margin notes: Two Bifhops religioufe fauourers of K. Arthures welfare. Of S. Dauid. Iltutus a Godly and learned father an other religioufe fauourer of Ar. K. Arthure his iourney to Ierufalem. His zeale & fpeciall good will towardes the Church men of Glaftenbury.]

Principis thus wryteth. For, aboue all the Churches in his Kingedome he fauoured and beare beſt good will vnto the Church of our Lady *S. Mary* at *Glaſtenbury*, and with greater deuotion aduanced the ſame before other Churches. *Polidorus* (according to his equitie and iudgment, and ſo farre as his auctoritie ſerueth him) declareth there was no Monaſterie at *Glaſtenbury* in *Arthures* time: So exquiſite a iudge is he of Antiquitie and ſpecially concerning *Brittaine*. He alſo contendeth that euen all the whole worlde by this rule (but in deede a moſt vniuſt rule) is conſtrayned to embrace, maintaine, and beleeue that which is ſpoken of him touching Antiquitie, as that which is pronounced for an Oracle. To that he ſaith and writeth in truth, will I as *Virgill* ſaith. *Enſe leuis nudo parmaque inglorius alba.* That is, (*With naked ſword and ſclender bright ſheelde without boa*[12]*ſting* eaſely defend his auctoritie and iudgment ſo auncient. But what he falſy or vntruly declareth, (which thing he doth ſomewhat oftener through all partes of his Hiſtory) I may not beare with all, I can not abide it, neyther will I ſuffer it, but the truth, (ſo much as it ſhall ſtand me vpon) will I reſtore to her comelyneſſe, fame, and glory, as one cheerefull and nothing fearefull in ſo doing, though the enemies of truth burſt them ſelues with inwarde mallice. For, vnto this moſt honeſt opinion that I ſhould couragiouſly cleaue in this behalfe, the thing done by thoſe two Apoſtles of the *Brittaines*, namely *Fugatius* and *Damianus*, and the Epiſtle of *Patritius* the great which I haue in my cuſtody confirming the ſame (to omit for breuitie ſake the teſtimonies of many others) do will me, or rather commaund me. *Henry Plantagenet* (the Nephew of *Henry Beauclarcke King* of *England* by the daughter of *Mathilda*) affirmeth, by preſcript and manifeſt wordes in a certaine deede of gift, that he ſaw, (and that it ſhould not want vpright credit) that hee read the couenants and articles concerning a certaine beneuolence of *Arthures*, extended towardes the religiouſe perſons inhabiting *Aualonia*. But I will hereunto annexe the very wordes of *King Henries* gift, out of the originall deede.

Moreouer what thinges ſo euer haue beene giuen me from my Predeceſſors, William *the firſt*, William *the ſecond*, and Henry *my Vnckle. Yea of their Anceſtors, namely of* Eadgar *the father*

[1] Text, *of*.

Iohn Layland a bearer with Polidorus. So farre as he bringes forth the truth, and otherwiſe his enemy.

Alias Faganus and Diruuianus. This was king Henry the 2. Sonne of Geoffrey plantagenet, brother to king Henry the firſt ſucceding him. An. 1154 *raigned* 3. *yeares,* 9. *monethes, &* 12. *dayes, and was buried* [at][1] *Founteuerard in Fraunce. Wordes contayned in*

K. *Arthure* 39

of Sir Edwarde *of* Edmond, &*[1] of his father* Edward, *and of* Ealfred *the Grandsire of the same, of* Brinwalchius Kenwinus, Baldredus, Ina, Cuthredus, *and of* Arthure, *and many other Christian Kinges.* And *also of* Kenwalchius *the Pagan King,*
5 *whose priuileges and writings I haue diligently caused to be searched and to be presented & read in my presence.* Thus far the deed of gift. If these witnesses of sure credit make not sufficient for most apparant knowledge of the truth, surely there can nothing at any time auaylably serue. For not to be satisfied with these being
10 receyued and knowen at full, is neyther the parte of a wise head, no nor yet of a good iudgment.

King Henry the 2. his deede of gift proceding from king Arthures beneuolence towardes the Church men at Aualonia.

[12 back]

Cap. viii.
King A[r]thures[2] Seale.

ANd because I haue againe entred into the Misteries of sacred Antiquitie and am descended a curious searcher into the bowels
15 thereof, it liketh me to bring forth to light an other matter, namely *Arthures* Seale, a monument most cunningly engrauen, aunciant, and reuerent. Concerninge which, *Caxodunus* maketh mention, yet breefly and sclenderly in his preface to the history of *Arthure*: which the common people readeth printed in the
20 English tongue. Being moued with the testimony of *Caxodunus* whatsoeuer it were, I went vnto *Westminster*, to the end that what so as an eare witnesse I had heard, I might at length also as an eye witnesse behold the same. Pondering well that sayinge of *Plautus*, in my minde. *Pluris valet oculatus testis vnus quam*
25 *Auriti decem.*

He meaneth Robert Caxton who translated the history of K. Arthure. K. Arthures Seale kept at Westminster in Iohn Leylandes dayes.

Of more force standes eye witnesse one,
Than ten eare witnesses among.

The keeper of those secretes being requested of mee to shew me this monument, by and by delyuered it both to bee seene and
30 handled. The sight of the Antiquitie pleased me at full, and for a long time the Maiestie thereof not onely drewe away but also detayned myne eyes from me to the beholding thereof. Of such force it is for a man aptly to chaunce vpon a thing with greate care desired. The substance which tooke the most lyuelyest

His reporte in praise thereof, describing the properties

[1] Text, *and* after *&*.   [2] Text, *Atthures*.

figure of *Arthure* imprinted vpon the Seale, (and which as yet doth firmely keepe the fame ftill) is waxe of redde coloure, which by fome mifhape, or iniury of long time perifhed, is crazed here & there into peeces. But fo yet notwithftanding as no part of it is altogether lacking. For the fragmentes or litle peeces thereof being beforetime by fome mifchaunce crazed, are fo clofed vp together with filuer plates which is of rounde forme, fuch as is the vtter fide of the Seale, that no parte of them may fall off. For vpon the vtterfide of this feale it is thus engraued with thefe breefe, but in very deede moft excellent, moft hauty, and moft magnificent tytles. That is to fay. [13]

The Infculpture of K. Arth. Seale and the Infcription ther of,

PATRICIVS ARTVRIVS BRITTANNIÆ, GALLIÆ, GERMANIÆ, DACIÆ IMPERATOR.

And of trueth this infcription circleth the outermoft compaffe of the Seale. The former parte thereof is moft bright fhining by a circle of chriftall, which being taken off, ftreightway may any man touch the wax, which by reafon of the Antiquitie is moft harde. But the portracture of *Arthure* printed thereupon, refembleth I wotte neare what Heroyical Maieftie. For the *Prince* as it were inuefted with purple, royally fitteth vpon a halfe circle, fuch one as we fee the raine boe is. Hauing a crowne vpon his heade he fhineth like the funne. In his right hand rifeth vp a fcepter wrought with a *Flowerdeluce* at the toppe: And his left hand holdeth a globe adorned with a croffe. His bearde alfo groweth comely, large, and at length, and euen that is a maieftie. The other fide of the Seale is altogether couered ouer with a thinne plate of Siluer. By meanes wherof alfo it is vncertaine of what fafhion it is. There hangeth downe at the fame a ftring chainefafhionlike twifted of Siluer. Certes Reader, I pray God I be deade but thou wouldeft defire to fee the fame, fuch and fo greate is both the antiquitie and alfo the maiefty of the thing. At length the keeper of thofe fecretes was there requefted by me to fignifie vnto me, if he had learned any thing ouer and befides this, as touching the feale hanging thereat.

K. Arthures maieftie reprefented on the feale. Nota.

The feale, one of the ornaments which were about. tombe

For, amongeft very many ornaments which glittering with Gold & precious ftones did adorne the tombe of *Edwarde* the *Simple*, King of England, euen this alfo was worthie of memorie. But he coulde fay nothing to thefe demaundes fauing onely this, that

hee thought the fame was by yͤ king laid in yͤ place to yͤ of K. Edwarde
perpetuall memorie of the moſt high and mighty prince *Arthure*. the ſimple.
Surely if a man might lawefully by any coniectures gather and
ſet downe the trueth in writing, I would not thinke that ſuch
5 a ſeale had be[en]e [1] tranſlated from *Glaſtenburie*: vppon which It was tranf-
monaſtery (by misfortune of fire moſt filthily debaſed) the moſt lated from
bountifull prince beſtowed ſuch rewardes, as hee for his excellent to Weſt-
godlines might more eaſily giue, then thoſe monckes might hope minſter.
for. *K. Henrie* himſelfe as I haue aboue [13 back] mentioned,
10 made teſtimony of *Arthures* free gift, and ſo farre forth as he
both ſawe and read the ſame. By meanes whereof alſo it might
come to paſſe, that the parchment beeing eaten out with little
wormes, and moathes by long tract of time, ſo famous a monument of antiquitie being founde, he deliuered the ſame to the
15 Monaſterie of firſt fame, there to be kept ſafe, and to be ſeene
for euer of the nobylitie in all poſterities. Certes (except my
coniecture faileth me) the expences or charge is ſmall in deede,
yea, none at all. This yet in the meane time pleaſeth me, that
while we intreate of *Arthure* and of things done by him,
20 *Glaſtenbury* is alwaies at hand and moſt friendly promiſeth his
endeuour towardes aſſured knowledge of things. From whence
in deede all yͤ fruite of our labour at this preſent is to be fetcht,
as it were from a moſt plentifull running fountaine. Neither He meaneth
ſurely is there any thing apparant, (that I doe knowe of) which either yͤ
25 more euidently approueth that *Arthure* was liuing, then the ſame as Chronica
Seale doth. Which thing, if God ſo would, ſome perſons Gleſſobur-
(leaning rather to their opinion, ſelfe will, and finally raſhneſſe, either els
then vnto any vpright reaſon) doubt not to deny. But after Patricius
this we will chuſe a place, wherein by full & whole aboundance fis.
30 of argumentes, wee may ouerthrowe the violent rabble of
ſlaunderers. In the meane ſeaſon wee muſt more ſubtilely
diſcuſſe the inſcription of the Seale. For, this hath her miſteries,
which when they ſhall receiue light, ſhall both with greater
pleaſure, and alſo apter grace fill yͤ eares of honeſt readers, and
35 being filled ſhal wonderfully delight them: which thing is worth
the trauell, & that in deede largely.

The name PATRICIVS is taken as from the maieſtie of the Patricius
Romans. The noble men of Rome are called by that name, whence it
hath originall.

---

[1] Text, *benee*.

42   *The Aſſertion of*

viz. ſuch as are come of the firſte Senatours: That ſeemeth *Tacitus* to ſignifie by theſe wordes. *In thoſe dayes Caeſar* tooke into the number of Noble men, euery one moſt aunciant of the Senate, or which were of noble perſonage. *Liuius* makes this mention. *Romulus* created 100 Senators, which were called *Patres* or *Fathers*, by reaſon of honor done to them & alſo *Patricij* or noble men by reaſon of their progeny. Therefore it is euident that *Arthure* receiued that ſame no-[14]table fame of his name from his parentes and Aunceſters. Whereupon alſo it appeareth that as yet, the glory of *Romane* Maieſtie (tranſlated or applyed vnto the *Brittaines*, in their titles) waxed not cold in thoſe dayes. I haue alſo beleeued that the name of *Arthure* tooke his beginning from the *Romane Arthures*. For *Iuuenall* the Poet in his thirde *Satyre* writeth thus.

marginalia: Patres & Patricii why ſo called. From whence the name of Arthure was firſt deriued.

Cedamus Patria, Viuant *Arturius* iſtic,
& *Catulus*.

*From our countrie departe let vs:
There* Arthure *liue and* Catulus.

ALthough *Brittaine* was by *Claudius* brought into one only countrie, it was yet a thing moſt familier amongſt ye noble men of *Brittaine*, partly to take vnto them ye names of the *Romans*, & to giue them moſt often vnto their children, by this perſuation (as I veryly beleeue not fooliſh) ſo moued, that herehence they would procure honour vnto them & theirs, & gaine themſelues fauour of the *Romans*. *Lucius* whome the *Brittaines* ſirnamed the great, *Conſtantine* and he alſo the great, *Aurelius Ambroſius*, & *Arthure* vnto theſe not inferior, doe mightely ratifie this mine opinion. The ſame thing alſo is performed in ye attribution of names vnto noble women. For example, ſuch were *Claudia Ruffina* a woman ſincerelie learned, as *Martiall* the Poet witneſſeth. *Helena* the moſt holy matron, and *Vrſula* that *Cynoſura* or glittering Starre ſo called. And where as the inſcription of ye Seale by a certaine circumſtance of words calleth him *Emperor of Brittaine, Fraunce, Germany* & finally of *Denmarcke*. This alſo commeth to paſſe through ye cuſtome of the *Romans* & their dilligence, yt together with their triumphes the titles alſo of nations conquered might accrewe or encreaſe vnto the conqueror. For a token hereof the *Bowes* were vſed

marginalia: Anno a Chriſto nato. 44. Perottus in Cornucopia nameth her a Nimph, & one of Iupiters nieces. Bowes vſed for

in triumphes at Rome, and the Coynes of *Caefar* with their figures were with like care ſtamped. But the name of the Emperor, as by *Auncientie*, (after the teſtimony of *Caesar, Cicero*, and *Liuius* apparant) pertained vnto the gouernors of yᵉ legions: wherupon *Arthure* is called Emperor by [14 back] an apt worde, ſignificant, and as it were a pure *Latine* Phraſe. And where as the inſcription hath not *Arturius* but *Arturus* (leauing out the letter .i.) that doe I impute vnto the errour or negligence of the ingrauer only. Proper names of the *Romaynes* by a certaine compoſition or methode, & by a certaine nature of theirs, doe runne at length more delicately & more familiarly, & doe end in *ius* rather then in *us* : as *Æmilius, Ma*n*lius, Claudius, Cornelius, Tere*n*tius, Vergilius, Horatius*, and *Ouidius*. I haue ſaide before my minde touching *Arthures* triu*m*phes by reaſon of his battles proſperouſly acco*m*pliſhed againſt the *Saxones* & *Frenchmen*. It now remaineth (that being put in minde of yᵉ inſcriptio*n* of his ſeale) co*n*cerning GERMANIE & DENMARCKE I ſhoulde ſpeake ſomewhat. But heere the authoritie of auncient hiſtoriographers (while I would proceede to ſo honeſt a purpoſe) doth not miniſter vnto me (according as my deſire is to write) ſufficient matter in this poynte. And of truth in the meane time not to defend the cauſe I haue taken vpon me, were no doubt a matter of controuerſie. I will be ſo bold therfore as one fully co*n*firmed with this ſo aſſured & manifeſt teſtimonie of inſcriptio*n*, to promiſe the reader faithfully yᵗ *Arthure* hauing vanquiſhed the French men by ſome memorable garboile did feight hand to hand with yᵉ *Germains* and the *Dacians*. Except any man contend yᵗ the victory refpected thus farre, yᵗ *Arthure* in the ciuill battle ſharply tamed yᵉ *Saxons* & *Cymbrya*ns of the Germaine and Danſike people. *Cherſoneſus* of the *Cymbrians* was in times paſt yᵉ part of *Germany* which is now called by later termes or names *Denmarcke* and *Norway*. The more ancient kinges of theſe natio*n*s (as I haue heard) did in their priuileges write themſelues rulers not of yᵉ *Danes*, but of yᵉ *Dacia*n*s*. And yet there are amongſt yᵉ learned ſorte which affirme yᵗ the *Dacia*n*s* inhabited that regio*n* which is now called *Moldauia*, & *Valachia*. *Volateranus* in his 3. booke of *Geography* affirmeth, yᵗ part of *Fraunce*, of *Norway*, and of *Dacia* was conquered by *Arthure*. Alſo *Tritemius* writeth on this manner. *Which thing*

triumphes at Rome.

Arthure aptly called Emperour.

K. Arth. conqueſtes in forraigne countries.

44   The Aſſertion of

when the kinges of Dacia *and of* Norway *did heare they comming thether of theyr owne freewill and* [15] *voluntarie mindes, became ſubiect vnto his gouernment.* Here muſt the Reader be admon-

Iohn Stow.   iſhed of me, that not onely yᵉ *Saxones, Engliſh* men, & *Iuites* otherwiſe *Vites* ſo called, came into Brittaine, but alſo the 5 inhabitantes of al yᵉ Coaſtes of *Germany.* Otherwiſe they had beene vnmeete matches for ſo many battelles and broyles. Now haue I deſcribed out the Seale with the inſcription thereupon in his colours after a ſorte. The next enterpriſe, ſhall be to ſette downe in wryting *Arthures* returne out of *Fraunce,* and the 10 bloody battelles betweene him and *Mordred.*

Cap. ix.
King Arthures returne out of Fraunce.

Mordred was with Guenhera in Arthures abſence, practiſing miſcheefe with Cerdicius that Saxon.

ARthure had aduertiſement both by letters and alſo by meſſengers of ſpetiall credit, that *Mordred* his too much familier friend was wᵗ *Guenhera,* whiles himſelfe was abſent : and beſides 15 this, that he had entered a League (againſt the oath of his aleageance) with *Cerdicius* the King and with the *Saxons*: yeelding vp vnto them (to the infinite daunger of the common weale) almoſt all the Countrie which extendeth towardes the South part of *Brittaine.* An other miſcheefe alſo happened 20 hereunto: then which more pernicious was none. This ſame moſt lewde reuolt, and most vngracious betrayer of his Lord, and Land, (al bondes of amitie, aliance and alegeance being broken) takes vpon him the purple roabe not fitte for thoſe his ſholders, and truſting to a new vpſtart tyranny of his, mountes vp to yᵉ 25

K. Arthures expedition againſt Mordred.

royall ſeate. *Arthure* could no longer abide ſo notable an iniury howſoeuer done vnto him by this periured perſon : although he alſo a few yeares before had determined his iuſt reuenge vpon him, (being yet letted by his warres in *Fraunce*) but that he would vtterly ſubuert by might and maine, ſo horrible, ſo ingent, 30 and ſo cruell a monſter. His nauy therefore being prepared, from the Cittie *Bononia* bordering vpon the coaſtes of *Belgia* vnto the ſhoare of *Richeborow* (as witneſſeth *Mattheus Florilegus*

Iohn Stow.   together wᵗ others) he laboureth the Seaes with proſperouſe windes. The moſt lew-[15 back]deſt ſeruant of all vnderſtood before, the comming of his gracious Lord, and with a full appoynted Hoaſt not without counſell and helpe of *Pictes, Scottes, & Weſt Saxones,* moſt boldly meetes him, returning home. The Coaſt of *Kent* ratled with all manner noyſe of weapons: and now the Captaines ſtood orderly before their enſignes: the troupe of *Cheualliers* alſo conquerours of the world w^t chearefull aſſaults toſſed their weapons, parte of them drew out their fierie flaſhing blades, and part ſhaked their ſhiuering ſpeares with ſtrong handes. They had all one voyce. The battells were warrelike fightes. *Arthure* moſt iocund with this prompt alacritie and ſtoute courages of his Souldiours, as the miracle both of all manhood, and alſo of ripe wiſdome by experience, made ſuch a like Oration vnto them by lifting vp his eyes from the earth vnto heauen, and with cherefulneſſe of countenance together with a certaine maieſtie mixed, ſaying on this manner.

Yee Cheualiers *the moſt noble lightes of martiall proweſſe, and you the other multitude of moſt approued valiancie, do ſee whither our fortune and aſſociate of ſo great victories hath brought vs, as what we haue with moſt ſtrong hand gotten abroade, wee may not onely keepe vpright, but alſo get vs more greater booties with ſome ſtraunge and large increaſe: the which thing that it may at this inſtant be brought to paſſe and more eaſely, ſuch occaſion is now offered vs, as all good happes could not in deede, if they would, more plentifully, nor more proſperouſly offer themſelues to fauour vs frendly. Let vs therefore go to this geare with moſt manly courages, whither as* Fortune, Valiancie, *and finally* victory *calleth vs. Now is the moſt impudent* Mordred *at hand, yet one moſt neareſt to me in bloude, whome I haue brought vp and loued in hope of greate fame, and ſo far forth made much of, and that in very many booties beſtowed vpon him in deede, and thoſe no leſſe beneficiall as when I ſhould paſſe into* France *to aduenge me of mine enemies, he ſo ſeeming to be then vndoubtedly of profound counſell, vnto him I did both commit my wife & [16] ſtate, (and that which is much more) my natiue country to keepe, and to gouerne our affaires as our deputie, finally to defend the ſame moſt valiantly from the dayly aſſault of* Saxones, Scottes, & Pictes. *But he in meane time forgetfull of my moſt bountifull liberallity towards him, & of our familiaritie, (which for moſt part in humaine*

Mordred meetes him.

The armies of them both encamped.

K. Arthures noble Oration vnto his fouldiours & ſubiectes going to fight againſt Mordred and his company.

46 The Assertion of

affaires, hath vndoubtedly cheefest importance) and not remembring the solemne oath of warelike order, wherby he is to me most deeply bounden, like a false periured and mightie contemner of God and man, yea an adulter also, (as Fame reporteth) now entertayneth me, a King and Conquerour of Nations, and his Liege soueraigne Lord returning into mine owne Countrie (if God so would permit him) euen with open hostilitie, hauing ready for his complices the Pictes his kinsmen, the Scottes their neighbours, and last of all the Saxones to helpe him.

Nota. Their first battell fought in Kent.

And neither doth this so notable mischeefe only touch me, but in deede it toucheth you all. Wherfore you most inuincible Champions, my only care, & you most valiant fellow souldiers, with present prowesse, handle your comune cause, and let vertue now shine forth in you, which I haue hetherunto perceiued to be ready, valiant & wonderful alwayes. Sir Gallouinus you the most praise worthy garland of warlike prowesse, whose glory for manie causes, and cheefly this, is most commendable vnto the world (in that you haue set at nought, Mordred our commune enemie, and in respect of equitie & oath of your alegeance to vs made, haue despised him your brother in Law.) Stand you here on your¹ right hand, as the most apt furnished horne with strength of Souldiours. For the first shares of hand stroakes and of renome shal light in this troupe of yours. Sir Augusellus as the bulwarke of most approued valiancie shall cast himselfe to encounter with our enemies at the left wing. I my selfe (& God to friend) will in the middest of you fight it out continually and will be present as your onely safegard, but to the enemies will I be a terrour, a scourge, and a deserued destruction. [16 back] But what neede many wordes, which neyther in deede adde nor take away valiant courage. Your valiancy is enlarged by custome, exercise, and sustayning of labour, watchinges and penury, yea finallie by shedding of the enemies bloud, and spoyling the same enemies: For the which considerations both I to you, and you to me againe (God fauouring so iust a cause) do promise assured victory. Go to, make immortall tryall of your manhoodes, and slay down right those traytours at a pinch. When he had thus saide, they altogether at their Gouernours commaundement showted aloude, and with a cherefull onsette, bestowing in order their ensignes, far and wide shewed forth the valiant

Sir Gallouinus his charge.

Sir Augusellus his charge.

The apparant promptitude of K. Arth. his souldiours.

¹ For our?

tokens of warlike attempt. So at the length partly their
enemies being flaine, and partly put to flight, *Arthure* obtayned His victory.
the victory with an horrible ouerthrow of his enemies. But
there were flaine in that battell fough[t] at the hauen of *Dorcefter*,
5 both *Gallouinus* and *Augufellus* the two thunderbolts of the Two of his Cheualiers
battell, as *Graius* maketh mention in his booke called *Scale-* or knightes
cronica, and as other Authours of fame not to be defpyfed, do flaine.
witneffe. *Mordred* blaming *Fortunes* vntowardneffe, with a Nauy
recouered, & the remnant of his Hoaft therein, got him with
10 fhame enough to the hauen of Tammeroth[1] on the Sea coafte of
Cornwaile. The noble coarfe of *Gallouinus* was entombed in
a certaine Chappell within the Caftle of *Dorcefter*. But *Arthure*,
(the death of two fo excellent famoufe men being fully knowne
to him) fore bewailed the fame: and with often prayer as, alfo
15 with very deepe greefe of heart, fuppreffing forrow from
their handes, (nobly minded and of Godly difpofition as he was)
fatherly tooke care ouer them. And then in deed hauing a frefh
prepared with incredible expedition a full Hoaft and army, he
determined with long iorneyes to purfue his lewde enemie, and
20 as it were vpon the fnappe to ouerthrowe the fugetiue. *Mordred* Mordredes
yet was more craftie, then of power able to withftand: here- preparation againft
upon found he out a meane for vnacuftomed inuentions. He King Arthure,
had manifeft knowledge giuen him by efpyals, that *Arthure* moft the fecond time.
abfolutly furnifhed for the battell, was comming at hand. [17]
25 Wherefore he commanded euery fouldier wearied vpon yͤ land,
& againe wᵗ toile vpon yͤ fea, as alfo penury of corne, to departe
for a feafon, & hauing refrefhed their induftrie, labour, & dilligence, as alfo furnifhing them with munition, fo well as he could
through yͤ mountayny foiles of *Cornwale*, by yͤ way yᵗ leadeth
30 to the banckes of *Seuerne*, not farre thence diftant conducteth he
his hoaft with eafie iornies: and in a place which of yͤ common
forte of writers is called Camblan (where as are wafte grounds &
partly a natural moift plaine, & a little hill rifing vp to yͤ vfe of
a watch or a profpect) did he pitch his tents. Here am I com-
35 pelled to interpofe or fet downe by the way my iudgment concerning the place where it was fought by both parts: and for yͤ
caufe yᵗ I fhould not thinke to bring hether anything amongft
yͤ reft, as if it were out of Iupiters braine, but that with yͤ good

[1] For *Tamermouth*? Cf. 49/2.

leaue of ye learned fort I might explane my coniecture, without all bitternes or difdaine as it were touching it by the way. In which behalfe I freely confes my felfe hardly to hold opinion with *Hector Boetius* the Scot, which (as his maner is) applieth all moft famous facts of antiquity in *Brittaine* to ye commenda- 5 tion of his owne country, beyond all meane & meafure. And here he boldly affirmeth y^t *Arthure* (with his laft enfignes) fought it out not far from ye great flowing riuer of *Seuerne*, which he barbaroufly calleth *Humbar* not knowing the circumftance of the phrafe. But the hiftory of *Brittaine* beleeueth otherwife, & 10 affirmeth that he fcourged his enemies in his laft battle in *Corn- wale*: fo yet notwithftanding as he mentioneth how *Mordred* was ye fecond time vanquifhed and put to flight by *Arthure* at *Winchefter*.

Graius vndoubtedly an excellent champion in behalfe of ye 15 truth & a ftoute affertor of *Arthures* glory, holdes ye fame opinion. Neither fingeth the found cenfured fociety of learned witneffes any other Song. But truely our coniecture is not of the places, but of the name of the place. Surelie I am almoft brought to that poynte, to beleeue that the Riuer *Alaune* 20 is eafily chaunged by the faulte of vnlearned Lybraryes into *Camblan*. This Riuer ryfeth in *Cornewale* a fewe Myles aboue the Towne *Athelftowe* otherwife *Padftowe*, a fifher Towne not farre [17 back] fcituate from the Salte water of *Seuerne*: by meanes wherof, (but yet mixed with falte waters) it runneth 25 downe lower into the countrie. Aboute the heade fpringes of that Originall in Champion grounde, and a certaine wafte plaine, there is a famous place, fomewhat more fruitfull of graffe then of corne. The reporte (amongeft the inhabitants fo many ages preferued) declareth that of olde time, there was made a notable 30 garboile by fighting in y^t place, but in meane time the truth of the hiftorie is vnknowne vnto ye common forte. Many things no doubt euen in this our age are founde out of ye fame place by ploughmen & thofe that delue at the Riuer: fuch as are thefe quoynes which fhewe the gouernments of aunciet perfonages, 35 ringes, fragments of harneffe & brafen ornaments for Bridles vnguilte, for trappers & alfo Saddles for Horfes. This is my coniecture, both by reafon of the fcituation of the place, & alfo for ye name of ye riuer *Alaune*, running hard by, yet not far

---

Nota.
Arthures
fecond
battle with
Mordred,
and the place
where.

Graius a
writer in the
fauour of
Arthure.

M. Cambden.

K. Arthure 49

diſſonant (if a man behold it more throughly) from *Camblan*.
Arthure now draweth neare, & paſſing ouer yᵉ riuer of T*amer*- M. Camden.
mouth, by knowne paſſages, yet otherwiſe a ſtreame moſt violent
in many places & moſt deepe (the enimy fugitiue not being
5 regarded) he pitcheth tents againſt tents. Behold, deſperation
(as oft times it hapneth) reſtoreth vnwonted boldnes to the ouer-
co*m*med part. And wherupon both partes prouoke battle,
burning with hope of ſpoyle & of victory, as alſo fearing nothing
leſſe then death.

10   Quis cladem illius pugnæ, quis funera fando
      Explicet ? aut poſſit lachrymis æquare labores ?

Who ſhall that bloodie broyle expreſſe or the dead corpſes name ?
Or who can iuſtly tell the toyles, with iuſt teares for the ſame ?

MOrdred the firſt forman of all miſchiefe (this battle being Mordred
15 attempted) and he thruſt through with yᵉ ſword, receiued a iuſt ſlaine out-
rewarde for his breach of faith or periury. Let him be an right.
example, & that for euer, to ſuch as for deſire of gouernment
infringe and violate their faith. There was ſlaine together with
yᵉ tyrant a great nu*m*ber of noble perſonages & of old beaten
20 ſouldiers: But neither was the victorie without bloodſhedde
befallen vnto *Arthure*. For in that broyle and [18] fierce fight, K. Arthure
himſelfe was either ſlaine outright, or wounded paſt recouery, receiued his
ſo that a little while after with publike lame*n*tation of all wound, &
Brittaine (but ſpecially of his heauie hearted cheualyers for the yet had the
25 miſchance of ſo noble a *Prince*) he was carried away fro*m* victorie.
thence. And this in deede was the end or death of the moſt
puiſſant *Prince Arthure*.

Chap. x.

K. Arthures Commendation.

ARthure is nowe deade (if ſo hee may bee ſayde to haue
30 dyed well) whoſe fame, memory, and prayſe fully and wholly
liue, and ſhine forth in the worlde.

Our anceſtors, both *Poets* and alſo hiſtoriographers were ſo
friendly, honeſt, and thankefull towardes *Arthure*, that they both
enobled his fame and factes, and alſo adorned them with eternall

L

The Assertion of

Auncient Authors, as Poets, & Historiographers, writing in commendation of K. Arthure.

memorie and commendation. T*heliesinus Melchinus*, who is also called *Meuinus*, *Ambrosius Maridunensis*, & *Merlinus Caledonius* the most excellent starres of *Brittaines* antiquitie haue performed this effect. *Nennius* and *Samuell*, historiographers of *Brittaine* haue performed no lesse memorie bestowing their statelie stiles of commendations accordingly. Touching whome and others also wee haue before fitly spoken in their places, affying in the authoryty of *Galfredus, Aluredus, Henry* of *Huntington*, Iohn termed the *Golden Historiographer, William of Malmesburie, Graius*, and *Boccace*.

Chrisistoriographus.

Iscæ.

But if it now auayle any man to knowe anything as yet more in matter and larger discourse: I will not refuse (in the best dilligence that I can) to restore to light a fewe wordes taken out of the most approued Authors. *Iosephus* the writer brought vp at *Exceter* in *Deuonshire*, and the Golden floud of Greeke and Latine eloquence in his dayes, extolleth *Arthure* to the very cloudes, not onely for his excellent prowesse, as in his *Antiochides* appeareth by thefe verses, contending for the victorie with the *Romane* antiquitie.

> Hinc cælebri fato fælici claruit ortu,
> Flos Regum *Arthurus*: Cuius cum facta stupori
> [18 back]
> Non micuere minus, quòd totus in aure voluptas,
>   Et populo narrante fauus, Quæcunque priorum,
> Inspice: Pelleum commendat[1] fama Tyrannum.
>   Pagina Cæsareos loquitur Romana tryumphos,
> Alciden domitis attollit gloria monstris.
>   Sed nec Pinetum Coryli, nec sydera solem
> Æquant. Annales Latios, Graiosque reuolue.
>   Prisca parem nescit, æqualem Postera nullum
> Exhibitura dies. *Reges* supereminet omnes,
>   Solus, præteritis melior, maiorque futuris.

Hence florished by famous fate, and origin prosperous
  Arthure *the flowre of kinges, whose deedes shined no lesse merueilous*
Then that both peoples eares & tongues did in his praise delite:
  As. *If thou view of former wights, what euer bookes recite.*

---

[1] Text, *comemndat*.

K. Arthure

Fame doth Pelleus *tyrant blaze: and Romane hiftories*
Extoll their Caefars *tryumphes greate, after their Victories.*
Renoume aduanceth Hercules *fubduing Monfters greate:*
But not Coryli, Pinetus, *nor* Stars *the* Sunne *his heate*
5 *Coequate. Search the Cronicles of Greekes & Latines both:*
Ancient age knoweth not his like, ne yet pofteritie doth
His match declare. All kinges, alone in deede furmounteth he,
Better then thofe are deade & gone, Greater then any fhall be.

THere hath beene feene latelie at *Glaftenburie* a little Booke
10 of matters touching Antiquitie, gathered by a certaine moft
ftudious Moncke of yᵉ fame Cloyfter: who by exercife of
Rethoricall coulour as it were handling an other matter, doth
famoufly mention of *Arthure* in thefe wordes. I paffe ouer with
filence alfo to fpeake of *Arthure* the noble King of *Brittaine*
15 buried with his wife betweene two Pyramedes within the church-
yard of thofe Monckes, & many princes alfo of yᵉ *Brittaines.*
Siluefter Giraldus Meneuenfis, a chiefe fauourer of Antiquitie in
his booke entituled the Inftitution of a *Prince,* enobleth *Arthures*
fame with this maner fpeach.

20 The memorie alfo of *Arthure* yᵉ noble king of *Brittaine* ought Siluefter
not to be buried or vtterly troden vnder foote, whom yᵉ hiftories Giraldus his
of yᵉ monaftery of *Glaftenbury* (whofe chiefe patron, [19] bene- testimony of
factor and mightie fupporter he alfo was in his dayes) do much K. Arthure.
aduaunce. *Iohannes Anneuillanus* no doubt a wittie *Poet* of his Iohannes
25 time, and no leffe elegant, folemnizeth *Arthures* praife in thefe Anneuillanu
verfes, which euen at this day appeare in his booke *Architrenio.*

    Alter *Achilles*
    Arthurius, teretis menfæ genitiua venuftas,
    A *Ramo Phrygius,* dandi non vnda fed æquor.
30 *An other* Achilles
    Arthure *was, whofe firft growne grace, through out his table*
      rounde
    Him Phrigius *made as of a* Branch *with fruites which doth*
      a bound
35 *For liberall hand, not* Riuer *he, but a maine* fea *Yfound.*

BUt here if ouer & befides this I fhould endeuour largely, to
adorne *Arthure* with praife as the multitude of Authours do moft
truly write and agree vpon him: fooner fhould copy of eloquence

52   The Affertion of

faile me, then magnificencie of lightfome teftimony howfoeuer.
Be it fufficient then that we vfe at this prefent the moft famoufe
commendations, though of fewe writers. I pray you, what is
the caufe that T*rittemeus* in his breefe Crounicle maketh fo
excellent mention of *Arthure.* Doubtleffe[1] the caufe is plaine
enough. For by reafon he learned the fame of others in plaine
trouth, therefore did he as thankfull commit it vnto pofteritie:
which thing doubtleffe he would neuer haue done, had he
doubted of the veritie of the caufe.[2] But now let T*rittemius* him
felfe in prefence fpeake.

*Which Arthure excelling in great humanitie, wifdome, clemencie
and manhood, ftudied by all endeuour to fhew himfelfe beloued and
reuerenced of all, and to excell all : becaufe alfo he abounded in
valiancie of minde with wonderfull liberalitie towardes all men,
and fpecially towardes Church men, vnto whome for zeale to God-
wardes, he gaue very many benefittes, yea and alfo rewardes.   He
droue out of* Brittaine *both* Saxons *and* Pictes.   *He mightely fubdued, the* Scottes, Irifhmen, *and* Orcades *vnto his kingdome.*

Volateranus in his third booke of *Geography* honoureth the
fame of *Arthure* & diligently celebrateth his valiant actes.

[19 back] Furthermore alfo *Iacobus Philippus* of *Bergoma* in
his 9. booke of *Cronicles,* aduanceth A*rthures* valiancie euen
with moft condigne commendations.

And neither doth *Nauclerus*, in his hiftory make any leffe
relation of him. Thefe teftimonies doubtleffe (men both moft
learned & moft exercifed in Antiquitie would neuer haue fet
downe) if they had not firft beene fully perfwaded, that A*rthure*
in times paft was aboundantly notable by all ornamentes of
valiancie. But fuch is the lewdneffe of many men, and their
difdainefull minde, that they altogether being feduced with
ignorance, (and that in deede very rude) do not manifeftly fee at
full, but blindly neglect, contemne, and altogether reiect the
truth. Such Cenfors or Iudges in auncient hiftories let them go
a Godes name, and let them enioy their foolifhneffe at full,
I will not fay their madneffe. What if I fhould bring forth
amongft the reft, that notable teftimony of *Hector Boætius,*
a writer in our time, touching ye immortall glory of *Arthure?*

---

[1] Text, *Ddoubtleffe.*   [2] Text has , instead of .

Trittemius his teftimony, who was famoufe Anno. 1484.

Trittemius his wordes in commendation of king Arthure.

Volateranus.

Iacobus Philippus Bergomas.

Nauclerus his teftimony.

Hector Boætius a Scottifh writer.

Surely by this accompt nothing fhal fall from his dignitie, but very much fhall be added therto for this caufe, that ẙe Scots in old time (I know not by what inftinct of nature) hated the Brittaines as ẙe Prouerbe fayeth. *Odio Vatiniano.* Whereupon, to be prayfed of an aduerfarie, enemie and euen a deadly foe, ftandeth in place of a rewarde for victory. Thefe are then his words. King Arthure *was no leſſe famouſe in glory for notable exploytes, & for maieſtie, then the Kinges of* Brittaine, *which liued before his dayes: whereupon the* Brittaines *during his raigne very much encreaſed in riches & power.* _{Hector Boætius his commenda- tion of K Arthure.}

Thus far faith *Boætius*. What iuft occafion wifh I here to be giuen me of *Polidorus* the *Italian*, that euen by fome memorable teftimony of his, I might alfo aduance *Arthures* countinance, & make him looke aloft? He handleth *Arthures* caufe in deed, but by the way, he yet is fo fainte harted, luke warme & fo negligent ẙt he makes me not onely to laugh, but alfo to be angry (as while he is contrary to truth, and filled ẘt *Italian* bitterneffe) I know not whether he fmile or be angry. For he wrefteth him felfe wretchedly in the aptneffe of the hiftory, which yet that he might frame after a fort, he is compelled, will hee [20] nill hee, to come in fauour ẘt *Geoffry of Monmouth*: whom before (as it seemed vnto him) he had in many words (proceeding mightely rather of bitter ftomacke, then of good difgeftion) corrected alfo at his owne controlment. Whom for ẙt as an interpreter I haue once or twife only defended in a caufe as no doubte moft iuft. (A danger in deed great might redound vpon my heade) if I fhould paffe beyond ẙe boundes of equity. I will take heede therefore, and trufting onely in ẙe veritie of the caufe, I will continually beare the fame aboute ẘt me for a bulwarcke & fure defence. Though *Polidore* hold his peace it is not needfull by and by for the whole worlde to be mute: And although *Italy* in times paft fo efteemed of *Arthure*, and yet ftill doth, when bookes printed both of his proweffe, & victories (as I haue learned) are read in the *Italian* tongue yea in ẙe Spanifh, and alfo in the *French* tongue: whereupon alfo the *English* collection of *Thomas Mailerius* his trauaile, is publifhed abroade. The aduerfarie I know will fay, that many lyes haue crept into thofe bookes. Wherefore this is nothing els, but to *Teach him which is fully taught.* As I contemne fables, fo I _{Polidorus Virgillius a corrupt witneffe of King Arthures worthineffe.}

_{Bookes printed of Arthure in forraine languages.}

reuerence & imbrace yᵉ truth of the hiſtory: neyther will I ſuffer this to be taken away from mee at any time, but with loſſe of life. Unthankfull perſons I vtterly eſchew and I betake me vnto thoſe Rockes & monuments, the true witneſſes of *Arthures* renoume and maieſtie. And in this behalfe, *Silueſter Geraldus Meneuenſis*, entertayneth me comming to him wᵗ theſe wordes taken out of that worke of his called Itenerarium. He vnderſtandes concluſiuely that *Brecania* or *Brecknock* rounde about is the Land ſo called as it were by reaſon of the loftie blaſtes from yᵉ North winde. From *Zephirus* or the Weſterly winde, it hath the mountaine places of *Canter Veha*n, alias yᵉ leſſe *Vehany*, from *Auſter* or the ſoutherly winde, it hath hilles ſouthwarde, whereof the principall is called in the *Brittaine* language *Cair Arture*: that is to ſay *Arthures Caſtle*, by reaſon of the two toppes of the hilles aſcendinge vpwardes ſhewinge them ſelues in maner of a Caſtle. And becauſe the Chaire of State is there erected in a high and harde place it is by a common name aſſigned vnto [20 back] the high and mightie *Arthure King* of *Brittaine*. Theſe faith *Silueſter, Giraldus*. Now muſt I take my iourney from the hilles of *Brecania* vnto *Baldwine*, a Towne in olde time famouſe, which for foure hundreth yeares and more agone, (of *Roger* then gouernoure of *Mountgomerie*, and Earle of *Shrowsbury*),[1] was called *Mountgomerie*. Here amongeſt the ruinous olde Cotages of the walles, is a place by common reporte knowne, which the remnant of the citizens of later age do call *Arthures gate*. Truly the people of *Wales* have alwayes beene and as yet are with a certaine Gentlemanly feruent affection bent to ſet forth the praiſes of their *Princes*. Through which title euen at this day ſhyneth forth the fame together alſo with the commendation not vulgar of *Arthure* firnamed the greate: who is alſo called in the Brittaine language **Arthure Vaur**. **Maur** In the Brittiſh tongue ſignifieth great: but the fond pronunciation of the welch tongue (in the worde **Copulatiue Maure**) turneth M. into V. Like as alſo in other wordes by reaſon of their proper tearming, B. is oftentimes turned into V.

---

[1] ꜱText lacks).

K. Arthure 55

Cap. xi.

The Antiquitie of *Aualonia*.

THe circumftance of fpeach, here admonifheth me that I expreffe fomewhat touching *Arthures* buriall; whereof as I haue made fufficient mention, fo iudge I it fpecially (for the lightfome
5 order) conuehient that I fhould firft with exquifite diligence confecrate vnto pofteritie the Antiquitie of that place, whither vnto the deade corpes was caried. *Aual* in the Brittifh tongue fignifieth *Malum*, (or as I may with a more common phraife interprete it) *Pomum*, an Aple: and *Aualon* fignifieth *Pomarium*, or
10 Orcharde. By reafon whereof alfo, of *Merlinus Caledonius*, (as *Geoffrey Arthurius* of *Monmouth* interpreteth the fame) it is called the Ifle of Apples, in thefe wordes. Diffinition of *Aualonia* the place where King Arthure was buried. Geoffry of Monmouth his teftimony thereof.

    Infula pomorum quæ fortunata vocatur,
    Ex re nomen habet, quia per fe fingula profert.
  [21]
15 Non opus eft illi fulcantibus arua colonis:
    Omnis abeft cultus nifi quem natura miniftrat.
    Vltro fœcundas fegetes producit & Vuas:
    Nataque poma fuis, prætonfo germine fyluis.

The Ifle of Apples, which called is fortunate,
20 *Of effect hath name, for it bringes forth all thinges:*
The feeded ground no neede of Plowmen hath,
    All tillage wantes, faue that which Nature bringes.
Of it owne accorde it beares both Grapes & Corne,
    And apples grow in woods, firft grafts being pruned & fhorne.

25 MELchinus the *Brittaine* makes mention of *Aualonia* and of the religious place there. *Siluefter Giraldus* in his booke *De Inftitutione Principis*, thus fpeaketh. And yᵉ ifland which at this day is called Glaftenbury, *was called in aunciẽt time* Aualonia: *For it is an Iflande altogether environed with moorifh*
30 *or fenny groundes: Whereupon in the Brittifh tongue it is called* Aualon, *that is, an Ifland fruitefull of apples: For with apples* (*which in the Brittifh tongue are called* Aual) *this place aboundeth*. Melchinus. Siluefter, Giraldus &

Patricius the Apoſtle or teacher amongeſt the *Iriſhmen* in a certaine Epiſtle makes mention of this place, but by another name, whoſe wordes alſo I will hereunto annex.

> *I haue conuerted Ireland vnto the way of truth, and when I had grounded them in the chriſtian faith, I returned at length into Brittaine, & as I beleeue (by the guidance of God, who is the way and the life) I chaunced into the Iſland* Iniſwitrine, *wherein I found a holy and auncient place choſen of God, and conſecrated vnto the Virgin* Mary, *and there alſo founde I certaine Brethren inſtructed with the rudiments of the Chriſtian faith, which ſucceeded the Diſciples of* Fugatius *and* Damianus.

Marginal notes: Patricius, all 3. witneſſes of Avalonia. | Alias Ciuitas, vitrina, nunc Glaſtenbury. | Suppoſed rather to be Faganus & Diruuianus, vt ante.

Thus farre ſayth *Patricius*: who in that place of his epiſtle alſo recyteth the names of twelue religious perſons: where of two were noble perſonages: Of all which twelue, he had chiefe Rule, as by theſe wordes it is manifeſt.

> *So they preferred me (though againſt my will) before* [21 back] *themſelues.*

Marginal note: Faganus and Diruuianus.

And againe, in the ſame Epiſtle the brethren ſhewed me writings of thoſe holy men *Fugatius* and *Damianus*, wherein was conteyned that the twelue Diſciples of *S. Philip* and *Iacob* the Apoſtles had founded and erected that auncient Church: and that three Pagan kinges had giuen ſo many poſſeſſions of land vnto thoſe twelue.

Marginal note: Vt ante dixi. Faganus & Diruuianus.

And laſt of al how that *Fugatius* & *Damianus* had builded a chappell on a high hill, not farre from *Aualonia* in the honor of *God* and *S. Michaell.* Heere is enough at this preſent (euen touch and goe) to haue vnderſtanding of the reuerend father *Patricius* his Epiſtle.

Marginal note: W. of Malmeſburie his teſtimony.

Gulielmus Meildunenſis, in his booke of the antiquitie of the religious houſe at *Glaſtenburie*, and in his firſt booke of kinges vnto *Henrie Bleſenſis* otherwiſe *Soliaſenſis* Biſhop of *Venta Simenorum* or *Wincheſter*, writeth not vnlike matters. Wherupon alſo by good coniecture it may bee ſeene that this *William*, tooke his tranſlations out of the Epiſtle of *Patricius*. *Silueſter Giraldus* in his booke *De Inſtitutione Principis*, not inconueniently explaneth the *Etymon* or true interpretation of the name. It was alſo in times paſt called in the brittiſh language Iniſwitrine: by yᵉ which word the *Saxones* which came thether afterwarde called that place *Glaſtenbury*. For **Gles** in their tongue

Marginal note: Silueſter Giraldus his teſtimony and explanation of Glaſtenburie.

K. Arthure 57

fignifieth *Vitrum* or glaffe, and **Bury** fignifieth *Caftrum* or Caftle, and is called together the city of *Glaftenburie*. Thefe doth he affirme. Truly vnto me this feemeth to bee a foule faulte in writers of bookes that they heere do recite **Byry** for
5 **burg** or **berg**: **Byry** in the Saxon tongue is in Latine *Curia*: As for example, *Aldermanburie*, that is to fay *Seniorum Curia*. Alfo **Litlebyry**, that is *Parua Curia*. **Canonbyry** commonly called *Canbyry*. *Burg* otherwife *Borow*, fignifieth a hill, and high places of earth caft vp. Finally **Berg** is in the Latine
10 tongue called *Caftrum*: by reafon wherof I more truly beleeue we muft reade *Berg* or *Burg*, for a Caftle: which worde *Giraldus* vfeth or maketh it to ferue for a Towne: although as I may freely confeffe, I find the name written diuerfly amongeft the ancients viz. *Gleffenbyry Gleftonbury* and *Gleffenburg*. And
15 there are which pronounce *Glas* for *Gles*: Although [22] *Gles* is more perfect and more Auncient, as by the name of the Iflandes of *Glaftenburie* it appeareth plainly.

Chap. xii.

K. Arthures Buriall.

NEither can I, nor wil I publifh for trueth, whether *Arthure*
20 dyed out right in the battle fought at *Alaune*, which is commonly called *Camblan*, or at *Aualonia*, while his wounds were in healing. The writers of *Brittaine* with one voyce holde argu- Writers of ment, that he dyed at *Aualonia*, through griefe of the fame brittaine affirming woundes: But touching the place of his buriall, they doe all where
25 agree as one. Arthure died.

This one thing dare I be bolde to affirme, the *Brittanes* were The Brit- fo forowfull for the death of their Soueraigne Lorde, that they taines forow- endeuored by all meanes to make the fame famous, and to death of leaue the name of their Gouernour euen for euer fearefull and to K. Arthure.
30 bee trembled at amongeft the *Saxones*: So farre foorth as they with a certaine plaufible and ftraunge inuention did fpreade abroade Rumors both of his comming againe, and of his ruling againe. Touching the againe comming (of *Arthure* fo wounded to death) into *Aualonia* aforefaid, certaine Brittaines did blindly

58 The Affertion of

Merlinus Caledonius a writer his verfes of K. Arthures death.

write. But none more at large nor more lightfome, then *Merlinus Caledonius* being inftructed (as fome men fuppofe) of T*heliefinus* the *Poet*: whofe verfes alfo I will heere annex, felected out of his little booke of prophecy, *Geoffrey Arthurius* beeing interpreter thereof.

Illuc poft Bellum *Camblani* vulnere læfum,
 Duximus *Arthurum*, nos conducente *Barincho*.
Æquora cui fuerant, & cœli Sidera nota.
 Hoc Rectore ratis, cum Principe venimus illuc,
Et nos quo decuit *Morgan* fufcepit honore,
 Inqu*e* fuis thalamis pofuit fuper aurea Regem
Fulcra, manuqu*e* fibi detexit vulnus honefta,
 Infpexitqu*e* diu: tandem redire falutem,
[22 back]
Poffe fibi dixit, fi fecum tempore longo
 Effet, & ipfius vellet Medicamina fungi.
Gaudentes igitur, Regem commiffimus illi,
 Et dedimus ventis redeundo vela fecundis.

*T*he English.

Thether after the battle was at Camblan *fiercely fought,*
 Barinchus fo conducting vs) we Arthure *wounded brought.*
Who knew the feas, & of the ftars the Clymats perfectly,
 By this guider of the helme with Prince we thether ply.

Morgan a faithfull friend and true fubiect vnto Arthure.

And Morgan *vs receiued as it behoued with honor dewe,*
 In Chamber his on Golden hearfe, and laide the king to view.
And with his friendly hand forthwith did Arthures *wound vnhill,*
 Long looking thereon, faid, may be life come againe yet will.
If he along time were with him, & would his medicines vfe,
 Therfore with ioy the King to him we did betake to chufe,
And hoift our failes with profperous wind: by our returne our porte to finde.

Morgans wife made prouifion for Arthures buriall.

Syluefter Gyraldus writeth in his *Speculo Ecclefiaftico*, that *Morgans* noble wife made prouifion for *Arthures* buriall. And againe, in his booke *De Inftitutione Principis* he makes relation of thefe thinges. *Whereupon alfo the noble wife of Morgan,* and Gouerneffe of thofe partes againe as *Patroneffe* there and alfo neare of blood vnto *Arthure*, after the battle at *Kemelen* caufed

K. Arthure 59

him to be conueyed into an Iſle (which now is called *Glaſconia*) to cure and heale vp his woundes.

The interpretor of the Britiſh hiſtory, writeth of the death of *Arthure*, on this manner, as in his ſixt booke appeareth. *Arthure being wounded vnto death at the battle at* Camblan *went vnto* Aualonia, *his kingdome being left vnto* Conſtantine *the sonne of* Cadorius *Duke of Cornwale.* {Brittanic Hiſtoriæ Interpres teſtimonium dat de morte Arthurii.}

Iohannes Burgenſis Abbot, in his Annales hath left theſe wordes in credible writinges. When Arthure *was at the pointe of death, he kept him ſelfe ſecret, that his enemies ſhould not inſult at ſuch and ſo great a miſhap, nor his friends be diſcomforted as troubled in minde.* Thus far he. {Iohannes Burgenſis teſtimonium de eodem.}

Now muſt wee ſpeake of the reli[gi]ous place at *Aualonia*, wherein *Arthure* was buried.

[23] *Melchinus* ſpecially makes mention of this and alſo of *Arthure* buried there.

Gulielmus a Medulphi curia both els where, and ſpecially in his booke *De antiquitate Gleſſonburgenſi*, religiouſly celebrateth this place where *Arthure* was buried. {Aualonia commended by 3. writers. viz. Melchinus, & Malmsbury Giraldus.}

The ſame thing doth *Giraldus Meneuenſis* alſo in his *Speculo Eccleſiaſtico*, and in his booke *De Inſtitutione Principis*, religiouſe houſes were not at that time ſo common, and in ſo many places of *Brittaine*, as they be in theſe dayes.

Saxons of noble linage, a people without knowledge of God if happely being ſicke they dyed at home, were buryed in pleaſant gardens: if they were ſlaine abroade, and in battell, they were then buryed in graues digged out of the earth, which they called *Burghs*, neare vnto their tentes: but the baſe common people were buried euen in medowes and open fieldes. {Burying places how and for whom in thoſe dayes.}

There was at that time a religiouſe place neare vnto the olde Church, in very greate eſtimation. By which title and of the whole nobilitie in all the weſt Prouinces of *Brittaine*, it was choſen as a place allotted for their burials. The ſame was afterwardes often done by ſuch *Saxons* as had the knowledge of God. As at *Douer* of the *Kentiſhmen*, at *Yorke* of the *Brygantes*, at *Lindiſſarna* or *Lyland* and ſo forth in other places. Concerning the place of his buriall it is now ſufficient manifeſt.

It remayneth that I make declaration of the ceremony and manner of his buriall. There was preſent (but ſecretly) {Ceremonies uſed at King}

60   *The Aſſertion of*

Arthure his buriall. a Troupe of Noble perſonages which mourned for yᵉ death of their foueraigne Lord bereft from them by ſuch ſiniſter fate.
Morgans noble wife alone prouided for Kinge Arthures buriall. The wife of *Morgan* alone prouided for the buriall thinges needfull: a woman doubtleſſe of incomperable godlineſſe, who performed all ceremonies and ſeruices with greefe of minde, and floudes of teares. The manner in thoſe dayes was to bury in the graues, and to lay them as a ſurceaſing from ſorrow to the vſe of Tombes or ſepulcres great boules or bodyes of Alder trees, whereof the places about *Aualonia* neare adioyning were moſt fruitfull. For the Alder tree hath I know not what propertie with the naturall [23 back] moyſt ground, ſuch as is a Churchyarde: ſo farre forth as the ſubſtance thereof laide on this forte, more deepe in the Earth, ſhould be reputed for euerlaſting not onely. The body of *Arthure* thus bewailed and
How he was interred in the earth. mourned for, was buryed in a graue of ſufficient depth, with the greate boale of Alder tree therein laide hollow. And becauſe he liued moſt magnificent in fame, factes, and rule of his kingdome (they folowing diligently the cuſtome and integritie of *Chriſtians* in this poynt) beſtowed vpon the Tombe of *Arthure* ſo buried,
Monumentes of him. a toaken of perpetuall memory namely a *Croſſe*, ſignyfyinge *Mnemoſynen vitæ perpetuæ*: that is to ſay, the remembrance of life euerlaſting. It was made of a leaden plate, one foote long more or leſſe, which I haue beholden with moſt curiouſe eyes, and handled with feareful ioyntes in each part, being moued both with the Antiquitie and worthineſſe of the thing. It conteyneth vpon it theſe wordes in thoſe not ſo greate Romane letters, but indifferent cunningly grauen, viz.

HIC IACET SEPVLTVS INCLITVS REX
ARTHVRIVS, IN INSVLA AVALONIÆ.

But here peraduenture ſome curiouſe perſon would ſearch out for what purpoſe the inſcription was commended to our memory vpon the leaden plates. It was a moſt vſual manner in that age, and endured euen vntill latter times to beſtow vpon Noble mens Tombes leaden plates engrauen. Of which not a fewe haue I ſeene in euery place throughout all *Brittaine*. Leade of his nature is eaſilie engrauen, and when it is once grauen continueth
This was ſet vp in both a very long time, and alſo moſt firmly, as witneſſeth experience. The myne hilles where leade groweth much, are ſcarce

K. Arthure

fiue miles diftant from *Aualonia*. The *Romans* as Lordes of places where riches, were not afhamed to fet up a ftandard of ftone vnto enemies were vanquifhed *Claudius Cæfar* by a very long table of leade, almoft in the very by the bottomes of thofe hilles at the heade fpringes of the fabulus Emperour.
5 little floude *Ochides* within the iurifdiction of *Fontanus* the Bifhoppe, engrauen on this manner

   Ti. Clavdio Cæsari. Avgvst. P.m.
   Tr. P. viiii. Imp. Xvi. De Britan.

This [24] Standard of Stone a few yeares paft was turned vp out In tempore
10 of the earth by the plowe, and tranflated vnto the houfe of regni Henrici Reg. 3.
Thomas Howarde, Duke of *Northfolke* at *London*.

Cap. xiii.

The two *Pyrameds* in that religious place.

WIthin the burying place which was confecrated at *Aualonia* Within the ftand two *Pyramedes* of moft auncient buylding, bearing a fhew burying place were fet vp
15 of figures & letters, but the windes, ftormes, and time which 2. Pyrameds. confumeth all thinges, finally enuy of man from time to time haue fo defaced the notable figures and infcription of auncient workes, that they can fcarce be difcerned by any neuer fo fharpe fight of the eye. The continuall trauell of writers commendeth Auncient
20 thefe, and fpecially the diligence of *Gulielmus Meildunenfis* that writers commending greate *Antiquary*: whom alfo *Siluefter Geraldus* euen he a louer the fame. of Antiquities, doth follow at an inche. Doubtleffe both of them handle their matters learnedly: The one whereas by exquifite labour he reftored to light a frefh, both titles and figures which
25 were not altogether raced out of knowledge for foure hundreth yeares before, according as in his famoufe and elegant little booke *De Antiquitate Gleffoburgenfi*, appeareth. The other in that he leaning vnto founde argumentes and relation of auncient writers, proueth that *Arthures* Tombe was in times paft eyther
30 erected betwene the two *Pyrameds*, or in a place not far diftant King Arthures from them. Of *Giraldus* we wil fay more in the Tombe of Tombe where it was erected. *Arthure* found.

In the meane time, I wil herevnto annex the difcription of the *Pyrameds*, artificially purtrayed out by the very pencilles of the

62   *The Aſſertion of*

<small>The meaning and diſcription of thoſe two Pyramedes.</small>

ſame *Gulielmus*, as it were in a plaine table to the eyes of the be‑ holders. And where as that no doubte is vnknowne vnto all men, I would willingly publiſh it, (if I could poſſibly expreſſe the truth) what thoſe *Pyrameds* do meane, which being erected in a litle ſpace from the olde Church do after a ſorte include 5 the Churchyarde of thoſe religiouſe perſons.

<small>Tabulatus.</small>

[24 back] Undoubtedly the more ſtatelyer, larger, and nearer *Pyramed* vnto the Church hath fyue ſtoryes height or flooers boorded, & is in height, 26. foote. Thus although it foreſhewed ſome decay by reaſon of yᵉ too much oldneſſe, yet hath it a few 10 apparant ſpectacles of Antiquitie, which may be plainely reade, although they can not fully be vnderſtode. For in the vpper ſtory or floore boorde is made an image in likeneſſe of a Biſhoppe.

<small>Note the blindneſſe of that time in preferring a Biſhop before a king.</small>

In the ſecond is an Image expreſſing a Kingly ſtate, and letters: *Her. Sex. & Bliswerh*. In the third neuertheleſſe are names. 15 **Wem Creſte, Bantomp, Winewegn**. In the fourth. **Hate, Wulfredi & Franflede**. In the fifte, and which is the loweſt, an image and this writing. **Logwor. Weſllelas & Bregdene. Swellwes, Huyrgendes berne**. But the other Pyramed hath 18. foote height and foure ſtoryes or flooers boorded wherein 20 theſe wordes are reade, **Hedde**, *Epiſcopus* & **Bregorred & Beorwalde**. What theſe may ſignifie I do not raſhly define: but I gather by ſuſpition, that within or about the ſame place are laide in hollow ſtones the bones of them whoſe names are reade on the outſide. Surele **Logwor** for certaine is affirmed to be the 25 perſon by reaſon of whoſe name **Logweres Beorh**, was ſo called, which is now called **Montacute**. **Beor walde** neuertheleſſe was Abbot after **Hemgiſelus**. Theſe ſaith *Meildunenſis* (vnto whom the learned ought to referre theſe *Pyrameds*) as from him by all meanes borowed, and moſt famouſly ſet forth. Now yᵉ lady 30 *Guenhera* offereth herſelfe to be ioyned wᵗ *Ar[t]hure* her Huſband.

Cap. xiiii.

What manner Perſon *Guenhera* was.

I Haue eaſely beleeued, that *Guenhera* was deſcended out of the progeny of the Dukes of *Cornwale*: both leaninge vnto 35 other argumentes, and alſo for this cauſe ſpecially, that the Hiſtory

K. Arthure 63

of *Brittaine* makes mention y^t she was brought vp in ye Pallas of Cadorus Duke of *Cornwale*, & also from hence taken vnto wife by *Arthure*. The coniecture is, and that not altogether vncertaine this name of *Guenhera* foundeth in the *British* language the same that *Bella Dona* [25] doth in the Italian & in french. *Belle Dame*, no doubt the name was giuen for some fame: as *Guenllean*, that is *White* or *fayre Leonora*, or of coniecture *Helena*: so as ye worde *White* may signifie faire, beautifull, or amiable. But as it is sufficiently apparant y^t she was beautifull, so it is a thing doubted, whether she was chaste yea or no. Truly so far as I can with honestie I would spare the impayred honor and fame of noble wome*n*: But yet the truth of ye historie pluckes me by the eare, & willeth not onely, but commandeth me to declare what the Ancients haue deemed of her. To wrestle or contend with so greate authoritie were in deede vnto me a controuersie and that greate. The historie of Brittaine affirmeth, that she had not onely carnall knowledge of *Mordred* the *Pict*, but also that she was ioyned to him in mariage. O mischiefe, O lewd life, O filthy dayes.

The writer of the historie of *Gildas* is in deede an Auncient Author, (but in mine exemplar that same *Anonymus*) declareth these things of *Guenhera* the adultresse.

Arthure in despite of *Melua* the ruler, beseeged the fenny countries neare vnto Glesconia: which noble man had defiled *Guenhera* being stolne away and carried thether. This testimonie as touching a Queene, though hee say she was stolne away, is scarce honourable. Women of such beauty are now and then stolne away by their owne good will. How soeuer it was, most assured is this, that she liued no long time after the Death of her Husband, and the Adulterer. But whether through any disease of the bodie, or with vnfayned sorrowe she dyed (which I doe sooner beleeue) it appeareth not playnely. Writers make mention, that she beeing mooued with repentance did put vpo*n* her a holy *Veyle* at *Ambrosia*, and that there she dyed and was also buried, vntill both the dilligence and also Godlinesse of S*ir* *Lancelot* the most courteous and most inuincible knight had translated the bones and ashes afterwardes vnto *Aualonia*. Heere aryseth a doubt against the suspition of this Adulterie.

Where the Lady Guenhera was brought vp.

Her description.

Beautie & Chastitie seldom agree inuiolably.

Anonimus.

A writers testimonie touching Guenhera.

Sir Lancelot, knight, a friend of Guenheras after her death.

Whether fo notable a Louer or friend of *Arthure*, and the fame a reuerencer of his royaltie had committed fuch a fact that hee woulde burie the Adultreffe in the moft Religioufe [25 back] place fo neare her hufbands graue in the earth. The hiftory of the cloifter at *Glaftenbury* which was dilligently collected, fully 5 fheweth that *Guenhera* was buried in the religious place neare her hufbandes Tombe, and that her bones and afhes were found the fame time that her hufbandes were.

<small>Nota. where she was buried.</small>

Siluefter Giraldus Meneuenfis confirmeth this in his booke *De Inftiiutione Principis* fpeaking of *Arthure* in thefe wordes. 10

<small>Siluefter Giraldus his teftimony both of Arthure and of Guenheraes dead corpfes.</small>

For hee had two wiues, whereof in deede the laft was buryed with him, and her bones founde at one time with her hufbandes bones, fo yet feparated that the two parts of the graue towardes the head, namely (which fhould containe the bones of her hufband) had beene afcribed vnto him: But the third part at the feete contained 15 *the bones of a woman vpwardes. Where as alfo a yeallow locke of a womans haire, with the former integrity & coulour was found, which as a certaine Moncke defiroufly caught vp in his hand & lifted it vp, it altogether ftreightway perifhed into duft or pouder.* 20

The fame *Giraldus* recyteth fuch like matters in his booke intituled *Speculo Ecclefiaftico*: Hee doubtleffe might well with fome authority fpeake concerning this geare, for fo much as, euen then he (beeing eftablifhed in the fauour of *K. Richard coeur de Lion*, king of England) came the very fame time that 25 the Sepulchre was found at *Glaftenbury*, and as an eye witnes (by conduction of *Henry de Soliaco* nephew vnto *K. Henry* by *Adela* and cofen germaine of *K. Richard* beeing the prefident of *Glaftenburie*, but afterwardes Bifhop of *Winchefter*) learned full and whole all thinges which vnto *Arthure* appertained. 30

<small>De Soliaco.</small>

Yet notwithftanding, if it were lawfull for me heere to fpeake all thinges which I thinke, I would furely affirme that thofe thinges are of farre better credite, which are delyuered vs of *Arthures* buryall, then of *Guenheras*. And yet woulde I not doe any iniurie vnto the Authorytie of Auncyent wryters, that euen 35 the pofteritie in time to come myght not handle mine Authoritie or allegation in a worfe manner. At *Glaftenbury* vppon the Tombe of [26] *Lydias Marble* or *Touchftone* Artyficially engrauen (and erected for *Arthure* and alfo for *Guenhera*) thefe

<small>Arthures and Guenheras Tombe erected at Glaftenbury.</small>

two little verses, sauoring of that his time, are written in this manner.

> Hic iacet *Arturi* coniux tumulata secunda,   Her Epitaph.
> Quae meruit cœlos, Virtutum prole fæcunda.

5 *The second wife of* Arthure *heere, entomed lo doth ly,*
Who for the fruites of Vertuous life deserued the heauens on hye.

THere bee which say that *Henry Suynesius* Abbot of *Glastenbury* was the composer of these verses: Except any man thinke that *Henry Blesensis* alias *Soliacensis* chaunged his name into 10 Suynesius, in whose time the bones and ashes both of *Arthure* and also of *Guenhera* were founde.

But what *Giraldus* & *Henricus* do meane by the name of *Second wife*, truly I doe not sufficiently vnderstand. For so much (as I can remember) I haue neither hard of the name nor 15 memorie of a second wife untill this day.

But let credite remaine with Authors: by the latter part of the second litle verse (*Virtutum prole fæcunda*) it appeareth y^t *Guenhera* was more vertuous then apt to beare children. Neither am I ignorant what *Boetius* writeth here, that in times past there 20 was a sharp battle fought betweene *Arthure* and *Mordred*, at the riuer of *Humber*, and y^t *Guenhera* being euen there caried away of ye Picts, into their tents, afterwards died and was buried at *Horestia* in the streete *Angusia*. But I leaue *Hector* to the reporte of *Veremundus* & *Turgotus* those obscure writers. And 25 it might so bee, that the Tombe was there erected for another *Guenhera* not Queene.

Nota. How Guenhera was stolne away of the Pictes.

Chap. xv.
K. Arthures Tombe found.

When the *Saxones* powre grewe to some force after *Arthures* death, & that the *Picts* & *Scots* by and by were put to flight, 30 & chased away beyond the vale of *Seuerne*, [26 back] The same Saxones began not so much to feare, and much lesse to esteeme of, but rather openly to set at nought the remnauntes of those vanquished *Brittaines*. Wherefore, the glory of them beganne to floorish, but of the *Brittaines* to decrease and fade away: 35 Yet so, as the *Saxones* left almost nothing (touching affaires

After Arthures death, the Saxons florished, but the Brittaines perished.

Saxones were negligent in

the fame of Britones their pofteritie. paffed betweene them and the *Brittaines*) at that time perfectly written for the pofterytie.

For, thofe thinges which were written (after *Chrift* was knowne vnto them) concerning the firft victories of the Saxones, are deliuered by the reportes of the common people, & fo receiued, 5 and in writinges fo committed: or els the *Brittaines* being vtterly worne away by fo many battles, beftowed fcarce any iuft or right dilligence in writing of the hiftorie. Only there are *Iohn Stowe.* extant certaine fragments of *Gildas* the Moncke of the City *Bangor* rather flaying aliue, difmembring, and wounding to death 10 the *Brittaines*, then allowing them with any value of vertue, fo farre foorth as he feemeth a Rethorician thorowly moued to make euyll reporte. By this meanes were the affaires of *Brittaine*, *Bardi were fuch as fung to the harpe the famo[u]s[1] factes of noble perfonages.* through calamitie of battles left obfcure or vnrevayled. The hiftoricall fingers only ftudied to preferue alfo with muficall 15 meanes the famous memorie of Nobles in thofe daies. They fung the famous facts of noble perfonages vpon the harp. This ftudie or practife wonderfully profited knowledge, as it were deliuered by hand vnto pofterity. Whereupon in deede it fo commeth heere to paffe alfo, that the name, fame, and glory of 20 *Arthure* might fo be preferued after a forte.

O factum bene.
    Si quid mea Carmina poffunt,
        Aonio ftatuam fublimes vertice Bardos.
    Bardos Pieridum cultores, atque canentis,   25
        Phœbi delitias, quibus eft data cura perennis,
    Dicere nobilium clariffima facta virorum
        Aureaque excelfam famam fuper aftra locare.

The Englifh.

O well done.   30
If anything my verfes may auayle,
    Thefe ftatelie fingers then aduance Will I, [27]
That high Parnaffus mount for to affaile.
    As fingers honouring the Mufes friendes duly,
    And Phoebus his delightes finging fweetly.   35
The famous actes of noble men to blafe,
    And ftately fame I'th golden heauens to place.

[1] Text, *famons*.

K. Arthure 67

William A Norman had conquered the Nation of Englishmen Anno. 1067.
by permission of God, and now came the kingdome of *England*, a Christo
vnto *Henry* the second of that name, Nephew by *Matildes* nato.
the daughter of *Henry Beauclercke*, and the Sonne of *Geoffry* 1154. Regni.
5 *Plantagenet*, Duke of *Gaunt*. This man endeuoring by all Anno. 1.
meanes to enlarge the limittes of his kingdome, applyed also
his minde vnto the kingdome of *Ireland*. *Richard* of *Clare* 1154. Regni.
Erle of *Chepstowe*, (so called by reason of the wanderinge Riuer) Anno. 1.
a man both most noble by birth, fortune, and vertue, went into
10 *Ireland*, beeing before requested of *Deronutius* the ruler of
Lagenia, so to do: in which expedition hee behaued him selfe
so valiantly, that (they being cast out by heapes put to flight,
and vanquished which withstood the Ruler) he purchased him Giraldus.
selfe fame an[d] immortall glory and (if this also might Cambrensis
15 anything auaile to the purpose) he obtayned besides greate Richard
riches vnto himselfe thereby, taking to wife *Eua* the daughter Strongbowe
of *Deronicius*, and heire by right nougth. *King Henry* had Chipstow.
vnderstanding of the successe of *Richard* the Erle of Iohn stow.
Chepestowe, and whether he enuyed his glory, or (which is
20 most like) that hee earnestly sought the pray of this rich
kingdome, hee forbad this *Richard* in the meane time to
beare rule in *Ireland*, not disdayning yet to proffer him reward. He being wise, fully knowing the *Princes* purpose, gaue
place vnto his right. In the meane seaſon *Henry* hauing
25 prepared no small part of an Hoast, came into *Cambria* or 1157. Regni.
Wales, and purposing there to appoynt the residue, he thence Anno. 3.
straight sayled from *Meneuia* or *Sanct Dauids* into *Ireland*, with
hope of which kingdome to obtaine, hee burned as hote as fire.
Whiles he busieth him selfe here aboutes being (for his worthi- Iohn stow.
30 nesse as befitted) receyued of the Gouernoures of *Wales*, at
his banquettes there (vsing [27 back] an Interpreter) he gaue
eare not with out pleasure vnto the historicall singers, which
singe to the Harpe famous actes of noble men. Truly there
was one amongst the rest most skilfull in knowledge of Antiquitie.
35 He so sunge the praises and noble actes of *Arthure* comparing
Henry with him as Conquerour in time to come for many King Henry
respectes, that hee both wonderfully pleased, & also delighted the second
the Kinges eares: at what time also ye King learned this valiancy com-
thing especially of the historical singer, that *Arthure* was pared to K.
Arthure and

M 2

was inquifi-tiue after his monument.

King Arthures Tombe found. Anno Ric. Regis. 1.

Siluefter Giraldus Malmsbury.

The place where King Arthure his Tombe was found at that time, and the manner therof.

buried at *Aualonia* in the religioufe place. Whereupon fending away the faide finger as witneffe of fuch a monument moft liberally rewarded, he had conference with *Henricus Blefenfis*, alîas *Soliacenfis* his nephew, who euen then or a litle after was made of an Abbot in the Ifle of *Bermundfege*, cheife 5 Magiftrate ouer *Glaftenbury* that he might with moft exquifite diligence fearch out thorowly the Tombe or burying place of *Arthure* within the compaffe of that religioufe houfe. It was affayed by him otherwhiles and at length founde out with greate difficulty, in the laft dayes, as fome fuppofe of *Henry* 10 the fecond, King of *England*: but as others thinke (vnto whom I eafely affent) in the beginning of the raigne of *Richard* the firft, his Sonne.

Touching both this fearching for, and finding out of the bones, two perfons fpecially amongft others haue written their 15 mindes: of which two one was a Moncke of Glaftenbury, and by name vnknowne to me, but the other was *Siluefter Giraldus*. Furdermore there had beene hereunto added alfo *Gulielmus Meildunenfis*, as the third witneffe to be conferred with them both, but that death had taken him away in his aged yeares 20 before the Sepulcre or Tombe was found. The teftimonies of thefe men will I vfe efpecially, and at this inftant I will bring hether the wordes of *Annonymus* the Moncke. *King Arthure* was entombed, like as (by *K. Henry* ye fecond) *Henry* ye Abbot had learned, whofe cofen germaine & familier friend he of late 25 was. But ye King had often times heard this out of the actes of the *Brittaines*, & of their hiftoricall fingers, that *Arthure* was buried neare vnto the old Church in the religioufe place betweene two [28] *Pyramedes* in times paft, nobly engrauen, and erected as it is reported for the memory of him. 30

And King *Arthure* was buryed verie deeply for feare of the *Saxons*, whom he had often times vanquifhed, & whome he had altogether reiected or caft out of the Ifle of *Brittaine*. And whome *Mordred* his mifcheeuous Nephew had firft called backe againe and brought thither againft him: leaft they (fhould alfo 35 with mallice of minde raige in crueltie towardes the deade body) which had laboured by tooth & naile euen now to poffeffe againe the whole Ifland after his death. Againe for and in refpect of the fame feare, he was laide in a certaine broade ftone, (as it

K. Arthure 69

were at a graue) found of them which digged there, of feauen foote as it were vnder ye earth: when yet notwithftanding *Arthures* Tombe was founde more lower, of nyne foote depth.
5 There was moreouer founde a leaden croffe not fet into the vppermoft but rather neathermoft parte of the ftone, hauing thereon thefe letters engrauen.

HIC IACET SEPVLTVS INCLITVS REX
ARTHVRIVS IN INSVLA AVALONIÆ.

And the Croffe taken out of the ftone, (the faide Abbot *Henry*
10 fhewing the fame) we haue feene with our eyes, and haue reade thefe letters. But like as the Croffe was infixed to the neathermoft parte of the ftone: So that parte of the croffe engrauen (to the ende it might be more fecrete) was turned towardes the ftone. Doubtleffe a wonderfull induftrie and exquifite wifdome of the
15 men in that age, who by all endeuoures defired to hide in fecret manner the body of fo greate a perfonage, and their Soueraigne Lord, efpecially the *Patrone* of that place, by reafon of the inftant troubled ftate: And who yet had further care that at one or other time afterwardes (when the trouble furceafed, by the
20 perfect order of thofe letters engrauen in the Croffe and found out other whiles) they might make apparànt teftimonies of his buriall.

And as the forefaide King *Henry* had before declared all the matter to the Abbot: fo the body of *Arthure* was found not in
25 a marble Tombe (as it befitted fo notable a Kinge) [28 back] not in a ftony place, or grauen out of the white *Paris* ftone, but rather in a wodden Tombe made hollow for this purpofe, and of fixtene foote deepe in the earth, more for the haftie then the honourable burying of fo puyffant a *Prince*, that time of trouble
30 requyring the fame.

Anno Domini. 1189. The *King* befetting the place, with Caldrons, on a certaine day, commanded them to digge there. Herehence the Deluers hauing fearched an exceeding depth, & now almoft being paft hope, beholde yet they found out a
35 wodden Tombe of a wonderfull greatneffe faft clofed rounde aboute. Which being lift vp, and opened, they found therein the Kinges bones of an incredible bigneffe, fo as the bone of his fhinne, might reach from the ground vnto the middle of the

Margin notes:
- Nota His infcription & the fubtile deuife of the Workmen in thofe dayes.
- King Arthure buried in a wodden Tombe of 16. foote deepe. An. 1. Ricardo Regis. prmi.
- King Arthures Tombe found where as alfo the Queene

<small>was with him laide.</small> legge in a tall man. They alſo found a leaden croſſe on the other ſide. Thus engrauen.

> Hɪᴄ Iᴀᴄᴇᴛ Sᴇᴘᴠʟᴛᴠs Iɴᴄʟɪᴛᴠs
> Rᴇx Aʀᴛʜᴠʀɪᴠs Iɴ Iɴsᴠʟᴀ Aᴠᴀʟᴏɴɪæ.

Herehence they opening the Tombe of the Queene buried [5] with *Arthure* founde a yealow locke of womans heaire, both faire of it ſelfe, and alſo twiſted together with wonderful curioſitie : which when they had touched, mouldred away too nothing. Then the Abbot and his conuent, taking vp their Lyneaments tranſlated the ſame with ioy into the greater [10] Church, placing them in a new Tombe (nobly engrauen and pulliſhed in the inwarde partes) after a twofold faſhion : That is to ſay, the Kinges body by it ſelfe at the heade of the Tombe : The *Queene*, at the feete of him, namely in the Eaſte parte : <small>Their tranſlation vnto another place.</small> where, vntill this day preſent, they honourably take their reſt. [15] But this Epitaph is engrauen vpon their Tombe.

<small>King Arthures old Epitaph.</small>   Hic iacet *Arthurius* flos regum, gloria regni,
   Quem, mores, probitas, commendant laude perenni.

Here lyeth Arthure *the floure of kinges, & glory of his king-*
  dome, [20]
Whome life and honeſtie commende with laſting praiſe to come.

THus farre moſt diligently, and alſo moſt faithfully haue we conuerted theſe things out of yᵉ booke at *Glaſtenbury* into this preſent vſe. But becauſe the Epitaph ſeemeth vnto me to ſound out I knowe not what after the manner [29] of a harſh grating [25] inſtrument, and to draw with it the faulte of that age ſcarce eloquent, as alſo finally to be more briefe & baſe the*n* might ſeeme conuenient for ſo mightie a Monarcke, wee haue dedicated another therefore (in commendation of him) vnto the Sacred memorie and poſteritie of the learned, viz. [30]

<small>Iohannis Leylandij Antiquarij Encomion funerale In vitam, facta mortemq*ue*, Regis Arthurij Inclitiſſimi.</small>
Saxonicas toties qui fudit marte cruento
  *T*urmas, & peperit ſpolijs ſibi nomen opimis.
Fulmineo toties *Pictos* qui contudit enſe,
  Impoſuitq*ue* Iugum *Scotti* ceruicibus ingens.
Qui tumidos *Gallos, Germanos* quique feroces [35]
  Perculit, & *Dacos* bello confregit aperto :

K. *Arthure* 71

Deniq*ue Mordredum* è medio qui fuſtulit illud
    Monſtru*m*, horrendu*m* ingens, diru*m* ſeuumq*ue* Tyra*n*nu*m*,
    Hoc iacet extinctus monumento *Arturius* alto,
    Militiæ clarum Decus, & Virtutis Alumnus:
5   Gloria nunc cuius terram circumuolat omnem,
    Ætherijq*ue* petit ſublimia tecta tonantis,
    Vos igitur gentis proles generoſa *Britannæ*
    Induperatori ter magno aſſurgite veſtro :
    Et tumulo ſacro Roſeas inferte Corollas,
10   Officij teſtes redolentia munera veſtri.

*T*he Engliſh.

He that ſo oft the Saxons troupes, in bloody fight did foile,
And got him fame by noble facts, with manie a full rich ſpoile,
He that with fierie flaſhing ſworde, ſo oft the Picts *deſtroide,*
15 *And laid a yoake vpo*n *the* Scots, *their necks which greatly noid.*
*He that did daun*t *the lofty* French, *&* Germanes *fierce did ſmite*
With open war the Dacians, *& their force did vanquiſh quite.*
20 *He laſt*[*l*]*y*[1] *which bereft of life* Mordred *that Monſter thoe,*
Both horrible mightie, Dyre, and cruell tyraunt foe:
Arthure (*euen he*) *lieth buried in this loſtie monument,*
Of warlike force the garland braue, & friend to Vertue bent.
Whoſe glorie now & greate renowme, flieth all the world about,
25 *And mounts vnto the climates hie of thu*n*dering skies throghout.*
Ye Gentlemanlie Offſpring then of Brittaines nation braue,
Towardes this ſo puiſſant Emperor, due Honor ſee you haue.
And on his Tombe gay garlands lay of Roſes *fragrant smell,*
Sweete ſauoring giftes as witneſſes, your duties forth to tell.

Iohn Leyland Antiquary his funerall commendation vpon yᵉ life, deeds & death of the moſt Noble K. Arthure.

[29 back]

30   NOw in fit time comes forth *Silueſter Giraldus*, that ſame eye witneſſe of *Arthures* bones and aſhes found, and aptly adioyneth his accounte vnto theſe wordes.

    And his body (*which as it were fantaſticall in the end and as it were by ſpirites tranſlated vnto places a farre off, and not ſubject*
35 *vnto death, fables ſo fully had fayned*) *was in theſe our dayes by wonderfull and as it were meruailous tokens founde out buried more*

Silueſter Giraldus his teſtimonie of Arthure his Tombe found.

---

[1] Text, *laſty.*

deeper in the earth at Glaftenburie *betweene two Pyrameds, in old time fet vp within the religious place, and by a hollow Oake marked or knowne, & was with honor tranflated into the Church, & decently beftowed in a Marble Tombe.* Whereupon a leaden croffe being engrauen in the ftone not in the vpper part as it is accuftomed (*but on the lowermoft part rather*) which we alfo haue feene (*for we haue handled the fame*) conteyned thefe letters engrauen and not eminent and extant, but rather inwardlie turned to the ftone.

   Hic Iacet Sepvltvs Inclitvs Rex
   Artvrivs In Insvla Avaloniæ.

And thefe wordes follow euen there.

And feeing there were fome euident tokens of finding the bodie there by his infcriptions, and fome by the Pyramedes engrauen (although as very much defaced and ouerworne by too much oldneffe of time:) *yet moft chiefely and moft euidentlie did* Henry *the second King of* England declare and manifeft full and whole vnto thofe Monckes, according as he had harde of that aunciont hiftoricall Mufician the Brittaine: namely that they fhould finde him buried deepely in the earth for xvi. foote at the leaft, & not in a Tombe of ftone, but in a hollow *Oake*. And therefore his body (beeing laide and as it were hidden fo deepe, to the end that it might not be founde of the *Saxons*, inhabiting the Ifland after his death, whome he in his life time had fo puiffantly fubdued & almoft deftroyed) might f[c]arcely at any time be found.

A wife pollycy of workmen in thofe dayes.
  And for this caufe were the letters as teftimonies of truth engrauen vpon the croffe turned inwardes to the ftone, to the end they fhould at that time kepe in fecret, what they conteyned and that fometime alfo according to the place & time [30] requifite they might difcouer or manifeft that fame meaning. Moreouer alfo he writeth thefe words euen in the fame place.

We muft alfo know that the bones of Arthures *bodie which were found, were fo greate, that even that faying of the poet might feeme in thefe words to be fulfilled.*

   Grandiaque effoffis mirabitur offa Sepulchris.

And the Tombes being digged forth right:
He fhall maruaile at the greate bones in fight.

FOr the bone of his fhinne beeing layde to the fhinne of

K. Arthure

a moſt tall perſon (which alſo the Abbot ſhewed vs) and as it
was faſtned vnto that grounde neare vnto his foote, retched it
ſelfe largely, three fingers ouer his knee.

 Alſo the ſcalp of his head as it were a wonder or ſpectacle,
5 was capable and groſſe, in ſo much as betweene the eye bryes
and the eyes it largely conteyned a hande bigneſſe. There
appeared in this, tenne or moe woundes: all which (except one
only greater then the reſt which gaped wide and which onely
ſeemed to bee a deadlie wounde) grewe together into one whole
10 ſcarre. Nowe if it ſhall auaile any man either to repeate ye
very ſelfe ſame thinges which I haue ere while recited out of
Giraldus, or not much vnlike to theſe, let him read his booke
viz. *Speculum Eccleſiaſticu*m, where as two chapters lightſomly
entreat of this matter. In meane time yet I haue ſomwhat
15 which holds me doubtfull. For *Giraldus* affirmeth y^t his burying place was of Oake, which as I doe not ſtreyght way affirme
to be falſe: So I will inſinuate thoſe thinges, which vehemently
perſuade me to ye contrary. Firſt, the number of greate Alder
trees which by a certaine nature are growing commodious for the
20 ground there. Moreouer agayne, I thinke the inhabitants of
Aualonia, were not ſo ignorant of natural things, y^t they ſhould
beleeue ye Oake would continue longer in ſomwhat a moyſt
ground, then the watery Alder tree, which is growing in the
grounde.

25 They which haue written of *Trees*, willingly attribute ſomwhat
moiſt grounds to be apt both for Alder & Elme trees to be
brought forth in them. There alſo remaineth another doubt,
which, (if I any thing rightly iudge) ſhall rather ſeeme a plaine
errour, then any doubt at all. *Gyraldus* confirmeth that
30 *Arthures* Tombe was founde betwene two [30 back] Pyrameds
in the religious place, at *Aualonia*: In which opinion, (as it
were, ſo confirmed with teſtimonie of ancient writers) euen I alſo
remaine. But I am ſo farre from beleeuing any thing to be
engrauen in them, which thing *Arthures* tombe (as *Giraldus*
35 declareth ye verie ſame) ſhould ſhew, expreſſe, or make famous,
that in deede vnto me may appeare nothing leſſe like to be true.
If there had beene any ſuch thing, I pray you who more truly
or more playnly ſhould haue manifeſted y^e ſame, then *Gulielmus
Meildunen*ſis? vnto whom alone all poſteritie ought to refer both

Marginal notes: The largneſſe of K. Arthures Lineaments. Nota. Ten woundes diſcerned in his ſcalp. A relation to a further teſtimony of Giraldus. in Speculo Eccleſiaſtico yet par[t]ly doubted. Alder trees in Aualony. Where Giraldus affirmeth K. Arthures Tombe to be found. viz. betweene two Pyrameds at Aualonia alias Glaſtenbury. A doubt. Malmesbury.

74   *The Affertion of*

their portractures & infcriptions. But hee in deede fpeaketh not fo much as one worde of *Arthure*, whom elfwhere he diligently extolleth. Doubtleffe it is a coniecture probable, that *Giraldus* was vtterly ignorant what infcriptions thofe Pyrameds contayned, feeing he faith the letters were worne out by antiquitie or oldnes 5 of time.

But I let paffe *Giraldus* (a man truly otherwife learned & a great & greedy deuourer of ancient knowledge) as I am prouoked by another care not vnprofitable for the purpofe: Namely that I fhould not onely by the teftimonie of two, whom 10 I haue aboue named, but alfo by a full number of writers, con-firme, eftablifh, and perfuade as it were ratified, *Arthures* Tombe founde. Alfo to the end that that thing may more commodi-oufly be done, I think there are caufes agreeable why I may more profoundly repeate all and finguler teftimonies of famous 15 men within a certaine conuenient and euydent fcope of matter. In which behalfe *Claudius* a frenchman (to the end the reader may vnderftand that the credible report of *Arthures* Tombe found hapned euen vnto ftraungers vpright and perfect) fhall be a greate witneffe in matter aboundant.   20

Anno 1217. The bodie of *Arthure* that noble king of *Brittaine*, (which had lyen buried. 600. and moe yeeres) was found in the Church of *S. Mary* at *Glaftenbury*.

Heere, in computation of the yeeres, either by the Authors negligence (or as more fincerelie the Interpreter faith) by the 25 negligence of the booke writer, did there creepe in a foule error. For, *Henry* the *Second* of that name king of England dyed about the yeere after *Chriftes* byrth a thoufand [31] one hundreth and nyntie: and the Tombe was founde in the firft yeare of the raigne of King *Richard* the 1. his fonne. The 30 Cronicles of *Perfor Abbey* doe make relation of thefe thinges.

Anno Domini 1191. the Tombe of *Arthure* Kinge of *Brittaine* was found at *Glaftenbury*: the leaden croffe vpon his breft, de-claring that his name was there written. *Iohannes Fiberius* who is alfo commonly called *Beuer*, writeth thefe thinges moft 35 briefly, and by way of running it ouer.

Anno Domini 1191. were founde at *Glaftenbury* the bones of *Arthure*. *Matthew Paris* Moncke of the Monafterie of *S. Albane* at the racing and feege of that moft auncient Cittie

[marginalia:]
Iohn Ley-lands infer-tion of famous men for proofe of Arthures Tombe found.
Claudius a Frenchman.
Anno Domini 1190.
Perforana. Iohn Stow.
Anno Domini 1191.

K. Arthure

Verolamium, nere vnto S. *Albones* in the Countie of *Hartford*, thus mentioneth of the Tombe. *The bones of the moſt famouſe King Arthure were founde at* Glaſtenbury, *laide vp in a certaine moſt auncient Tombe there, about the which ſtoode erected two moſt auncient* Pirameds *wherein the letters were engrauen, but by reaſon of the too much rudneſſe and deformitie they could not be reade. And they were found by this occaſion. For as they digged there, to bury a certaine Moncke, which with a vehement deſire in his life time, had before wiſhed for this place, as to be therein buried: they founde a certaine cloſe Tombe, vpon the which was put a leade croſſe, wherein was engrauen:* HIC IACET INCLITVS BRITONVM REX ARTVRIVS, IN INSVLA AVALONIÆ SEPVLTVS. *But that place beinge rounde about encompaſſed with Mariſh groundes, was in times paſt called the Iſle of* Aualon, *for truth that is the Ile of Aples.* [By what chaunce Arthures Tombe was founde (as Matthew Paris ſaith) which yet Iohn Leylande affirmes he neuer heard of to be true.]

Like as by Good right I fauour verie much the authoritie of this *Matthew*, ſo I am ſory that a fewe wordes chaunced redounding to this declaration in the inſcription. Certes that which he mentioneth of the Moncke, I neuer hearde of before, neyther doth he ſo farre forth perſwade mee of the truth.

Ranulphus Higeden of *Cheſter* alſo maketh mention of [31 back] King *Arthure* his Tombe. I omit to mention other Authours, and that with employed diligence, becauſe I would not ſeeme to affectate the number of witneſſes in a matter ſo manifeſtly knowne and credited. [Ranulphus Higeden of Cheſter mentioneth of Arthures Tombe.]

Cap. xvi.

The Tranſlation of King Arthures bones.

I Remember that in my Epiſtle dedicatory, I haue ſpoken of *Arthures* Lyneamentes, three times tranſlated. Whereof, which was the firſt, (becauſe it appeareth not euident enough by the greater Church at *Glaſtenbury*, from whence they write theſe were firſt of all conueyed) I will ſomewhat more manifeſtly and more lightſomely notify. I learned of the Monckes at *Glaſtenbury* moſt diligent referuers no doubte of the Antiquitie pertayning

Arthures bones & afhes tranflated into the greate Church at Glaftenbury.

to their Cloyfter, that *Arthures* Lyneamentes were tranflated into the greate Church (which worke was greatly augmented by the liberallitie of *Henry Plantagenet*) from the religioufe place: but not laide in that place at that time where they now be. There is a porch towardes the South parte, and a Chappell from whence they go into the Treafury. In this place men affirmed that *Arthures* bones remayned for a certaine feafon:

The remouing of them into the midle Iles of the Queare.

after that againe, that they were tranflated to the midle Iles of the Queare.

By which interchaunge of time, a newe, ftately, and magnificent Tombe out of blacke Marble (fuch as we fee the *Lydian* or tutch ftone) was both heawne and cut out, & at that time together framed, by vnaccuftomed workmanfhippe and witty deuife: concerning which, and alfo the tranflation thereof, to write at this prefent, it were vndoubtedly a needleffe thinge, feeing that in the chapter before going touching *Arthures* Tombe founde, all thofe matters appeare together in their order.

The third tranflation of King Arthure in the dayes of King Edward, firnamed the long, alias the firft of that name.

Therefore let our hiftory apply it felfe vnto the third tranflation: which was made in yᵉ dayes of *Edward*, firnamed *Longfhanke*, K. of *England* not only the cheefeft patrone of *Arthures* praife, but alfo yᵉ louer, & great reuerencer of his fame, when as all yᵉ Lyneamentes of them remayning [32] in the moft ftately Tombe (where they tooke their reft together before) fauing the fhinne bones of the King, and of the Queene, which he commaunded to be kept abroade, it was no doubte a fpectacle of Antiquitie very acceptable vnto the nobilitie thithei reforting. And to the ende now that fo noble a deede of King *Edwarde* (who neuer enough can bee commended) may enioy eternall fame: I will recyte al and fingular fuch teftimonies hetherunto pertayning, as were moft faithfully taken out of the Arches of the Monaftery of *Glaftenbury*, Authour of which things alfo was the fame Monck of *Glaftenbury*, who had in him a moft earneft care to extoll *Arthure* with due commendations, and with a founde faith to aduance vnto the pofteritie thefe actes done by him. The writer neyther wanted lightfome order, nor wit in handling his matters: But that age had neyther familierly *Greeke* nor *Latine* eloquence. What manner thinges fo euer thefe bee, as he write them, so will I recyte them in order, yet pondering by the way, that poynt in time conuenient: not with how greate

K. Arthure 77

elegancie, but how worthie and howe true thofe thinges are, which he maketh mention of.

Anno Domini 1276. *King Edward*, the Sonne of *Henry* the thirde came with the Queene his wife vnto *Glaftenbury.* But vpon Tewfday next folowing the Kinge and all his Court was entertayned there at the Monafteries chardges. On which day in the twylight time he caufed to be opened *Arthures* Tombe, where, (in two Coffines theire portractures and Armes being depainted thereon) hee founde the bones of the faide Kinge, of a wonderfull thickneffe and largeneffe feperated. The picture of the Queene in deede was made with a Crowne vpon her heade. The Crowne of the Kinges picture was made lyinge downe, with the abfcifion of his left eare, and with the euident fignes of that wounde whereof hee dyed. Upon euery one of thefe was founde a manifeft plaine infcription.

The fame King and his wife. viz. King Arthures Tombe.

King Edward the firft, and Queene Elyanor his wife behold King Arthurs Image & the Queenes his wife with their infcriptions.

The day folowing, namely being wednefday, the Kinge fhutting vp the Kinges bones, and the Queene his wife the Queenes bones, folded vppe in feuerall wrappers [32 back] of precious preferuatiues and putting to their feales, commaunded that the fame Tombe fhould be with all fpeede placed before the hye Alter, outwardly retayning ftill the heades of them both to be feene, engrauen by reafon of the zeale of the people, inwardly fetting therein fuch a like fentence. *Hæc funt offa nobilifsimi Regis Arthurij quæ Anno Dominicæ incarnationis. 1278. Decimo calend. Maij per. Dominum* Edwardum *Regem Angliæ illuftrem hic fuerunt fic collocata, præfentibus* Leonora *ferenifsima eiufde*m *Regis conforte, & filia Domini* Edwardi [1] *Regis Hifpaniæ:* Magiftro Gulielmo *de* Midleton, *tunc* Norwicenfi [2] *electo Magi-ftro.* Thoma *de* Becke, *Archidiacono Dorcelenfi & predicti Regis T*hefaurario, Domino Henrico *de* Lafcey *comite* Lin-colniæ, Domino Amadio *comite* Sabaudiæ, *& multis magnatibus Angliæ.* Thus farre mentioneth the Moncke of *Glastenbury.*

Theire commandement made for preferuation of the Lyniamentes of K. Arthure & his Queene entombed, & for continuall referuation of theire memoriall.

Go now *William Paruus* together with thy fucceffour in place, and ftoutly deny thou that eyther *Arthure* liued not, or was not victorioufe in times paft. Surely thou fhalt neyther haue me partaker, nor fauourer, no nor yet one in loue with thine opinion, nay rather errour, at any time. Undoubtedly it

William Paruuf an enemy of K. Arthures fame.

---

[1] Leland has *Ferrandi.*   [2] Text, *Noowicenfi.*

were a greate and greeuoufe crime, not onely worthie of ſtripes, but alſo of all kinde of puniſhment, if any man ſhould derogate from her the glory due to his Cuntrie, ſhould enuy the fame of his *Princes*, which haue moſt iuſtly deſerued well of the common weale, and ſhould not finally ſtand vp with valiancy and famouſe actes by all meanes to adorne and illuſtrate the fame.

<small>Iohn Leylandes petition to the friendly Readers.</small>

Truly, I hope (moſt friendly Readers) it will fall out, (that the equitie of the cauſe being knowne) and alſo ye truth, I ſhall haue you my friendly healpers herein: and that (ſuch is your good will, humanitie, and integritie) you will alſo willingly render me thankes for my duety towards the common weale. In the meane time I truſting to this good fortune will doubtleſſe endeuour all that I may, ſo as hauing taken a freſh courage vnto me, and that moſt confirmed, I may boldly enterpriſe to buckle with hand to hand, and by might and maine ouermatch the broode of backbyters which [33] importunatly, greeuously, and enuiously murmure at, and inueigh againſt the commendations of *Arthure*, for ſo, as it were to make an end of my worke, haue I by all meanes determined with my ſelfe.

Chap. xvij.

A confutation and ouerthrow of Slaunders raſhly affirming that Arthure was not liuing.

<small>Writers varying what time K. Arthure liued.</small>

HIſtoriographers do contend, and as yet the controuerſie is before the iudge, at what time *Arthure* floriſhed. And this contention hath ſo encreaſed, and gathered force, that doubts, (concerning uniuerſall credite of the hiſtorie, which declareth his exploits done) as yet ſticke to the feeble[1] conceipts of the Readers.

But this is ſo weake a ſlaunder, that it needes not any diligent anſwere. *Valerius* faith that he floriſhed in the time of *Zenon* the Emperour. But *Hector Boetius* reporteth in the time of *Iuſtinian* the *Barbarians* then inhabiting Italy. Finally others write otherwiſe: concerning the time I doe not much force vpon, were it euen now. Although yet from hence, the time is eaſily gathered, namely from the raigne of *Aurelius Ambroſius*, of whome alſo *Paule* the Deacon makes mention. Perhaps

<small>Valerius. Hector Boetius.</small>

<small>Paulus Diaconus.</small>

---

[1] Text, *feoble*.

K. Arthure

some of the aduersaries will say, How comes it to passe, that *Paule* remembreth not *Arthure?* I answere, *Paule* had other matters to busie himselfe with, then doubtfully to make famous the Brittaines, which were not as yet forsaken of the Romans.
5 In ye meane time he takes away nothing from *Arthures* dignitie or historie, becaufe he is not named of him: seeing by the way a good number of noble personages throughout the whole worlde are of the same Author passed ouer with silence.

Undoubtedly y^t seemeth to haue greate effect, where as *Gildas*
10 the writer of *Brittaine* wrytes nothing at all of *Arthure.* There be which cyte the testimonie of *Gildas*, both in his fauour and praise also. But that *Gildas* in deede is a [33 back] fabler, and layde foorth as an open praie vnto silly wormes and Moathes, at *Oxenforde*, in the Lybrary.

Gildas a fabler.

15 *Gildas* his historie is published abroade of *Polidorus*, vn- doubtedlie a fragment of ye old *Gildas*, but it is lame, out of order, and maimed, so farre forth, as if he were now againe restored to life, the father would scarce knowe his chylde. It is euidently knowne that he wrote bookes which by him were
20 entituled *Cambriedos*, found out eight hundreth yeres and more agone in the Islandes of *Ireland*, and caried ouer in to *Italy.* Admitte the Historie of *Gildas* bee true: How coulde he as an eye witnesse declare anything truely of *Arthure*, when he himselfe saith, y^t he was borne in the yeere when the battle
25 was fought at *Bathe*, where *Arthures* victorie (and that in deede most famous) fell vnto him, as *Nennius* witnesseth. The enemy gathereth. *Gildas* makes no mention at all of *Arthure*: *Ergo* he was neuer liuing. Undoubtedly a subtile gathering, such a one as this is: *Gildas* remembreth not *Aruiragus, Lucius*,
30 or *Constantine* the greate, and therefore they were not liuing. O straunge force of Logicke! And yet being hartened with this so weake argument (as it seemeth to him in deede) he thinkes he hath easily gotten the best game. Is this an Italian reason? For certainly, now can I hardly any longer abyde to
35 be called *Vltramontanus*, or one that goeth beyond his boundes: And surely why?

Maldunensi.

Cælum non animum mutant, qui trans Mare currunt.
The ayer, not mind change they,
Which take their voyage ouer the Seay.

Gildas an vnthankefull perſon & reprochfull towardes his countrie of Brittaine.

I know yet in the meane time, what yᵉ Wealch Writers doe iudge of *Gildas* his ſilence, ſo much as vnto Arthure appertaineth: namely, for that *Hoel* the coſengermaine of *Gildas* was ſlaine of *Arthure*: this was yᵉ cauſe his name was neglected. But I will not ſo much reſt vpon this helpe or ſauegard: being rather ready to fight out the battle with him, becauſe (as vnthankefull and the ſame ſcarſe wiſe, I will not ſay vngodly) hee hath blemiſhed his countrimen the *Brittaines* with this blot or error of his.

Britanni nec in Bello fortes, nec in pace fideles. 10

[34] Surely but that I ſhould ſeeme to fauour mine owne affection, or feede the choller of my ſtomake, I my ſelfe woulde heere coragiouſly enforce my weapon & that in deede ſharpe againſt this ſlanderous enemy of yᵉ *Brittaines*. But I will moderate mine anger, being ready to bring hether from another place (amongſt theſe) moſt valiant or ſtoute defenders of yᵉ truth, leaſt mine affection may ſeeme to haue iniured any man.

Siluester Giraldus promiſed to confute the ſlanders of Gildas.

Siluester Giraldus (in his Topographia or deſcription of *Wales*) promiſeth that he will anſwere this ſlander of *Gildas*, in his Topographie or deſcription of *Brittaine*: which booke yᵗ he hath ſo written in times paſt, I doubt not; but ſo far as I know it is not in theſe our dayes extant in any place. What hee in meane while writeth in his 2. booke of yᵉ *Deſcription of Wales*,

Nota. Siluester Giraldus his praiſe of the Brittaines. Anno. ante Chriſt. natiuit. 50.

I wil now amongeſt others bring forth to light. But for ſo much as *Iulius Cæſar*, who was ſuch a manner of man, as yᵉ teſtimony of the whole worlde vnder *Caſſiuilane* yᵉ Duke ſheweth, viz. when, as *Lucane* yᵉ Poet ſaith.

Territa quæſitis oſtendit terga Britannis.

Vnto the Brittaines by him ſought, 30.
He ſhewed his trembling backe for nought.

An. ante Chriſt. natiuitat. 401. Poſt Chriſtum 107. Brittaines alwaies approued.

Were not thoſe Brittaines valiant and coragious perſons? Againe, what were they when *Bellinus* & *Brennus* added yᵉ Romane Empyre vnto their victories? what were they in yᵉ daies of *Conſtantine* the Emperor, & ſonne of *Helen* ſometime heere Queene? what were they in yᵉ raigne of *Aurelius Ambroſius* Anno, poſt *Chriſt.* 466. whom alſo *Paule* the Deacon

K. Arthure 81

extolleth with praifes? And to conclude, what fellowes were valiant they in yᵉ daies of our famous *Arthure.* *An. poſt Chriſt* 516. perſons, & eue*n* in *Ioſephus* the writer brought vp at *Exeter* in *Deuonſhire* in his Arthure booke *Antiochiedes*, thus ſingeth.

his time
An. 540.
Iſcae.

5   Inclita fulſit.
Poſteritas Ducibus tantis, tot diues Alumnis,
   *T*ot fæcunda Viris præmerent qui viribus orbem,
Et fama veteres. Hinc *Conſtantinus* adeptus,
   Imperium, Romam tenuit, Bizantion auxit.
10 Hinc Senonum ductor, captiua Brennius vrbe,
   Romuleas domuit, flammis Victricibus artes,[1]
Hinc & ſæua ſatus, pars non obſcura tumultus.
[34 back]
Ciuilis, magnum ſolus qui mole ſoluta
Obſedit, meliorq*ue* ſtetit pro *Cæſare* murus.

Laudes,
veteru*m*
Heroum &
Regis Arthurij
præcipue.

15   Hinc celebri fato fœlici floruit ortu,
Flos Regum *Arthurus*: Cujus cum facta ſtupori
   Non micuere minus, totus quod in aure voluptas,
Et populo narrante ſauus, Quæcunq*ue*, priorum,
   Inſpice: *Peleum* commendat fama Tyrannum,
20 Pagina *Cæſareos* loquitur formoſa tryumphos,
   Alciden domitis attollit gloria monſtris,
Sed, nec *Pinetum Coryli*, nec ſydera ſolem
   Æquant. Annales Latios, Graioſq*ue* reüolue.
Priſca parem neſcit, æqualem Poſtera nullum
25   Exhibitura dies. *Reges* ſupereminet omnes
Solus, præteritis melior maiorq*ue* futuris.

The Engliſh

Noble poſteritie.
With ſo great Princes richlie ſhined, & *Patrons ſo many,*
30 *So ſtored with men which conquered the world with valiancy.*
And fame extolleth auncients. Hence had Conſtantine *poſſeſt*
The Empyre; Rome he ſurely kept, and Bizance eke encreaſt.
Hence Brennus *the* Italians *guide, (in Citie captiued ſo)*
With conquering flames the ſtately towers of Rome did ouerthrow.
35 *And hence thoſe cruell Impes, a part (of ciuil broile) not baſe,*

The praiſes of
ancient Po-
tentates &
amo*n*geſt them
of K. Arthure
eſpecially.

[1] Leland, *arces.*

Alone befiedge their mightie Prince, the huge hoafte letting paffe.
Defence & fauegarde fo, whereby to Cæfar was.
Hence florifhed by famous fate, & origin profperous
Arthure *the flowre of kinges, whofe deedes fhined no leffe mar-
ueilous :*   5
Then *that both peoples eares & tongues did in his praife delite :
As, if thou view of former wights, what euer bookes recite.*
Fame doth Peleus *tyrant blaze : and* Romane *hiftories*
Extoll *their* Cæfars *tryumphes greate, after their victories,*
Renoume aduanceth Hercules *fubduing monfters greate :*   10
But not Coryli, Pinetus, nor Starres *the* Sunne *his heate
Coequate. Search the Cronicles of Greekes & Latines both :
Auncient age knoweth not his like, ne yet pofteritie doth
His match declare. All kinges alone in deede furmounteth he,
Better then thofe are dead & gone, Greater then any fhall be.*   15

Gildas his former difpraife of the Brittaines here ouermaftered with praife worthineffe.

[35] HOw or in what manner thefe may not anfwere the prayfes by *Gildas* before recyted, the difcreete Reader at large fully feeth : and perceyueth *Arthures* commendations hereunto (amongeft the reft added) to agree fo well vnto this place, that I almoft haue no neede to reckon them as (I truft) with any 20 fault of mine, but in deede (good Readers) if I iudge aright, with your very much pleafure and delight. For the verfes before going haue their right father or authour that he in deede fhould then be liuing. Moreouer againe they fo pleafantly allure the eares of vncorrupt fenfe, with a certaine apt concinnitie or 25 proper agreement, with pure elegancie and equall Maieftie (that except fancy faile me) they fhall fully & wholy pleafe the Reader, yea were it fo that I reckoned them ouer ten times.

Ponticus virunnius an Italian, commending the Brittaines.

Ponticus Verunnius an *Italian* but yet one that loued the *Brittaines* well, beinge iuftly angry with *Polidorus* the *Italian*, 30 thundereth forth thefe wordes.

O admirabile tunc genus Britonum qui eum, (Caefarem intelligit) *bis in fugam expulerunt, qui totum orbem fubmiferat occidentis : Cui quafi totus mundus poftea nequiuit refiftere illi etiam fugati refiftunt, parati pro patria & libertate mortem*[1] *fubire.* 35
Which may thus be englifhed.

O wonderfull nation of the *Brittaines* in that age, which twife put him (he meaneth *Cæfar*) to flight, who had conquered the

[1] In Leland's text *mortem* precedes *pro*.

whole weft part of the world: whom as it were, when the vniuerfall world could not refift afterwardes, euen they them felues being put to flight, refifted, being ready to dy for their Country and the libertie thereof.

5 Hereupon fingeth *Lucane* the *Poet* vnto their praifes, (writing *Lucanus.* of *Cæfar*) as before is faide.

> Territa quæfitis oftendit terga Britannis.
> *Vnto the* Brittaines *by him fought,*
> *he fhewed his trembling backe for nought.*

10 IF in this place I fhould rather endeuour to mende the matter with multitude of teftimonies, then with vpright truth of effect, I could alfo take out of *Iohannes Anneuillanus* his *Architrenio* (that litle booke wittily in praife hand-[35 back] ling the fame) certaine litle verfes concerning the valiancy 15 and proweffe of the *Brittaines*: For fo fhould I fhutte vp the mouthes of brabling backbyters againft the praifes of thefe *Brittaines*, and that with a fufficient frontier framed for the purpofe. But me feemeth that I make more a dooe about thefe bablers then is conuenient. Let them with fhame enough 20 come to naught and burft them felues in their enuy: for fo much as the honour of *Brittaine* neyther ftandeth nor falleth by meanes of fuch foggy miftes. But by the way, leaft I fhould feeme not mindefull enough of my promife, I come againe to the encounter ready to vanquifh the force of argumentes which the aduerfaries 25 haue gotten. The *Romane* writers (fay they) made no mention of *Arthure*, wherefore, like it is to be true, that he was not liuing.

Iohannes Anneuillanus in Architrenio alfo commending the Brittaines.

If no thing be true, but that which appeareth by truth of *Romane* writers, it fhould go euill to paffe with the hiftory of the whole worlde. The infinite force of thinges worthie of memory, 30 and of noble effect confifteth rather of eye witneffes at home refident and inhabiting, then of the vncertaine relation made by forraine writers. For the *Romanes* made almoft all the whole worlde bond flaues: and writers which proceeded amongeft them, and were there borne applyinge their mindes to the ftudy of 35 eloquence, made their owne exploytes euen admirable or wonderfull; but the enterprifes & actes of other Nations they dyd[1] euen fo obfcure and debafe, that almoft they made them none at all.

Romanes careful for their owne fame, but negligent in all other mens.

[1] *Text,* dyed.

For the matter was fo handled by them, that they woulde elegantly and not truly pleade their caufe. They painted out fuch thinges in writinges, which they might rather lawfully hope for, then fee at that time, done by the moft prudent Gouernours. And vndoubtedly maruell it is not, that they made no remembrance at all of *Arthure*. The *Goathes* at that time had inuaded *Italy*, and barbaroufe ftyle with phrafe of writing and fpeaking was brought in, in fteade of eloquence, fo farre forth, that honour vnto learning was rare, & rewardes for the fame, were moft rarely vnderftoode off. And yᵉ matter was not handled by writers but by warriers. Wherefore if any certaine thing were written as touchinge [36] *Arthure* the fame might rather bee done of the *Brittaine* writers what manner perfons fo euer they were, then of the nouicy and ignorance of the *Romanes*, not onely declyning from the function or office of writing, but alfo carefully thinking vpon their owne wretched eftate and calamitie, dayly faling vpon them by many meanes, lettinge paffe all other thinges.

An other brabler after this alledgeth, more vaine matters are in *Arthures* Hiftory conteyned then that they may tollerably be allowed of him that is of ripe iudgement, and difcreet knowledge. If he meane touching that Hiftory which is reade amongeft the common forte in the *Italian*, *Spanifh*, *Frenche* and *Englifh* tongues, I do not much ftriue with him. Although the vpright reader fhall call to minde, the fame thing hath beene often times done euen in the Hiftory each where forraine of *Charles*, *Rowlande*, *Godfrey*, *Guy*, and *Belloufe*, that I may let paffe many others. Neyther yet notwithftanding are their names, or credit of the true Hiftory taken away the more. It is no noueltie, that men mixe triflinge toyes with true thinges, and furely this is euen done with a certaine employment that writers might captiuate yᵉ fimple common people with a certaine admiration at them when they heare of marueyloufe matters. So was *Hercules*, fo was *Alexander*, fo *Arthure*, and fo alfo *Charles* commended. But there is an other farre greater reafon incident to the Hiftory of *Arthure*, then I do conceaue of. For thofe thinges which are not apparant in courfe of ages, which are not probable, which as aliable helpes agree not with the credit of Authours, which are not embraced in long exercife of yᵉ ages,

K. Arthure 85

and furderance of learned men, & by them comprobate or fully
ratified I do not vnaduifedly allow off. Many yeares againe,[1]
Graius the Authour of the booke *Schalecronicon* (as I fuppose) Graius the Author of that booke Schalecronica had much adoe with fuch backbiters.
had great contention with this rable of backbyters. Unto him
was *Beda* obiected, who paffed ouer *Arthure* with great filence.
Paraduenture this holy man refufed to mention ye Prince,
becaufe he was borne in adulte[r]y.[2] And it might alfo be, y^t
when he had heard fome one or other prophecies fpoken of
him, by thofe hiftorical fignes y^t it a-[36 back]lienated his minde Beda more religioufly then Hiftorically addicted.
vtterly from the whole hiftory. But they neyther adde, nor take
away credit. That is moft true, whereas *Beda* otherwife a good
man and a learned, did not onely flenderly efteeme of the glory of
Brittaines name, but alfo defpyfed or neglected it. For, there
was fome what a dooe betwene them and the *Saxons* concern-
ing the rule ouer *Brittaine*. The Romifh Bifhoppe practized by Nota The tyranny of the Romifh Bifhop betwene the Saxons and Brittaines of olde time.
all meanes to keepe vnder his iurifdiction (which hee had moft
wickedly obtayned) the Englifh *Saxons*. For this caufe the
Brittaines curfed him. He againe with a certaine hatred
moued, fette the *Saxons* and them together by the eares. Then,
I pray you what praifes might the *Brittans* hope for at the *Saxon*
writers? Undoubtedly, cold commendations or rather none at
all. Adde hereunto, that *Beda* alfo was ignorant in ye affaires
of *Brittaine* before the dayes of *Gildas*; fo farre forth as hee
neither knew of ye monument in memory of *Arthures* Coronation at *Ambrofia*, nor of ye fame thereof. A thing credible it is,
that the calamitie of thofe warres which had confumed and
deftroyed Churches, together with libraries infinite, had vtterly
raced out of knowledge, manifeft or euident monumentes of
Antiquitie. Whereupon to him that fhould then take in hand to
write of Antiquitie touching *Brittaine*, all thinges were moft
obfcure and vnknowne. There are which thinke many thinges
haue beene tranflated into *Armorica* or the leffer *Brittaine*,
although at this day verie fewe thinges may be hoped for from
thence, fauing that a few notes are extant in moft auncient
exemplars of the liues of holie men thither reparing, and which
intermixe light with darkneffe.

Gulielmus Paruus of *Bridelington*, in his Prologue before his William Paruus his flaunder of Arthure.
Hiftory thus thundereth out his errour.

[1] For *agone*!   [2] Text, *adultely*.

Galfridus Hic dictus eſt, cognomen habens Arthurij, *qui diuinationum illarum nenias ex Britannica lingua tranſtulit, quibus vt non fruſtra creditur, ex proprio figmento multa adiecit.* William *Paruus* there faith: This man is called *Geoffry* bearing the firname of *Arthure*, who tranſlated yᵉ Fabulus Dreames of thoſe prophecies out of yᵉ *Brittaine* language: whereunto he (as men do not credit [37] vainelie hath alſo added many thinges after the deuice and imagination of his owne braine. Theſe wordes vttereth he vpon a ſtomake and contempte. But I will ſing him a contrarie ſonge euen for euer and a day. That men beleeue him in vaine, except he prooue this rather by reaſon, then by naked or playne wordes.

Well I knowe, and that too well, manie fables and vanities are diſperced throughout the whole hiſtory of *Brittaine*. Yet, therein are matters (if a man behold the ſame more thorowly) ſuch as might not be deſired without greate hinderance of auncient knowledge, and which beeing rather reade then vnderſtood by *William Paruus* beare not any ſhewe at all of commodity. Againe, I will alſo heere ſet downe another honourable teſtimony, namely not onely touching the Interpreter of the hiſtorie, but alſo concerning *Arthure* himſelfe. Plainly it appeareth, that whatſoeuer thinges this fellow publiſhed in writing (concerning *Arthure*, and *Merline* to feede yᵉ curioſitie of the not ſo diſcreete perſons) were fainedly inuented of lying and diſſembling Authours. Let him cogge and foyſte ſixehundreth times, if hee will. *Merlinus* was in very deede a man euen miraculouſly learned in knowledge of thinges naturall, and eſpecially in the ſcience Mathematicall: For the which cauſe he was moſt acceptable and that deſeruingly vnto the *Princes* of his time, and a farre other manner of man, then that hee woulde repute himſelfe as one ſubiect vnto yᵉ iudgement of any cowled or loytering groſſeheaded Moncke. But I will let paſſe *Arthure* and *Merline*, the one more valiant, the other more learned, then that they ought to regarde eyther the pratling or importunitie of the common people. And that ſeemeth vnto me a thing moſt vnequall and againſt all right, that one Moncke beareth enuie towardes another Moncke, which is euen dead and gone. *William Paruus* might haue hoped for greater victory of the liuing, then of the deade Perſons. This yet by the waye did

Monacus
Monaco
Inuidet.

hee count for aduauntage, to ſtrike him that woulde not ſtrike againe.

But if the Spirites of dead men haue any knowledge [37 back] of humane matters, he ſhall ſo farre perceiue that beyond equity and honeſty hee beares away no victorie from *Geoffrey*, that dead is, but that by his wounde he hath procured him ſelfe a perpetuall wounde and bloodſhedde. Neither is there cauſe why hee ſhould hope for the preſent helpe of that Phiſition *Polidorus* from the Citie *Vrbinas*, for as much as hee him ſelfe alſo languiſhing of like diſeaſe hath very greate neede of a cunning mans cure. And there remayneth as yet another wounde, wherewith *W. Paruus* ſuppoſed that hee had euen quite diſpatched *Geoffrey* out of this life. For, ſo hee inſulteth.

Nec vnum quidem Archiepiſc[op]um vnquam habuere Britones.

Neither (ſaith hee) *had the Brittaines in deede ſo much as one Archbiſhoppe at any time.*

Didſt thou learne this amongeſt the *Brigantes*?

Aſſerius Meneuenſis, ſometimes the Schoolmaſter of *Alfredus* ſirnamed the greate, king of England, taught mee another manner of matter in theſe wordes, in the booke of his Cronicles. Qui ſæpe depredabatur (*Hemeidum* Regulum intelligit) illud Monaſterium & Paræciam S. *Degwi*, id eſt, *Dauidis*, aliquando expulſione Antiſtitum qui in eo præeſſent, ſicut & nobis Archi- epiſcopum propinquum meum & me aliquando expulſit, ſub ipſis. *Which did oftentimes ſpoyle (he meaneth* Hemeidus *the Duke) that ſame Monaſterie and parriſh of Saint* Degwy *that is S.* Dauid, *in times paſt by baniſhing of the Biſhoppes which bare ſway therein, like as he baniſhed ſometime from vs the Archbiſhoppe my neighboure, and me alſo vnder them.*

Vixit Alfredus circiter. Annum. 842. & poſt 28. ann.

Gyraldus makes mention and with verie good credite that *Dubritius* was *Archbiſhop* of *Exceter*. For *Iſca* ſo called is the moſt noble Cytie of *Deuonia*, and moſt auncient of others, (by reaſon of the Ryuers and floude bearing the ſame name) there edyfied, which alſo was called of the Romans, the citie of *Caerlegion* or *Cheſter* vpon *Huſke*. The Biſhoppes Sea beeing tranſlated from thence vnto *Sainte Dauids*, where the moſt holy and the ſame moſt Learned *Dauid* floriſhed in the dignity of an *Archbiſhop*.

Iſcanus & Iſcae.

Iohn Stow.

[38] Sampson a man of famous memorie, Archbishop of *S. Dauids* in *Wales* shunning the sickenesse or disease of the Iaundice, went vnto *Armorica*, or the lesse Britaine: wherevpon came the originall of the Archbishopricke of *Dolence*. And from *Sampsons* time vnto yᵉ victories of yᵉ *Normans* ouer the Welchmen all the Bishops beyond *Seuerne* as yt were of solemne orders were confecrate by the bishop of *Sainte Dauids* their *Primate*: who when the *Paule* sayled him, with tooth and nayle retayned still all his title and interest.

Moreouer, it appeareth by yᵉ *Dialogue* of *Siluester Giraldus* that the Cannons at *S. Dauids* (in the time of *Dauid* the Bishop which succeded *Bernharde*) had a treatie with *Richarde* the greate, Archbishop ouer the Kentish men (in presence of *Hugucion* the Cardinall) concerning the Metropolitane tytle of their Church; whereof the same *Giraldus*, handled earnestlie an entreatie at Rome, being afterwardes chosen Bishop of *S. Dauids*.

And that I may recite more Ancient testimonies, *Ptolomeus Lucensis*, (who wrote the liues of the Romish Bishops) declareth yᵗ in *Eleutherius* his time three chiefe flammins in *Brittaine* were conuerted into so many Archbishops. *London*, in old time called T*roynouant*, & *Yeorcke* then also called *Brigantum*, without doubt florished famously with this dignitie or prerogatiue. Where then is the third Bishops Sea? Where els but in *Wales*.

3. Bishops Sees. London, Yeorcke, and Caerlegion vpon Huske in Walles.

In which poynte that I my selfe say nothing, *Trittemius* surely in his abridgment of Cronicles is also a lightsome and plaine witnesse. May not then *William Paruus* the Schoolemaster be ashamed to haue inculcate into the eares of *Polidorus* his scholler farre better Learned then himselfe such vaine tales. But, beholde, by one euill another euill chauncing. The ingrafted error so far forth hath now infected a number, yᵗ scarce is this disease curable by any *Helleborus*, no though they fayle into *Anticyria* for yᵉ same. And yet for sooth are they compelled, I knowe not by what violent Authoritie in the meane time to haue a good opynyon [38 back] of this their Schoolemaster. These I say before hand, are hard poyntes to beleeue. Surely I wish all thinges prosperous vnto my Schoolemasters. But when the matter is in handling concerning truth and credite of the cause, doubtlesse I beare no parciall affection towardes any

K. Arthure 89

of them: No certainely if I fhoulde by and by knowe that they woulde euen catch and conquere for mee all mine enemyes at once.

A Peroration or briefe Conclufion

To the Readers

HEtherto (moft courteous Readers) haue I defcribed *Arthure* in his coloures, not without diligence, laboure, and finally a ready good will: but yet in meane while, whether with like eloquence, grace, and good fucceffe I haue done this, let that by the iudgement of honeft and learned perfons bee determined. For I knowe very well, *How flender Furniture I haue at home*: For the which caufe I challenge not any thing at all vnto my felfe: Vndoubtedly I might foone appeare both rafh & vnwife, if I fhould fo doe. Onely I purpofed of good wil to make tryall of my wit in a matter honeft, to helpe the hiftory languifhing, to aduance the glory of my country, hindred by enuy, and beeing enthralled vnto the crafty deceiptes of euill willers, reftore the fame honeftly vnto liberty. I knowe it will come to paffe, that moft mighty enemies will affaulte my doinges: Let them ouercome with powre, if they can, fo the trueth be ours. I will imitate the Noble *Palme Tree*, which beeing preffed downe with heauie burdens yet falleth not to the ground at any time. And neither at this inftant doe I feeke for any reward: fo you vouchfafe me your courtefy, good will & fauour, truly I may perfuade my felfe I haue al thinges that I rightlie looke for. And for amendes, on my part alfo fhall hereunto enfue moft requifite promptitude & expedite alacrity, enflamed alfo by vertue of en-[39]couragement vnto like enterprifes not onely, but alfo to imparte you greater matters which fhall ftirre vp your learned eares, and being ftirred vp, may long detaine them, and fo deteyned as it were by a certaine land floude of pleafant delight therewith bring them vnto fragrant fieldes. And all thefe thinges do I eafily promife my felfe, trufting in your honeftie and helpe, as one doubtleffe fully bent vpon hope thereof. Surely my mufe (fuch as it is) altogether is youres: neyther tendeth fhe to any other purpofe at any time, but vnto your behoofe, and the commoditie of all men. I count it a bafe feruice to fatiffie the common peoples humor: but to performe you my continuall induftrie differeth not far from a kingdome, fuch a one as by a iuft caufe I may prefer euen before the kingdome of *Alexander*. For what more referued hee vnto him felfe wholy (when he dyed) of fo greate Riches, poffefsions and dominions, fauing fame onely. This, (though by many accomptes in example inferior) obteyned by your meane fhall I yet fo earneftly aduance, that nightes and dayes fhall fhe watch for your welfare & emolument. And at lengthe (thofe fame moft thicke miftie cloudes in deede of ignorance beeing fhaken off, & vtterly dafhed afide) the light of *Brittifh* Antiquitie with difplayed beames farre and wide fhall fhine forth. God giue you long life and wellfare, moft fincere fauorers of vertue and good learning.

FINIS.

LONDON.

Imprinted by *Iohn wolfe*, dwelling in *Diftaffe Lane* ouer againft the figne of the *Caftell*.
1582

ASSERTIO
inclytissimi Arturii
REGIS BRITANNIAE
JOANNE LELANDO
Antiquario
autore.

Ad candidos lectores.

Delituit certe multis Arturius annis
  Vera Britannorum gloria, lumen, honos.
Dispulit obscuras alacer Lelandius umbras,
  Sidereum mundo restituitque iubar.
Plaudite lectores studiosa caterua diserti,
  Præstitit officium candidus ille suum.
Hinc procul at fugiant Codrino felle tumentes:
  Ne proprio crepitent ilia rupta malo.

LONDINI. ANNO
1544.

Henrico Octavo

*inuictifsimo Regi Angliæ, Franciæ, ac Hiber
niæ, Fidei defenfori, Anglicæ ac Hibernicæ
eccleliæ proxime a Chrifto fupremo
capiti, Ioannes Lelandus Anti-
quarius. S. P. D.*

*Cura femper merito maxima eruditis fuit Rex longe ferenifsime,
ut fortia illuftrium uirorum facta facrofanctæ pofteritati accurate,
fplendide, magnifice confecrarent: ne rerum undecunque memora-
bilium, confpicuum lumen crafsa filentii umbra aliquando obdu-
ceretur. Hinc Hebræi Iudam Maccabæum magnis extollunt
præconiis. Hinc Homerus Græcus poëtarum gloria Hectora, et
Achillem commendatiffimos orbi reliquit. Nec fegniori ufi funt
Græci diligentia in exornando Alexandro bellatorum inuictifsimo.
Romani uero Cæfaris facinora tantum non ad fidera tollunt.
Burgundiones Gotthofridum Boillionenfem Saracenorum flagellum
ab infigni fortitudine exquifite collaudunt. Nec defuere Britanni
uiri, tum eruditione, tum rerum cognitione præcellentes, qui
Arturii nobilifsimi, inuictifsimique, genus, uitam, uirtutem, felicitatem, famam denique, folicita, at iufta interim diligentia, orbi
teftatifsima reliquerint. Applaufit eruditorum confenfus multis
iam fæculis tam celebri præftantifsimorum Ducum memoriæ, et res
ab eis geftas magno quidem cum ftudio, maiori uero uoluptate,
et admiratione plane maxima lectitat. Hiftoriæ de Arturio
fcriptæ nota a nefcio quo Gulielmo Paruo Nouoburgenfi, homine,
ut ego iudico, magis pio, quam in Britannica antiquitate erudito,
temere, et præter commune iudicium omne, inufta eft: qui cum
poft ducentos, et quinquaginta annos in manus Polydori Vergilii
incidiffet, ita in præfatione hiftoriæ quam de Nortomannis Angliæ
regibus fcripfit, in Arturium rhetoricatus, aut potius cornicatus
est, ut Italum perfuafione noua, fed uiolenta, uirum alioqui probum,*

Affertio inclytiffimi Arturii

et eruditum in fuam pertraxerit hærefim, et pertractum, ne alio dilaberetur, tam adamantinis arcte conftrinxerit uinculis, ut illum coegerit, ædita etiam hiftoria, gloriam, nomenque, fi diis placet, Arturii, tanquam folem, de medio tollere. Vnde et graue quidem iam bellum non modo a Gulielmo Paruo, uerum etiam a Polydoro Galfredi Monæmuthenfis manibus indictum eft, hac præcipue calumnia, quod is primus affertor gloriæ Arturii, Arturius et ipfe, effe uideatur. Durum me Hercle, et impium cum manibus decertare. Quid enim nobis cum laruis? Nennius Britannus fcriptor, ut illa ferebant tempora, non ignobilis, Arturii gloriam luculenta celebrauit oratione. Vixit enim ille tempore inclinationis Britannici imperii: Tantum abeft ut Arturius recentioris Galfredi Monæmuthenfis fit inuentum, et fabula. Vt taceat Nennius, Theliefinus uates, Merlinus Caledonius, et Melchinus antiquioris notæ homines Arturii illuftrem fecere mentionem. Certe nunquam temere id imbibam, quod me a fide hiftoriæ Arturii auertat: adeo uero non magni æftimo, aut Gulielmi Parui qualemcunque opinionem, aut Polydori in hac parte iudicium, cuius tamen alioqui eruditionem excolo, eloquentiam adprobo, ingenium fufpicio, et in bonis denique artibus autoritatem complector. Non hic de eloquentia, non de orationis fplendore, non de ftyli perfpicuitate, fed de folida fide, et hiftoriæ ueritate agitur, qua fretus aufim audacter pronunciare, neque enim eft quod metuam umbras obuerfanteis, olim fuiffe, regnaffe, atque adeo in precio ftetiffe magno Arturium. Mentiar, nifi palam, liquide, et manifefte teftetur ingens nobilium fuis temporibus fcriptorum numerus Arturii originem, uitam, res longe fortifsime geftas, mortem, fepulchrum, denique inuentionem eius reliquiarum, unamque, et alteram, ac etiam tertiam earundem latifsime famofam tranflationem: Quarum quæ ultima fuit, regnante Eadueärdo Longo Angliæ rege uictore fortunatifsimo, facta eft. Quo tempore ftipatus magna nobilium caterua præfens Arturii ofsa præfentia, referato fepulchro, Aualonia uidit, et contrectauit, ut ex eius diplomate, cui fyngrapham adfixit, luculente apparet. Quare ut orbis uniuerfus pofthac intelligat quanta, et quam præclara Arturii fama olim fuerit, non grauabor uel uniuerfam eius uitam, et quid ueteres de eo fenferint autores, lucido quodam ordine perfcribere. Sic enim lucem obfcuris, antiquitati fuum decus, uacillantibus præ ignorantia iuftum robur, certitudinem controuerfiæ, veritati poftremo suffragium dediffe uidebor. Tu Princeps

Regis Britanniæ

*maxime, uictorque felicissime nouo libello tuis alacriter in lucem
prodeunti auspiciis faue quæso, quo munere non modo præsentis
famam opusculi, una cum successu, promouebis, augebis,
ornabis, uerum etiam lætissimo mihi igniculos ad
alia quoque non inferiora propediem ædenda
excitabis. Nam et Cygnus meus
tuarum encomiastes uirtutum
ad te conuolare mirifice
cupit. Vale Regum
ornamentum
unicum.*

NOMENCLATVRA AVTORVM
quorum teftimoniis præfens utitur libellus.

Externi.

Lucanus.
Iuuenalis.
Martialis.
Cornelius Tacitus.
Paulus Diaconus.
Claudius Gallus.
Ioannes Annœuillanus.
Valerius.
Boccatius.
Diuionenfis.
Ponticus Virunnius.

Britannici.
Theliefinus.
Ambrofius Maridunenfis.
Merlinus Caledonius.
Melchinus.
Patricius Gleffoburgenfis.
Gildas Bannochorenfis.
Anonymus.
Nennius.

Samuel.
Beda Girouicanus.
Afferius Meneuenfis.
Gulielmus Meildunenfis.
Galfridus Monęmuthenfis.
Aluredus Fibroleganus.
Henricus Venantodunenfis.
Jofephus Ifcanus.
Syluefter Giraldus.
Matthęus Parisius
Ioan: chryfifloriographus.
Gulielmus Paruus.
Ioannes Fiberius.
Thomas Vicanus.
Ranulphus Higedenus.
Matthæus Florilegus.
Ioannes Burgenfis.
Thomas Meilorius.
Scalæchronica.
Chronica Durenfia.
Chronica Gleffoburgenfia.
Chronica Perforana.

Assertio incompara
BILIS ARTVRII:

autore Ioanne Lelando
Antiquario

HERCVLEM ex Alcmena adulterio Iouis fuisse natum, magno scriptorum Græcorum, & Latinorum consensu liquet. Qualis vero quantusque olim fuerit, arbitror vel mediocriter eruditis notius esse, quam vt in præsentia vlla prorsus egeat insinuatione. Fuerunt & alii complures ex adulterio geniti, vt ex veteri abunde constat historia, quorum virtus domi, militiæque eximie claruit. Inter quos & noster Arturius Britanniæ ornamentum maximum, & sui sęculi miraculum vnicum effloruit. Liceat mihi igitur cum bona gratia Gulielmi Parui, atque adeo eius fortissimi Succenturionis Polydori Arturium conterraneum meum vel iustis prosequi laudibus: & eadem opera Britannicæ historię à Galfredo Monæmuthensi viro non omnino inerudito, quicquid alias calumnientur scioli antiquitatis ignari, interpretatæ præsidio inniti firmo, potius quam externorum ficulneo. Fa|bulis vero, quæ in Arturii historiam irrepserunt, non magis applaudo quam Polydorus censor. At vt perterritus alicuius vel senio, vel eloquentia, vel autoritate demum veritatis partes vecors, atque idem desertor indefensas relinquam, committam plane nunquam. Alio me æquum, honestum, famæ ratio, hinc & amor patriæ iustus, ac ipsa veritas, qua nil mihi charius vna, perducunt. Sed neque bellum cum doctis mihi suscipiendum puto. Liberum interim per rationem erit, patriæ & veri maxime partes diligentia summa, industria expedita, labore alacri, consilio prompto, iudicio acri, denique modis omnibus erectissimas facere. Aggrediar igitur, candidorum lectorum beneuolentia,

O

humanitate, ac gratia fretus, Arturii originem ab ouo aliquanto accuratius reperere.

 Eſt locus Abrini ſinuoſo littore ponti
Rupe ſitus media, refluus quem circuit æſtus.
Fulminat hic late turrito vertice caſtrum
Nomine Tindagium veteres dixere Corini.

 Conſtans fama eſt per ora multorum tradita, & ſcriptis confirmata etiam eruditoru*m*, Gorloiden Coriniæ regulum hic ſedem habuiſse ſibi, ſuiſq*ue*. Erat ei Igerna vxor fœmina formæ plane venuſtifsimę, at pudicitiæ improbatæ. Huc ſepiuſcule recreandi animi gratia Vtherius rex Britannorum cognomine Pendraco, a ſerpentina, vt ego arbitror, prudentia ſic dictus, cuius & Gorlois beneficiarius erat, diuertebat.

 Architrenius libro, ſi recte computo, quinto hæc ſcribit.

  Hoc trifido mundum Corinei poſtera ſole
  Irradiat pubes, quartiq*ue* puerpera Phœbi
  Pullulat Arturum, facie dum falſus adulter
  Tintagol inrumpit, nec amoris Pendragon æſtum
  Vincit, & omnificas Merlini conſulit artes,
  Mentiturq*ue* ducis habitus, & rege latenti,
  Induit abſentis præſentia Gorlois ora.

 Conſuetudo, familiaritas, conuictus amori igniculos ſubminiſtrabant. Et quoniam, vt inquit poeta quidam. Lis eſt cum forma magna pudicitiæ: euicit libido continentiam. Vnde & poſtea Arturius, vna cum Anna virgine egregia genitus eſt. Illud non eſt omittendum quod refert Hector Boethius. Vtherium videlicet Gorloiden tandem ob Nathaleodem regulum contra Saxones pugnantem ab eo derelictum e medio tuliſſe; vel potius, vt Igerna liberius potiretur. Nomen vero Arturiorum Romanis nobile, iuxta ac familiare vel hinc fuiſſe dinoſcitur quod Iuuenalis Poeta hæc Satyra .3. ſcribat:. Cedamus patria, viuant Arturius iſtic. Et Catulus. Samuel ſcriptor Britannicus Arcturium per Cappa pingit ad vrſam alludens, vt a Græco fonte etymon trahat. Non hic aut vitio, aut conuitio eſſe debet Arturio, quod pater adulter filium ad fortitudinem, felicitatem, & triumphos genitum reliquerit: quando per eum non ſtetit, quo minus a legitimo naſceretur coniugio. Neque vſque adeo refert quo parente quis procedat, modo is in virum aliquando fortem probumque euadat.

Nam genus & proauos, & quæ non fecimus ipfi,
Vix ea noftra puto.

Immenfum quantum accreuit puer uirtuti, & iam pater qui viribus, confilio, iudicio quoque non fine gloria floruerat diem vitæ obiit Verolamii, deftinata ante | imperii dignitate filio notho, quod legitimum non haberet. Fol. 2 back.

Corona Arturii.

Britannica adfirmat hiftoria Arturium infulis regni decimo quinto ętatis fuæ anno initiatum fuiffe a Dubritio vrbis Legionum epifcopo. Ioannes Aureæ fcriptor hiftoriæ videtur octodecim adnumerare annos Arturio regiam fedem confcendenti. Scalæchronica, cuius libri vt coniectura ducor, quidam Graius autor fuit, aiunt Arturium coronæ infignia Ventæ accepiffe. Pictorum & Scottorum duo reguli Lotho, cui Anna foror Aurelii Ambrofii regis Britannorum nupferat, & Conranus cui Ada foror Annæ coniunx data fuerat, cœperunt tam lætis Arturii fuccefsibus inuidere : nam vterque, fed præcipue Lotho, ad Britanniæ imperium afpirabat. Hinc factum poftea vt ille, adiuncto fibi Ofca, alias Occa homine impurifsimo, bellum Arturio intulerit. Tandem ad manus peruentum eft, victusque Pictus peioreis partes tulit, partim Hoeli inuictifsimi præfidio, qui tunc ducem ibi agebat. Libellus de imperio Britannorum, & Anglorum in Scottos beneficiarios adfirmat hanc victoriam Eboraci ab Hoelo partam : vtque deuictis Scottis antiquas fedes precibus motus Arturius reliquerit fub Augufello fuo, quem eis regulum præfecit. Nęc fors melior Saxones excepit, interfecto Colgrino duce, Baldrico autem, & Cheldrico fugientibus. Victoriam fecuta eft concordia. Lotho fe Britanno dedidit. Mordredus, & Gallo|uinus filii Lothonis ex Anna, fauorem Arturii miris ambiebant modis, & tandem familiares illi facti funt. Duxerat interea Arturius Guenheram Cadori Corinienfis alumnam raræ, formæ fœminam. Deinde & Saxones bellis cruentifsimis contudit. Fol. 3.

100 Affertio inclytiffimi Arturii

Duodecim bella ab Arturio gefta.

Nennius Britannus bonæ, & antiquæ fidei fcriptor inter alios multos luculentifsimam eius bellorum mentionem facit: cuius verba quanuis librariorum incuria, & temporis iniuria aliquantulum luxata fint, tamen, quia ad rem præfentem pluri- 5 mum faciunt, & venerandam quandam fecum adferunt antiquitatem, lubet hic apponere, & fuo ordine. Arturius pugnauit contra illos, videlicet Saxones, cum regulis Britonum: Sed ipfe Dux erat. Primum bellum fuit in oftio fluminis Glein, alias Gledy. Secundum, tertium, quartum, & quintum fuper aliud 10 flumen quod vocatur Dugles, quod eft in regione Linueis. Sextum fuper flumen quod vocatur Baffas. Septimum fuit in fylua Caledonis, id eft Catcoit celidon. Octauum in caftello Guinion. Nouum bellum geftum eft in vrbe Legionis. Decimum in littore quod vocatur Traitheurith, alias Rhydrhwyd. 15 Vndecimum in monte, qui dicitur Agned cathregonion. Duodecimum in monte Badonis in quo multi corruerunt vno impetu Arturii. Hactenus Nennius. Ioannes aureæ fcriptor hiftoriæ hæc eadem de bellis duodecim aduerfus Saxones comprobat. Aluredus etiam Fibroleganus hifto|ricus fimilia narrat. Atque adeo 20 hæc funt Henrici Venantodunenfis verba .2. hiftoriæ fuæ libro. Arturius belliger illis temporibus Dux militum, & regulorum Britanniæ contra Saxones fortifsime pugnabat. Duodecies dux belli fuit: duodecies victor. Et ibidem. Hæc autem bella, & loca bellorum narrat quidam hiftoriographus. Videtur hic 25 Venantodunenfis incidiffe in Nennii hiftoriolam, cuius nomen exemplari, vt videtur, non erat adfcriptum. Hinc filentium illud. Neque erat libellus ille id temporis in manibus frequens, & noftra hac ętate plane rariffimus. Tantum tria eius exemplaria me vidiffe memini. Ioannes Rhefus antiquitatis amator, atque idem 30 fedulus illuftrator habet libellum Gilde titulo infcriptum, qui quantum ego, ex eius oratione colligo, non Gildam, fed Nennium parentem habuit. Elenchus bibliothecæ Bellici monafterii Gildæ hiftoriam inter fuos numerabat thefauros. Sedulo quæfitus a me liber, at non inuentus tamen. Fama prędicabat exemplar 35 Brecheniacum tranflatum fuiffe. Hæc obiter inferui. Nunc repetenda bella. Scriptor non inelegans vite D. Dubritii archiepifcopi vrbis Legionum talia commemorat. Perempto

Regis Britanniæ

tandem per venenum Aurelio rege, & regnante paucis annis Vthero eius fratre, Arturius filius eius, ope Dubritii fuccefsit: qui Saxones audacter pluribus præliis aggreffus eft, nec tamen illos a regno funditus extirpare potuit. Subiugauerant enim
5 fibi Saxones totam partem infulę, quæ ab Humbro flumine vfq*ue* ad Cattenefsinum æquor protenditur. Ea propter conuocatis regni primatibus, quid potifsimum co*n*tra paganorum Saxonum irruptionem faceret, co*n*fuluit. Com|muni tandem con- Fol. 4. filio mittit ad Armoricam, id eft minorem Britanniam ad
10 Hoelum regem nuncios, qui ei calamitatem Britanniæ notam facerent. Qui cum quindecim millibus armatorum Britanniam ueniens ab Arturio, & D. Dubritio honorifice fufceptus ad vrbem Lindocollinum a Saxonibus obfeffam proficifce*n*tes, commiffo bello, sex millia Saxonum vel fubmerfi, vel telis percuffi perie-
15 runt. Cæteri uero ad nemus Caledonis fugientes a Britannis obfefsi ad deditionem coacti funt: & fufceptis obfidibus de tributo annuatim foluendo cum folis nauibus eos patriam repetere permifit. Elapfo paruo deinde tempore, peractæ pactionis Saxones puduit, & viribus reparatis fœdus fuum irritum
20 fecerunt, vrbemq*ue* Badonis obfidione vallant, quæ nunc Bathonia dicitur: quo audito Arturius congregato exercitu, confpectis hoftiu*m* caftris, fic alloquitur. Quoniam impiifsimi Saxones fidem mihi obferuare dedignantur, ego fide*m* Deo meo feruans fanguinem ciuium meorum vlcifci conabor. Proditores ergo
25 iftos viriliter aggrediamur, quos procul dubio,[1] fuffragante[2] Chrifto, cum votiuo triumpho[3] deuincemus: Et irruens in Saxonum cuneos adiutus Dubritii precibus multa milia profternendo victoriam obtinuit, & paucos, qui ftragem aufugerant, ad deditionem coegit. Boccatius in libro de ftagnis, & paludibus fic
30 fcribit. Murais ftagnum eft Arturii Britonum regis victoria claru*m*. Aiunt enim Scottos, Pictos, & Hibernienfes ab eodem in ftagno obfeffos, in deditionem coactos. Idem libro octauo de viris illuftribus illuftrem Arturii facit mentionem, religione quadam ductus, ne tantum, talemq*ue* virum in|grato præteriret Fol. 4
35 filentio. Neque hic a noftro aliena inftituto funt, quæ in back. chronicis cuiufdam Diuionenfis comparent. Cerdicius cum Arturio co*n*fligens fæpius, fi vno menfe vinceretur, in alio menfe acrior furrexit ad pugnam. Tandem Arturius tædio

[1] Text, *dudio*.   [2] Text, *suffragante*.   [3] Text, *ttiumpho*.

fatigatus poſt duodecimum annum aduentus Cerdicii, fidelitate
ſibi iurata, dedit ei Auoniam meridianam, & Somariam, quam
partem vocauit Cerditius Viſiſaxoniam. Gulielmus a Meildulphi
curia ſcriptor tum elegans, tum eruditus, & quod in hiſtoria
primum fidelifsimus, hæc de Arturio primo de regibus Britannicis 5
libro infert. Et iam tum profecto peſſum iſſent, Britannos intelligit, niſi Ambroſius ſolus Romanorum ſuperſtes, qui poſt
Vortigernum monarcha fuit, regni intumeſcenteis barbaros
eximia bellicoſi Arturii opera prefsiſſit. Huc etiam pertinere
videntur [1] hæc, quæ in Gildæ Britanni fragmentis ad hunc legun- 10
tur modum. Vires capeſſunt Britanni victores prouocantes ad
prælium, quibus victoria, Domino annuente, ex voto ceſſit.
Ex eo tempore nunc ciues, nunc hoſtes vincebant, vt in iſta
gente experiretur Dominus ſolito more præſentem Iſrahelem,
vtrum eum diligat, an non, vſque ad annum obſeſsionis Badonici 15
montis, nouiſsimeque ferme de furciferis non minimæ ſtragis, qui
& meæ natiuitatis eſt. Hęc ille. Ecce adeſt calumniator, &
feroculus a me rationem exigit, cur Gildas Arturii, ſi tum fuit, hic
non meminerit. Ad hæc reſpondeo me inferius de Gilda dicturum.
Interea meminerit aduerſarius Gildam tempore Badonici belli 20
infantulum fuiſſe: quo nomine, & eius res geſtæ, aut non ab eo,
aut leuiter admodum intellectæ. Gulielmus a Meildulphi | curia
paulo ſuperius ita honorificum contulit Arturio teſtimonium, vt
parum abfuerit, quin, ſi non ſuperiorem, ęqualem cum Ambroſio
ſtatuerit. Nennius uero non malæ fidei autor tantum præſtitit in 25
gratiam Aurelii Ambroſii, quantum Gildas in Arturii: nempe vt
illius omiſſo nomine, huic, & merito decus omne Badonici belli
integre attribuat. Sed neque hi ſoli hoc præſtant. Numerus eſt
bonorum autorum, qui idem autoritate quadam iuſta confirmant:
Niſi interim tam iniquus ſit cenſor, vt nihil admittat, quantumuis 30
fidele, quod non ſpiret Ciceronianum, aut Liuianum, cum ipſe
potius interim ſpiret neſcio quid Aemilianum, id quod mihi non
diſplicebit, vbi eum hoc ingenue fateri intellexero. Interea
recitabo Ioannis, qui auream ſcripſit hiſtoriam, de Arturio teſtimonium. Hoc anno decimo Cerdicii regis Viſiſaxonum ſurrexit 35
apud Britones Arturius belliger.

[1] Text, *videntnr*.

Regis Britanniæ

Arturii in Gallos expeditio.

Britannicæ hiftoriæ liber fextus fufe loquitur de rebus ab Arturio in Gallia geftis: quam non ante petiit, quam maturo, vt tum quidem videbatur, confilio Britanniæ immunitati profpexerat. Erat ei nepos quidam Mordredus nomine, filius Lothonis Pictorum regis, & Annæ fororis Aurelii Ambrofii regis Britanniæ. Huic, quia ei fanguine, & familiaritate fuerat coniunctifsimus, omne regnum fuum, vna cum Guenhera fuauifsima coniuge concredidit. Erat enim Mor|dredus fortitudinis nomine commendatifsimus, tum præterea ingenio acri, & gerendis rebus expedito: quas virtutes, nifi libidine dominandi flagrantifsima, fed interim principio ob metum tacita, & adulterii nota obfcuraffet, merito quidem inter clarifsimos viros numerandus effet. Iam Galliam Arturius inuaferat, & debellatis regulis virtutis fuæ fpecimen vel illuftre oftenderat. Ecce adfuit tyrannus immanis, truculentus, ferox, qui Helenam neptem Hoeli Armoricani raptam, & ex Britannia abductam, ad littus Gallicum vitiauerat, vnde & obiit. Non tulit Arturius tam infignem Helenæ factam contumeliam, & ftatim tyranni iugulum petiit, ac monftrum ingens, horrendumque e medio fuftulit. Nec multo poft ab Hoelo erectus Helenæ facer tumulus in infula qua periit, & Tumba Helenæ loco nomen apte inditum, quod vel hodie feruat, Chronica Diuionenfis fcriptoris magna Arturium laude in Gallia militantem huiufmodi verbis attollunt. Arturius per nouem annos Galliam fibi fubiugauit, commiffo regno, & regina fua Mordredo nepoti fuo. Ille vero regnare appetens, fed folum Cerdicium timens dedit ei vt fibi faueret feptem alias prouincias Sudofaxoniam, Sudorheiam, Berrochiam, Vilugiam, Duriam, Deuoniam, & Coriniam. Cerdicius autem his confentiens fuas prouincias accitis Anglis inftaurauit, & coronatus eft more gentili apud wintoniam. Mordredus vero fuper Britones apud Londinium. Et ita Cerdicius cum regnaffet tribus annis obiit, manente ad huc Arturio in Galliis. Cui fucceffit Kinrichus, cuius anno feptimo Arturius rediit. Hactenus e chronicis. Habent, quæ modo citaui, non | folum fuam antiquitatem, verum etiam fidem, & ferie quadam hiftoriæ confonant. Vtque triumphis Arturii de Gallis aliquanto indulgentius faueam multa præterea funt, quæ ego ftudio plane quodam omitto. Illud tamen tanquam in

104   *Affertio inclytiffimi Arturii*

tranfcurfu attingendum eft, conftare ex infcriptione figilli Arturii magni, de qua nos fuo loco accurate dicemus, eum aliquando Gallici cognomento infignitum fuiffe. Neque enim hoc fine luculenta vnquam factum caufa. Nam de figilli & antiquitate, & cognitione vel certifsima, adeo plane non dubito, vt 5 certe confidam, adfint modo iudices candidi, & veterum monumentorum gnari, confpicuis probaturum me rationibus genuinum effe illud, & ab archetypo profectum. Quin hæc rectius fuo loco. Tantum in præsentia adiiciam Valerium quendam triginta regnorum ab Arturio deuictorum meminiffe. Nam eo fęculo 10 ingens regulorum turba infulas, vna cum Gallia, & Germania fub ditione tenebant.

Pugiles Arturio familiares.

Expectaret hic forfitan aliquis, vt & Arturii contra Romanos victorias, quarum & Britannica meminit hiftoria, tuba magna 15 perfonarem. Hiftorici in hac parte certant, & adhuc fub iudice lis eft. Ego vero temere nihil pronunciabo : quandoquidem manifeftifsime conftat, obfcura, & abfurda inrepfiffe in Arturii hiftoriam : id quod a curiofis facile deprehenditur. At hæc non
Fol. 6 back.
fatis quidem iufta caufa eft, ut | quis hiftoriam alias luculentam, 20 & veram negligat abiiciat, proterat. Quanto rectius, abiectis nugis, refectis anilibus fabulis, & auctariis in fpeciem vero magnificis, at nihil ad fidem pertinentibus, demptis, quæ ex autoritate confonantia funt legere, difcutere, conferuare. Nam quod longo iam tempore a doctis receptum magno confenfu eft : 25 non debet momento temporis quocunque oblatrante, vna cum fide e medio tolli. Aliter in tanto hactenus non ftetiffet honore hiftoria. Ergo quia maioris operis eft, quam in præfentia agimus, exquifite, curiofe, & ad unguem facta Arturii omnia excutere,[1] omittamus tantifper Romanos, & familiares illius 30 calamo illuftremus. Hoelus Armoricæ regulus in hoc celebri nobilium choro proximum a primo locum iure quodam fuo pofcit, de cuius in Britanniam aduentu, & virtute bellica fuperius in titulo de bellis ab Arturio geftis fcripfimus. Huc accedunt Mordredus, & Gallouinus germani fratres Arturio fanguine, 35 & confuetudine coniuncti : quorum ille tandem veluti perfidus, atque idem defertor nunquam fatis vituperandus, vt de nota

[1] Text, *excutete*.

Regis Britanniæ 105

adulterii nihil loquar, occifus eft bello, Hectore parum vero tefte,
Abrino, at, vt ego cum iudicio colligo, rectius Alaunico. Hic
autem perpetuo fui fimilis, fidelifsimam operam præftitit cum
bellis externis omnibus, tum præcipue in Dorenfi conflictu, sub
5 reditum Arturii ex Gallia in Britanniam, qui illi contra Mordredum
fupremus fuit. Melchinus vates Britannicus Gallouini
celebrat nomen. Idem facit Ioannes Annæuillanus in fuo
Architrenio, non ineleganti opere, his verfibus.

Et Vualganus ego, qui nil reminifcor auara.
10 Illoculaffe manu: non hæc mea fulgurat auro,
Sed gladio dextra: recipit quo fpargat, & enfes,
Non loculos ftringit: Nec opes in carcere miles
Degener, & cupide cumulato rufticus ære.
Et me bella vocant: et tua forfitan vrget
15 Sollicitudo. Vale.

Hiftoria quoque Arturii fabulofa quidem illa, quæ vulgo
vernacula lingua fcripta circumfertur, adfirmat Gallouinum Dori
in facello quodam fepultum fuiffe. Qua parte qualifcunque liber,
adeo non omnino fallit, vt idem Scalæchronicon aperte referat:
20 & caftellani eius offa pene Gigantea etiam nunc miraculi
oftentent loco. Quodque olim tempore Lucii magni facellum in
Durenfi caftro, prædicantibus Fugatio, & Damiano Britannis
euangelium, Seruatori Chrifto optimo maximo pofitum fit, ex
eiufdem urbis annalibus uenerandam antiquitatis prę fe ferentibus
25 imaginem, liquido apparet. Vt fit receptifsimum, iuxta ac
verifsimum quod fupra de Gallouini & cæde, & fepultura intuli:
non tamen per me ftabit, vt Gulielmi a Meildulphi curia iudicium
de morte, & fepultura Gallouini, nunquam fatis a fortitudine
collaudati, aut intercidat, aut emoriatur. Quare operæ pretium
30 duco illius verba ex tertio libro de regibus Anglicis hic apponere,
vt hinc prudens lector, veluti ad Lydium lapidem verifulgorem
genuinum ab adulterino curiofe excutiat. Tunc in prouincia
walliarum, quæ Rofsia vocatur inuentum eft waluuini fepulchrum,
qui fuit haud degener Arturii ex forore nepos. Regnauit in ea
35 parte Britanniæ, quę ad huc waluuithia vocatur miles virtute
nominatifsimus, fed a fratre, & nepote Hengifti, de quibus in
primo libro dixi, regno expulfus, prius multo eorum de|trimento
exilium compenfans fuum: communicans merito laudi auunculi,

106 *Assertio inclytissimi Arturii*

quod ruentis patriæ cafum plures annos diftulerit. Sed Arturii fepulchrum nufquam vifitur, vnde antiquitas Nęniarum ad huc eum venturum fabulatur. Cæterum alterius buftum, vt præmifi tempore Gulielmi primi regis Angliæ repertum eft fuper oram maris quatuordecim pedes longum, vbi a quibufdam, vt afferitur, 5 ab hoftibus vulneratus, & naufragio eiectus : a quibufdam dicitur a ciuibus in publico epulo interfectus. Sic Meildunenfis de Gallouino. Ego vero fi mihi liceret tyroni cum Meildunenfi veterano ad dandos repellendosque ictus exercitatifsimo his telis cominus cum eo periculum virium facerem. Non eft verifimile 10 homines giganteæ altitudinis, vt ex fepulchro quatuordecim pedes longo colligo, fuiffe fęculo Gallouiniano. Quare, mea quidem fententia, credibile magis fepulchrum alicuius gigantis indigenę fuiffe. Nanque[1] taleis Albionem primum incoluiffe, & externorum, & noftrorum fcriptorum autoritate conftat. 15 Quorum vnius, Iofephi fcilicet Domnonienfis Britanni poetæ omnibus numeris elegantiffimi fidem fecutus, defumptis his paucis verfibus ex eius Antiocheide opere immortali, teftimonio breuitatis ftudio vtar.

> His Brutus auito 20
> Sanguine Troianus Latiis egreffus ab oris
> Poft varios cafus confedit finibus, orbem
> Fatalem nactus, debellatorque gigantum,
> Et terræ victor nomen dedit.

Architrenius libro fexto de gigantibus Albionicis hæc refert. 25

Fol. 8.
> Hos auidum belli Corinei robur auerno
> Præcipites mifit : cubitis ter quattuor altum
> Gogmagog Herculea fufpendit in aere lucta,
> Anthæumque fuum fcopulo detrufit in æquor.

Nec me fugit caftellum olim fuiffe nomine Gallouinum in littore, 30 de quo fupra Meildunenfis, cuius vel ad huc veftigia comparent. Sed illud non fuit fedes gigantis, vt neque forfan Gallouini Arturiani, fed recentioris alicuius fubreguli eiufdem nominis. Quod autem refert de fepulchro Arturii eo tempore verifsimum eft. Nemo homo vnquam curiofius illo excufferat omnes bibliothecæ 35 Gleffoburgenfis thefauros. Hoc tantum hic defuit ei ad cognitionem, quod Arturii fepulchrum ignorauerit moriens circa primos

[1] *Sic.* [2] Text, *Corineus.*

annos Henrici fecundi¹ regis Angliæ, cum fepulchrum poftea inuentum fit principio imperii Richardi Leonii. Quin in gratiam de qua nec adhuc aperte excidi redeo cum Gulielmo Meildunenfi, per quem, virum fuo fęculo in omni genere bonarum literarum
5 plane eruditifsimum, & in eruenda antiquitate ingenio, diligentia, cura fingularem, fateor, & quidem ingenue me in cognitione antiquitatis frequenter adiutum fuiffe. Candoris plane eft agnofcere per quem profeceris. Lubet hic ad coronidem addere notationem, quam ipfe ex lingua Britannica colligo, nominis
10 Gallouini. Walle Gallum fignificat. Guin album, perinde ac fi quis hoc vocabulo virum bellum, elegantem, & forma confpicuum defignaret, nifi quis rectius putet a Saxonica barbarie originem fumpfiffe. Waulwine Gallus amicus, vt Leofwine charus amicus. Aldwine vetus amicus. Inftat Augufellus de
15 quo pauca fuperius, qui in tam flagran|ti apud Arturium gratia fuit, vt merito Scottis regulus beneficiarius præfectus fit. Retulit ille par pari. Accitus inter alios multos principes, vt fe Arturio comitem in expeditione Gallica præftaret, adeo iniunctam fibi prouinciam non recufauit, vt magno virtutis exemplo ibi
20 ædito, maius multo in Rutupino littore domum rediens, bello ciuili Mordredo victo, & fugato ipfe inter arma cadens, fanguine, & vita exhiberet, vt teftis minime malus eft autor Scalæchronicorum, vti ego arbitror, Graius. Et quoniam de euocatione principum Arturio audientium fuperius verba fecimus, iuuat hic
25 fignificare multas, & celebres ab eo fuiffe indictas. At illa omnium celeberrima, quæ in Ifca, alias vrbe Legionum enituit, quo tempore ad arma in Gallos conclamatum eft. Quid mufis cum Marte? profecto aut parum, aut nihil. Si iufta effet tamen inter eos confuetudo exorarent Martem vt fua caufa magnas,
30 merito gratias agerent Arturio, qui myftarum chorum eruditum in Legionum vrbe, fi vera referunt Galfredus, Ioannes Burgenfis, & Roffus Verouicenfis, aut reftaurauit, aut inftituit. Hoc interim conftat ex Anonymi hiftoria Amphibalum, Iulium, & Aarona martyres Chriftum, atque adeo literas in vrbe Legionum coluiffe,
35 a quibus & alios eafdem per manus accepiffe credibile eft. Eft in Archiuis etiam Grantæ Giruiorum tabula diplomatis ab Arturio aliquando erogati in gratiam ftudioforum. Fidem tamen facti non dum fatis excufsi. Iderus olim cultor Arturianæ

¹ Text, *fefecundi*.

aulæ maximus ad pugilum numerum accedit. Hic Arturio fanguine coniunctus virtutis fortia exempla multa exhibuit: & lateri Principis fui perpetuo adhęfit, ac demum, | nefcio quo cafu, moriens maximum fui defiderium Arturio reliquit, qui & eius folicite funus Aualoniæ curauit. Legi Gleffoburgi libellum de antiquitate eiufdem, a monacho quodam illius loci diligentifsime collectum, in quo de officiis Arturii erga hunc mortuum, & munificentia eiufdem ob cognati caufam in Eremitas monachos ibidem incolenteis, multa explicat. Appendebat nuper tabula columnę Gleffoburgenfi ecclefiæ, quæ Iderum inter patronos, & reftauratores Gleffoburgenfis ecclefiæ numerabat. Lancelotus fama notifsimus locum inter Pugiles vel clarifsimos fibi dari poftulat: cui ego voto facile annuo, hoc in eius dicturus præconium, quod infigni quodam candore erga Arturium adfectus fit. Virtus eius abunde enituit eo prælio, quod inter Mordredum proditorem, & Arturium geftum eft. Superfuit vero pugnæ, & vt femel, atque iterum legi tranftulit Guenheræ, a morte Arturii velatæ, corpus ab Ambrosii curia ad Gleffoburgum. Cęterum Giraldus vno, aut altero loco videtur integre eius fepulturam, vt in Speculo ecclefiaftico, & in opere de Inftitutione Principis, Gleffoburgo attribuere. Quanquam magis mihi arridet, vt primum Ambrofiæ tumulum acceperit. Caradocus nobilæ virtutis bellicæ nomen Gallicana expeditione Arturium fecutus eft, & domum rediens in ora Rutupina bello vt videtur ciuili interfectus eft. Annales Durenfis portus opus antiquitatem redolens meminere Carodoci. Caftellani ibidem vel hodie Caradoci memoriam refricant iactantes penes fe effe nefcio quas eius exuuias. Nec fic contenti Arturii aulam, & Guenheræ cubiculum deprædicant. Iam illuftrium bellato|rum Arturianæ turmæ numerus fe ingerit: fed ego, modo id fiat fine eorum offenfa, quia præftantifsimos tantum nominandos, & collaudandos fufcepi, reliquos, laudatos alioqui, pręterire ftudii, ac poftremum adiungere Cadorum Corinianum illum. Is fuit de nobiliffimo ftemmate regum Britanniæ, & genti ad Corinum promontorium imperabat. Titulorum fui Principis defenfor fane acerrimus fuit, perpetuamque necefsitudinem cum Britannis continentis habuit. Poftremum moriens filium reliquit Conftantinum, qui mortuo Arturio Britanniæ præficitur. Is ne Mordredi proditoris filii alumni, et nepotes Gallouini aliquando, paternum imitati

exemplum, regno afpirarent, gladio iugulandos curauit. Factum vero aut hoc, aut fimile narrat Gildas Britannus his verbis. Cuius tam nefandi piaculi non ignarus eft immundæ leenæ Damoniæ tyrannicus catulus Conftantinus, qui hoc anno poft
5 horribile iuramenti facramentum, quo fe deiunxit, nequaqu*am* dolos ciuibus Deo primum, iureque iurando fa*n*ctorum demu*m* choris, & genitrice comitantibus, facturum, in duarum venera*n*dis matrum finibus, ecclefiæq*ue* carnalis fub fancto abbate Amphibalo latera regiou*m* tenerrima puerorum, vel præcordia
10 crudeliter duum, totidemq*ue* nutritorum, inter ipfa, vt dixi facrofancta altaria nefando enfe, haftaq*ue* pro dentibus lacerauit, quorum brachia nequaquam armis, quæ nullus pene hominu*m* fortius hoc eis tempore tractabat, fed Deo, altariq*ue* portenta in die iudicii ad tuæ ciuitatis portas Chrifte veneranda patientiæ, ac
15 fidei fuæ vexilla fupendent. Hactenus de pugilibus.

Orbicularis Arturii menfa. Fol. 10.

Nunc locus eft peroportunuus[1] pauca fed electa, fplendida, deniq*ue* magnifica de orbiculari menfa, & epulis Arturii in medium adferre. Non hæc patebat omnibus nobilibus, fed
20 illis tantum,

Lucida quos ardens euexit ad æthera virtus,
Virtus fola virens nullis moritura diebus.

Hanc ut ferunt pompam frequentiufcule celebrauit præcipue vero in vrbe Legionum, quem locum infigniter coluit. Idem
25 fecit Ventæ Simenorum, & Camaleti Murotrigum. Vulgus fcriptorum indoctum illud arbitratur Ventam alio nomine Camaletu*m* dici. Quin vulgi iudicium non moror. Fama publica Murotrigum radices Camaletici montis incolentium prædicat, attollit, canticat nomen Arturii incolæ aliquando caftri, quod
30 idem olim, & magnificentifsimum, & munitifsimum, atq*ue* in æditifsima fpecula, vbi mons co*n*furgit, fitum eft. Dii boni quantum hic profundifsimarum foffarum? Quot hic egeftæ terræ valla? Quæ demum præcipitia? Atq*ue* vt paucis finia*m*, videtur mihi quidem effe & artis, & naturæ miraculum.

35 At feges eft vbi Troia fuit ftabulautur in vrbe,
Et foffis pecudes altis, valloq*ue* tumenti,
Taxus, & aftutæ pofuere cubilia vulpes.

[1] *Sic.*

Atque hæc quidem humanarum vicissitudo rerum est. Hanc calamitatem hinc Iscalis vrbs antiqua: hinc Clarus fons frequens emporium mœstis inspiciunt oculis, lachrimisque indulgent. Incolæ interealoci solum a|ratro vertunt, & annis singulis numismata aurea, argentea, ærea Romanorum imagines tantum non viuas exprimentia, quærentes inueniunt, ex quibus & ego pauca dono ab eis accepi. Franciscus Hastingius Comes Venantodunensis nobilium iuuenum regiæ Britannicæ ornamentum egregium, & alumnus olim in bonis literis meus Camaleti rudera una cum latifundiis vicinis, vtpote hæres Piperellorum, Boterellorum, & Hungrefordorum possidet. Ioannes Annequillanus in Architrenio sphæricam pro dignitate sua collaudat mensam. Idem facit & Volateranus libro tertio Geographie his verbis. Domi quoque luculentus mensa inter proceres vtebatur rotunda, ne quod his discrimen ex ambitione foret. Ventæ Simenorum in castro fama notissimo appendet muro aulæ regiæ mensa, quam & rotundam a maistate Arturiana vocant. Quid? quod nec memoria, nec societas Orbicularis chori recentioribus seculis ex animis nobilium, excidit. Eadueardus Longus, vt fama refert, Orbicularem illam societatem plurimi fecit, fabricata in eos vsus, si credere dignum est, tabula sphęrica, & tripodibus ex auro solido. Sunt qui scribant Mortimarium quendam hos thesauros decoxisse. Illud interim certissimum ex historia Thomæ Vicanii, Rogerum Mortimarium celebrasse conuiuium maximum Keneluorti, quo pugiles præstantissimos, tanquam chorum Arturianum [1] ad sphęricum illud insigne magnanimus euocauit: hinc virtutis signa equestris plurima quidem ædita, quæ sedula posteritas chartis commissa auide leget. Sed nunc tantisper ab armis ad pietatem transeo.

Pietas Arturii.

Quanta, & quam syncera religione adfectus sit erga rem publicam Christianam Arturius, autoritate veterum scriptorum liquet. Vsus est Dubritii episcopi vrbis Legionum, viri cum eruditione, tum vitę continentia singularis, familiaritate, vsque adeo vt in bello Badonico eius preces victor vtileis persenserit. Dauid preterea Meneuensis homo sanctitatis plane infinitæ Arturii tum gratiam, tum munificentiam sensiit, vsque adeo, vt

[1] Text, *Artutianum.*

Regis Britanniæ

Meneuenſes translatam ad ſe ab vrbe Legionum epiſcopalem ſedem Arturio acceptam referant. Horum æqualis Iltutus vir vitę incomparabilis, audita eius ſingulari illa magnificentia, & in Deum pietate, auſus eſt, vt eius vitæ illuſtrator ſcribit, præſens præſentem non modo inuiſere, verum etiam ſalutare, atque adeo conuenire Arturium, qua pia plane audacia tantum abeſt, vt Principem offenderit, vt gratias abunde magnas præmium me hercle candidum retulerit. Deiparam virginem aſsidue coluit, cuius & imaginem, ſi vera antiqui ſcriptores, et fama conſtans referunt, depictam habuit Martio illo clypeo, quo multis in preliis, & maxime in Badonico vſus eſt. In eiuſmodi minutiis non admodum laboro. Illud interim piis non indignum auribus quod Samuel ſcriptor Britannus, & Elbodi epiſcopi diſcipulus, qui annis ab hinc pene nongentis floruit, expeditionis, aut peregrinationis potius Arturii ſic meminerit. Arturius Hieroſolimam petiit, vnde & crucis ſignum ex ligno ſecum tulit inſtar ſalutiferæ, cuius ad huc fragmenta ſeruantur in wedale uilla Lodoneiæ ſex milli|bus paſsuum a Mailros. Denique Gleſſoburgen- Fol. 11 ſes monachos heremitas illos infinitis excoluit modis, vt partim back. ſuperius in Idero, & hic fuſius oſtendam. Sylueſter Giraldus in Principis inſtitutione ſic ſcribit. Præ cunctis enim eccleſiis regni ſui S. Dei genitricis Marie Gleſconienſis eccleſiam plus dilexit, & præ cęteris longe maiori deuotione promouit. Polydorus pro ſuo iure, atque adeo autoritate pronunciat non fuiſſe monaſterium Aualoniæ tempore Arturii: tam exquiſitus cenſor eſt antiquitatis & maxime Britannicę. Contendit etiam vel orbem vniuerſum hac lege, ſed plane iniquiſsima, conſtringere, vt quod ab eo de antiquitate, tanquam e tripode dictum amplectantur, foueant, ac ſuſpiciant. Vt vera dicat, ac ſcribat ego facilæ aſſurgam enſe leuis nudo, parmaque inglorius alba, illius & autoritati, & iudicio vtpote veterani. At vt falſa pronuntiet, id quod frequentiuſcule per omneis hiſtoriæ ſuæ partes facit, non feram, non ſinam, non patiar, quin veritatem, rumpantur vt ilia Codris omnibus, ſuo nitori, fame, gloriæ alacer, & intrepidus, quantum per me ſteterit, reſtituam. Nam me huic ſententiæ in hac partæ honeſtiſsimę vt fortiter inhęream geſta ab ipſis Britannorum apoſtolis Fugatio, & Damiano, & epiſtola Patricii Magni, quæ penes me eſt eadem confirmans, vt multorum aliorum teſtimonia breuitatis cauſa omittam, iubent, aut potius imperant. Henricus Plantagenifta Henrici Belloclerici regis Angliæ ex Mathilde filia nepos præfcriptis, & liquidis verbis adfirmat in donatione quadam fe vidiffe, atque, ne quid ad fidem defit integram, legiffe tabulas cuiufdam munificentiæ Arturii erga monachos heremitas Aualoniam | incolenteis. Quin ipfa Henricianæ donationis verba ex archetypo fubfcribam. Quæcunque etiam a prædeceſſoribus meis Gulielmo primo, Gulielmo fecundo, & Henrico auo meo. Sed ab antiquioribus videlicet Eadgaro patre S. Eadueardi, ab Eadmundo, & patre ipfius Eadueardo, & Ealfredo auo eiufdem. Brinwalchio. Kenwino, Baldredo, Ina, Cuthredo, & Arturio, & multis aliis regibus Chriftianis. Sed & a Kenwalchio rege pagano, quorum priuilegia, & chartas diligenter feci inquiri, & coram me prefentari, & legi. Hactenus diploma. Hi tam certæ fidei teftes fi non fatis ad excufsifimam veritatis cognitionem faciunt, nihil profecto vnquam faciet. Nam his auditis, & percognitis non adquiefcere, nec fani capitis, fed neque iudicii erit.

Sigillum Arturi.

Et quoniam in facrofanctæ antiquitatis penetralia, receſſus, ac vifcera curiofus indagator defcendi, lubet in lucem aliud proferre, videlicet figillum Arturii monumentum faberrime infculptum, antiquum, & venerandum, de quo Caxodunus, fed obiter, & leuiter in præfatione hiftoriæ Arturianæ, quam vulgus lingua Anglica impreffam legit, mentionem facit. Motus qualicunque Caxoduni teftimonio Vifimonafterium me contuli, vt, quæ auritus teftis audiueram, oculatus tandem cernerem, illud animo expendens meo. Pluris valet oculatus teftis vnus, quam auriti decem. Rogatus Myftagogus, vt oftenderet mo|numentum, ftatim uidendum, & contingendum exhibuit. Perplacuit fpectaculum antiquitatis, & aliquandiu fua maieftate non modo mihi attraxit, uerum etiam detinuit oculos. Tanti momenti eft commode incidiffe in rem ftudio defideratam magno. Materia quæ ipfiffimam figilli formam impreffam accepit, & ad huc fideliter retinet, cæra coloris rubri eft, quæ uiolentia aliqua, uel temporis iniuria longi comminuta, in partes hinc inde diffinditur: ita tamen ut nulla prorfum defideretur. Nam fragmenta cafu aliquo prius concuffa, fic argenteæ lamina, quæ orbicularis

Regis Britanniæ 113

figuræ, qualis & figilli facies, eft, undique concluduntur, ut eorum pars recidat nulla. Infcribitur enim his titulis in fpeciem breuibus, fed re ipfa fplendifsimis, amplifsimis, magnificentifsimis. PATRICIVS ARTVRIVS BRITANNIAE, GALLIAE,
5 GERMANIAE, DACIAE IMPERATOR. Atque hæc quidem infcriptio figilli orbem extimum circinat. Anterior eius pars per circulum cryftallinum pellucida eft, quo remoto, tangi fe patitur cæra iam præ antiquitate durifsima. Effigies vero Arturii impreffa refert nefcio quam heroicam maieftatem.
10 Purpura enim regaliter indutus Princeps fedet fuper hemicirculum, qualem videmus pluuium arcum. Capite coronato fulget. In dextera confurgit fceptrum ipfo liliatum vertice. Siniftra vero orbem cruce infignitum complectitur. Barba quoque prominet, & illud etiam maieftatis eft. Pars altera
15 orbiculari lamina argenti tota obducitur: vnde & incertum cuius forme fit. Appendet catenulæ ex argento intortæ. Dispeream lector nifi vidiffe velis: tanta eft tum rei antiquitas, tum maieftas. Rogatus tandem a me | myftagogus, vt mihi Fol. 13. fignificaret, fi quid præterea didiciffet de appenfo figillo, nam
20 inter ornamenta, quæ plurima auro, & gemmis micantia Eadueardi Simplicis regis Angliæ fepulchrum exornabant, & hoc quoque memorabile fuit. Ille autem ad hæc nihil, præterquam quod a rege aliquo putaret eo repofitum loco in perpetuam Arturii terque, quaterque magni memoriam. Certe fi fas effet
25 coniecturis vllis collineare verum, tantum non crederem, figillum a Gleffoburgo translatum fuiffe, cui monafterio cafu per ignem fœdifsime deturpato tali munificentifsimus præmia contulit, qualia ille pietate fua infigni facilius dare, quam monachi fperare, potuit. Henricus ipfe, vt fupra retuli, fecit mentionem Arturianæ dona-
30 tionis, atque adeo eam vidiffe, & legiffe fe. Vnde & fieri quidem potuit, vt ex efa membrana a blattis, & tineis longo temporis curfu, repertum tam illuftre antiquitatis monumentum, monafterio primi nominis conferuandum, & a nobilitate perpetuo videndum tradiderit. Vt mea me fallat coniectura difpendium quidem
35 leue, immo plane nullum. Hoc interim blanditur mihi, quod cum de Arturio agitur, & de rebus ab eo geftis, Gleffoburgus femper inftat, & operam ad certam cognitionem candidifsime pollicetur fuam. Vnde quidem & noftri in præfentia laboris fructus omnis, tanquam e fonte profluentiffimo deriuandus. Nec

P

certe, quod ego fciam, extat quicquam quod luculentius ipfo figillo comprobet Arturium fuiffe: id quod, fi diis placet, impudenter pernegare aliqui non dubitant, opinione, voluntate, temeritate denique, potius quam ratione vlla iufta nixi. Sed inferius deligemus locum, quo iuftis argumentorum | copiis hanc violentam calumniatorum turbam profternamus. Interea figilli infcriptio fubtilius excutienda. Habet enim fua myfteria, quę, vbi lucem receperint, maiori cum voluptate, tum gratia aures candidorum lectorum imbuant, & imbutas mirifice delectent: id quod operis precium & quidem amplum eft. Patricius nomen a maieftate Romana defumptum. Dicti funt eo nomine Romani nobiles, qui a primis fenatoribus oriundi. Id videtur Tacitus his verbis fignificare. Iifdem diebus in numerum patriciorum afciuit Cæfar vetuftifsimum quemque ex fenatu, aut quibus clari parentes fuerant. Liuius hæc refert. Romulus centum creat fenatores, qui patres ab honore, patricii quoque progenie eorum appellati. Liquet igitur Arturium hanc nominis famam infignem illam a parentibus, & maioribus fuis accepiffe. Vnde etiam apparet, non dum id temporis Romanæ maieftatis gloriam ad Britannos translatam in titulis refrixiffe. Crediderim Arturii etiam nomen originem ab Arturiis Romanis accepiffe. Iuuenalis poeta fatyra tertia ita fcribit. Cedamus patria, viuant Arturius iftic, Et Catulus.

Quanquam, redacta in prouinciam a Claudio Britannia, familiarifsimum erat Britannis nobilioribus Romanorum nomina fibi partim defumere, & filiis frequentifsime indere, hoc, vt ego plane arbitror, confilio non inepto ductis, quod hinc & fibi, fuifque honorem, fimul & a Romanis gratiam facile compararent. Lucius, cui Britanni cognomen Magni attribuerunt. Conftantinus, & ille quoque Magnus. Aurelius Ambrofius, & his Arturius non inferior meam vehemen|ter comprobant fententiam. Idem quoque in nobilium nomenclatura fœminarum factum eft. Exemplo funt Claudia Rufina, tefte Martiali poeta, eruditifsima, Helena fanctifsima, & Vrfula Cynofura illa. Quod autem infcriptio figilli ferie quadam eum Britanniæ, Galliæ, Germaniæ, Daciæ denique imperatorem vocet, confuetudine, & diligentia hoc quoque factum Romana, vt una cum triumphis, & tituli deuictarum gentium victori accrefcerent. Inditio funt arcus triumphales Romæ, & numifmata Cæfarum cura fimili infcripta.

Regis Britanniæ 115

Imperatoris vero nomen antiquitus, vt ex Cæsare, Cicerone, & Liuio manifestum est, ad Duces pertinebat legionum: vnde est Arturius imperator dictus est vocabulo apto, significanti, & pure pute Latino. Illud vero quod inscriptio non Arturius, sed Arturus
5 amissa i litera habet, sculptoris tantum vel errori, vel incuriæ imputo. Propria Romanorum nomina compositione, & natura quadam sua mollius, & consociantius defluunt, & terminantur in ius quam us, vt Aemilius, Manilius, Claudius, Cornelius, Terentius, Vergilius, Horatius, Ouidius. Dixi superius de
10 triumphis Arturii ob feliciter gesta contra Saxones, & Gallos bella. Superest vt inscriptione sigilli admonitus de Germania, & Dacia aliquid loquar. Sed hic expeditum me ad tam honestum munus historiographorum veterum autoritas non satis ex voto scripturienti mihi materiam subministrat. Causam vero interim susceptam non
15 defendere, religio plane esset. Audebo igitur hoc tam certo, & manifesto inscriptionis testimonio confirmatus fidem lectori facere, Arturium, fusis memorabili aliqua clade Gallis, cum Germanis, | atque Dacis manus conseruisse. Nisi quis uictoriam huc pertinere Fol. 14 contendat, quod domestico bello Saxones, & Cimbros gentes Ger- back.
20 manicas, & Dacicas acriter castigauerit. Cimbrorum Cherfonesus ea Germaniæ pars olim fuit, quæ nunc Dania, & Noruegia recentioribus uocabulis. Harum gentium reges antiquiores in suis diplomatibus, ut ego accepi, non se Danorum, sed Dacorum gubernatores scribebant. Sunt tamen inter eruditos, qui adfir-
25 ment Dacos inhabitasse eam regionem, quæ nunc Moldauia, & Valachia dicitur. Volateranus libro 3, Geographiæ adfirmat Arturium partem Galliæ Noruuegiæ, & Daciæ ab Arturio deuictam fuisse. Trittemius quoque hæc scribit. Quod cum reges Daciæ, Noruuegiæque audissent, ultro venientes eius se dominio
30 subdiderunt. Hic mihi lector admonendus est non solum Saxones, Anglos, & Iutas, alias Vitas soles venisse in Britanniam, verum etiam totius littoris Germanici accolas. Alioqui tot bellis, & cædibus impares fuissent. Sigillum iam vna cum inscriptione suis vtcunque depinxi coloribus. Proxima cura erit Arturii
35 reditum e Gallia, & cruentos conflictus inter eum, & Mordredum chartis committere.

P 2

Arturii ex Gallia reditus.

Intellexerat Arturius cum per literas, tum etiam per nuntios optimæ fidei Mordredum nimium familiarem abfente ipfo apud Guenheram fuiffe : tum preterea fœdus contra fidei facramentum cum Cerdicio rege, & | Saxonibus iniiffe, ditione pene omni, qua Britannia meridiem fpectat, illis, damno rei publicæ infinito, tradita. Accefferat & aliud malum, quo non perniciofius vllum. Ruptis ille omnibus amicitiæ, fanguinis, ac fidei vinculis, defertor pefsimus, ac domini, & patriæ proditor fceleftifsimus, purpuram non illis aptam humeris induit, ac regiam confcendit fedem tyrannide noua fretus. Non tulit vltra Arturius tam vndecunque infignem fibi factam a perfido contumeliam, quanquam & ante aliquot annos iuftam decreuerat fed impeditus bello Gallico, vindictam, quin totis viribus tam horrendum, ingens, crudele monftrum protereret. Claffe igitur comparata a Gefforiaco Morinorum ad Rutupinum littus, tefte vna cum aliis, Mattheo Florilego, fecundis velis contendit. Præfenferat aduentum optimi Domini feruus longe omnium pefsimus, & iufto exercitu confcripto, non fine confilio, & auxilio Pictorum, Scottorum, & Vififaxonum, redeunti confidentifsimus occurrit. Cantianum littus omne armorum perfonabat ftrepitu, & iam Duces pro fignis ftabant, & chorus Pugilum victores orbis alacri impetu tela vibrabant, pars gladios fulminantes exeruere, pars haftas validis manibus crifpabant. Vox omnibus vna, bella Martia bella. Lætifsimus hac expedita alacritate, & militum magnis animis Arturius miraculum omnis cum fortitudinis, tum maturæ per experientiam prudentiæ, huiufmodi oratione, oculis a terra ad cœlum, & fuos leuatis, vultufque ferenitate cum feueritate, & maieftate quadam mixta, vfus eft. Vos Pugiles, illuftriffima virtutis martiæ lumina, & vos cętera notifsimæ fortitudinis turba videtis quo nos deduxerit fortuna | & tantarum victoriarum comes, vt quæ foris fortiffima peperimus manu, non modo integra conferuemus, verum etiam nouo aliquo, & luculento incremento maiora comparemus, id quod vt in præfentia, & facilius fiat talis occafio oportune me hercle oblata iam eft, vt fi vellent bonæ fortunæ omnes in gratiam amice coniurare noftram non equidem poffent, vel fufius vel felicius obtuliffe.

Eamus igitur maximis animis quo fortuna, quo virtus, quo denique victoria vocat. Adeſt Mordredus confidentiſsimus, & mihi ſanguine coniunctiſsimus, quem adoleſcentem in ſpem magni nominis foui, amaui, atque adeo tam magni feci, ero-
5 gatis prædiis quidem bene multis, nec minus fertilibus, vt in Galliam vindex profecturus, confilio, vt tum videbatur plane fano, vni illi & vxorem meam, & fortunas, & quod multo maximum patriam conferuandam, ac vicaria opera regendam, a Saxonum, Scottorum, & Pictorum denique afsiduo impetu
10 fortifsime defendendam crediderim. Ille interim oblitus profuſiſſimæ liberalitatis erga ſe meæ, & necefsitudinis, quæ plerunque in rebus humanis maximum plane momentum habet, ac ſacramenti militaris, quo mihi eſt deuinctifsimus, perfidus, & contemptor magnus, adulter etiam, vt fama prædicat, me regem,
15 & gentium cum domitorem, tum dominatorem ad penates redeuntem, aperto, ſi diis placet, marte accipit, Pictis cognatis ſuis, Scottis eorundem vicinis, denique & Saxonibus in præſidium comparatis. Neque enim hæc me ſolum tangit inſigne flagitium, veſtra certe omnium intereſt. Quare vos Pugiles mea vnica
20 cura inuictiſsimi, & vos commilitones ſtrenuiſsimi agite præſentiſsimis | viribus communem cauſam, eluceatque nunc virtus, Fol. 16. quam ego hactenus in vobis expeditam, validam, admirabilem ſemper eſſe perſenſi. Tu Gallouine militiæ decus laudatiſsimum, cuius gloria, multis nominibus, & hoc maxime, orbi commenda-
25 tiſsima eſt, quod Mordredum hoſtem communem noſtrum, germanum fratrem tuum æquitati, & ſacramento fidei poſtpoſueris, concede hinc ad dextrum cornu robore militum inſtructiſsimum : nam primæ certaminis, & gloriæ partes hac turma tuæ erunt. Auguſellus exploratiſsimæ fortitudinis vallum hoſtibus ſe ad
30 ſiniſtram alam obiiciet. Ipſe in medio pugnator afsiduus bonis auibus adero, vobis præſidium vnicum, hoſtibus vero terror, flagellum, crux merita. Sed quid verbis opus eſt, quæ virtutem nec certe dant, nec adimunt. Veſtra virtus ex conſuetudine, exercitatione, patientia, laboris, vigiliarum, & inediæ, denique ex fuſo ſan-
35 guine, & ſpoliis enata eſt : quibus nominibus & vos mihi, & ego rurſus vobis, ſuperis tam iuſtæ cauſę fauentibus, uictoriam polliceor. Agite, facite immortalia ueſtrarum uirium pericula, & proditores punctim occidite. Dixerat. Vniuerſi imperio Ducis adſonabant, & alacri procurſu, collatis ſignis, fortia virtutis indicia

longe, lateque ædebant. Sic tandem partim interfectis, partim etiam fugatis hoſtibus, uictoria potitus eſt cruenta Arturius. Cecidere eo prælio ad portum Durenſem commiſſo Gallouinus, & Auguſellus belli fulmina, ut refert Graius in Scalæchronicis, atque alii non contemnendæ notæ autores. Mordredus inclinationem fortunæ accuſans, recuperata claſſe, cum reliquiis exercitus Tamarinum inglorius portum limitem Coriniæ petiit. Gallouini nobile | funus in quodam facello Durenſis caſtri tumulatum eſt. Ingemuit Arturius, percognita cęde duorum virorum tam eximie illuſtrium, & eorum manibus frequenti prece, alto corde dolorem premens, generofus, idemque pius parentauit. Deinde vero, iuſto exercitu incredibili cum celeritate refecto, ſtatuit magnis itineribus hoſtem improbum perſequi, & quaſi ex improuiſo fugitiuum opprimere. Callidior erat Mordredus, quam fortior. Hinc illi methodus ad artes non infuetas. Cognouit liquido per exploratores aduentare Arturium ad bellum inſtructiſsimum. Quare militem in terram vtpote feſſum, tum falis tædio, tum annonæ penuria, defcendere iufsit, ac reparatis induſt[r]ia, labore, diligentia, quanta potuit maxima, armis, per montana Coriniæ, qua ſpectat littora Sabrinaica non longe difsita, exercitum lentis itineribus ducit, & in loco qui a vulgo fcriptorum Camblan appellatur, vbi vaſta, ac partim etiam vliginoſa planities, & colliculus in ſpeculæ confurgens vfum, caſtra metatus eſt. Hic meum cogor interponere iudicium de loco in quo depugnatum eſt, & eius nomine, non quod hinc me in medium allaturum putem aliquid, tanquam e Iouis cerebro, ſed vt bona cum eruditorum gratia, coniecturam meam citra fumum, faſtumque omnem, veluti in tranſcurſu, paucis explicem. Qua parte ingenue fateor ægre ſentire me cum Hectore Boethio Scotto, qui pro more ſuo illuſtrifsima quæque in Britannia antiquitus facta pręter modum, & menfuram omnem in patrios deducit agros, atque hic audacter pronunciat extremis Arturium depugnaſſe ſignis non procul ab Abro æſtuario maximo, quod ille Humbrum barbare, ignota vocabuli no|tatione, appellat. At aliter fentit Britannica hiſtoria, & in Cornubia supremo conflixiſſe bello, adfirmat: ita tamen, vt meminerit Mordredi fecundo ab Arturio victi, & fugati Ventæ Simenorum. Graius hoc idem fentit egregius profecto fatelles, & Arturianæ aſſertor gloriæ rigidus. Nec aliter literatorum argutus chorus concinit.

Regis Britanniæ 119

At noftra non eft equidem de loco, fed de loci nomine coniectura. Ego certe pene adducor vt credam Alaunum fluuium facile degeneraffe vitio indoctorum librariorum in Camblan. Oritur hic fluuius in Corinia paucis paffuum millibus fupra.
5 Athelftouam alias Padeftow oppidum pifcatorium, non adeo procul a Sabrino æftu pofitum, per quod, fed falfis mixtus aquis, delabitur. Circa fontes eius originis in campeftri, & vafta quadam planitie eft locus fama celeberrimus, graminis, quam frumenti aliquanto feracior. Fama tot fæculis apud incolas
10 conferuata prædicat hoc loco infignem olim pugnando ftragem fuiffe factam, fed hiftorię veritas interim ignota vulgo. Multa quidem vel hac noftra ætate ibidem ab aratoribus, & fofforibus ad ripam eruuntur : qualia funt numifmata antiquorum imperium oftentantia, annuli, fragmenta armorum, & ænea ornamenta
15 inaurata ex frenis, phalerifque, & ephippiis equorum. Hæc mea eft coniectura, tum propter loci fitum, tum Alauni fluminis vicini nomen, non admodum, fi quis penitius infpiciat, a Camblan diffonum. Arturius inftat, & traiecto per vada cognita Tamaro fluuio multis alioqui in locis, & rapidifsimo, & profundifsimo,
20 contempto hofte fugitivo, caftra caftris opponit. Ecce defperatio, vt fere fit, infolitam victis audaciam retulit : vnde & pars vtraque | martem prouocat, ardens, fpe prædæ, & victoriæ, & nihil minus quam mortem metuens.

Quis cladem illius pugnæ, quis funera fando
25 Explicet? aut pofsit lachrimis æquare labores?

Mordredus commiffa pugna malorum præcentor omnium gladio confoffus perfidiæ iuftum tulit precium. Exemplo fit ille, & perpetuo fidem violantibus ob imperii cupiditatem. Cecidit vna cum tyranno ingens nobilium, & veteranorum militum numerus.
30 Sed neque victoria Arturio incruenta fuit. Nam in illo ftrepitu, & furore aut interfectus, aut ad defperationem vulneratus paulo poft publico totius Britanniæ luctu, fed præcipue Pugilum mœrentium ob tam inclyti Principis cafum elatus eft. Atque hæc quidem Arturii ter maximi finis erat.

120   *Affertio inclytiffimi Arturii*

Laus Arturii.

Arturius mortuus eft, fi modo is recte mortuus dicendus, cuius fama, memoria, laudes toto viuunt, & prænitent orbe. Fuerunt maiores noftri cum poetæ, tum hiftoriographi adeo erga Arturium faciles, candidi, grati, vt illius & nomen, & facta celebrauerint, 5 & æternitate quoque donauerint. Theliefinus, Melchinus qui & Meuinus, Ambrofius Maridunenfis, ac Merlinus Caledonius clarifsima Britannicę fidera antiquitatis hoc præftiterunt. Nennius, & Samuel Britanni hiftoriographi non minorem exhibuere memoriam, colla|tis laudum niueis calculis. De quibus, atque 10 aliis fuperius oportune, & fuis locis diximus, freti autoritate Galfredi, Aluredi, Henrici Venantodunenfis, Ioannis Chryfiftoriographi, Gulielmi a Meildulphi curia, Graii, & Boccatii. At fi nunc quem iuuat maius & luculentius ad huc aliquid cognofcere, non recufabo pauca ex probatifsimis defumpta autoribus luci, 15 diligentia qua pofsum optima, reftituere. Iofephus Ifcæ Domnoniorum alumnus, & aureum fuo fæculo vtriufque eloquentiæ flumen, fic Arturium in Antiocheide ab eximia fortitudine tantum non ad fidera ipfa attollit, vt ex his verfibus cum antiquitate Romana de palma contendentibus liquer. 20

Hinc celebri fato felici claruit ortu
Flos regum Arturus: cuius cum facta ftupori,
Non micuere minus, quod totus in aure voluptas,
Et populo narrante fauus, Quæcunque priorum
Infpice. Pellęum commendat fama tyrannum.   25
Pagina Cæfareos loquitur Romana triumphos.
Alciden domitis attollit gloria monftris.
Sed nec pinetum coryli, nec fidera folem
Aequant. Annales Latios, Graiofque reuolue.
Prifca parem nefcit, æqualem poftera nullum   30
Exhibitura dies. Reges fupereminet omnes
Solus, præteritis melior, maiorque futuris.

Libellus rerum antiquarum Gleffoburgi · nuper comparuit, collectus a quodam eiufdem cœnobii monacho ftudiofifsimo, qui per occupationem colorem rhetoricum, tanquam aliud agens 35 Arturium his verbis celebrat. Prætermitto, & de inclyto Arturio rege Britannorum loqui in cœmeterio monachorum inter duas |

Regis Britanniæ

pyramides cum fua coniuge tumulato, & multis etiam Britonum Fol. 18 Principibus. Syluefter Giraldus Meneuenfis cultor antiquitatis back. fummus hac oratione, in libro cui Principis inftitutio titulus, eius famam illuftrat. Arturii quoque Britonum regis inclyti memoria
5 non eft fupprimenda, quem monafterii Glefconienfis egregii, cuius & ipfe patronus fuis diebus fuerat præcipuus, & largitor, ac fubleuator magnificus, hiftoriæ multum extollunt. Ioannes Annæuillanus poeta fuis temporibus plane ingeniofus, nec minus elegans carmina hæc cecinit in laudem Arturii, quæ vel nunc in
10 eius Architrenio comparent.

 Alter Achilles
 Arturus, teretis menfæ genitiua venuftas,
 A ramo Phrygius, dandi non vnda, fed æquor.

 Hic vero fi præterea ftuderem Arturium a multitudine autorum
15 rectifsime de eo & fcribentium, & confentientium cumulate exornare: facilius me copia eloquentiæ, quam materiæ vndecunque luculentæ magnificentia defereret. Sit fatis in præfentia paucis fcriptorum, fed illuftribus fuffragiis, vti. Quid obfecro in caufa quod Trittemius in Compendio annalium tam egregiam de
20 Arturio mentionem faciat? Caufa quidem fatis aperta eft. Nam quod ab aliis bona fide didicit, eadem gratus pofteritati tradidit, id quod plane feciffet nunquam, fi de caufæ veritate dubitaffet. Quin præfens nunc loquatur ipfe. Qui Arturus multa probitate morum, prudentia, manfuetudine, fimul &
25 humanitate pollens, fe cunctis amabilem venerandumque cunctis præftare omni ftudio curabat: quia cum virtute animi etiam mira liberalitate affluebat in omnes & | maxime in ecclefiafticos, Fol. 19. quibus pro Chrifti amore plura conferebat munufcula, fimul & donaria. Saxones, & Pictos de Britannia expulit. Scottos
30 Hibernicos, & Orcades fuo regno potenter fubiecit. Volaternus libro tertio Geographiæ affurgit famæ Arturii, & eius facta fortia accurate celebrat. Porro & Iacobus Philippus Bergomas nono Chronicorum libro Arturii virtutem præconiis vel iuftifsimis attollit. Sed nec minora vlla Nauclerus eidem in fua contulit
35 hiftoria. Hæc plane feciffent nunquam viri cum doctiffimi, tum in antiquitate exercititatifsimi, nifi prius fibi perfuafiffent Arturium aliquando fuiffe omnibus virtutum ornamentis abunde infignem. Sed quæ multorum eft iniquitas, & animus contemptor, quæ

122 Assertio inclytissimi Arturii

statim ignorantia toti, & crassa quidem, obducti non liquido perspiciunt, stupide negligunt, contemnunt, ac prorsus reiiciunt. Valeant eiusmodi antiquæ censores historiæ, & sua perfruantur stultitia, ne dicam insania. Quid si nunc Hectoris Boethii scriptoris nost[r]æ ætatis testimonium conspicuum de Arturii gloria 5 immortali in medium protulero? Certe nihil hoc calculo eius dignitati decedet, accedet vero plurimum, hoc nomine, quod Scottus instinctu nescio quo naturæ Britannum odio, vt est in prouerbio, Vatiniano prosequatur. Vnde ab aduersario, inimico, vel hoste laudari palmarii loco est. Hæc itaque sunt eius verba. 10 Fuit rex Arturius rerum egregie gestarum gloria, & amplitudine non minus quam Britanniæ reges, qui ante eum vixere insignis: vnde opes, & vires Britannis, eo regnante, plurimum creuere. Hactenus Boethius. Quam hic vellem dari mihi occasionem a Polydoro Italo iustam, vt Arturio | Britanno cristas erigerem 15 eius quoque suffragio memorabili aliquo. Agit ille causam Arturii, sed patronus interim tam languens, tepidus, & remissus, vt mihi non risum modo, verum etiam stomachum, dum falsus, & Italo perfusus aceto nescio an rideat, an stomachetur. Torquet enim se misere in historiæ concinnatione, quam, vt interim 20 aliquam faciat, cogitur velit, nolit in gratiam redire cum Galfredo Monæmuthensi, quem ante, vt sibi videbatur, verbis multis ex felle potius, quam splene natis magnifice, & pro imperio castigauerat. Quem quia interpretem tantum semel, atque iterum defenderim in causa plane iustifsima periculum & quidem 25 magni meo etiam capiti, cum sim vltra montanus, imminet. Cauebo igitur, & rei veritate consisus vna, eam pro vallo, & fossa mecum vel perpetuo circumferam. Vt sileat Polydorus. Non statim necesse est, vt orbis sileat vniuersus. Quanquam & Italia Arturium in precio olim habuit, atque adeo iam habet: 30 quando libri de eius cum fortitudine, tum victoriis, impressi, vt ego didici, Italice legantur, Hispanice etiam, & Gallice. Vnde & collectio Anglica, autore Thoma Mailerio, prodiit. Dixerit aduersarius in illos mendacia irrepsisse multa Pernoui. Quare hoc aliud nihil quam edoctum docere. Vt fabulas contemno, 35 ita historiæ veritatem amplector, & suauior. Nec hanc patiar, nisi cum vita, a me unquam distrahi amicam. Ingratos refugio, & ad rupes, & saxa testes nominis, & maiestatis Arturianæ confugio. Hac quoque parte venientem me Syluester Giraldus

Meneuenfis his verbis ex Itinerario defumptis accepit. Motibus excelfis præterquam a borea hæc vndique terra, Brechaniam intelligit concluditur. A zephyro | montana de Canter Vehan : Fol. 20. ab auftro montes habet meridionaleis, quorum principalis Cair
5 Arture Britannice dicitur, id eft caftrum Arturii propter gemina promontorii cacumina in caftri modum fe præferentia. Et quoniam in alto cathedra, & in arduo loco fita eft, fummo, & maximo Britonum regi Arturio vulgari nuncupatione eft afsignata. Haec ille. A montibus Brechanicis ad Balduinum
10 nunc mihi commigrandum, vrbem olim celebrem, quæ quadringentis ab hinc annis & amplius a Rogero Montis Gomerici alumno, & Salopiæ comite Mons Gomericus dicta eft. Hic inter collapfa mœniorum rudera locus eft fama cognitus, quem ciuium reliquiæ Portam Arturianam appellant. Fuit profecto
15 femper, atque adeo nunc eft, gens Cambrorum generofo quodam impetu erga Principum fuo tum laudes, quo titulo vel hodie elucet nomen vna cum laude non vulgari Arturii cognomento Magni, qui & Britannice Arture vaur dicitur. Maur Britannice magnum fignificat. At linguę Cambricę idiotifmus in Maure coniugato
20 vertit. M. in V. quemadmodum & in aliis vocabulis propter euphoniam B. fubinde in V. vertitur.

Aualoniæ antiquitas.

Series orationes hic me admonet, vt de Arturii fepultura verba faciam, cuius vt fatis iam memini, ita lucido, ordini in primis
25 conuenire iudico, vt loci prius antiquitatem, quo funus perlatum eft, exquifita cura pofteritati confecrem. Aual Britannice ma|lum, Fol. 20 vel ut communiori vocabulo interpreter pomum, fignificat, Aualon back. vero pomarium : vnde & a Merlino Caledonio his verfibus interprete Galfredo Arturio Monæmuthenfi infula pomorum dicta eft.

30   Infula pomorum quæ fortunata vocatur
      Ex re nomen habet, quia per fe fingula profert.
      Non opus eft illi fulcantibus arua colonis.
      Omnis abeft cultus, nifi quem natura miniftrat.
      Vltro fœcundas fegetes producit, & vuas,
35   Nataque poma fuis prætonfo germine fyluis.

Melchinus Britannus Aualoniæ, & facri ibidem cœmeterii

meminit. Sylueſter Giraldus in libro de Inſtitutione Principis ſic loquitur. Quæ nunc autem Glefconia dicitur antiquitus infula Aualonia dicebatur. Eſt enim quaſi infula tota paludibus obſita, vnde dicta eſt Britannice Aualon, id eſt inſula pomifera. Pomis enim quæ Aual Britannica lingua dicuntur locus abundat. Patricius Hiber[n]orum apoſtolus in quadam Epiſtola mentionem huius loci facit, ſed alio nomine, cuius & verba ſubiiciam. Hiberniam ad viam veritatis conuerti, & cum eos in fide ſolidaſſem catholica, tandem in Britanniam ſum reuerſus, ac, vt credo, duce Deo, qui vita eſt, & via incidi in inſulam Iniſwitrine, in qua inueni locum ſanctum, & vetuſtum a Deo electum, & ſanctificatum Mariæ: ibique quoſdam fratres rudimentis catholicæ fidei imbutos, qui ſucceſſerunt diſcipulis ſanctorum Fugatii, & Damiani. Hactenus Patricius, qui & ibidem nomina recenſet duodecim religioſorum, quorum & duo nobiles, quibus omnibus ipſe præfuit, vt ex his verbis liquet. Sic me licet inuitum ſibi prætulerunt.

Fol. 21. Et rurſus in eadem epiſtola oſten|derunt mihi fratres ſcripta ſanctorum Fugatii, & Damiani, in quibus continebatur quod duodecim diſcipuli ſanctorum Philippi, & Iacobi ipſam vetuſtam eccleſiam conſtruxerant, & quod tres reges pagani ipſis duodecim, totidem terræ poſſeſſiones dederant. Poſtremo, vt Fugatius, & Damianus ſacellum in Turrito monte non procul ab Aualonia D. Michaeli poſuerint. Satis eſt in præſentia vel leuiter deguſtaſſe Patricii venerandi epiſtolam. Gulielmus Meildunenſis in libro de antiquitate Gleſſoburgenſis monaſterii ad Henricum Bleſenſem alias Soliacenſem epiſcopum Ventæ Simenorum, & libro de regibus primo non diſſimilia ſcribit. Vnde et coniectura iuſta Gulielmum ſua tranſtuliſſe ex Patricii epiſtola. Sylueſter Giraldus in libro de Principis inſtitutione etymon nominis non infeliciter aperit. Dicta quoque quondam Britannice Iniſwitrin fuerat: ex quo vocabulo ſuperuenientes poſtea Saxones locum illum Gleſſenbury vocabant. Gles enim eorum lingua vitrum ſonat & bury caſtrum, vel ciuitas appellatur. Hæc ille. Mihi quidem mendum eſſe videtur librariorum, quod hic ſcribant byri pro burg, aut berg. Byri ſaxonice curia: Vnde Aldermanbyri id eſt ſeniorum curia, Lytlebyri parua curia. Canonbyri, vulgo Canbyri canonicorum curia. Burg alias borow montem denotat, & egeſtæ terræ tumulos. Berg denique caſtrum Latine dicitur. Vnde ſentio rectius legendum Berg, aut Burg, vt caſtro, quo

Regis Britanniæ 125

Giraldus vocabulo vtitur, aut oppido fubferuiat. Quanquam, vt ingenue fatear, nomen varie apud antiquos fcriptum reperio, vt Gleffenbyri, Gleftonbyri, & Gleffenburg. Sunt qui & pronuncient Glas pro | Gles : quanquam Gles purius, & antiquius, ut ex
5 Gleffariarum infularum nomine liquido apparet.

Fol. 21 back.

Funus Arturii.

Nec poffum, nec uolo pronunciare num Arturius totus in bello Alaunico, quod uulgo Camblan, conciderit, an Aualoniæ inter curationem vulnerum. Britannici fcriptores omnes contendunt
10 vno ore eum Aualoniæ ex dolore eorundem periiffe. De loco autem fepulturæ conueniunt vniuerfi. Vnum hoc aufim adfirmare tam folicitos fuiffe Britannos de nece Domini fui, vt eam modis omnibus ftuduerint claram reddere, & nomen Ducis fui Saxonibus vel perpetuo tremendum relinquere : vfque adeo, vt plaufibili, &
15 nouo quodam commento fparferint rumores de eo cum redituro, tum iterum regnaturo. De Arturii vulnerati aduentu in Aualoniam fcripfere aliquot Britanni. At nullus vel fufius, vel lucidus, quam Merlinus Caledonius a Theliefino vate, vt quidam volunt, edoctus, cuius & hic verfus ex prophetico libello, interprete Galfrido
20 Arturio, delectos adfigam.

    Illuc poft bellum Camblani vulnere læfum
    Duximus Arturum, nos conducente Barincho,
    Aequora cui fuerant, & cœli fidera nota.
    Hoc rectore ratis cum Principe venimus illuc,
25   Et nos quo decuit Morgan fufcepit honore,
    Inque fuis thalamis pofuit fuper aurea regem
    Fulcra, manuque fibi detexit vulnus honefta,
    Infpexitque diu: tandemque redire falutem   Fol. 22.
    Poffe fibi dixit, fi fecum tempore longo
30   Effet, & ipfius vellet medicamine fungi.
    Gaudentes igitur regem commifimus illi,
    Et dedimus ventis redeundo vela fecundis.

Syluefter Giraldus in Speculo ecclefiaftico fcribit **Morganen** illuftrem fœminam curauiffe funus Arturii. Et rurfus in libro de
35 inftitutione Principis hæc refert. Vnde & Morganis nobilis matrona, & partium illarum dominatrix, & patrona, nec non

& Arturio fanguine propinqua poft bellum de Kemelen, Arturium ad fanandum eius vulnera in infulam, quæ nunc Glafconia dicitur, deportauit. Britannicæ interpres hiftoriæ libro fexto talia de morte Arturii fcribit. Arturius letaliter vulneratus in pugna ad Camblan contulit fe Aualoniam, relicto 5 imperio Conftantino Cadorii ducis Coriniæ filio. Ioannes Burgenfis abba in fuis Annalibus hæc fidis commifit chartis. Occuluit fe rex Arturius moriturus, ne cafui tanto infultarent inimici, amicique confufi moleftarentur. Hactenus ille. Nunc de facrofancto cœmeterio Aualoniæ, in quo Arturius fepultus 10 eft, dicendum. Melchinus in primis huius meminit, & Arturii ibidem fepulti. Gulielmus a Meildulphi curia cum alibi, tum præcipue in libro de antiquitate Gleffoburgenfi facrum hoc cœmeterium religiose celebrat. Idem facit & Giraldus Meneuenfis in fpeculo ecclefiaftico, & libro de inftitutione Principis. Non 15 erant eo fæculo in Britannia tam frequentia, quam nunc funt cœmeteria. Saxones nobiles gens Chrifti ignara in hortis amœnis fi domi forte ægroti moriebantur, fi foris, & bello occifi in egeftis per cam|pos terræ tumulis, quos burgos appellabant, iuxta caftra fepulti funt: vulgus autem promifcuum etiam in 20 pratis, & apertis campis. Erat tunc temporis facrum cœmeterium iuxta ueterem ecclefiam in precio maximo, quo titulo & a tota nobilitate occidentalium Britanniæ regiuncularum in fepulchri fortem cooptatum. Idem poftea a Saxonibus Seruatorem agnofcentibus factitatum eft: vt Durouerni Cantiorum, Eboraci 25 Brigantum, Lindiffarnæ, atque adeo alibi. De loco fepulturæ iam fatis conftat. Supereft, vt & ritum, & fepulchri formam demonftrem. Adfuit, fed fecreto, nobilium chorus Domini tam iniquo fato fublati funus perlugens. Curauit vna funus Morganis fœmina pietatis plane incomparabilis, & iufta fepulchro, lachri- 30 marum flumine irriguo, omnia anxie perfoluebat. Mos eius fæculi fuit alnorum ingenteis truncos, quarum, partes Aualoniæ vicinæ feracifsimæ erant, incauare, & in vfus fepulchrorum dedolare. Habet enim alnus nefcio quid commune cum vliginofo folo, quale cœmeterium eft: vfque adeo, vt eius materia in terra 35 huiufmodi altius pofita, tantum non æterna cenfeatur. Corpus Arturii deplorati, foffa bene alta facta, robore alneo excauato conditum eft. Et quoniam fama, factis, ditione magnificentifsimus vixit: fymbolum æternæ memoriæ Chriftianorum in hoc fedulo

tum confuetudinem, tum candorem imitati, crucem uidelicet perpetuæ vitæ Mnemofynen fepulchro mortui intulerunt. Erat ex lamina plumbea confecta, longa plus minus pedem vnum, quam & ego curiofifsimis contemplatus fum oculis, & folicitus
5 contrectaui articulis, motus & antiquitate rei, & dignitate. Literis Romanis maiufculis | illis, fed parum dextere infculptis hæc Fol. 23. verba continet. HIC IACET SEPVLTVS INCLYTVS REX ARTVRIVS IN INSVLA AVALONIÆ. Sed hic forfitan curiofus aliquis ⁺exquiret, quo confilio infcriptio laminæ
10 plumbeæ commendata fit. Mos eius ætatis erat receptifsimus, & durauit vfque ad recentiora fęcula, vt fepulchris nobilium laminas plumbeas infcriptas includerent. Quarum non paucas vidi pafsim per vniuerfam Britanniam. Plumbum fua natura facile recipit fculpturam, & acceptam cum longifsime, tum fide-
15 lifsime, tefte experientia, conferuat. Montes Minerarii plumbi admodum fertiles, vix quinque pafsuum millibus ab Aualonia diftant. Non puduit Romanos rerum Dominos trophæum ex oblonga plumbi tabula in ipfis pene eorundem montium radicibus ad fontes Ochidis fluuioli fabulofi ditionis epifcopi
20 Fontani Claudio Cæfari fic infcriptum erigere. TI. CLAVD. CAESAR. AVG. P. M. TR. P. VIIII. IMP. XVI. DE BRITAN. Hoc trophæum annis ab hinc paucis aratro erutum, & ad ædes Thomæ Houerti Icenorum Ducis Londinum tranflatum.

25   *Pyramides fancti cœmeterii.*

In fepulchreto, quod Aualoniæ facrofanctum eft, ftant duæ pyramides antiquifsimę ftructure, imagines, & literas præ fe ferentes, fed venti, procellæ, tempus edax rerum, poftremo inuidiofa vetuftas ita operum eximias olim figuras, & infcriptiones
30 deuenuftauerunt, | vt vix vllo labore deprehendi vel a lynceo Fol. 23 pofsint. Has frequens fcriptorum pagina commemorat, & præcipue back. Gulielmi Meildunenfis antiquarii cura magni, quem & Siluefter Giraldus, amator & ipfe rerum veterum fubfequitur. Vterque equidem docte: Ille quod labore exquifito imagines, & titulos
35 ante quadringentos annos tantum non obliteratos, luci in pulcherrimo, iuxta ac elegantifsimo libello de antiquitate Gleffo- burgenfi reftituerit: Hic quod iuftis fretus argumentis, & veterum

relatione fepulchrum Arturii, vel inter pyramides, aut loco ab eis
non longe difsito, aliquando pofitum fuiffe, probet. Plura de
Giraldo in fepulchro Arturii inuento dicemus. Interea de-
fcriptionem pyramidum ab ipfis Gulielmi pencillis graphice
depictam, velut in luculenta tabula, fpectatorum oculis fubiiciam. 5
Illud quod clam plane omnibus eft libenter predicarem, fi veritatem exculpere poffem : quid ille pyramides fibi velint, quæ
aliquantis pedibus ab ecclefia vetufta pofite coemeterium
monachorum prætexunt. Prœcerior fane, & propinquior ecclefiæ
habet quinque tabulatus, & altitudinem viginti fex pedum. Hęc 10
præ nimia vetuftate, & fi ruinam minetur, habet tamen antiquitatis non nulla fpectacula, quæ plane poffunt legi, licet non
pofsint plene intelligi. In fuperiori enim tabulatu eft imago
pontificali fchemate facta. In fecundo imago regiam prætendens
pompam, & literæ. Her. Sexi. et Blifwerh. In tertio nihilo- 15
minus nomina. Wem crefte. Bantomp. winewegn. In
quarto Hate. wulfrede, & Eanflede. In quinto, qui & inferior
eft imago, & hęc fcriptura. Logwor. Weslielas, & Bregdene.
Swelwes Hwingendes berne. Altero vero pyramis habet | octo-
decim pedes, & quatuor tabulatus, in quibus hæc leguntur. 20
Hedde epifcopus, & Bregorred, & Beorwalde. Quid hæc
fignificent non temere definio, fed ex fufpicione colligo eorum
interius in cauatis lapidibus contineri offa, quorum exterius
leguntur nomina. Certe Logwor is pro certo afferitur effe, de
cuius nomine quondam Logweresbeorh dicebatur, qui nunc Mons 25
acutus dicitur. Beorwalde nihilominus abbas poft Hemgifelum.
Hæc Meildunenfis, cui docti illuftratas pyramides omnino
acceptas ferre debent. Nunc Guenhera fe offert marito Arturio
comitem.

Qualis Guenhera. 30

Guenheram ex progenie regulorum Coriniæ ortam facile
crediderim, cum aliis argumentis innixus, tum hoc præcipue,
quod Britannica referat hiftoria eam in palatio Cadori Coriniani
educatam fuiffe, atque hinc ab Arturio in coniugem acceptam.
Coniectura eft, nec ea omnino incerta, nomen id Britannice fonare, 35
quod bella dona Italice & Gallice belle dame, Indubie a fama
nomen inditum, vt Guenllean id eft alba Leonora, vel a coniectura Helena : ita vt albę vocabulum pulchram, bellam, venuftam

exprimat. At vt de eius venuſtate ſatis conſtat, ita de pudicitia dubitatum eſt. Parcerem ipſe quidem pro meo candore heroinarum læſo honori, & fame : hiſtoriæ tamen veritas aurem vellit mihi, iubetq*ue*, & tantum non imperat, vt referam quid
5 veteres de ea ſenſerint. Tanto re|luctari imperio mihi quidem religio, & magna. Britannica hiſtoria adfirmat eam non modo rem cu*m* Mordredo Picto habuiſſe, verum etiam coniugio illi fuiſſe adiunctam. O ſcelera : o mores : o corrupta tempora. Vitæ ſcriptor Gildaicæ, autor quidem antiquus, ſed in meo
10 exemplari anonymus, hæc de Guenhera adultera prædicat. Arturius obſeſsit paludes vicinas Gleſconiæ in odium Meluæ reguli, qui eo Guenheram raptam, & perductam vitiauerat. Eſt hoc teſtimoniu*m* de regina quanuis raptam dicat, parum honorificum. Rapiuntur ſubinde eiuſmodi formæ ſua ſponte. Vtcun-
15 q*ue* fuerit, hoc certiſsimum non longo ſuperfuiſſe illam te*m*pore a nece coniugis, & adulteri. At an morbo corporis aliquo, an animi iuſto, quod ego facilius credo, mœrore obierit, non aperte conſtat. Scriptores referunt pœnitudine ductam eam velum ſacrum Ambroſiæ induiſſe, ibidemq*ue* mortuam, ac ſepultam,
20 donec humaniſsimi Lanceloti Pugilis inuictiſsimi cum cura, tum pietas reliquias poſtea Aualoniam tranſtuliſſet. Scrupulus hic contra adulterii ſuſpicionem ſuboritur. An commiſiſſet tam inſignis Arturii amator, atque idem cultor, vt adultera*m* in ſacratiſsimo cœmeterio propter illius ſepulchrum terræ commit-
25 teret? Hiſtoria Gleſſoburgenſis cœnobii accurate collecta perdocet Guenheram in ſacro cœmeterio fuiſſe ſepultam ad coniugis tumulum, & eius reliquias eodem tempore inuentas, ·quo & mariti. Confirmat hoc Sylueſter Giraldus Meneue*n*ſis in Inſtitutio*n*e Principis his verbis de Arturio loquens. Habuerat
30 enim vxores duas, quarum vltima ſcilicet cum ipſo ſepulta fuerat, & oſſa ipſius cum oſsibus viri ſimul inuenta, ſic diſtincta tamen, vt duæ par|tes ſepulchri verſus caput, ſcilicet oſsibus viri continendis, deputatæ fuiſſent : tertia vero ad pedes oſſa ſeorſum muliebria contineret. Vbi & trica comæ muliebris flaua cum
35 integritate priſtina, & colore reperta fuit, quam vt monachus quidam auide manu arripuit, & ſubleuauit, tota ſtatim in puluerem decidit. Idem Giraldus ſimilia refert in Speculo eccleſiaſtico. Potuit ille quidem cum autoritate aliqua de hac re loqui, qua*n*doquidem tum temporis in flagranti Richardi Leonii

regis Angliæ gratia confirmatus, venit ipſo tempore inuenti ſepulchri Gleſſoburgum, & oculatus teſtis, duce Henrico de Soliaco Henrici regis ex Adela nepote, & Richardi regis conſanguineo, tunc Præſide Gleſſoburgenſi, poſtea epiſcopo Ventę Simenorum, omnia, quæ ad Arturium attinebant perdidicit. Atta- 5 men ſi hic mihi liceret libere quæ ſentio dicere, adfirmarem profecto longe certioris eſſe fidei ea, quæ de Arturii quam Guenheræ, ſepultura traduntur. Nec tamen interim facio vim autoritati veterum ſcriptorum, vt & meam aliquando non deteriori tractet poſteritas modo. Leguntur Gleſſoburgi in tumulo Lydii mar- 10 moris fabre exculpto, & Arturio, iuxta ac Guenheræ poſito, hii duo verſiculi ſuum redolentes ſæculum

   Hic iacet Arturi coniunx tumulata ſecunda,
   Quæ meruit cœlos virtutum prole fecunda.[1]

Sunt qui dicant Henricum Suineſium abbatem Gleſſoburgenſem 15 fuiſſe autorem verſiculorum: niſi quis putet Henricum Bleſenſem alias Soliacenſem in Suineſii degeneraſſe nomen, cuius tempore inuentæ & Arturii, & Guenheræ reliquiæ.[2] Quid autem ſibi velint Giraldus, & Henricus nomine vxoris ſecundæ | non ſatis hercle intelligo, quando non alterius hactenus, quod meminerim quam 20 Guenheræ nomen, aut memoriam audiuerim. Sed ſit fides penes autores. Ex ſecundi verſiculi hemiſtichio: virtutum prole fecunda,[1] meliorem fuiſſe Guenheram, quam fœcundiorem apparet. Neque hic me latet Boethium ſcribere, acriter aliquando depugnatum fuiſſe inter Arturium, & Mordredum ad Humbrum fluuium, 25 & Guenheram a Pictis in caſtris ibidem captam, ac poſtea mortuam, ac ſepultam Horeſtiæ vico Anguſiæ. Relinquo Hectorem Veremundi, & Turgoti obſcurorum ſcriptorum fidei. Et fieri potuit vt illic alteri Guenheræ tumulus, non regine poneretur.

Inuentum Arturii ſepulchrum.   30

Inualeſcente Saxonum, a cæde Arturii potentia, & mox Pictis, ac Scottis ſtrenuiſsime profligatis, ac vltra vallum Seuerianum abactis, cœperunt Saxones deuictorum Britannorum reliquias non adeo timere, & multo minus magnificare, contemnere aperte potius. Quare illorum gloria florere cœpit, Britannorum 35 vero defloreſcere: Ita tamen vt nec Saxones amuſi quicquam pene de rebus inter ipſos,[3] & Britannos eo tempore geſtis

[1] Text, *fecunda*.   [2] Text, *teliquiæ*.   [3] Text, *ipſos*.

Regis Britanniæ   131

scriptum posteritati reliquerint, nam quæ post Christum cognitum, de primis Saxonum victoriis scripta sunt, ex historia per ora vulgi, & accepta, et chartis tradita sunt, aut Britanni tot bellis attriti, operam scribendi iustam vllum historiæ impenderint.
5 Tantum extant | fragmenta quædam Gildæ monachi Banno- Fol. 26. chorensis Britannos potius vellicantis, exagitantis, lancinantis, quam vllo virtutum calculo adprobantis, vsque adeo vt conductus ad male dicendum rhetor videatur. Hoc pacto res Britannica obscura per calamitatem bellorum relicta est. Bardi soli musicis
10 numeris, & illustri nobilium memoriæ conseruandæ studebant. Canebant illi ad lyram heroum facta inclyta. Profuit hoc studium mirifice cognitioni, tanquam per manus posteritati traditæ. Vnde equidem factum est vt Arturii quoque maximi nomen, fama, gloria vtcunque conseruarentur. O factum bene.

15 Si quid mea carmina possunt,
  Aonio statuam sublimeis vertice Bardos,
  Bardos Pieridum cultores, atque canentis
  Phœbi delitias, quibus est data cura perennis,
  Dicere nobilium clarissima facta virorum,
20 Aureaque excelsam famam super astra locare.

Deuicerat Anglorum gentem, superis id permittentibus, Gulielmus Nortomannus, & iam imperium Angliæ peruenerat ad Henricum eius appellationis secundum nepotem ex Matildę filia Henrici Belloclerici, filium vero Galfredi Plantageniste Ande-
25 gauensis. Hic fines imperii prorogare modis omnibus studens ad Hibernię quoque regnum animum adiecerat. Richardus Claranus Comes Strigulien̄sis propter Vagam fluuium, vir & natalibus, fortunis, ac virtute splendidissimus petierat, ante a Deronutio Lagenię regulo rogatus, Hiberniam: qua expedi-
30 tione tam fortiter se gessit, vt, proturbatis, fusis, ac victis regulo obaudientibus, famam, & gloriam immortalem, ac, si hoc quic- | quam ad rem pertinet, opes etiam sibi comparauerit, accepta in Fol. 26 vxorem Eua Deronicii filia, & ex asse hærede. Senserat Henricus back. rex Richardi Striguliensis successus, & siue eius inuidebat gloriæ,
35 seu, quod veri similius est, prædam tam opimi regni ambiebat, interdixit, proposito interim non contemnendo præmio, Richardum Hiberniæ imperio. Prudens ille, percognito Principis consilio, iuri suo cedere. Interea Henricus comparata

exercitus parte non minima in Cambriam peruenit reliquam conſcripturus, & inde recta a Meneuia in Hiberniam, cuius ſpe potiundæ totus conflagrabat, nauigare. Hæc dum agit, a Cambriæ regulis pro dignitate acceptus, in conuiuiis Bardos ad lyram concinenteis non ſine voluptate, interprete vſus, audit. Erat quidem vnus inter reliquos cognitione antiquitatis doctiſsimus. Is laudes, & inclyta Arturii facta, Henricum victorem futurum cum eo multis nominibus conferens, ita cecinit, vt aures regis mirifice & demulceret, & delectaret : Quo etiam tempore rex hoc præcipue a Bardo didicit ſepultum fuiſſe Arturium Aualoniæ in ſacro cœmeterio. Vnde munificentiſsime dimiſſo Bardo tanti monumenti indice, egit cum Henrico Bleſenſi alias Soliacenſi nepote ſuo, qui tum, aut paulo poſt ex abbate Bermundianæ inſulæ Præfectus Gleſſoburgenſis deſignatus eſt, vt diligentia exquiſitiſsima ſepulchrum in ſepto ſacri cœmeterii perquireret. Tentatum eſt aliquoties : & tandem magna difficultate inuentum, vltimis, vt quidam volunt annis Henrici ſecundi regis Angliæ, vt autem alii, quibus ego facile aſſentio, principio imperii Richardi primi eius filii. De hac reliquiarum cum indagatione, tum in|uentione ſcripſere inter cęteros multos duo pręcipue, quorum vnus erat monachus Gleſſoburgenſis, ſed nomine mihi ignotus : alter vero Sylueſter Giraldus. Acceſſiſſet porro & Gulielmus Meildunenſis teſtis tertius vtriſque conferendus, niſi mors eum de medio ante inuentionem ſepulchri ſenem abſtuliſſet. Horum in primis teſtimonio vtar, & in præſentia monachi anonymi verba huc adducam. Conditus fuit rex Arturius ſicut per regem Henricum ſecundum abbas Henricus didicerat, cuius conſanguineus, & dudum familiaris extiterat. Rex autem hoc ex geſtis Britonum, & eorum cantoribus hiſtoricis frequenter audiuerat Arturium ſepultum[1] fuiſſe iuxta vetuſtam eccleſiam in ſacro cœmeterio inter duas pyramides quondam nobiliter ſculptas, ac in eius memoriam, vt dicitur, erectas. Fuit autem rex Arturius ſepultus valde profunde propter metum Saxonum, quos ipſe frequenter expugnauerat, & quos ab inſula Britannica prorſus eiecerat, & quos Mordredus eius nepos peſsimus, contra ipſum primo reuocauerat, ne in mortuum etiam vindicis animi vitio deſęuirent, qui totam iam inſulam poſt mortem ipſius iterum occupare contenderant. Propter eundem etiam metum, in

---

[1] Text, ſepultum.

lapide quodam lato, tanquam ad fepulchrum, a fodientibus
inuento quafi pedum feptem fub terra: cum tamen fepulchrum
Arturii nouem pedum inferius inuentum fuerit. Reperta eft
etiam crux plumbea non fuperiori, fed potius inferiori parti
5 lapidis inferta literas has infcriptas habens. HIC IACET
SEPVLTVS INCLYTVS REX ARTVRIVS IN INSVLA
AVALONIA. Crucem autem extractam a lapide, dicto abbate
Henrico oftendente, | profpeximus, & has literas legimus: Sicut Fol. 27
autem crux inferius lapidi inferta fuit: fic crucis literata pars, back.
10 vt occultior effet, verfus lapidem verfa erat. Mira quidem
induftria, & hominum tempeftatis illius exquifita prudentia, qui
corpus tanti viri, Dominique fui, præcipue loci illius patroni
ratione turbationis inftantis, totis nifibus tunc occultare volebant.
Et tamen, vt aliquo impofterum tempore, tribulatione ceffante,
15 per literarum faltem eruci infertarum, & quandoque repertarum
indicia propalari poffet, procurarunt. Sicut autem prædictus
rex totum abbati prædixerat: fic Arturii corpus inuentum fuit,
non in fepulchro marmoreo, vt regem decebat tam eximium, non
in faxeo, aut Pariis lapidibus excifo, fed potius in ligneo ad hoc
20 cauato, & fexdecim pedibus in terra profundo, propter feftinam
magis quam feftiuam tanti principis humationem, tempore turbationis id exigente.

Anno Domini. 1189. Quadam die locum cortinis circun-
dans fodere præcepit. De hinc profunditate nimia a foſſoribus
25 exquifita, iam pene defperati farcophagum ligneum miræ
magnitudinis inuenerunt vndique claufum. Quo leuato, ac
aperto, regia inuenerunt offa, quantitatis incredibilis, ita vt os
tibiæ a terra vfque ad medium crus in magno viro attingeret.
Inuenerunt & crucem plumbeam altera parte fic infcriptam.
30 HIC IACET SEPVLTVS INCLYTVS REX ARTVRIVS
IN INSVLA AVALONIA. De hinc tumbam reginæ Arturio
confepultæ aperientes, tricam mulieris flauam, & formofam
miroque artificio confertam inueniunt, quæ tacta ab illis in
nihilum eft comminuta. Abbas igitur, & conuentus fufcipientes |
35 eorum exuuias cum gaudio in maiorem tranftulerunt ecclefiam Fol. 28.
in maufoleo nobiliter exculpto intrinfecus bipertito collocantes:
regium videlicet corpus per fe ad caput tumbæ: reginam ad
pedes fcilicet in orientali parte: vbi vfque in hodiernum diem
magnifice requiefcunt. Hoc autem epitaphium tumbæ infcribitur,

Hic iacet Arturus flos regum, gloria regni,
Quem mores, probitas commendant laude perenni.

Hucufque diligentifsime, fimul & fidelifsime ex Gleffoburgenfi codice in præfentem hæc conuertimus vfum. Sed quoniam videtur mihi epitaphium nefcio quid ftridulum petfonare, & vitium fæculi parum eloquentis fecum trahere, ac poftremo breuius, & humilius effe, quam vt tanto conueniat Imperatori, nos aliud facrofanctæ doctorum memoriæ, & pofteritati in eius laudem dedicauimus.

Saxonicas toties qui fudit marte cruento
Turmas, & peperit fpoliis fibi nomen opimis.
Fulmineo toties Pictos qui condidit enfe,
Impofuitque iugum Scotti ceruicibus ingens:
Qui tumidos Gallos, Germanos quique feroceis
Perculit, & Dacos bello confregit aperto:
Denique Mordredum e medio qui fuftulit illud
Monftrum, horrendum ingens, dirum, fęuumque tyrannum.
Hoc iacet extinctus monumento Arturius alto
Militiæ clarum decus, & virtutis alumnus:
Gloria nunc cuius terram circumuolat omnem,
Athereiique petit fublimia tecta Tonantis.
Vos igitur gentis proles generofa Britannæ
Induperatori ter magno affurgite veftro,
Et tumulo facro rofeas inferte corollas,
Officii teftes redolentia munera veftri.

Fol. 28 back.

Nunc oportune prodit Syluefter Giraldus ille oculatus inuentaram reliquiarum Arturii teftis, & calculum his verbis fuum commode apponit. Huius autem corpus, quod quafi phantafticum in fine, & tanquam per fpiritus ad longinqua tranflatum, neque morti obnoxium fabulæ confinxerant, his noftris diebus apud Glafconiam inter pyramides duas in cœmeterio facro quondam erectas, profundius in terra quercu concaua reconditum, & fignatum miris indiciis, & quafi miraculofis eft inuentum, & in ecclefiam cum honore tranflatum, marmoreoque decenter tumulo commendatum. Vnde & crux plumbea lapide fuperpofito; non fuperius, vt affolet, fed inferiori potius ex parte infixa, quam nos quoque vidimus, namque tractauimus, literas has infculptas, &

non emine*n*teis & extanteis, fed magis interius ad lapidem verfas continebat. HIC IACET SEPVLTVS INCLYTVS REX ARTVRIVS IN INSVLA AVALONIA. Sequuntur & hæc ibidem. Cum autem & aliqua indicia corporis ibi inueniendi
5 ex fcripturis fuis, aliqua ex pyramidibus imprefsis, quanquam nimia vt plurimum antiquitate deletis: maxime tame*n* & euidentifsime rex Angliæ Henricus fecundus, ficut ab hiftorico cantore Britone audiuerat antiquo, totum monachis indicauit: fcilicet quod profunde in terra per fexdecim pedes ad minus
10 inuenirent, & non lapideo in tumulo, fed in quercu cauata. Ideoq*ue* tam profunde fitum corpus, & quafi abfconditum fuerat, ne a Saxonibus poft necem illius infulam occupantibus, quos viuens tantopere debellauerat, & fere deleuerat, poffet vllatenus inueniri. Et ob | hoc literæ veritatis indices cruc Fol. 29.
15 impreffæ interius ad lapidem verfæ fuerunt, vt & tunc temporis quod co*n*tineba*n*t, occultare*n*t, & quandoq*ue* pro locis, & temporibus id propalarent. Preterea & hæc quoque ibidem fcribit. Sciendu*m* etiam quod offa reperta corporis Arturii tam grandia fuerunt, vt & illud poetæ completu*m* in his uideri poffet

20 Grandiaq*ue* effofsis mirabitur offa fepulchris.

Os enim tibiæ ipfius appofitum tibiæ longifsimi viri, quem & nobis abbas oftendit, & iuxta pedem terræ illius adfixum large tribus digitis trans genu ipfius fe porrexit. Os etiam capitis tanquam ad prodigium, vel oftentum capax erat, &
25 groffum, adeo, vt inter ciliu*m*, & oculos palmalem amplitudinem large contineret. Apparebant in hoc dece*m*, aut plura vulnera, quæ cu*n*cta præter vnum, maius cæteris, quod hiatum grandem fecerat, quodq*ue* folum letale videretur, in folidam concreuerant cicatricem. Nunc fi quem iuuabit vel ipfa eade*m*, quæ modo
30 recitaui ex Giraldo, vel his non admodum difsimilia repetere, legat eius librum Speculum videlicet ecclefiafticum, vbi duo huius materiæ capita elucent. Interim hic habeo quod me tenet dubium. Nam Giraldus adfirmat fepulchru*m* quercinum fuiffe, quod vt falfum effe non ftatim pronu*n*cio: ita infinuabo
35 ea, quæ mihi contrarium vehementer fuadeant. Primum alnorum ingentiu*m* numerus ibidem foli propicia quadam natura excrefcentium. Tum præterea Aualonianos tam ignaros rerum naturalium non fuiffe puto, vt quercu*m* crederent diuturniorem

futuram in subhumida terra, quam alnum aquaticam, & loci
incolam. Qui de arboribus scripsere humidiuscula loca alnis,
& vlmis producendis lubenter attribuunt. Superest & scrupulus
alter, qui, si ego quicquam recte iudico, excussus semel error
potius, quam scrupulus plane videbitur. Confirmat Giraldus
inuentum fuisse Arturii sepulchrum inter duas pyramides in sacro
Aualoniæ cœmeterio, in qua opinione, vtpote testimonio antiquorum scriptorum confirmatus, et ego quoque sum. At tantum
abest vt credam quicquam in illis exculptum, quod sepulchrum
Arturii, id quod agit Giraldus, indicet, exprimat, illustret, vt mihi
nihil fiat minus verisimile. Si quicquam fuisset, quis illud quæso
rectius, aut plenius Gulielmo Meildunensi, cui vni elucubratas
eorundem tum imagines, tum inscriptiones debet posteritas omnis,
explicuisset? At ille ibi ne Gry quidem de Arturio alias ab eo
accurate collaudato. Est equidem coniectura probabilis Giraldum penitus ignorasse quid inscriptionum pyramides continuerint,
cum dicat literas præ antiquitate deletas. Quin Giraldum virum
alioqui sane doctum, & magnum vetustæ cognitionis helluonem,
omitto, alia nec inutili prouacatus cura: nempe vt inuentum
Arturii sepulchrum non modo duorum, quos supra nominaui,
suffragio, verum numero scriptorum iusto confirmem, stabiliam,[1]
denique tanquam ratum persuadeam. Quoque id commodius
fiat, puto conuenire causæ, vt singula illustrium virorum, serie
quadam expedita, & lucida, testimonia altius repetam. Qua parte
Claudius homo Gallus, vt lector intelligat fidem inuenti sepulchri
vel ad exteros integram peruenisse, abunde magnus testis erit.

Anno D. 1217. Corpus inclyti[2] regis Britanniæ Arturii quod
sexcentis, & amplius annis delituerat inuen|tum est in ecclesia
D. Mariæ Glessenburiæ. Hic in annorum computatione aut
autoris, aut, vt candidius interpretor, librarii incuria irrepsit
mendum. Nam obiit Henricus secundus rex Angliæ circa
annum a Christo nato millesimum centesimum nonagesimum,
& inuentum est sepulchrum primis annis imperii Richardi eius filii.
Chronica Persorana hæc referunt. Anno D. 1191. Sepulchrum
inclyti regis Arturii apud Glasconiam, cruce plumbea super pectus
nomen eius inscriptum declarante, repertum est. Ioannes Fiberius,
qui & vulgo Beuer dictus, hæc breuissime, & in transcursu scribit.
Anno D. 1191. Inuenta sunt ossa Arturii Glesconiæ. Matthæus

---

[1] Text, *stabiliem.*   [2] Text, *incyti.*

Regis Britanniæ

Parifius monachus Fani Albani ad ruinas Verolamii vrbis antiquifsimæ Catieuchlanorum, fepulchri fic meminit. Inuenta funt apud Glafconiam offa famofifsimi regis Arturii in quodam vetuftifsimo recondita farcophago circa quod duæ antiquifsimæ
5 pyramides ftabant erectæ, in quibus literæ exaratæ erant, fed ob nimiam barbariem, & deformitate, legi non potuerunt. Inuenta autem funt hac occafione. Dum enim ibi effoderent vt quendam monachum fepelirent, qui hunc locum fepulturæ vehementi in vita defiderio præoptauerat, quoddam reperiunt
10 farcophagum, cui crux plumbea fuperpofita fuerat in qua exaratum erat. HIC IACET INCLYTVS BRITONVM REX ARTVRIVS IN INSVLA AVALONIA SEPVLTVS. Locus autem ille paludibus vndique inclufus, olim infula Aualonis, id eft pomorum infula eft vocatus. Vt merito autoritati
15 Matthæi plurimum faueo, fic dolet aliquot voculas redundanteis eius accefsiffe orationi in infcriptione. Illud | certe quod de monacho refert audiui ante plane nunquam, nec vfque adeo mihi fidem facit. Ranulphus Higedenus Caftrenfis meminit etiam Arturiani fepulchri. Alios data opera omitto ne numerum
20 teftium in re tam liquido cognita, & recepta adfectaffe videar.

Fol. 30 back.

Tranflatio reliquiarum Arturii.

Memini me in epiftola dedicatoria de exuuiis Arturii ter tranflatis locutum. Quarum quæ prima fuit, quia non fatis perfpicue per maius templum, quo fcribunt principio traductas fuiffe,
25 apparet, aliquid apertius, & lucidius lectori fignificabo. Didici a Gleffoburgenfibus monachis obferuatoribus antiquitatis fui cœnobii plane ftudiofifsimis reliquias in magnam bafilicam, quod opus in immenfum beneficio Henrici Plantageniftæ excreuit, fuiffe a facro cœmeterio tranflatas: at non eo tunc loco, quo
30 nunc funt pofitas. Porticus ad meridiem eft, & facellum, quo itur in gazophylacium. Hic adfirmabant offa aliquandiu quieuiffe. Deinde iterum tranflata fuiffe in prefbyterii finus medios: qua temporis intercapedine,[1] nouum, fublime, magnificum fepulchrum ex marmore nigro, quale Lydium effe videmus, infolita quidem
35 arte, & ingenio tum excifum, tum compactum eft, de quo vna cum tranflatione iam fcribere fuperuacaneum fane effet, quando capite præcedenti de Inuento Arturii tumulo, ea comparent fuo

---
[1] Text, *intercapidine.*

ordine omnia.   Ad tertiam igitur noftra fe conuertat oratio,
Fol. 31. quæ tempore Eadueardi Longi re|gis Angliæ non modo maximi
laudatoris, verum etiam admiratoris, peneque cultoris Arturianæ
famæ, facta eft, relictis in fepulchro magnificentifsimo, in quo
prius conquiefcebant, exuuiis omnibus præter Regis, & Reginæ
cranea, quæ iufsit foris feruari, gratum profecto nobilitati eo
confluenti antiquitatis fpectaculum.   Vtque nunc tam nobile
Eadueardi nunquam fatis laudati facinus æternitate gaudeat,
referam fingula huc pertinentia ex archiuis Gleffoburgenfis
monafterii fideliffime defumpta, quorum & autor fuit idem
monachus Gleffoburgenfis, cui cura ardentifsima inerat Arturium
iuftis celebrare præconiis, & res ab eo geftas fide integra pofteritati commendare.   Non defuit fcriptori ordo lucidus, aut
ingenium. Sed ętas illa nec Græcam, nec Romanam familiarem
habebant eloquentiam. Qualiacunque ea funt, vt ipfe fcripfit,
ita ego ordine recitabo, illud interim oportune expendens, non
quam elegantia, fed quam digna, & quam vera referat.

    Anno D. 1276.   Eadueardus rex Henrici tertii filius venit
cum regina fua Glefconiam.   Die vero Martis proxima fequente
fuit rex, & tota curia acceptus fumptibus monafterii.   Quo die
in crepufculo fecit aperiri fepulchrum inclyti regis Arturii, vbi in
duabus ciftis imaginibus, & armis eorum depictis, offa dicti regis
mirę groffitudinis feparata inuenit.   Imago quidem reginæ coro-
nata, Imaginis regiæ corona fuit proftrata cum abfcifione finiftræ
auriculæ, & veftigiis plagæ, vnde moriebatur. ·Inuenta eft fcriptura fuper his fingulis manifefta. In craftino videlicet die
Mercurii Rex offa regis, Regina offa reginæ in fingulis palleiis
Fol. 31 preciofis reuoluta in fuis ciftis recludentes, & figilla fua appo nentes
back.   præceperunt idem fepulchrum ante maius altare celeriter collo-
cari, retentis exterius capitibus vtriufque propter populi
deuotionem, appofita interius fcriptura eiufmodi : Hæc funt offa
nobilifsimi regis Arturii, quæ anno dominicæ incarnationis.
1278. decimo tertio Calend. Maii, per Dominum Eadueardum
regem Angliæ illuftrem hic fuerunt fic collocata, præfentibus
Leonora ferenifsima eiufdem Regis conforte, & filia domini
Ferrandi regis Hifpaniæ, magiftro Gulielmo de Midleton tunc
Norwicenfi electo, magiftro Thoma de Becke archidiacono
Dorfetenfi, & prædicti regis thefaurario. Domino Henrico de
Lafcey Comite Lincolnię. Domino Amadio Comite Sabaudiæ,

& multis magnatibus Angliæ. Hactenus monachus Gleffoburgenfis, cuius diligentia, memoria tam præclari facti immortalis facta eft. I nunc Gulielme Parue, vna cum Succenturione tuo, & fortiter pernega Arturium aliquando aut vixiffe, aut viciffe.
5 Me certe opinionis, immo erroris tui, nec participem, nec fautorem, fed neque riualem habebis vnquam. Flagitium me hercle non modo flagris, fed grauifsimo quoque fupplicio dignum, vt quis gloriæ patriæ fuæ deroget, Principibus de re publica rectifsime meritis fuam inuideat famam, virtuti denique,
10 & factis vndecunque illuftribus non affurgat. Spero equidem lectores candidifsimi futurum, vt vos adiutores, cognita caufæ tum ęquitate, tum veritate facileis habeam, & gratiam pro officio erga rem publicam meo, quæ veftra eft beneuolentia, humanitas, candor, magnam libenter relaturos. Hoc ego interim fretus
15 omine omnem plane mouebo lapidem, vt noua comparata fortitudine, eaque | confirmatifsima in harenam defcendam debella- Fol. 32. turus calumniatorum turbam laudibus Arturii importune, molefte, inuide obftrepentium. Sic etenim operi veluti colophonem addere omnino apud me conftitui.

20 *Conuulfio calumniarum temere adfirmantium Arturium non fuifse.*

Hiftorici certant, & adhuc fub iudice lis eft, quo tempore Arturius floruerit. Atque hoc certamen ita excreuit, & inualuit, vt fcrupuli de vniuerfa hiftoriæ fide, quæ eius res geftas prædicat,
25 lectorum fibris nunc hæreant. Quin hæc tam imbecillis eft calumnia, vt accurata non egeat refponfione vlla. Valerius eum floruiffe dicit tempore Zenonis imperatoris. Hector vero Boethius Iuftiniani tempore, barbaris Italiam ocupantibus. Denique alii, alia fcribunt, De tempore non admodum laboro,
30 fuerit modo. Quanquam vel hinc tempus facile colligitur videlicet ab imperio Aureliani Ambrofii, cuius et Paulus Diaconus mentionem facit. Dixerit forfitan aduerfariorum aliquis. Qui factum eft, vt Arturii non meminerit Paulus? Refpondeo aliud egiffe Paulum, quam vt Britannos a Romanis tantum non dere-
35 lictos anxie celebraret. Nihil interim detrahit dignitate Arturii, aut hiftoriæ, quod ab eo non nominetur: cum interim bona pars nobilium orbis totius filentio præmatur ab eodem. Illud magnum

Fol. 32 back.

plane videtur habere momentum, quod | Gildas scriptor Britannus nihil prorsus de Arturio scribat. Sunt qui citent Gildæ testimonium in eius tum gratiam, tum laudem. Sed ille quidem fictitius est Gildas, & blattis, & tineis ad Isidis vadum in bibliotheca Maridunensi prædæ expositus. Gildas a Polidoro editus, fragmentum indubie Gildæ veteris, sed mancum, luxatum, & mutilum, vsque adeo, vt, si iam vitæ restitueretur, vix foetum agnosceret parens. Scripsisse eum libros constat titulo Cambreidos, inuentos octuaginta, & amplius ab hinc annis in Hibernicis insulis, & in Italiam traductos. Vt sit historia Gildæ integra: qui potuit de Arturio quicquam recte tanquam oculatus testis pronunciare, cum ipsemet dicat se natum fuisse anno Badonici belli, quod Arturii victoria, & quidem clarissima, teste Nennio, fuit. Hostis colligit. Gildas nullam prorsus Arturii mentionem facit: ergo non fuit. Arguta plane collectio, qualis & hæc. Gildas non meminit Aruiragi, Lucii, aut Constantini Magni, proinde non fuerunt. O nouum dialectices acumen. Et tamen hoc tam infirmo corroboratus, vt sibi quidem videtur, argumento, palmarium facile se adeptum arbitratur. Hoccine est Italicum acumen? Profecto iam ægre vlterius non patiar dici Vltramontanus. Et plane. Coelum non animum mutant, qui trans mare currunt. Scio interim quid Cambrici scriptores de Gildæ silentio, quantum ad Arturium pertineat, sentiant: videlicet Hoelum Gildæ consanguineum ab Arturio occisum causam neglecti eius nominis fuisse. Sed nolo huic inniti præsidio: bellum potius cum eo gesturus, quod hac labe suos Britannos ingratus, ac idem parum prudens, ne dicam impius,

Fol. 33.

asperserit. Britanni nec in bello | fortes, nec in pace fideles. Nisi profecto viderer adfectui, aut stomacho indulgere, ipse in Britanno mastigem ferrum, & quidem acutum animose stringerem. Sed impetum temperabo meum, aliunde propugnatores in medium fortissimos adducturus, ne adfectus vim fecisse meus alicui videatur. Sylvester Giraldus in topographia Cambriæ promittit responsurum se huic Gildæ calumniæ in Britannica topographia, quem librum eum olim scripsisse non dubito, sed nostris temporibus nullo, quod ego sciam, loco extat. Quid interim scribat secundo libro de Cambriæ descriptione in medium proferam. Sed quando Iulius Cæsar, qui tantus erat, quantus & orbis, sub Casiuallano duce, Territa quæsitis ostendit terga Britannis.

Regis Britanniæ

Nunquid non fortes fuere? Quid etiam quando Bellinus, & Brennus Romanum imperium fuis addidere victoriis? Quid Helenæ noftræ filii Imperatoris tempore Conftantini? Quid Aurelii Ambrofii regno, quem & laudibus Paulus Diaconus
5 effert? Et Arturii noftri famofi tempore quanti fuere?

Iofephus Ifcæ Domnoniorum alumnus in Antiocheide fic canit.
       Inclyta fulfit
 Pofteritas ducibus tantis, tot diues alumnis,
10 Tot fœcunda viris, premerent qui viribus orbem,
 Et fama veteres. Hinc Conftantinus adeptus
 Imperium, Romam tenuit, Byzantion auxit.
 Hinc Senonum ductor captiua Brennius vrbe,
 Romuleas domuit flammis victricibus arces.
15 Hinc & Sæua fatus, pars non obfcura tumultus
 Ciuilis, magnum folus qui mole foluta
 Obfedit, meliorq*ue* ftetit pro Cæfare murus.
 Hinc celebri fato felici floruit ortu
 Flos regum Arturus, cuius cum facta ftupori,
20 Non micuere minus, totus quod in aure voluptas,
 Et populo plaudente fauus. Quæcunque priorum
 Infpice. Pellæum commendat fama tyrannum.
 Pagina Cæfareos loquitur famofa triumphos.
 Alciden domitis attollit gloria monftris.
25 Sed nec pinetum coryli, nec fidera folem
 Aequant. Annales Latios, Graiofq*ue* reuolue.
 Prifca parem nefcit, æqualem poftera nullum
 Exhibitura dies. Reges fupereminet omneis
 Solus, præteritis melior, maiorq*ue* futuris.

30 Quam hæc non refpondeant Gildæ titulis prudens lector abunde videt, & fentit laudes Arturii prius in medium adductas, huic loco tam bene conuenire, vt neceffe pene habeam eas repetere, nullo, vt fpero, meo vitio, veftra, fi vere iudico lectores, voluptate plurima. Habent enim verfus præcendentes fuum genium victu-
35 rum quidem illum. Tum præterea concinnitate quadam apta, elegantia pura, maieftate iufta, ita terfis adblandiuntur auribus, vt decies repetiti nifi me vehementer fallit meus adfectus, perplacebunt. Ponticus Virunnius homo Italus, philobritannus tamen, Polydoro Italo merito iratus hęc intonat. O admirabile tu*nc*

genus Britonum, qui eum, Cæsarem intelligit, bis in fugam expulerunt, qui totum orbem submiserat occidentis: cui quasi totus mundus postea nequiuit resistere, illi etiam fugati resistunt, parati mortem pro patria, & libertate subire. Hinc ad laudem eorum canit Lucanus de Cæsare.

>Territa quæsitis ostendit terga Britannis.

Hic si multitudine testimoniorum potius, quam solida rei veritate niterer, possem & Ioannis Annæuillani versiculos ex Architrenio libello argute canoro de fortitudine Britannorum desumere. Sic enim importune in Britannorum iustas laudes obstrepentium os præstructo occluderem uallo. Sed videor mihi pluris, quam conuenit, oblocutores istos facere. Dispereant, & inuidia rumpantur sua: quando Britannicus honor per huiusmodi tenebriones nec stat, nec cadit. At interim, ne non satis promissi memor videar, rursus repeto harenam, vim argumentorum ab aduersariis comparatam infirmaturus. Scriptores, inquiunt, Romani non fecerunt mentionem Arturii, quare verisimile est eum non fuisse. Si nihil sit verum, nisi quod ex Romana constet autoritate, male consultum esset historiæ vniuersi orbis. Infinita vis rerum memorabilium, & nobilitatis pendet potius ab incolis oculatis domi testibus, quam ex incerta exterorum relatione. Romani autem vniuersum pene orbem seruum reddiderunt, & scriptores apud eos nati, & educati sua facta vel admirabilia eloquentiæ innixi studio fecerunt. Cæterorum vero facta, vel ita obscurabant, vel eleuabant, vt nulla pene facerent. Agebatur enim vt elegantissime, non autem verissime causam dicerent. Talia pingebant in chartis, qualia sperare potius a prudentissimis Ducibus, quam facta videre liceat. Nec mirum plane est quod de Arturio nihil memoriæ prodiderint. Gotthi eo tempore Italiam inuaserant, & barbaries pro eloquentia inuecta, vsque adeo, vt literis honor rarus, præmia rarissima decernerentur. Et res non per scriptores, sed | per bellatores agebatur. Quare si quid certi de Arturio, illud potius a Britannicis scriptoribus qualibuscunque, quam ab infantia, & ignorantia Romanorum eo tempore non modo a scribendi functione declinantium, verum etiam de sua, relictis aliis rebus omnibus, calamitate multis quotidie modis irruente cogitantium. Subinfert alius vaniora esse in historia Arturii, quam vt a maturo, & sapiente facile admittantur. Si de illa sentit, quæ a vulgo

Italice, Hifpanice, Gallice, & Anglice legitur non admodum contendo. Quanquam meminerit æquus lector idem factitatum, & in hiftoria circumforanea Caroli, Rolandi, Gotthofridi, Guidonis, & Bellouefi, vt alios omittam multos. Nec inde tamen eorum nomina, aut veræ fides hiftoriæ, fublata. Non eft nouum fabulofa veris mifcere, ftudio certe hoc quodam factum, vt fcriptores plebem fimplicem admiratione quadam detinerent, auditis rerum miraculis. Sic Hercules, fic Alexander, fic Arturius, fic Carolus laudati. At alia longe ratio eft Arturianæ, quam ego complector, hiftoriæ. Nam quæ non conftant ratione temporum, quæ non funt probabilia, quæ non fubfidiaria autorum fide cohęrent, quæ non longo sęculorum vfu, & doctorum fuffragio funt recepta, & comprobata, non temere admitto. Fuit multis abhinc annis magna contentio Graio autori, vt opinor, Scalęchronicorum cum hac calumniatorum turba. Illi obiectus Beda qui filentio magno Arturium præteriit. Cui illi fic argute, feuere, prudenter refpondet. Forfitan repudiauit homo fanctulus Principem ex adulterio natum. Fieri etiam potuit, vt auditis aliquot Bardorum de eo vaticiniis, animum ab vniuerfa deflexerit | hiftoria. Sed illa nec fidem addunt, nec adimunt. Fol. 35 Illud veriffimum Bedam virum alioqui bonum, & doctum gloriam Britannici nominis non folum leuem facere, fed & contemnere [1] quoque. Nam inter illos, & Saxones de imperio Britanniæ agebatur. Romanus pontifex Anglo-faxones in imperio pefsime parto conferuare ftudebat. Britanni hoc nomine male eius capiti precari. Ille Saxones odio quodam rurfus in eos armare. Quas igitur laudes potuerunt Britanni a Saxonicis fperare fcriptoribus? Frigidas plane, aut nullas. Adde huc, quod & Beda rerum ante tempora Gildæ Britannicarum ignarus vt plurimum erat: adeo vt nec coronarii operis trophæum fpectabile ad Ambrofiam vel de fama nouerit. Credibile eft calamitatem bellicam, quæ ecclefias vna cum bibliothęcis exhauferat infinitis clara vetuftatis monumenta abrafiffe. Vnde fcripturienti de antiquitate Britannica occultifsima pleraque omnia. Sunt qui putent multa in Armoricam tranflata, quanquam & ab illa paucifsima hac ętate fperanda, præterquam quod in exemplaribus vetuftifsimis de vitis fanctorum e Britannia eo commigrantium pauca extent, fed quæ lucem obfcuris adferant. Gulielmus Paruus Brillendunenfis in prologo hiftoriæ fuæ fic fulminat.

[1] Text, conemnere.

Galfredus hic dictus eft, cognomen habens Arturii, qui diuinationum illarum nęnias ex Britannica lingua tranftulit, quibus, vt non fruftra creditur, ex proprio figmento multa adiecit. Hæc ille per ftomachum, & contemptum. At ego illi fruftra creditur, occinam vel perpetuo, nifi id rationibus potius, quam nudis probet verbis. Satis fuperque fcio multas fabulas, & vanitates per vniuerfam fparfas effe Britannicam hiftoriam. | Sunt ibi tamen, fi quis penitius infpiciat, talia, qualia magno defiderarentur antiquæ cognitionis incommodo, & quæ a Gulielmo lecta, potius quam intellecta, nullum præ fe tulerunt commodum, Rurfus apponam & aliud eiufdem honorificum fcilicet, non modo de hiftoriæ interprete, verum etiam de Arturio ipfo teftimonium. Liquet a mendacibus effe conficta, quæcunque de Arturio, & Merlino ad pafcendum minus prudentium curiofitatem homo ille fcribendo vulgauit. Vt fexcenties obganniat: fuit quidem Merlinus vir in rerum naturalium cognitione, & præcipue in Mathefi vel ad miraculum vfque eruditus: quo nomine Principibus eius ætatis merito gratifsimus erat, longeque alius, quam vt fe putaret fubiiciendum iudicio alicuius cucullati, & defidis monachi. Sed Arturium, & Merlinum, illum fortiorem, hunc eruditiorem, quam vt plebis vel dicacitatem, vel importunitatem curent, omittam. Illud, quod monachus monacho etiam mortuo inuidet mihi iniquifsimum videtur. Poterat Gulielmus Paruus maiorem a viuis, quam mortuis fperaffe victoriam. Hoc interim in lucro effe deputabat ferire non repercuffurum. At fi quicquam manes de humanis rebus fciunt, perfenferit adeo fe non reportaffe victoriam a Galfredo præter æquum, & honeftum exagito, vt eius de vulnere fibi perpetuum vulnus contraxerit, & fanguinem. Nec eft quod Vrbinatem medicum adfuturum fperet, cum & ipfe interim languidus periti cura vehementer indigeat. Supereft & aliud uulnus, quo Gulielmus putauit fe Galfridum uel iugulaffe. Sic enim infurgit. Nec unum quidem archiepifcopum unquam habuere Britones. Hoccine apud Bri|gantes didicifti? Afferius Meneuenfis, olim Alfredi Magni regis Angliæ præceptor aliud me docuit his uerbis in libro Annalium fuorum. Qui fepe depredabatur, Heimeidum regulum intelligit, illud monafterium, & parœciam S. Degwi id eft Dauidis, aliquando expulfione antiftitum, qui in eo præeffent, ficut & nobis archiepifcopum propinquum meum, & me aliquando expulit fub

ipsis. Giraldus refert, & fide optima, Dubricium Iscanum archiepiscopum fuisse. Est enim Isca Demetarum vrbs nobilissima, & antiquissima propter ripas fluminis eiusdem nominis sita, quae & Legionum ciuitas a Romanis dicebatur. Translata idem
5 Meneuiam dignitas, vbi sanctissimus, atque idem doctissimus Dauid archiepiscopi enituit dignitate. Sampson clarissimae vir memoriae archiepiscopus Meneuensis, Ictericiam pestem fugiens, Armoricam petiit: vnde origo Dolensis archiepiscopatus. A tempore autem Sampsonis, vsque ad Nortomannorum de
10 Cambria victorias, episcopi Transfabrini omnes tanquam a suffragiis consecrati sunt a Meneuensi primate suo, qui mordicus ius omne suum, cessante pallio, retinuit. Apparet etiam ex Dialogo Syluestri Giraldi Canonicos Meneuenses tempore Dauidis episcopi, qui Bernhardo successit egisse cum Richardo
15 Magno Cantiorum archiepiscopo, coram Hugutione Cardinale, de Metropolitano suae ecclesie iure, de quo & ipse Giraldus postea electus in episcopum Meneuensem Romae solicite tractabat. Atque, vt antiquiora repetam, Ptolemaeus Lucensis, qui vitas Romanorum pontificum scripsit, in Eleutherio narrat vt tres
20 Britanniae Protoflamines conuersi sint in totidem ar|chiepiscopos Londinium Trenouantum, & Eboracum Brigantum hac indubie splendebant dignitate. Vbi igitur sedes tertia? vbi? nisi in Cambria. Qua parte, vt ego sileam, testis & quidem luculentus est Trittemius in Compendio annalium. An non pudeat
25 Gulielmum Paruum praeceptorem tam vana Polydoro discipulo longe eo eruditiori inculcasse? Ecce autem aliud ex alio malum. Acceptus error vsque adeo multos iam infecit, vt vix vllo helleboro, etiam si Anticyram peterent, malum medicabile. Et tamen interim coguntur, nescio qua violenta autoritate, de praeceptore
30 bene sentire. Duras esse has partes ego praedico. Praeceptoribus profecto meis omnia felicia opto. At cum de veritate, & fide causae agitur adfectus erga illos plane nullus, non certe si mox scirem eos capiundos esse mihi vel hostes omneis.

Peroratio.

35 Hactenus lectores humanissimi Arturium suis expressi coloribus, non sine diligentia, labore, ac studio denique propenso: at interim an pari eloquentia, gratia, & felicitate, candidorum, iuxta ac eruditorum sit iudicium: Nam ego probe noui, quam

R

mihi fit curta domi fupellex: quo nomine nihil quicquam mihi vendico, temerarius plane, & parum prudens fi id committerem. Tantum uolui in re honefta periculum ingenii facere, hiftoriæ laboranti opem ferre, gloriam patriæ, inuidia interceptam, & feruam infidiis maleuolorum, | libertate candide reftituere. Scio futurum, vt infultent aduerfarii potentifsimi. Vincant potentia, modo veritas noftra fit. Imitabor generofam palmam, quę oneri preffa cedit nunquam. Sed neque in prefentia pro munere quicquam ambio. Adfit veftra humanitas, beneuolentia, gratia: certe omnia adeffe merito crediderim. Accedet vna quoque ad cumulum dextera promptitudo, expedita alacritas, ignefcens etiam per virtutem impetus non folum ad fimilia, verum ad maiora quoque exhibenda, quæ doctas excitent aures, excitatas longum detineant, detentas veluti torrente quodam voluptatis fecum ad amœna deducant. Et hæc mihi omnia, veftro fretus candore, auxilioque, in fpem plane erectifsimus facile polliceor. Veftra quidem mea tota quanta eft Mufa: nec alio vfquam quam ad vos, & publicam tendit vtilitatem. Abfurdum plebi feruire, at vobis perpetuam præftare operam, non procul a regno eft, quale merito vel Alexandrino præferam. Quid enim ille amplius ex tantis opibus, fortunis, ditionibus fibi moriens integrum conferuauit, præter famam. Hanc, licet multis calculis exemplo inferiorem, per vos partam tamen ita folicite promouebo, vt noctes, atque dies veftræ inuigilet
commoditati, ac tandem excufsis tenebris
ignorantiæ crafsifsimis quidem illis,
lumen antiquitatis Britannicæ
diffufis late radiis eluceat.
Viuite,[1] & valete bona-
rum literarum fau-
tores candi-
difsimi.

[1] Text, *Viuete.*

ARTVRIVS REDIVIVVS.

Optima spes rerum mœstos solata Britannos
Sorte reuicturum promisit, et omine læto
Arturum, obscuro lucem qui redderet orbi.
Tempus adest. Victor prodit rediuiuus in auras,
Festa triumphali redimitus tempora lauro.
Hoc quoque ueridici uates cecinere futurum.
Martia cœruleos repetit sic palma Britannos.

ΣΎΓΚΡΙΣΙΣ.

Contulit Hectoreis arguta uoce triumphis
Eduerdum Viduus doctissimus ille Nigellum,
Et facti pretium tulit immortale poëta.
Impetus hinc crescens animi generosus honesti,
Me iubet Henrici titulos extollere magni,
Et conferre quidem multis uictoribus unum.
Inter quos præstans Arturius eminet heros,
Sæpe Caledonios qui Scottos, quique superbos
Perdomuit Gallos indicti fulmine belli.
Præstitit hæc eadem, longe et maiora supremus
Henricus, felix Octaui nomine uictor.
Castra puellarum cecidere. Bononia fracta est
Adque suos rediit patriæ pater almus, et idem
Commissi sceleris uindex Arturius alter.
Nunc superest uictis tristissima mortis imago,
Et sua fata uocant Scotti, Moriniqᵤₑ sinistra.

Elenchus antiquorum nominum.

Abrinus ab Abro Britannico vocabulo, quod ostiorum in fluminibus nomen est. Ab hac appellatione nomen duobus æstuariis totius Britanniæ maximis inditum est, quorum vulgus scriptorum unum Sabrinam, alterum uero Humbrum barbare, et corrupte uocant.

Alaunus frequens fluuiorum nomen, Britannice Alaun, Saxonice Aile, cuius & appellationis tres funt in Corinia.

Ambrosia vicus non incelebris Vilugianæ prouinciæ propter trophęum coronarii operis sepultura nobilium illustre, Aurelianus

Ambrosius originem loco dedit. Noftra ætas vicum Saxonice Ambresbyri appellat.

Armorica nunc Britannia continentis fic dicta quod littoralis. Sonat enim fuper mare.

Aualonia. Britannice Inis Aualon, Latine infula pomifera. Dicitur præterea Britannice Inis witrin a vitreo aquarum vicinarum colore.

Badonicus mons, Britannice Cair badon. Ptolomęo Græco Thermæ, Antonino Latino Aquæ folis, aliis quoque Balnea. At illud parum appofite, cum balnea humana caleant induftria. Badonicus mons mifere a Polydoro quæfitus, at non inuentus, apud Brigantes inter montes Blachemorinos.

Brigantes qui nunc Eboracenfes, & a Saxonibus partim Deiri. Boethius Scottus ftrenue dormitat in hac parte.

Brillendunum, vulgo Bridlington, oppidulum, et portus Ifurouicanæ alias Eboracenfis prouinciæ. Locus quidem olim illuftratus a Gualterio Gisbrithi Gandauenfis filio.

| Caledonii dicti a Romanis Britanni Caledoniæ fyluæ incolæ, quæ magnam Scotiæ partem olim penetrauit.

Clarus fons, Saxonice Shirburne, nomine quidem appofito, vocatus. Aldelmus doctifsimus epifcopus fedem ibi pofuit Inæ regis Vififaxonum liberalitate.

Camaletum caftrum olim magnificentifsimum in ipfis Murotrigum limitibus. Britannice Camalete, alias Cairmalet.

Catyeuchlani celebres Ptolomęo, quorum ciuitas prima Verolamium Romanis nota fcriptoribus. Erant in primis Chiltrenicorum montium cultores.

Corinia vulgo Cornewalle a Corino paleftrita fic dicta.

Domnonii, vnde & nunc corrupte Deuonia regio occidentalis. Hæc & a quibufdam Damonia dicitur.

Doris, Britannice Dour, corrupte Douer, portus olim celebris.

Duria, a Duro flumine præterlabente, vulgo Dorfetshire.

Durouernum Cantiorum metropolis, Saxonice Cantewarbyri.

Fontanus a fonte deriuatum. Fontes numero multitudinis vrbs clara in ipfis Minerariorum montium radicibus fita, quæ Saxonice welles appellatur. Ab Ina autem rege loci illuftratore Fontanetum, at antiquitus a Theodoro regulo Theodorodunum dicta eft.

Gefforiacum, nunc mutato nomine Bononia. Non defuerunt

qui Icium portum, qui Sclufam, qui Grauelinum pro Gefforiaco pofuerint. At frequens recentiorum imperatorum, addo hoc etiam & veterum traiectus a Bononia in Britanniam breuis, vt nihil inte|rim de Ammiano Marcellino, charta Militari, Fol 39.
5 Peutingero, aut Beato Rhenano loquar, aliud mihi plane perfuadent.

Gleffoburgus, Saxonice Gleffenburgh a paludum aquis cæruleum referentibus colorem nomen retinet: vnde & Dugles nigrocæruleus.

10 Giruii, qui & Fennicolæ partim Grantaniam, partim Venantoduniam, partim etiam Hollandiam Lindifinam, & limites orientalium Anglorum incolebant.

Granta vrbs olim notifsima, & a fcriptoribus tum Britannicis, tum Saxonicis celebrata, videlicet Felice, & Beda. Britanni hanc
15 fua lingua Cairgrant a fluuio vicino vocabant, Saxones vero a ponte conftructo Grantebridge, nunc corrupte Camebridge.

Ifca, Britannicæ Cairwiske, quæ & ciuitas Legionum propter Ifcam fluuium a Nigro Cambriæ monte in Ventaniam inferiorem illam defluentem.

20 Ifcalis vrbs antiqua Murotrigum, quæ Saxonice ab Iuelo fluuio Iuelceftre, contracte vero Ilcefter dicitur.

Ifidis vadum, Saxonice Oufeford, corrupte Oxford.

Lindocollinum a Lindo fluuio, & colle edito nomen traxit, vnde alias & Lindifpharos a fpecula. Lindum nomen vrbis
25 antiquum.

Lindisfarna Saxonice Halig Eilande propter littus orientale.

Morini quafi maritimi dicti gens Galliæ Belgicæ.

Murotriges, qui & Somurotriges vulgo Somerfetshire menne.

Moridunum vulgo Somerton vrbs olim clara Murotrigum.

30 Meildulphi curia nomen a Meildulpho Scotto literatifsimo accepit. Ante enim Britannice Cairbladon vrbs dicta eft.

Minerarii, montes altifsimi Somariæ, vulgo Minedepe hilles.

Nouus burgus vicus Brigantum difparatus ab Eboraco plus minus decem paffuum millibus, notoque illuftris Molbreiorum
35 monumento.

Ochis Anglice Oukey amniculus in fabulofo fpecu Minerarii montis oriens.

Strigulia nunc Chepeftow. Antiquum nomen, vt ego colligo, a fluminis Vagæ alueo vicino inditum.

Simeni, meo iudicio, olim fuerunt, qui nunc Auoniani ad meridiem.

Tamar flumen difterminans Corinios a Domnoniis.

Vaga fluuius Limonio oriens in monte, Britannice Gowy.

Venta Simenorum ad differentiam Ventæ Belgarum, Ventę Icenorum, Ventæ Sylurum. Crediderim Sylures a fyluarum vmbris, quas frequentabant, fuiffe dictos.

Vilugia, Anglice wilugfhire, corrupte wilefhire.

Verouicum, Saxonice werenwike, vulgo werwike.

Verolamium a fluuio vicino indubie nomen fumpfit. Saxones hanc dixere a publica via Veteliniana wethelingceftre. Nunc emporio nomen Fanum Albani.

Venantodunum id eft venatorum mons Saxonice Huntendune.

ERRATA.

Typographus frequentiufcule errauit tum in voculationibus, tum notulis incifionum, quas vel temere fubduxit, vel præfixit. Hic reliqua fuis detorta locis in ordinem accurate rediguntur. In epiftola nuncupatoria linea. 16. lege collaudant, Addenda & hæc nomina catalogo externorum autorum. Ptolemæus Lucenfis, Tritemius, Volateranus, Philippus Bergomas. Folio primo facie 2. linea. 15. lege repetere. Folio 4 facie 2 linea 16, lege prefsiffet. Fol. 7 facie prima linea 5, lege & te tua. Ibidem verfa pagella linea 13, lege comminus. Folio. 10. prima facie linea 23, lege ftabulantur. Ibidem facie fecunda, linea 16, lege maieftate. Folio 12 vltimi tres verfus terminandi, argento, tum, me. Folio 14 facie prima, linea 13, lege & pro eft. Ibide*m* linea 19 lege co*n*fonantius. Fol. 18 facie prima, linea 13, lege liquet. Folio 19 facie fecunda, linea 12 lege magnum. Ibidem linea 29 lege accipit, & linea 30, lege montibus, linea 31 lege concluditur. Folio 25 facie fecunda, linea vltima, lege vllam. Folio 27 facie prima, linea 8 lege, Conditus hic fuit. Fol. 28 facie prima, linea 12 lege perfonare, & ibidem linea 19 lege pro condidit contudit. Fol. 29 prima facie linea 26, lege propitia. Fol. 31 facie prima, linea 30, lege palliis. Fol. 35 facie prima, linea 4 lege contemnere. Fol. 36 facie prima, linea 13 lege inde pro idem. Et ibidem, linea 14 lege pro dignitate, autoritate.

Impreffum Londini apud
Ioannem Herford.
Anni 1544.

Corresponding references in present edition:

line 7. p. 98, l. 2.   p. 102, l. 9.   14. p. 123, ll. 1, 3.
     8–9. p. 105, l. 14.   p. 106, l. 10.   15–16. p. 131, l. 4.   p. 132, l. 26.
     9. p. 109, l. 35.   16. p. 134, l. 5.
     10. p. 110, l. 17.   p. 113, ll. 16,   17–18. p. 134, l. 12.   p. 135, l. 36.
        17, 18.   18. p. 138, l. 27.
     11–12. p. 115, l. 2.   19–20. p. 143, l. 22.   p. 145, l. 5.
     12–13. p. 115, l. 7.   p. 120, l. 20.   20. p. 145, l. 6.
     13. p. 122, l. 26.

NOTES

TO RICHARD ROBINSON'S *ASSERTION OF KING ARTHURE*.

7/28. *Arthure Maur*, i. e. Arthur the Great. Cf. 54/32.

20, side-note. The date 316 given for Arthur's coronation is an obvious blunder for 516.

39, side-note. *Robert Caxton who tranflated the hiftory of K. Arthure*. This blunder in calling William Caxton Robert and crediting him with Malory's translation is wholly Robinson's. Leland obviously knew Malory's work, whereas Robinson apparently had never read Caxton's preface to the *Morte Darthur* or the romance itself. One may wonder what he thought of Leland's reference to Thomas Mailerius, 53/36.

GLOSSARY

TO ROBINSON'S *ASSERTION OF KING ARTHURE*.

abject, *vb.*, reject, disparage, 27/23.
aliable, *adj.*, trustworthy, 84/38.
approued, *pp.*, shown, proved, 24/23.
auoyde, *vb.*, prevent, 29/34.

boules, *sb.*, boles, trunks, 60/8.
brabler, babbler, chatterer, 84/19.

comprobate, *adj.*, proved, 85/1.
conquerouse, *adj.*, conquering, 7/32.
crazed, *adj.*, cracked, 40/4. Cf. Fr. *écrasé*.
cuftomer, *sb.*, custom-house official, 3.

difburdenance, *sb.*, unburdening, freedom from, 25/22.
difcommendable, *adj.*, not to be commended, 28/12.

enioyned, *adj.*, entrusted, 32/3.
enfewe, *vb.*, follow, 28/9.
eye bryes, *sb.*, eyebrows, 73/5.

factes, *sb.*, deeds, exploits, 49/34.
forman, *sb.*, originator, 49/14.
furderance, *sb.*, help, service, 32/32.

garboyle, *sb.*, conflict, tumult, 23/29.
glofe, *vb.*, deceive, cheat, 19/5.

hand ftroakes, *sb.*, blows, 46/22.
hetherto, *adv.*, hitherto, 27/33.
hetherunto, in addition, 28/9.

inconueniently, *adv.*, unfittingly, 56/35.

magnanimitie, *sb.*, ability, 25/28.
maugre, *prep.*, despite, 8/14.
mountayny, *adj.*, mountainous, 47/29.

nouicy, *sb.*, inexperience, 84/14.

odible, *adj.*, hateful, 7/4.
otherwhiles...otherwhiles, sometimes...sometimes, 24/22.

performe, *vb.*, make, 32/2.
portracted, *pp.*, portrayed, 13/18.
puyfant, *adj.*, powerful, 30/33.

quoynes, *sb.*, coins, 48/35.

renoumed, *adj.*, renowned, 3, 8/1.

fincere, *adj.*, pure, unmixed, 29/23.
smally, *adv.*, in slight degree, 24/37.

their, *adv.*, there, 27/4.
then, *conj.*, than, 5/37, 13/22, 17/5, 17/18, 20, 26, &c. Cf. than, 27/35.
there, *poss. pron.*, their, 27/8.

vtterfide, *sb.*, outside, 40/9.

witty, *adj.*, clever, 76/13.
write, *pret.*, wrote, 25/15.

INDEX

TO ROBINSON'S *ASSERTION OF KING ARTHURE* AND TO LELAND'S[1] *ASSERTIO INCLYTISSIMI ARTURII*.

Arthur's arms, 13.
Arthur's bones transferred to Glastonbury abbey church, 75-8; L. 137-9.
Arthur's burial, 57-61; L. 125-7.
Arthur's coronation, 20, 21; L. 99.
Arthur's expedition against the French, 25-7; L. 103-4.
Arthur's existence, proofs of, 78-89; L. 139-45.
Arthur's godly disposition, 37-9; L. 110-12.
Arthur's knights, 14, 15, 27-34; L. 104-9.
Arthur, praise of, 49-54; L. 120-3.
Arthur's return from France, 44-9; L. 116-19.
Arthur's Round Table, 34-6; L. 109-10.
Arthur's seal, 39-44; L. 112-15.
Arthur's tomb found, 65-75; L. 130-7.
Arthur's twelve battles, 21-5; L. 100-2.

Authorities used in the *Assertion*, 11, 12.
Avalonia (Glastonbury), antiquity of, 55-7; L. 123-5; pyramids at, 61, 62; L. 127-8.

Dedicatory epistle addressed to Henry the Eighth, L. 93-5.

Guenhera, character of, 62-5; L. 128-30.

Introductory epistle, 3-9; introductory chapter, 17-20; L. 97-9.

Pyramids at Avalonia (Glastonbury), the two, 61, 62; L. 127-8.

Round Table, Arthur's, 34-6.

[1] Indicated by L.

The manufacturer's authorised representative in the EU for product safety is Oxford University Press España S.A. of El Parque Empresarial San Fernando de Henares, Avenida de Castilla, 2 - 28830 Madrid (www.oup.es/en or product.safety@oup.com). OUP España S.A. also acts as importer into Spain of products made by the manufacturer.
Printed and bound by CPI Group (UK) Ltd, Croydon, CR0 4YY

22/04/2026

02094916-0006